Duncan Petersen's

CHARMING SMALL HOTEL GUIDES

BRITAIN & IRELAND

Duncan Petersen's

CHARMING SMALL HOTEL GUIDES

BRITAIN & IRELAND

Consultant editor Fiona Duncan

Hotel critic of *The Sunday Telegraph*

Duncan Petersen

17th edition

Conceived, designed and produced by
Duncan Petersen Publishing Ltd,
Studio 6, 82 Silverthorne Road, Battersea, SW3 8HE

Editorial director Andrew Duncan
Consultant editor Fiona Duncan
Editor Alex Douglas
Contributing editors Jonathan and Joan Noble, Belinda and Hamish Alexander, David Perkins
Production editor Alex Douglas
Cover design Nicky Collings
Maps Map Creation Ltd
Photo credits see below for individual details

A CIP catalogue record for this book is available from the British Library

ISBN 978-0-9575759-1-2

DTP by Duncan Petersen Publishing Ltd
Printed in Slovenia by Almarose d.o.o.

Grays Court credit (page 313): Dominic Wright
Red Lion Freehouse credit (page 100): Nick Cunard
Cover photos: Gravetye Manor Hotel & Restaurant (front), Airds Hotel (back), Cley Mill (spine)

Contents

In this introductory section:

From the consultant editor, Fiona Duncan

Welcome to the 17th edition of Charming Small Hotel Guides Britain & Ireland – a guide with a long history. It was first published in 1988 by my husband Andrew Duncan, his co-director Mel Petersen and with Chris Gill as the editor. I took over as editor in the mid 1990s and looked after several editions until 2006 when I began writing my hotel column in *The Sunday Telegraph*. Since then it has been looked after by Duncan Petersen with myself as consultant editor, giving advice on new entries and which to drop.

Because this new edition has so many new entries my contribution has been greater than usual. Its focus on smaller places, usually with four to 12 bedrooms, is especially close to my heart – and to my view on hotel keeping – which is that small is, mostly, beautiful because large places find it hard to create a place with that elusive quality of character and charm, where the guest feels like a person, not just a customer.

I have not been able to visit every single entry in the guide, though most are known to me in some way. Though all the entries are faithful to our idea of a charming small hotel, I do like some better than others; and I have had to trust that the detailed work of updating facts has been done well. Those aside, I believe that the guide is as unique and as valuable as it was when first published in 1988. I hope you agree.

Happy travels.

Introduction

There have been major changes to this new edition:

• It's much larger than ever before – the number of hotels has increased from 350 to nearly 500.

• There's a new cover to reflect the changes, which is being used title by title for the whole series.

We hope that you will think these real improvements, rather than change for its own sake. In all other respects, the guide remains true to the values and qualities that make it unique (see next page), and which have won it so many devoted readers. It has sold hundreds of thousands of copies in the U.K., U.S.A. and in five European languages.

Why are we unique?

This is the only independent (no hotel pays for an entry) UK-originated accommodation guide that:

• concentrates on places that have real charm and character;

• is highly selective and fussy about size. Most hotels have fewer than 20 bedrooms; if there are more, the hotel must have the feel of a much smaller place. Time and again we find that a genuinely warm welcome is *much* more likely to be found in a small hotel;

• gives proper emphasis to description – doesn't use irritating symbols;

• is produced by a small company with like-minded reporters.

Above all, the text doesn't read as if it's an advert, paid for by the hotel, which is the case with most other guides. Our reviews are honest: objective, distanced and they mention negatives *and* positives.

Plantation Farmhouse, Bungay

So what exactly do we look for?

Our selection criteria

- A peaceful, attractive setting. Obviously, if the entry is in an urban area, we make allowances.
- A building that is handsome, interesting, historic or characterful.
- Adequate space, but on a human scale. We don't go for places that rely too much on grandeur.
- Good taste and imagination in the interior decoration. We reject standardized, chain hotel fixtures, fittings and decorations.
- Bedrooms that look like real bedrooms, not hotel rooms, individually decorated.
- Furnishings and other facilities that are comfortable and well maintained. We like to see interesting antique furniture that is there to be used, not simply revered.
- Proprietors and staff who are dedicated and thoughtful, offering a personal welcome, but who aren't intrusive or overly effusive.
- Interesting food.
- A sympathetic atmosphere; an absence of loud people showing off their money; or the 'corporate feel'.

No fear or favour

To us, taking a payment for appearing in a guide seems to defeat the object of producing a guide. If money has changed hands, you can't write the whole truth about a hotel, and the selection cannot be nearly so interesting. This seems to us to be proved at least in part by the fact that pay guides are so keen to present the illusion of independence: most only admit taking payment in small print inside.

Not many people realize that on the shelves of British bookshops there are many more hotel guides that accept payments for entries than there are independent guides. This guide is one of the few that do not accept any money for an entry.

A fatter guide, but just as selective

In order to accommodate extra entries with a whole or half page description and colour photograph, we've had to print more pages. But we have maintained our integrity by keeping the selection to around 500 entries. Since our last edition, the number of places to stay that deserve to be in the guide has increased substantially – many new revamped inns and restaurants-with-rooms have opened. But the guide is all about places that are more than just a bed for the night. Every time we consider a new hotel, we ask ourselves whether it has that extra special something, regardless of category and facilities, that makes it worth seeking out.

Types of accommodation in this guide

Despite its title, the guide does not confine itself to places called hotels or places that behave like hotels. On the contrary, we actively look for places that offer a home from home (see page 10). We include small and medium-sized hotels; pubs; inns; restaurants-with-rooms; guest-houses and bed-and-breakfasts. Some places, usually private homes which take guests, operate on house-party lines, where you are introduced to the other guests, and take meals at a communal table. If you don't like making small talk to strangers, or are part of a romantic twosome that wants to keep itself to itself, this type of establishment may not be for you. On the other hand, if you are interested in meeting people, perhaps as a foreign visitor wanting to get to know the locals, then you'll find it rewarding.

Home from home

Perhaps the most beguiling characteristic of the best places to stay in this guide is the feeling they give of being in a private home – but without the everyday cares and chores of running one. To get this formula right requires a special sort of professionalism: the proprietor has to strike the balance between being relaxed and giving attentive service. Those who experience this 'feel' often turn their backs on all other forms of accommodation – however luxurious.

Our pet dislikes

Small hotels are not automatically wonderful hotels; and the very individuality of small, owner-run hotels, makes them prone to peculiarities that the mass-produced hotel experience avoids. For the benefit of those who run the small hotels of Britain – and those contemplating the plunge – we repeat once more our list of pet hates:

Price too high Prices tend to be higher, like for like, than in France and Italy. This is not always the fault of hotels, but it is disappointing.

Not entirely child-friendly Again, compared with mainland European hotels, children are much more often seen as a nuisance by hoteliers.

Poor English at reception The surge in recent years of foreign workers, prepared to work for low wages, means guests sometimes have to adapt to a non-fluent English speaker. Especially irritating if you arrive tired after a long journey.

'Contemporary-formulaic' decoration Too many hotels think they can appeal simply by putting 'modern' paint on the walls. The more we see of this, the more of a cliche it becomes.

The hushed dining room Owners have a duty to create an atmosphere in which conversation can flow.

The ordinary breakfast Even hotels that go to great lengths to prepare special dinners are capable of serving prefabricated orange juice, sliced bread and tea made with tea bags at breakfast.

The schoolteacher mentality If you run a hotel, you should be flexible and accommodating enough to deal with the whims of travellers.

The inexperienced waiter Or waitress. Running a small operation does not excuse the imposition on the paying public of completely untrained (and sometimes ill-suited) staff who can spoil the most beautifully cooked food.

The lumpy old bed Beds have improved much in recent years. There's no excuse for a creaking frame or an old mattress.

The erratic boiler It doesn't often happen, but tepid baths are unforgiveable. Even the cheapest places should regard this as a basic.

Check the price first

In this guide we have adopted the system of price bands, rather than giving actual prices as we did in previous editions. This is because prices were often subject to change after we went to press. The price bands refer to the approximate price of a standard double room (high season rates) with breakfast for two people. Prices for Ireland are quoted in Euros. They are as follows:

£	under £80	€	under 120 euros
££	£80 – £150	€€	120 – 180 euros
£££	£150 – £200	€€€	180 – 240 euros
££££	more than £200	€€€€	more than 240 euros

Always check what is included in the price (for example service, breakfast, afternoon tea) when booking.

How to find an entry

In this guide, the entries are arranged in geographical groups. First, the whole of Britain and Ireland are divided into five major groups, starting with Southern England and working northwards to Scotland; Ireland comes last. Within these major groups, the entries are grouped into smaller regional sub-sections such as the South-West, Wales, the Midlands and the Highlands and Islands – for a full list, see page 5. Within each sub-section, entries are listed alphabetically by nearest town or village; if several occur in or near one town, entries are arranged in alpha order by name of hotel.

To find a hotel in a particular area, use the maps following this introduction to locate the appropriate pages.

To locate a specific hotel, whose name you know, or a hotel in a place you know, use the indexes at the back, which list entries both by names and by nearest place name. The name of the county follows the town name in the heading for each entry.

The five main sections of the book (Southern England, Central England, The North, Scotland and Ireland) are introduced by area introductions.

Using the guide

We use three different hotel entry formats in order to give you perspective on the character and quality of the places to stay. Although all are worthy of the guide, some are better than others. The **whole page** entries are the cream of our selection – mainstream charming small hotels that tick all or most of our boxes. **Half pages** shouldn't be overlooked or under-rated. They are also true charming small hotels, some of them good, some excellent. Usually, but no means always, because of their larger size, they don't conform as closely to our criteria as the whole page hotels. They are grouped at the end of each regional section, after the whole page entries. **Section opener** entries are useful back-up entries with small photos and brief descriptions. They are found on the five area introduction pages – see above. Again, don't overlook these: they are great places that have attracted our attention but not quite as faithful to our criteria as whole and half page entries.

So within each region you need to look in three different places to get the whole range of recommendations, and the entire contents are also easily accessible by using the maps on pages 15-25 and the indexes on pages 402-415.

How to read an entry

Postal address and other key information.

Places of interest within reach of the hotel.

This sets the hotel in its geographical context and should not be taken as precise instructions as to how to get there; always ask the hotel for directions.

Rooms described as having a bath usually also have a shower; rooms described as having a shower only have a shower.

This information is only an indication for wheelchair users and the infirm. Always check on suitability with the hotel.

Essential booking information.

THE SOUTH-WEST SOUTHERN ENGLAND

Gittisham, Devon

Gittisham, Honiton, Devon
EX14 3AD

Tel (01404) 540 400
e-mail stay@thishotel.com
website www.thishotel.com

Nearby Gittisham village, Honiton antique trail, Dartmoor National Park, Jurassic Coast, Ottery St Mary
Location set in 3,500 acres of grounds, 2 miles from A30 and Honiton with ample car parking
Food breakfast, lunch, dinner
Price ££££
Rooms 16 including cottage; all en suite with plasma TV, phone, hairdryers; most rooms have wi-fi internet
Facilities two bar/lounge rooms, two dining rooms, Georgian kitchen, extensive parkland, helipad; fishing, shooting and riding all nearby
Credit Cards MC, V
Children welcome
Disabled access to restaurant only
Pets well behaved dogs, £7 per night
Closed last two weeks of January
Proprietors Ken and Ruth Hunt

Combe House
Country hotel

Through delightful unspoiled Gittisham village, up a long drive, past wild flower meadows you find this large manor house dating from Elizabethan times. Perhaps it's not as mellow as some photos make it look, but you're definitely in the isolated world of an old country estate. Inside, old and new rub shoulders amusingly, perhaps eccentrically. In the main public space downstairs, the hall, gay splashes of colour contrast effectively with magnificent dark, heavy old panelling. Antique wallpaper has been preserved in a little reception room off the hall and the dining room walls are charmingly hand painted by former owners. It's full of quirky corners and surprises (including an outdoor bath house) to keep you amused. You'll see the odd imperfection downstairs, which could not matter less, because this is far from being a haphazard operation. Ruth and Ken Hunter are natural but astute hoteliers who have built up Combe House's reputation from nothing over a decade of hands-on hard work. Now, all the basics are right: award-winning food; upstairs, fresh, imaginative rooms, some traditional, some more contemporary, some pretty, at a useful range of prices. For a treat, book the Linen Suite with its copper bath tub. People of most ages can feel comfortable here.

50

City, town or village, and region, in which the hotel is located.

Name of hotel.

Type of establishment.

Description – never vetted by the hotel.

Breakfast is normally included in the price of the room. Other meals, such as afternoon tea, may also be available. 'Room service' refers to food and drink, either snacks or full meals, which can be served in the room

Always let the hotel know in advance if you want to bring a pet. Even where pets are accepted, certain restrictions may apply, and a small charge may be levied.

Children
Where children are welcome, there are often special facilities, such as cots, high chairs, baby listening and high teas. Always check whether children are accepted in the dining room.

We list the following credit cards:
AE American Express
DC Diners Club
MC Mastercard
V Visa
Most hotels accept many other credit cards.

Reporting to the guide

Please write and tell us about your experiences of small hotels, guest houses and inns, whether good or bad, whether listed in this edition or not. As well as hotels in Britain & Ireland, we are interested in hotels in Austria, France, Italy, Spain, Germany and Switzerland.

Readers whose reports prove particularly helpful may be invited to join our Travellers' Panel. Members give us notice of their own travel plans; we suggest hotels that they might inspect, and help with the cost of accommodation.

The address to write to us is:

Editor, *Charming Small Hotel Guides*
Studio 6, 82 Silverthorne Road, Battersea, SW8 3HE.

Checklist

Please use a separate sheet of paper for each report; include your name, address and telephone number on each report.

Your reports will be received with particular pleasure if they are typed, and if they are organized under the following headings:

Name of establishment
Town or village it is in, or nearest
Full address, including postcode
Telephone number
Time and duration of visit
The building and setting
The public rooms
The bedrooms and bathrooms
Physical comfort (chairs, beds, heat, light, hot water)
Standards of maintenance and housekeeping
Atmosphere, welcome and service
Food
Value for money

We assume that in writing you have no objections to your views being published unpaid, either verbatim or in an edited version. Names of major outside contributors are acknowledged, at the editor's discretion, in the guide.

Hotel location maps

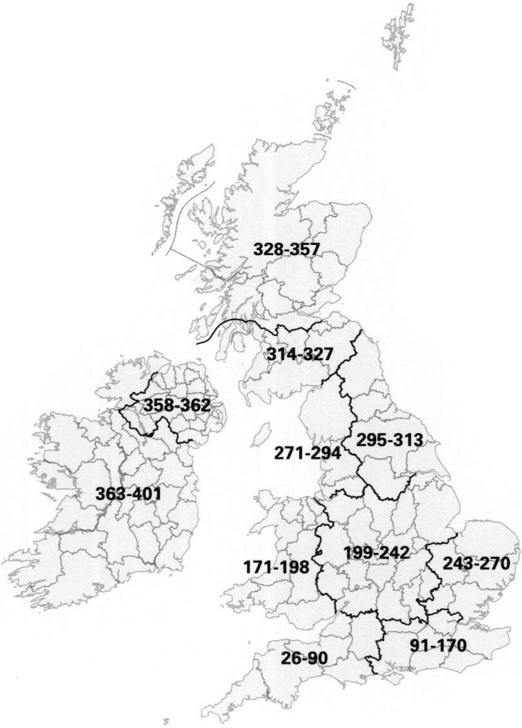

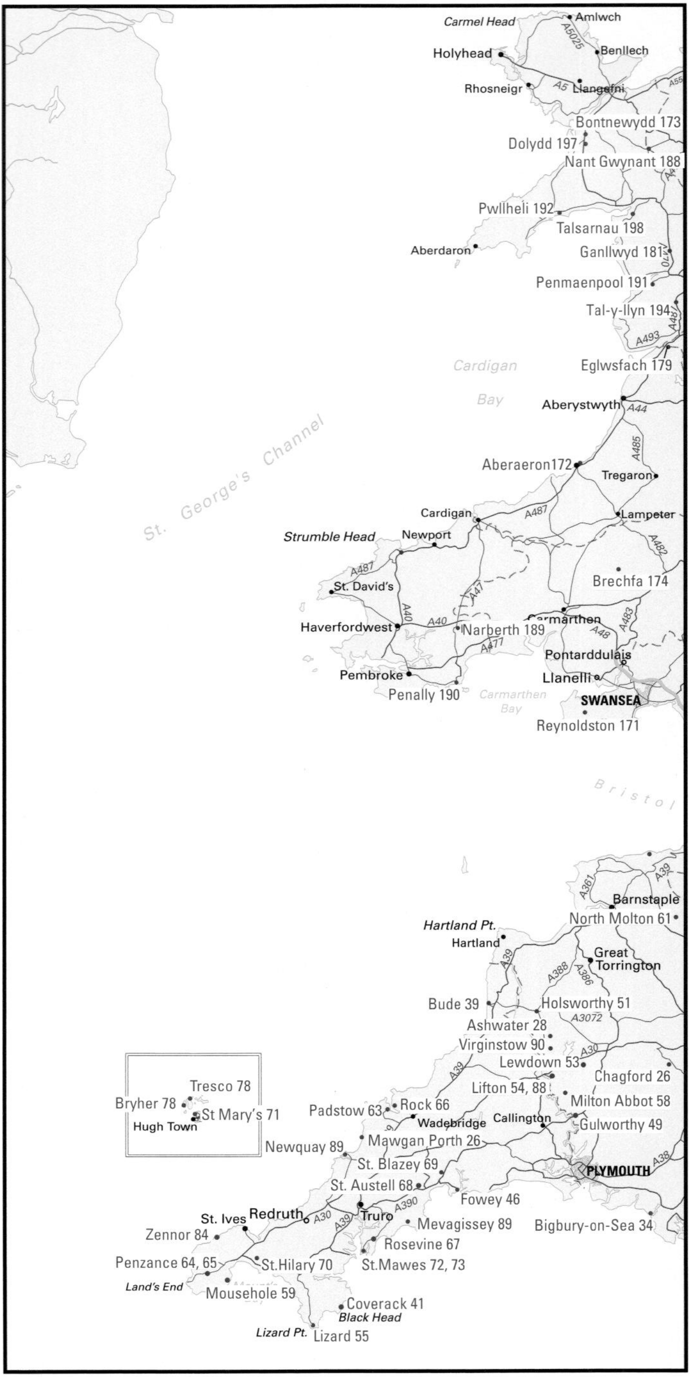
Carmel Head
Amlwch
A5025
Holyhead
Benllech
Rhosneigr
A5
Llangefni
Bontnewydd 173
Dolydd 197
Nant Gwynant 188
Pwllheli 192
Talsarnau 198
Aberdaron
Ganllwyd 181
Penmaenpool 191
Tal-y-llyn 194
A493
Cardigan
Bay
Eglwsfach 179
Aberystwyth
A44
A485
St. George's Channel
Aberaeron172
Tregaron
Cardigan
A487
Lampeter
Strumble Head
Newport
A482
A487
St. David's
Brechfa 174
A40
A40
Haverfordwest
Carmarthen
Narberth 189
A483
A477
Pontarddulais
Pembroke
Llanelli
Penally 190
Carmarthen
Bay
SWANSEA
Reynoldston 171
Bristol
A39
A361
Barnstaple
North Molton 61
Hartland Pt.
Hartland
Great
Torrington
A39
A388
A386
Bude 39
Holsworthy 51
A3072
Ashwater 28
Virginstow 90
A30
Lewdown 53
A39
Chagford 26
Lifton 54, 88
Tresco 78
Milton Abbot 58
Bryher 78
St Mary's 71
Padstow 63
Rock 66
Hugh Town
Wadebridge
Callington
Gulworthy 49
Newquay 89
Mawgan Porth 26
St. Blazey 69
PLYMOUTH
A38
St. Austell 68
Fowey 46
St. Ives
Redruth
A30
A39
Truro
A390
Mevagissey 89
Bigbury-on-Sea 34
Zennor 84
Rosevine 67
Penzance 64, 65
St.Hilary 70
St.Mawes 72, 73
Land's End
Mousehole 59
Coverack 41
Black Head
Lizard Pt.
Lizard 55

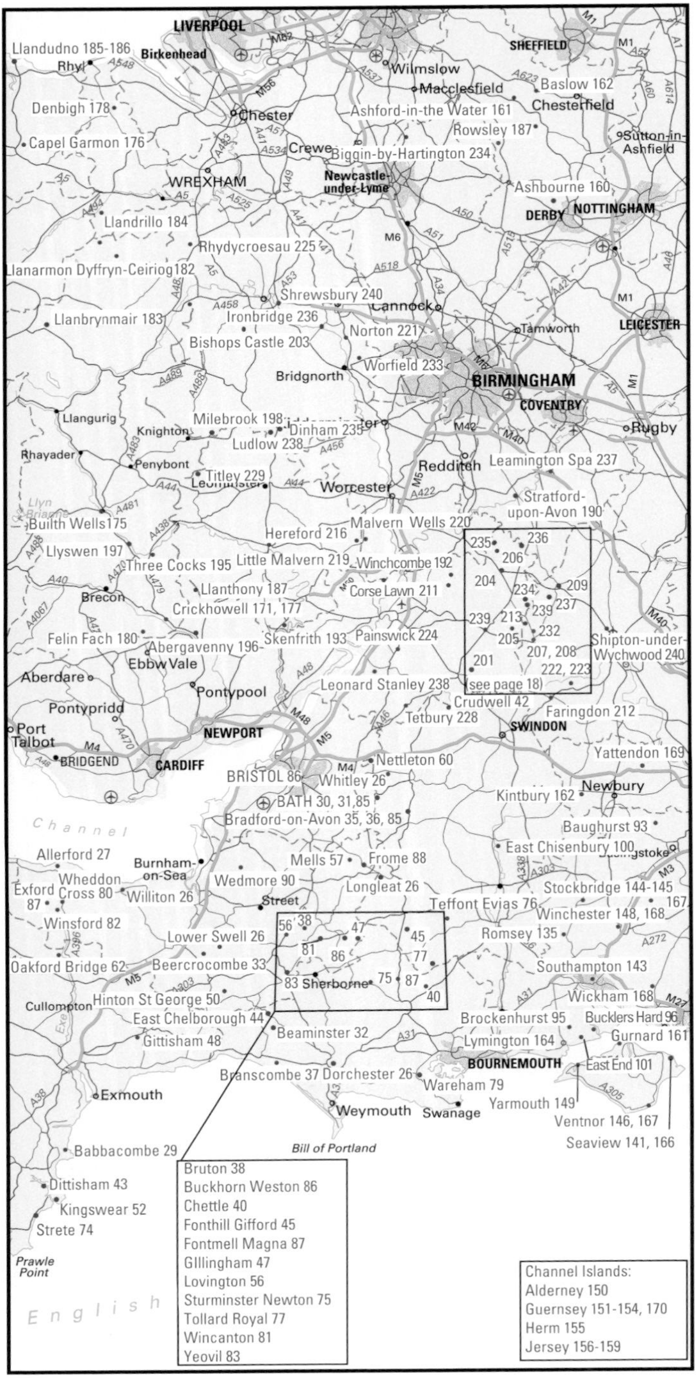
LIVERPOOL
Llandudno 185-186
Birkenhead
Rhyl
Wilmslow
Macclesfield
SHEFFIELD
Baslow 162
Chesterfield
Denbigh 178
Chester
Ashford-in-the Water 161
Rowsley 187
Sutton-in-Ashfield
Capel Garmon 176
Crewe
Biggin-by-Hartington 234
WREXHAM
Newcastle-under-Lyme
Ashbourne 160
DERBY
NOTTINGHAM
Llandrillo 184
Rhydycroesau 225
Llanarmon Dyffryn-Ceiriog 182
Shrewsbury 240
Cannock
Llanbrynmair 183
Ironbridge 236
Norton 221
Tamworth
LEICESTER
Bishops Castle 203
Worfield 233
Bridgnorth
BIRMINGHAM
COVENTRY
Llangurig
Milebrook 198
Dinham 235
Knighton
Rugby
Ludlow 238
Rhayader
Penybont
Redditch
Leamington Spa 237
Titley 229
Worcester
Stratford-upon-Avon 190
Builth Wells 175
Malvern Wells 220
Hereford 216
Llyswen 197
Three Cocks 195
Little Malvern 219
Winchcombe 192
Llanthony 187
Corse Lawn 211
Brecon
Crickhowell 171, 177
Felin Fach 180
Abergavenny 196
Skenfrith 193
Painswick 224
Shipton-under-Wychwood 240
Ebbw Vale
Aberdare
Pontypool
Leonard Stanley 238
(see page 18)
Pontypridd
Crudwell 42
Faringdon 212
Tetbury 228
Port Talbot
NEWPORT
SWINDON
BRIDGEND
CARDIFF
Nettleton 60
Yattendon 169
BRISTOL 86
Whitley 26
Newbury
BATH 30, 31, 85
Kintbury 162
Bradford-on-Avon 35, 36, 85
Baughurst 93
Allerford 27
East Chisenbury 100
Burnham-on-Sea
Mells 57
Frome 88
Wheddon Cross 80
Wedmore 90
Exford 87
Williton 26
Longleat 26
Stockbridge 144-145
Street
Teffont Evias 76
Winchester 148, 168
Winsford 82
Lower Swell 26
Romsey 135
Sherborne
Oakford Bridge 62
Beercrocombe 33
Southampton 143
Hinton St George 50
Wickham 168
Cullompton
East Chelborough 44
Brockenhurst 95
Bucklers Hard 96
Beaminster 32
Gittisham 48
Lymington 164
Gurnard 161
BOURNEMOUTH
East End 101
Branscombe 37
Dorchester 26
Wareham 79
Exmouth
Yarmouth 149
Weymouth
Swanage
Ventnor 146, 167
Seaview 141, 166
Babbacombe 29
Bill of Portland
Dittisham 43
Kingswear 52
Strete 74
Prawle Point
English Channel
Bruton 38
Buckhorn Weston 86
Chettle 40
Fonthill Gifford 45
Fontmell Magna 87
GIllingham 47
Lovington 56
Sturminster Newton 75
Tollard Royal 77
Wincanton 81
Yeovil 83
Channel Islands:
Alderney 150
Guernsey 151-154, 170
Herm 155
Jersey 156-159

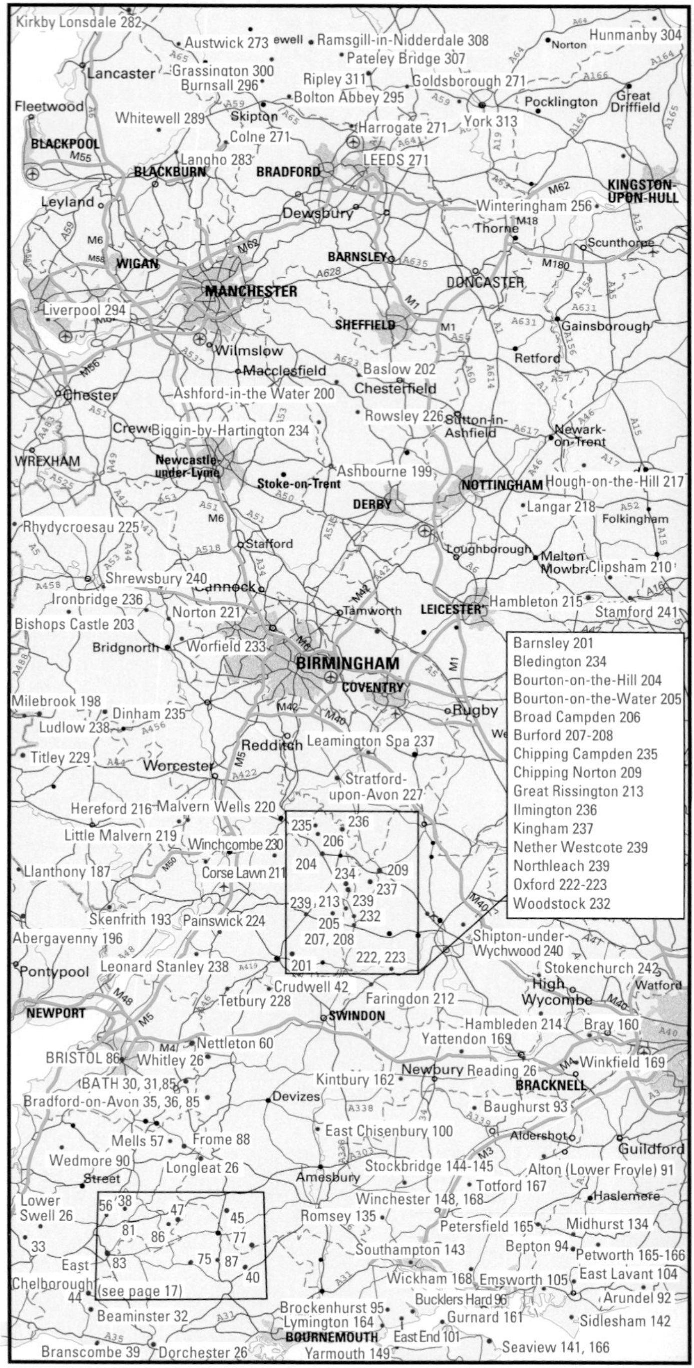

Kirkby Lonsdale 282
Austwick 273
Ramsgill-in-Nidderdale 308
Pateley Bridge 307
Norton
Hunmanby 304
Lancaster
Grassington 300
Burnsall 296
Ripley 311
Goldsborough 271
Fleetwood
Whitewell 289
Skipton
Bolton Abbey 295
Pocklington
Great Driffield
York 313
Colne 271
Harrogate 271
BLACKPOOL
M55
Langho 283
BLACKBURN
BRADFORD
LEEDS 271
KINGSTON-UPON-HULL
M62
Leyland
Winteringham 256
Dewsbury
Thorne
M18
M6
Scunthorpe
WIGAN
M62
BARNSLEY
A635
M180
A628
MANCHESTER
DONCASTER
Liverpool 294
SHEFFIELD
M1
A631
Gainsborough
Wilmslow
Retford
Macclesfield
Baslow 202
Chester
Ashford-in-the Water 200
Chesterfield
Rowsley 226
Sutton-in-Ashfield
Crewe
Biggin-by-Hartington 234
Newark-on-Trent
WREXHAM
Newcastle-under-Lyme
Stoke-on-Trent
Ashbourne 199
NOTTINGHAM
Hough-on-the-Hill 217
DERBY
Langar 218
M6
Folkingham
Rhydycroesau 225
Stafford
Loughborough
Melton Mowbray
Clipsham 210
Shrewsbury 240
Cannock
Ironbridge 236
Tamworth
LEICESTER
Hambleton 215
Norton 221
Stamford 241
Bishops Castle 203
Bridgnorth
Worfield 233
BIRMINGHAM
M1
COVENTRY
Milebrook 198
Dinham 235
Rugby
Ludlow 238
M42
M40
Redditch
Leamington Spa 237
Titley 229
Worcester
M5
Stratford-upon-Avon 227
Hereford 216
Malvern Wells 220
Little Malvern 219
Winchcombe 230
Llanthony 187
M50
Corse Lawn 211
Skenfrith 193
Painswick 224
Abergavenny 196
Pontypool
Leonard Stanley 238
M48
235
236
206
204
234
209
237
239
213
239
232
205
207, 208
201
222, 223
Barnsley 201
Bledington 234
Bourton-on-the-Hill 204
Bourton-on-the-Water 205
Broad Campden 206
Burford 207-208
Chipping Campden 235
Chipping Norton 209
Great Rissington 213
Ilmington 236
Kingham 237
Nether Westcote 239
Northleach 239
Oxford 222-223
Woodstock 232
M40
Shipton-under-Wychwood 240
Stokenchurch 242
Crudwell 42
Tetbury 228
Faringdon 212
High Wycombe
Watford
NEWPORT
M5
SWINDON
Hambleden 214
Bray 160
M4
Nettleton 60
Yattendon 169
BRISTOL 86
Whitley 26
Newbury
Reading 26
Winkfield 169
BATH 30, 31, 85
Kintbury 162
BRACKNELL
Bradford-on-Avon 35, 36, 85
Devizes
Baughurst 93
East Chisenbury 100
Aldershot
Guildford
Mells 57
Frome 88
M3
Wedmore 90
Longleat 26
Stockbridge 144-145
Alton (Lower Froyle) 91
Street
Amesbury
Totford 167
Lower Swell 26
56
38
47
45
Winchester 148, 168
Haslemere
81
86
77
Romsey 135
Petersfield 165
Midhurst 134
33
Bepton 94
East
83
75
87
Southampton 143
Petworth 165-166
40
East Lavant 104
Chelborough
44
(see page 17)
Wickham 168
Emsworth 105
Arundel 92
Bucklers Hard 96
Brockenhurst 95
Beaminster 32
Lymington 164
Gurnard 161
Sidlesham 142
BOURNEMOUTH
East End 101
Seaview 141, 166
Branscombe 39
Dorchester 26
Yarmouth 149

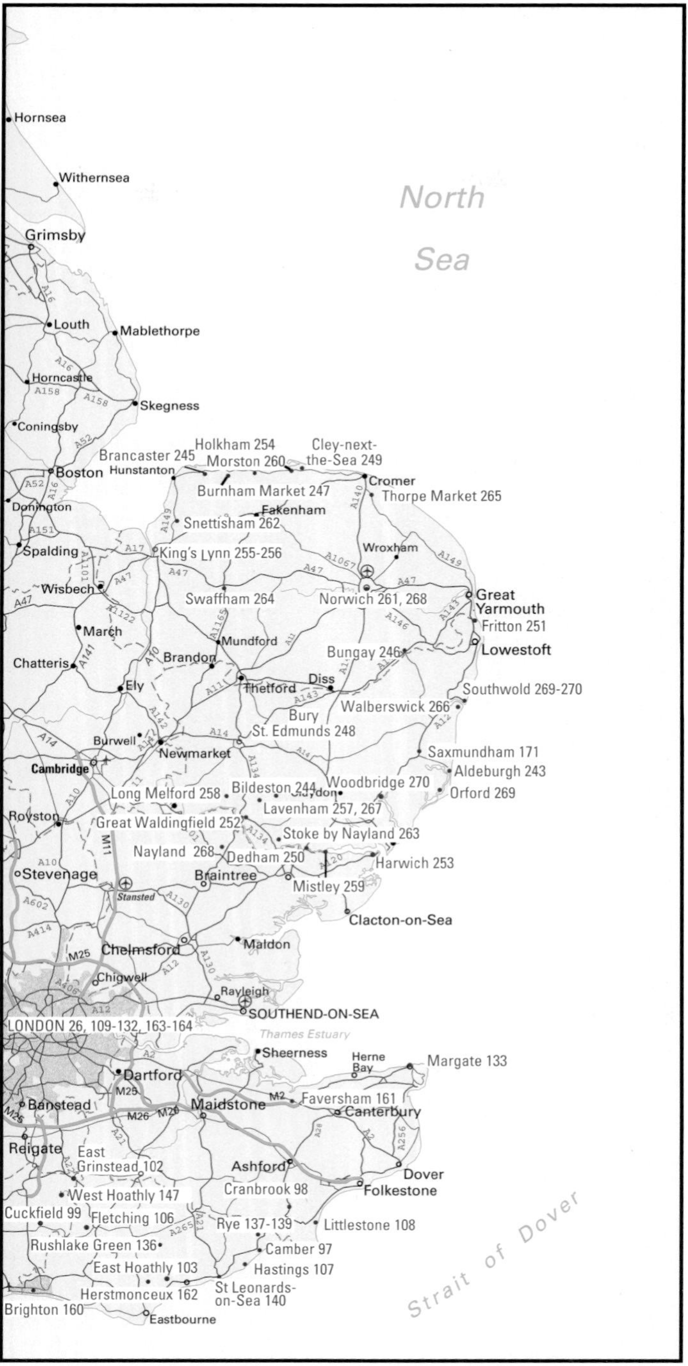

Hornsea
Withernsea
North
Sea
Grimsby
Louth
Mablethorpe
Horncastle
Skegness
Coningsby
Holkham 254
Cley-next-
the-Sea 249
Brancaster 245
Morston 260
Boston
Hunstanton
Cromer
Burnham Market 247
Thorpe Market 265
Donington
Fakenham
Snettisham 262
Spalding
King's Lynn 255-256
Wroxham
Wisbech
Swaffham 264
Norwich 261, 268
Great
Yarmouth
Fritton 251
March
Mundford
Lowestoft
Bungay 246
Chatteris
Brandon
Ely
Thetford
Diss
Southwold 269-270
Walberswick 266
Bury
St. Edmunds 248
Burwell
Newmarket
Saxmundham 171
Cambridge
Aldeburgh 243
Long Melford 258
Bildeston 244
Woodbridge 270
Orford 269
Lavenham 257, 267
Royston
Great Waldingfield 252
Stoke by Nayland 263
Nayland 268
Dedham 250
Harwich 253
Stevenage
Braintree
Mistley 259
Stansted
Clacton-on-Sea
Chelmsford
Maldon
Chigwell
Rayleigh
SOUTHEND-ON-SEA
LONDON 26, 109-132, 163-164
Thames Estuary
Sheerness
Herne
Bay
Margate 133
Dartford
Banstead
Maidstone
Faversham 161
Canterbury
Reigate
East
Grinstead 102
Ashford
Dover
Folkestone
West Hoathly 147
Cranbrook 98
Cuckfield 99
Fletching 106
Rye 137-139
Littlestone 108
Rushlake Green 136
Camber 97
East Hoathly 103
Hastings 107
Herstmonceux 162
St Leonards-
on-Sea 140
Brighton 160
Eastbourne
Strait of Dover

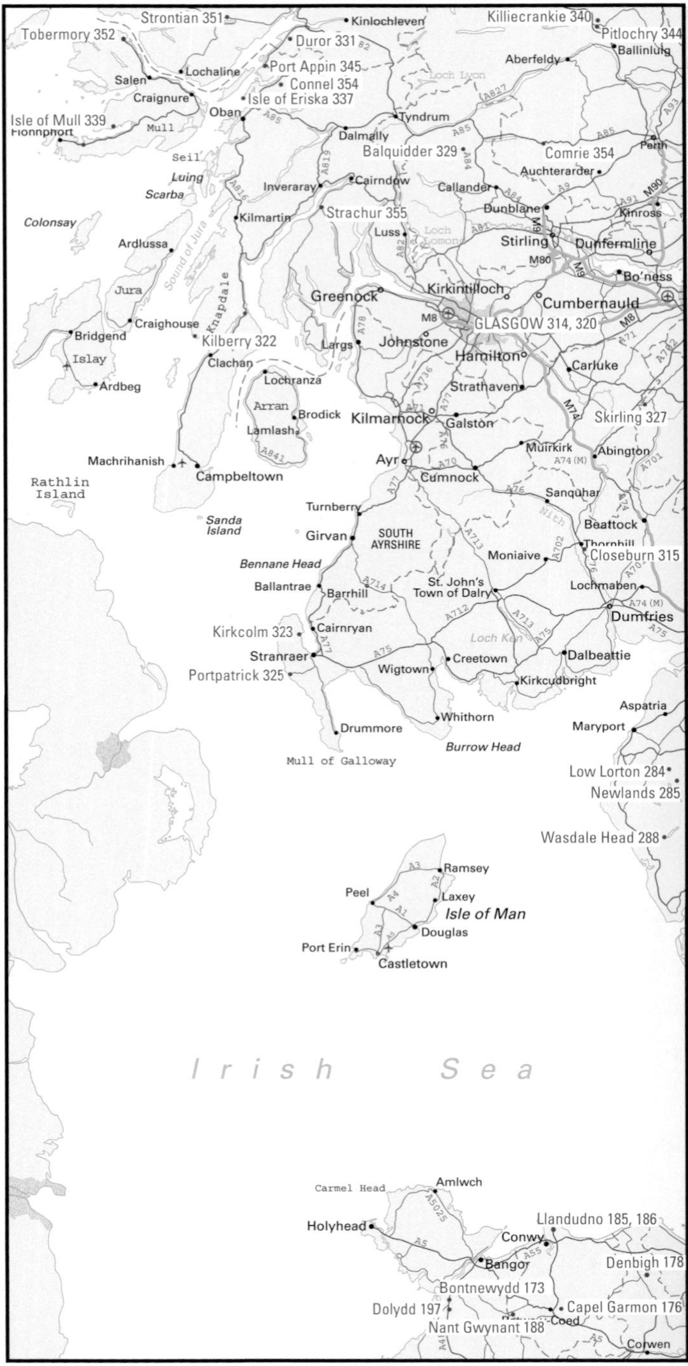
Strontian 351
Kinlochleven
Killiecrankie 340
Tobermory 352
Duror 331
Pitlochry 344
Ballinluig
Aberfeldy
Lochaline
Port Appin 345
Loch Lyon
Salen
Connel 354
Craignure
Isle of Eriska 337
Oban
Tyndrum
Isle of Mull 339
Fionnphort
Mull
Dalmally
Perth
Balquidder 329
Comrie 354
Seil
Luing
Auchterarder
Scarba
Inveraray
Cairndow
Callander
Strachur 355
Dunblane
Kinross
Colonsay
Kilmartin
Luss
Loch Lomond
Stirling
Dunfermline
Ardlussa
Sound of Jura
Knapdale
Jura
Bo'ness
Greenock
Kirkintilloch
Cumbernauld
Craighouse
Bridgend
GLASGOW 314, 320
Kilberry 322
Largs
Johnstone
Islay
Clachan
Hamilton
Carluke
Ardbeg
Lochranza
Strathaven
Arran
Brodick
Kilmarnock
Galston
Skirling 327
Lamlash
Muirkirk
Abington
Machrihanish
Ayr
Campbeltown
Cumnock
Rathlin Island
Sanquhar
Turnberry
Nith
Sanda Island
Beattock
Girvan
SOUTH AYRSHIRE
Thornhill
Moniaive
Closeburn 315
Bennane Head
Ballantrae
St. John's Town of Dalry
Lochmaben
Barrhill
Dumfries
Kirkcolm 323
Cairnryan
Loch Ken
Stranraer
Dalbeattie
Creetown
Portpatrick 325
Wigtown
Kirkcudbright
Aspatria
Whithorn
Maryport
Drummore
Burrow Head
Mull of Galloway
Low Lorton 284
Newlands 285
Wasdale Head 288
Ramsey
Peel
Laxey
Isle of Man
Douglas
Port Erin
Castletown
Irish Sea
Carmel Head
Amlwch
Holyhead
Llandudno 185, 186
Conwy
Bangor
Denbigh 178
Bontnewydd 173
Dolydd 197
Capel Garmon 176
Nant Gwynant 188
Corwen

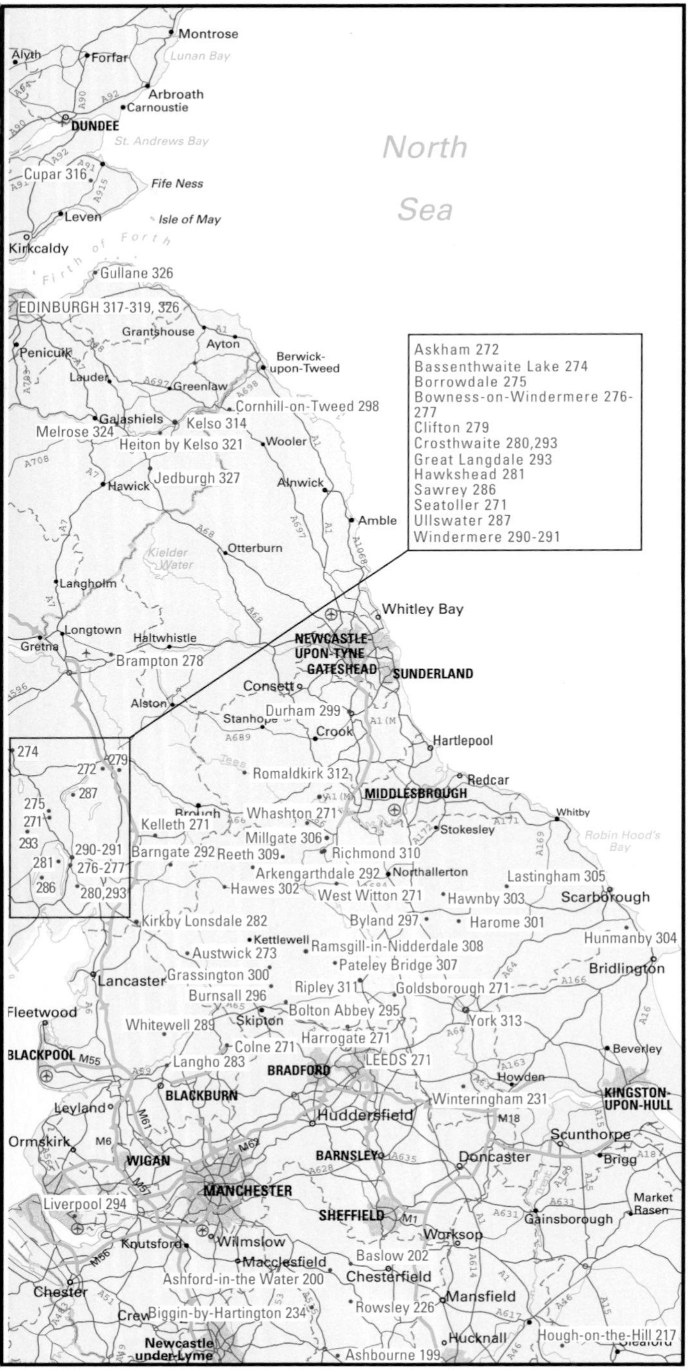
Montrose
Alyth
Forfar
Lunan Bay
Arbroath
Carnoustie
DUNDEE
St. Andrews Bay
North Sea
Cupar 316
Fife Ness
Leven
Isle of May
Kirkcaldy
Firth of Forth
Gullane 326
EDINBURGH 317-319, 326
Grantshouse
Ayton
Penicuik
Berwick-upon-Tweed
Lauder
Greenlaw
Cornhill-on-Tweed 298
Galashiels
Kelso 314
Melrose 324
Heiton by Kelso 321
Wooler
Hawick
Jedburgh 327
Alnwick
Amble
Kielder Water
Otterburn
Langholm
Whitley Bay
Longtown
Gretna
Haltwhistle
Brampton 278
NEWCASTLE-UPON-TYNE
GATESHEAD
SUNDERLAND
Consett
Alston
Durham 299
Stanhope
Crook
Hartlepool
Askham 272
Bassenthwaite Lake 274
Borrowdale 275
Bowness-on-Windermere 276-277
Clifton 279
Crosthwaite 280,293
Great Langdale 293
Hawkshead 281
Sawrey 286
Seatoller 271
Ullswater 287
Windermere 290-291
274
272
279
287
275
271
293
281
286
290-291
276-277
280,293
Romaldkirk 312
Redcar
MIDDLESBROUGH
Brough
Whashton 271
Kelleth 271
Millgate 306
Stokesley
Whitby
Robin Hood's Bay
Barngate 292
Reeth 309
Richmond 310
Arkengarthdale 292
Northallerton
Lastingham 305
Hawes 302
West Witton 271
Hawnby 303
Scarborough
Kirkby Lonsdale 282
Byland 297
Harome 301
Kettlewell
Hunmanby 304
Austwick 273
Ramsgill-in-Nidderdale 308
Pateley Bridge 307
Bridlington
Lancaster
Grassington 300
Ripley 311
Goldsborough 271
Burnsall 296
Bolton Abbey 295
Fleetwood
Whitewell 289
Skipton
York 313
Colne 271
Harrogate 271
Beverley
BLACKPOOL
Langho 283
BRADFORD
LEEDS 271
Howden
BLACKBURN
Winteringham 231
KINGSTON-UPON-HULL
Leyland
Huddersfield
Ormskirk
Scunthorpe
WIGAN
BARNSLEY
Doncaster
Brigg
MANCHESTER
Market Rasen
Liverpool 294
SHEFFIELD
Gainsborough
Worksop
Knutsford
Wilmslow
Baslow 202
Macclesfield
Chesterfield
Ashford-in-the Water 200
Chester
Mansfield
Rowsley 226
Crew
Biggin-by-Hartington 234
Hucknall
Hough-on-the-Hill 217
Newcastle under-Lyme
Ashbourne 199

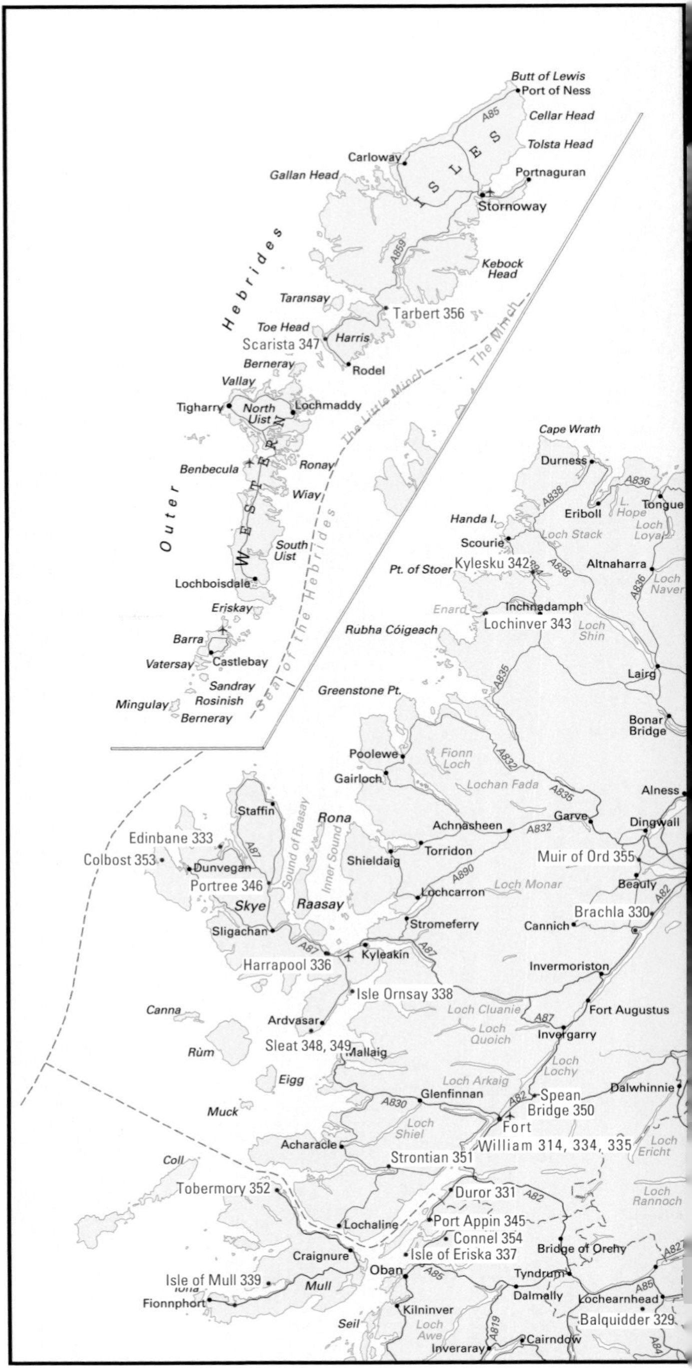

Butt of Lewis
Port of Ness
Cellar Head
Tolsta Head
Carloway
Gallan Head
Portnaguran
Stornoway
ISLES
A85
A859
Kebock Head
Hebrides
Taransay
Tarbert 356
Toe Head
Harris
Scarista 347
Berneray
Rodel
Vallay
Tigharry
North Uist
Lochmaddy
The Little Minch
The Minch
WESTERN
Benbecula
Ronay
Outer
Wiay
South Uist
Lochboisdale
Eriskay
Sea of the Hebrides
Barra
Vatersay
Castlebay
Sandray
Rosinish
Mingulay
Berneray
Cape Wrath
Durness
A836
A838
Tongue
Eriboll
L. Hope
Loch Loyal
Handa I.
Scourie
Loch Stack
Altnaharra
Pt. of Stoer
Kylesku 342
Loch Naver
Enard
Inchnadamph
Lochinver 343
Loch Shin
Rubha Cóigeach
A835
Lairg
Greenstone Pt.
Bonar Bridge
Poolewe
Fionn Loch
A832
Gairloch
Lochan Fada
Alness
Staffin
Rona
Garve
Dingwall
Edinbane 333
Achnasheen
Colbost 353
Dunvegan
A87
Sound of Raasay
Inner Sound
Shieldaig
Torridon
Muir of Ord 355
Portree 346
A890
Loch Monar
Beauly
Skye
Raasay
Lochcarron
A82
Brachla 330
Sligachan
Stromeferry
Cannich
Kyleakin
Harrapool 336
Invermoriston
Isle Ornsay 338
Canna
Loch Cluanie
Fort Augustus
Ardvasar
Loch Quoich
Invergarry
Sleat 348, 349
Rùm
Mallaig
Loch Lochy
Eigg
Loch Arkaig
Glenfinnan
Spean Bridge 350
Dalwhinnie
Muck
A830
Fort William 314, 334, 335
Loch Shiel
Loch Ericht
Acharacle
Coll
Strontian 351
Tobermory 352
Duror 331
Loch Rannoch
Lochaline
Port Appin 345
Connel 354
Isle of Eriska 337
Bridge of Orchy
Craignure
Oban
Tyndrum
A827
Isle of Mull 339
Iona
Mull
Dalmally
Lochearnhead
Fionnphort
Kilninver
Balquidder 329
Seil
Loch Awe
A819
Cairndow
Inveraray
A84

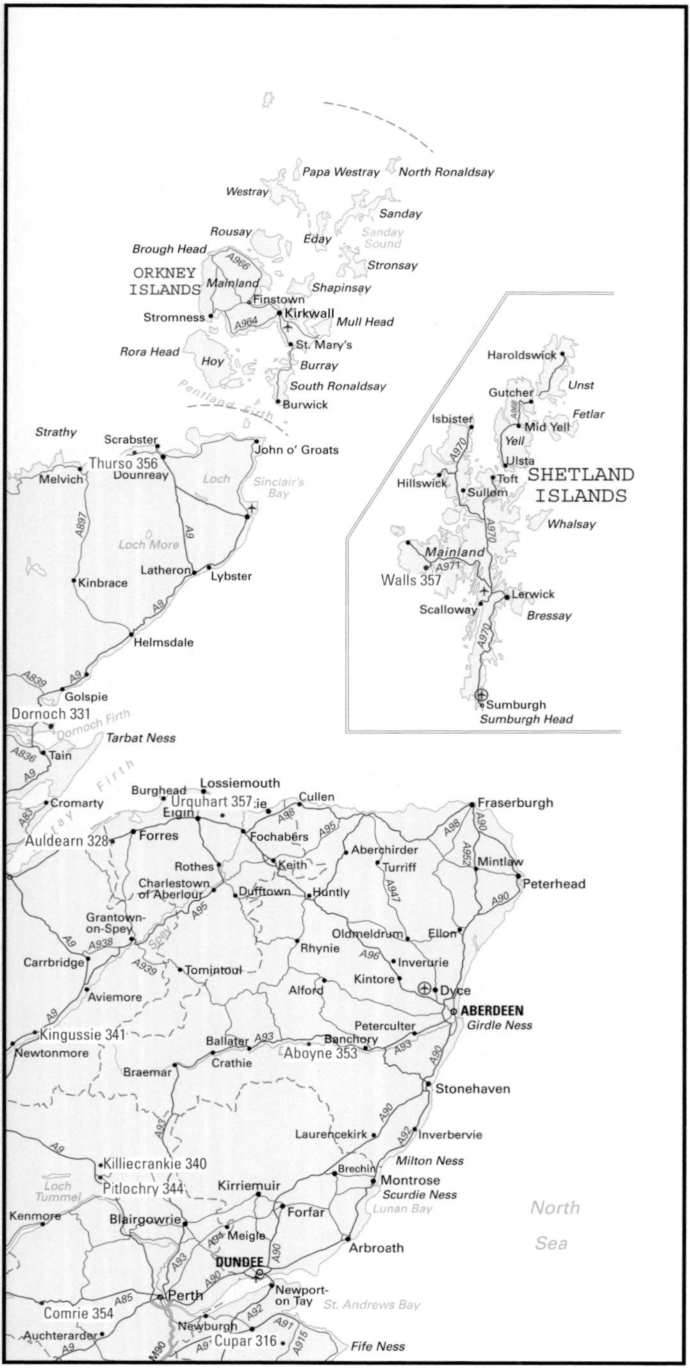

Papa Westray
North Ronaldsay
Westray
Sanday
Rousay
Eday
Sanday Sound
Brough Head
Stronsay
ORKNEY ISLANDS
Mainland
Shapinsay
Finstown
Stromness
Kirkwall
Mull Head
St. Mary's
Rora Head
Hoy
Burray
South Ronaldsay
Pentland Firth
Burwick
Strathy
Scrabster
John o' Groats
Thurso 356
Melvich
Dounreay
Loch
Sinclair's Bay
Loch More
Latheron
Lybster
Kinbrace
Helmsdale
Golspie
Dornoch 331
Dornoch Firth
Tarbat Ness
Tain
Haroldswick
Unst
Gutcher
Fetlar
Isbister
Mid Yell
Yell
Ulsta
Toft
SHETLAND ISLANDS
Hillswick
Sullom
Whalsay
Mainland
Walls 357
Lerwick
Scalloway
Bressay
Sumburgh
Sumburgh Head
Lossiemouth
Burghead
Urquhart 357
Cullen
Fraserburgh
Cromarty
Elgin
Auldearn 328
Forres
Fochabers
Aberchirder
Turriff
Mintlaw
Peterhead
Rothes
Keith
Charlestown of Aberlour
Dufftown
Huntly
Grantown-on-Spey
Oldmeldrum
Ellon
Rhynie
Inverurie
Carrbridge
Tomintoul
Kintore
Alford
Dyce
Aviemore
ABERDEEN
Girdle Ness
Peterculter
Kingussie 341
Newtonmore
Ballater
Banchory
Aboyne 353
Crathie
Braemar
Stonehaven
Laurencekirk
Inverbervie
Milton Ness
Killiecrankie 340
Brechin
Montrose
Scurdie Ness
Loch Tummel
Pitlochry 344
Kirriemuir
Lunan Bay
North Sea
Kenmore
Blairgowrie
Forfar
Meigle
Arbroath
DUNDEE
Newport-on Tay
Perth
St. Andrews Bay
Comrie 354
Newburgh
Auchterarder
Cupar 316
Fife Ness

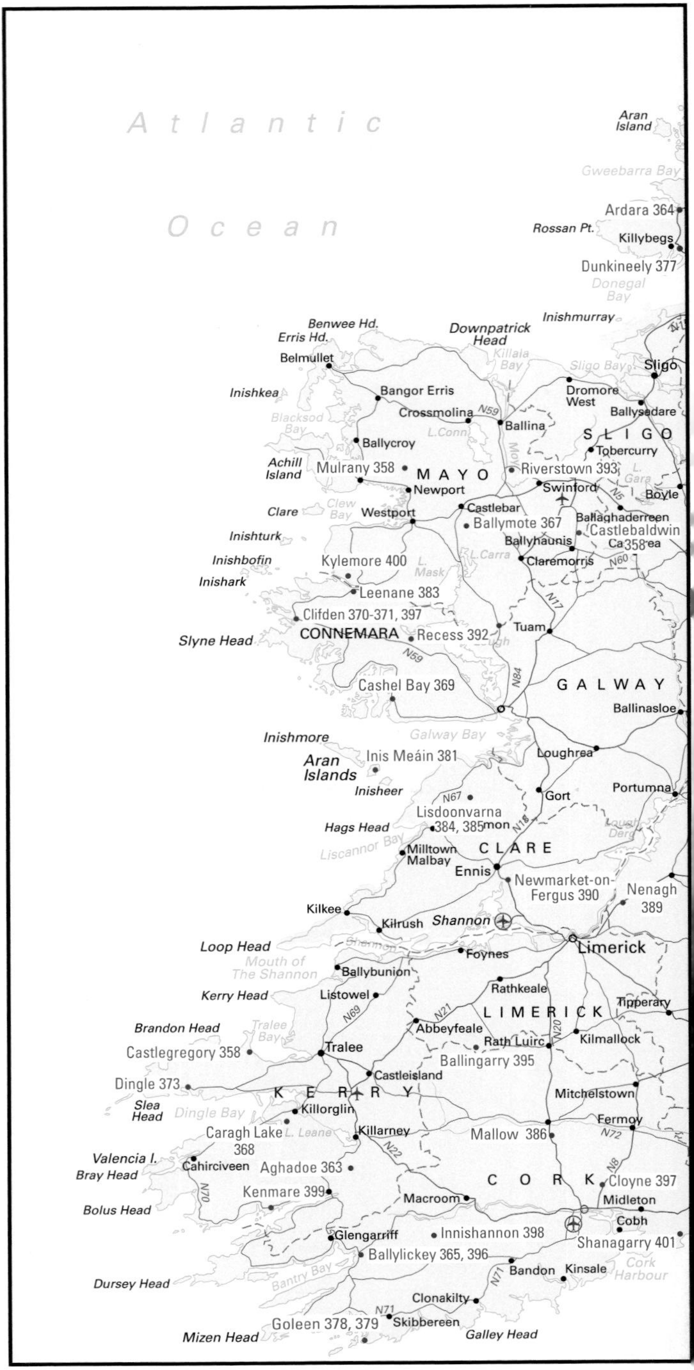
Atlantic Ocean
Aran Island
Gweebarra Bay
Ardara 364
Rossan Pt.
Killybegs
Dunkineely 377
Donegal Bay
Inishmurray
Benwee Hd.
Erris Hd.
Downpatrick Head
Killala Bay
Belmullet
Sligo Bay
Sligo
Inishkea
Bangor Erris
Dromore West
Blacksod Bay
Crossmolina
Ballina
Ballysadare
L.Conn
SLIGO
Ballycroy
Tobercurry
Achill Island
Mulrany 358
MAYO
Riverstown 393
Newport
Swinford
Boyle
Clare
Clew Bay
Westport
Castlebar
Ballaghaderreen
Ballymote 367
Castlebaldwin
Inishturk
Ballyhaunis
Ca358ea
Inishbofin
Kylemore 400
L. Mask
L. Carra
Claremorris
Inishark
Leenane 383
Clifden 370-371, 397
Tuam
Slyne Head
CONNEMARA
Recess 392
Cashel Bay 369
GALWAY
Ballinasloe
Inishmore
Galway Bay
Aran Islands
Inis Meáin 381
Loughrea
Inisheer
Portumna
Gort
Lisdoonvarna 384, 385
Hags Head
Liscannor Bay
Milltown Malbay
CLARE
Ennis
Newmarket-on-Fergus 390
Nenagh 389
Kilkee
Kilrush
Shannon
Limerick
Loop Head
Mouth of The Shannon
Foynes
Ballybunion
Rathkeale
Kerry Head
Listowel
Tipperary
LIMERICK
Brandon Head
Tralee Bay
Abbeyfeale
Kilmallock
Rath Luirc
Castlegregory 358
Tralee
Ballingarry 395
Castleisland
Dingle 373
KERRY
Mitchelstown
Slea Head
Dingle Bay
Killorglin
Fermoy
Caragh Lake 368
L. Leane
Killarney
Mallow 386
Valencia I.
Cahirciveen
Aghadoe 363
Bray Head
CORK
Cloyne 397
Kenmare 399
Midleton
Bolus Head
Macroom
Cobh
Glengarriff
Innishannon 398
Shanagarry 401
Ballylickey 365, 396
Cork Harbour
Dursey Head
Bantry Bay
Bandon
Kinsale
Clonakilty
Goleen 378, 379
Skibbereen
Mizen Head
Galley Head

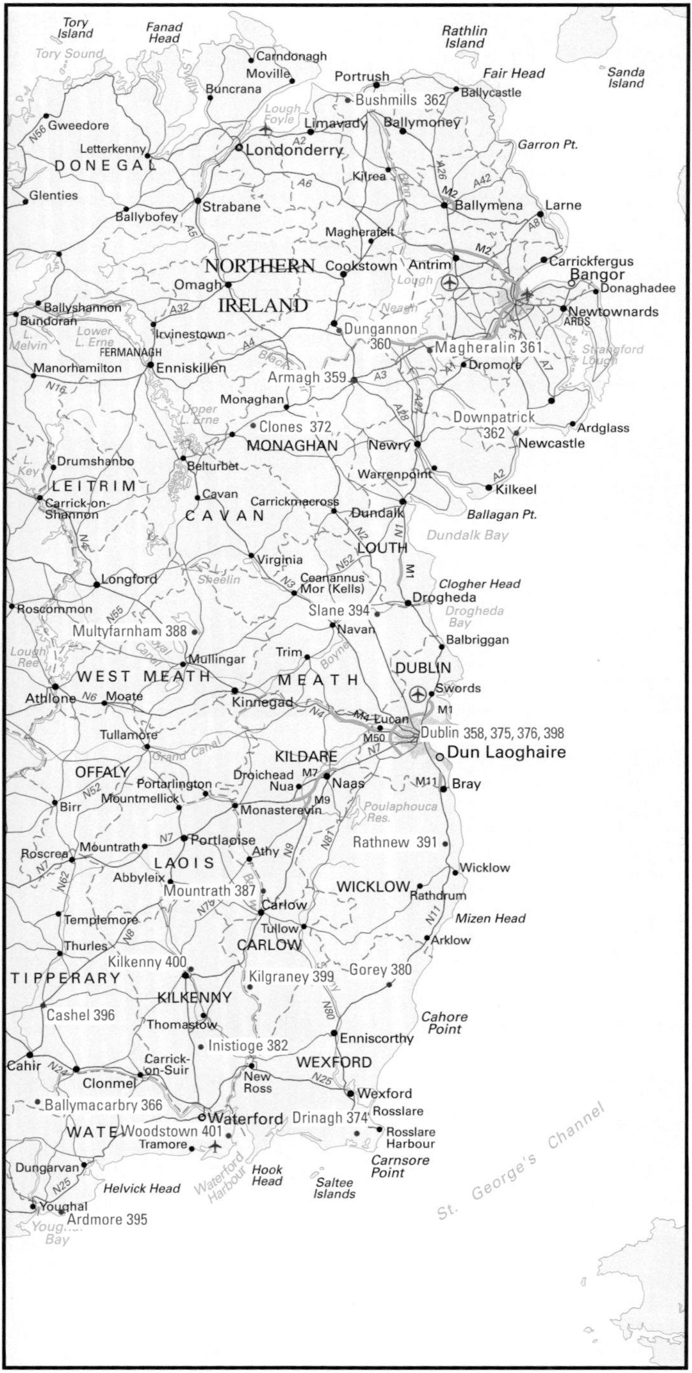

Tory Island
Fanad Head
Tory Sound
Carndonagh
Moville
Buncrana
Lough Foyle
Rathlin Island
Fair Head
Sanda Island
Portrush
Bushmills 362
Ballycastle
Gweedore
Limavady
Ballymoney
Letterkenny
Londonderry
Garron Pt.
DONEGAL
Kilrea
Glenties
Strabane
Ballymena
Larne
Ballybofey
Magherafelt
Carrickfergus
NORTHERN
Cookstown
Antrim
Bangor
Omagh
Lough Neagh
Donaghadee
IRELAND
Ballyshannon
Bundoran
Irvinestown
Dungannon 360
Newtownards
ARDS
Lower L. Erne
L. Melvin
FERMANAGH
Magheralin 361
Strangford Lough
Manorhamilton
Enniskillen
Dromore
Armagh 359
Monaghan
Upper L. Erne
Downpatrick 362
Ardglass
Clones 372
MONAGHAN
Newry
Newcastle
Drumshanbo
L. Key
Belturbet
Warrenpoint
LEITRIM
Cavan
Kilkeel
Carrick-on-Shannon
Carrickmacross
CAVAN
Dundalk
Ballagan Pt.
Dundalk Bay
LOUTH
Virginia
Longford
Sheelin
Ceanannus Mor (Kells)
Clogher Head
Drogheda
Roscommon
Slane 394
Drogheda Bay
Multyfarnham 388
Navan
Balbriggan
Lough Ree
Mullingar
Trim
Boyne
DUBLIN
WEST MEATH
MEATH
Swords
Athlone
Moate
Kinnegad
Lucan
Dublin 358, 375, 376, 398
Tullamore
Grand Canal
Dun Laoghaire
KILDARE
OFFALY
Droichead Nua
Naas
Bray
Portarlington
Birr
Mountmellick
Monasterevin
Poulaphouca Res.
Portlaoise
Rathnew 391
Roscrea
Mountrath
Athy
LAOIS
Wicklow
Abbyleix
WICKLOW
Mountrath 387
Rathdrum
Carlow
Templemore
Tullow
Mizen Head
Thurles
CARLOW
Arklow
Kilkenny 400
TIPPERARY
Kilgraney 399
Gorey 380
KILKENNY
Cashel 396
Thomastown
Cahore Point
Enniscorthy
Inistioge 382
Cahir
Carrick-on-Suir
WEXFORD
Clonmel
New Ross
Wexford
Ballymacarbry 366
Rosslare
Waterford
Drinagh 374
WATE
Woodstown 401
Rosslare Harbour
Tramore
Carnsore Point
Dungarvan
Hook Head
Waterford Harbour
Saltee Islands
Helvick Head
St. George's Channel
Youghal
Ardmore 395
Youghal Bay

Area introduction

This first section covers the most important summer tourist counties of Britai Devon and Cornwall, with their spectacular coastlines and wonderful patchwor countryside, their sunken lanes and timeless villages. Add to them Somerset an Wiltshire, Dorset and south-west Hampshire, and you have what is loosely known a the West Country – what used to be, more or less, the early medieval Kingdom c Wessex. The rest of the section consists of densely populated south-east England East and West Sussex, Kent, Berkshire and Greater London. Here, as elsewhere, yo can scarcely go a mile without discovering somewhere worth seeing: a picturesqu village, a Georgian town or a spectacular view. Charming small hotels are thick o the ground. We draw the border dividing southern England from Central Englan roughly along the M4, or a line linking London in the east with Bristol in the west.

Below are some useful back-up places to try if our main selections are fully booked:

Gidleigh Park
Country house hotel, Chagford
Tel 01647 432367
www.gidleigh.com
Luxury, fine dining.

The Bath Arms
Village hotel, Longleat
Tel 01985 844308
www.batharms.co.uk
Quirky country hotel on The Longleat Estate.

The Scarlet
Coastal hotel, Mawgan Porth
Tel 01637 861800
www.scarlethotel.co.uk
Eco-friendly, grown-ups only hotel for relaxation.

The White House
Town house hotel, Williton
Tel 01984 632306
www.whitehousewilliton.co.uk
Family-run guesthouse, comfortable Somerset base.

The Forbury
Town house hotel, Reading
Tel 01189 527770
www.theforburyhotel.co.uk
Artfully designed city hotel in centre of Reading.

Hotel du Vin
Town mansion hotel, Tunbridge Wells
Tel 084474 89266
www.hotelduvin.com
Elegant hotel in spa town.

The Casterbridge
Town guesthouse, Dorchest
Tel 01305 264043
www.thecasterbridge.co.uk
Relaxed guesthouse offerin bed-and-breakfast service.

Langford Fivehead
Restaurant-with-rooms, Lower Swell
Tel 01460 282020
www.langfordfivehead.co.u
'Farm to plate' fine dining.

The Pear Tree Inn
Restaurant-with-rooms, Whitley Tel 01225 70913
www.wheelerspeartree.com
Marco Pierre White's chic steakhouse in the Cotswol

B&B Belgravia
City bed-and-breakfast, London Tel 020 72598570
www.bb-belgravia.com
Upmarket, stylish bed-and breakfast accommodation.

The Mermaid Inn
Town inn, Rye
Tel 01797 223065
www.mermaidinn.com
Charming inn in pretty Ry dating back to 1420.

Longueville Manor
Country house hotel, St Saviour Tel 01534 725501
www.longuevillemanor.com
Traditional Relais & Chate hotel, high standards.

Allerford, Somerset

Allerford, Minehead, Somerset
TA24 8HW

Tel 01643 863276
e-mail info@crosslanehouse.com
website www.crosslanehouse.com

Nearby Exmoor National Park, Coleridge Way, West Somerset Rural Life Museum
Location just off the A39 in the village of Allerford
Food breakfast, lunch, dinner, picnic baskets on request
Price ££-£££
Rooms 3; 2 double with bathroom and 1 suite with bathroom
Facilities dining room, sitting room, terrace,
Credit cards MC, V
Children not under 16
Disabled access to ground floor only
Pets dogs welcome, not in public rooms
Closed Jan
Proprietors Max and Andrew

Cross Lane House
Village hotel

Cross Lane House has stood on the same corner of Allerford village for more than 500 years – but you'd be forgiven for not realizing this. Recent owners Max and Andrew have carefully renovated the late medieval building, turning it into a striking up-to-date hotel. Set back from the road by a charmingly haphazard stonewall and a trim, winding footpath, the exterior shows Max's and Andrew's attention to detail.

Wherever possible they have retained the house's original features – we especially like the dining room where the massive stone lintel over the fireplace and original timber panelling are good examples of their old-and-new style.

Upstairs the four generously sized bedrooms are decorated in country house style – each room has the kind of thought that we look for. The neutral tones are complemented with floral splashes, adding colour to an otherwise pastel palette.

The location – in Exmoor National Park – gives you access to some of the most beautiful walking routes in south-west England. It is also close to the Coleridge Way: a 36-mile (58 km) footpath noted as one of the UK's best autumnal walks.

Ashwater, Devon

Ashwater, Beaworthy,
Devon EX21 5DF

Tel (01409) 211224
Fax (01409) 211634
e-mail stay@blagdon.com
website www.blagdon.com

Nearby National Trust Coast; golf courses.
Location just off A388 Launceston – Holsworthy road, 4 miles (6.5 km) S of Holsworthy, in 20 acres; ample car parking and helicopter pad
Food breakfast, dinner
Price £££
Rooms 6; 3 double, 3 twin, all have bath/shower; all rooms have phone, TV, hairdryer
Facilities sitting room, library, dining room, bar; terrace, garden, croquet **Credit cards** MC, V
Children welcome over 12
Disabled access difficult **Pets** dogs welcome **Closed** 2 weeks in Nov and 2 weeks in Jan, see website
Proprietors Steve and Liz Morey

Blagdon Manor

Country house hotel

Don't be put off by Blagdon Manor's isolated situation: it lies plum in the middle of the West Country, so no place of interest is really very far away.

This Grade II listed former farmhouse, surrounded by rolling countryside, was derelict when previous owners Tim and Gill Casey discovered it and brought it back to life. Successors Steve and Liz Morey purchased Blagdon Manor in 2001 because, between them, they had worked in the hotel industry for 40 years and thought "it was time to do it themselves".

They told us that their goal isn't to make money, but to use their experience to provide quality. With that in mind, they completely refurbished all six rooms, and Steve took charge of the kitchen, which produces home-made jams, breads and ice-cream. What can't be made on the premises comes from local businesses.

The new conservatory makes an ideal spot for breakfast and lunch and with views toward the north side of Dartmoor, definitely adds to the place. Bedrooms are comfortable, with pretty fabrics and modern bathrooms.

The Moreys assured us that they will be at Blagdon for many years to come: "We want to be here until we retire." We would welcome comments on how they are doing.

Babbacombe, Devon

Oddicombe Beach Hill, Babbacombe, South Devon TQ1 3LX

Tel 01803 327110
e-mail enquiries@caryarms.co.uk
website www.caryarms.co.uk

Nearby Babbacombe Bay, Torquay.
Location turn onto Babbacombe Downs Road, continue along the Downs with the sea on your left then turn left onto Beach Road.
Food breakfast, lunch, dinner
Price ££££ **Rooms** 8; 6 with sea views and balcony/terrace, 1 with no balcony, 1 that sleeps 4; 4 with bath/shower, 2 with shower, 2 with bath; all rooms have phone,TV, hairdryer, tea/coffee facilities; 4 larger cottages **Facilities** residents' sitting room with fire, Yon-Ka Spa, conservatory, bar, dining room, wi-fi **Credit cards** MC, V **Children** welcome over 12 **Disabled** 1 ground-floor room **Pets** dogs in 2 bedrooms and the cottages **Closed** never **Proprietors** Lana de Savary

The Cary Arms

Beach inn

Special places need a special effort to reach them. Set beneath the cliffs on the beach at Babbacombe, the Cary Arms' location is spectacular, but its approach, via an alarmingly steep single-track road, is not for the faint hearted. Queen Victoria was equally enchanted 150 years ago, rowing ashore with Prince Albert from the Royal Yacht on several occasions.

The present hotel was built in the late 1880s: a solid, reassuring building with a stone walled, slate floored bar at its core. Here, superior gastropub dishes are served. Try the local Devon beef or Lyme Bay lobster.

There are eight bedrooms and three self-catering cottages, all delightful, with retro red leather bed-heads, pretty wardrobes, sticks of rock on snow white pillows and walls adorned by old posters advertising the delights of Devon and colourful photographs (recalling de Savary's passion) of racing yachts.

Chic and secluded doesn't come cheap, but it's worth it. As we went to press, double rooms were £155 in low season, rising to £225 in high – this price includes breakfast. The manageress, Jen, is superb.

1 Upper Oldfield Park,
Bath, Avon BA2 3JX

Tel (01225) 426336
e-mail info@dorianhouse.co.uk
website www.dorianhouse.co.uk

Nearby Bath centre.
Location from Bath, take A367 signposted Shepton Mallet, after 1 minute's drive, take first road on the right; with car parking
Food breakfast
Price ££
Rooms 13 doubles; all with bath or shower, all rooms have TV, phone, hairdryer, wi-fi
Facilities sitting room, dining room, honesty bar; garden
Credit cards MC, V
Children accepted by arrangement
Disabled access difficult
Pets not accepted
Closed 24th and 25th Dec
Proprietors Tim Hugh

Dorian House

Bed-and-breakfast

Although Bath has a large number of hotels, Dorian House stands out as a place of elegance and charm. Tim Hugh has made the most of this Victorian building built in 1880 of Bath stone, standing on a hill overlooking the city centre – bedrooms have splendid views towards Royal Crescent.

With high ceilings and large windows (including some impressive bay windows), rooms are drenched in light and, with tan, beige and cream tones, have a feeling of airiness. The house retains all of its original features and many rooms have fireplaces and fine antiques. Since our last edition there's been extensive redecoration in bedrooms, bathrooms and elsewhere.

Breakfast is taken in a tastefully decorated breakfast room, also with views of the city. The sitting room (with honesty bar) is equally refined. You can't have dinner here, but there are plenty of good restaurants in Bath and Tim provides a book of menus collected from the better restaurants in town. Tim happens to be a cellist for the London Symphony Orchestra and his concert recordings form part of Dorian House's own-label CD. His artistic flair is evident in this smart bed-and-breakfast.

Bath

Russel Street, Bath, Somerset BA1 2QF

Tel (01225) 447928
Fax (01225) 446065
e-mail reservations@thequeensberry.co.uk **website** www.thequeensberry.co.uk

Nearby Assembly Rooms; Museum of Costume; The Circus.
Location in middle of city, close to main shopping area; paved gardens behind; daytime car parking restricted – but valet parking available
Food breakfast, lunch, dinner
Price £££
Rooms 29, 1 with shower, rest with bath; all rooms have phone, TV, hairdryer, CD player
Facilities sitting room, bar, restaurant; courtyard
Credit cards AE, MC, V
Children welcome
Disabled accessible, lift/elevator
Pets guide dogs only
Closed never
Proprietors Laurence and Helen Beere

The Queensberry

Town house hotel

This Bath hotel is slightly large for our purposes, but cannot be allowed to escape the net. Laurence and Helen Beere bought this discreet, quiet and beautifully decorated haven right in the centre of Bath in 2003. It has the advantage of a lift to all levels, which cuts down on confusion in the maze of stairwells, corridors and different levels resulting from the linking of three buildings. Despite the small-scale appearance of the hotel, the majority of the bedrooms are surprisingly spacious, and are kitted out to the highest standards of comfort and elegance. Double beds generally mean king-size here, almost guaranteed to give you a good night's sleep, and are made up with lovely cotton sheets. Rooms on the first floor are largest, with armchairs and breakfast tables; bathrooms are lavish, with quality toiletries and proper towels.

All of the rooms have been refurbished in the last two years, successfully giving them a more contemporary feel, while still making use of the original features and antiques.

Downstairs, the principal sitting room is beautifully furnished in muted colours. The basement restaurant, the Olive Tree, attracts non-residents.

Beaminster, Dorset

Beaminster, Dorset DT8 3AY

Tel (01308) 862200
Fax (01308) 863700
e-mail enquiries@bridge-house.co.uk
website www.bridge-house.co.uk

Nearby Mapperton Gardens; Forde Abbey; Abbotsbury Swannery & Sub-Tropical Gardens.
Location on A3066 in centre of town; ample car parking
Food breakfast; lunch; dinner
Price £££
Rooms 13; 7 double, 3 twin, 1 single, 2 family, all with bath or shower; all rooms have phone, TV, wi-fi
Facilities sitting room, bar, restaurant, 2 conservatories; outdoor dining area, walled garden
Credit cards AE, MC, V
Children accepted
Disabled 4 bedrooms with easy access **Pets** dogs accepted in selected rooms **Closed** never
Proprietors Mark and Joanna Donovan

Bridge House Hotel

Country hotel

Dating from the 13th century, Bridge-House is reputedly a former clergy house and the oldest building in Beaminster. Whatever its antecedents, it is certainly a venerable and charming building and has been run as a hotel by Mark and Joanna Donovan for the last nine years. Mark, a former television producer, and Joanna, a former retail buyer, took on the hotel as a major change of lifestyle.Their aim has been to create a stylish country town retreat by 'updating where necessary, without destroying the building's unique charm'.

The sitting room and bar areas have medieval character; local artists' paintings hang on the cream walls. Lunch and dinner are served in the Georgian panelled dining room or the conservatory. In summer, guests can also eat outside under a large 'Gazova', which looks out on to the walled gardens. Head chef Steve Pielesz has an excellent reputation. The area is blessed with quality local produce: fish, meat and cheese all come from nearby. Bread, biscuits and ice-cream are all made in the Bridge House kitchens; even the marmalade that accompanies the satisfying breakfasts is made on the premises.

Bedrooms, with mahogany beds and Frette Italian linen, are all different, as would be expected in a building so full of nooks and crannies – including a priest hole.

Beercrocombe, Somerset

Hatch Beauchamp,Taunton,
Somerset TA3 6AF

Tel 01823 481883
email frogstreet@hotmail.com
website www.frogstreet.co.uk

Nearby Barrington Court; Vale of Taunton.
Location on SW side of village, 10 miles (16 km) SE of Taunton; in gardens, with ample car-parking
Food breakfast, dinner (for parties of 6 or more)
Price £
Rooms 4; 1 family suite, 2 doubles, 1 super king with private sitting room and entrace; all have bath/shower; all rooms have hairdryer, radio
Facilities sitting room, dining room; terrace, garden
Credit cards all major
Children accepted by arrangement
Disabled not suitable
Pets not accepted
Closed 6 weeks in the winter period
Proprietors Louise and David

Frog Street Farmhouse

Farm guesthouse

This longhouse dates back to the 15th century and can be found at the end of a lane in deepest Somerset. The house has considerable character and warmth, with Jacobean panelling and a handsome oak-beamed inglenook in the sitting room. Guests walk through the front door straight in to the highly polished dining room. Dinner is served for parties of 6 or more, and where possible Louise and David use their own produce: eggs come from their own hens, seasonal vegetables from the organic garden, with home-made bread and preserves at breakfast.

Bedrooms look out on to farmland, cider apple orchards and the pretty garden. They are all spacious and comfortable, with white duvets, and a mix of antique furniture. Since the last edition, the Orchard suite has been expanded into two bedrooms to incorporate families; The Snug has a private sitting room and entrance. The bathrooms in all rooms have been renovated and are airy, with freestanding roll-top baths or showers. The atmosphere is friendly, restful and unpretentious.

Bigbury-on-Sea, Devon

Folly Hill, Bigbury-on-Sea, Devon
TQ7 4AR

Tel (01548) 810240
Fax (01548) 810240
e-mail
thehenleyhotel@btconnect.com
website www.thehenleyhotel.co.uk

Nearby Burgh Island, Avon Estuary.
Location 20 minutes from A38 beyond Bigbury-on-Sea towards sea; ample car parking
Food breakfast, dinner
Price ££
Rooms 5; all double and 3 can be twin, all have bath/shower; all have phone, TV, radio
Facilities conservatory/dining room; garden, private cliff path and steps to beach, beach
Credit cards AE, MC, V
Children over 12 only
Disabled not suitable
Pets welcome
Closed Nov to March
Proprietors Martyn Scarterfield and Petra Lampe

The Henley

Coastal hotel

Recommended to us by an astute reader, The Henley was described to us as 'the sort of place that I always hope to discover on holiday, and alas, rarely do.' Originally built as a holiday cottage during Edwardian times, the hotel has a beach-house feel and spectacular views that stretch from the Avon Estuary around to Burgh Island. And if simply looking at the sea isn't enough, you can climb down the private cliff path to a stretch of pristine beach.

Although owner Martyn Scarterfield was a PE and Art teacher in a previous life, he comes from a family hotel in Sidmouth and has been in the trade for many years. Co-owner Petra Lampe brings both charm and a sense of warmth and elegance to the hotel. Together, they create a relaxing atmosphere that is, above all, unpretentious.

Bedrooms are simple, yet comfortable and spacious. The dining room has Lloyd Loom furniture and overlooks the sea. Martyn does the cooking and it can be described as 'real home cooked food' – excellent quality without any artificial presentation. The menu features a choice of three starters and two mains, one of which will be fresh, locally caught fish.

A winning combination of great food, beautiful views and friendly owners.

Bradford-on-Avon, Wiltshire

4 Masons Lane, Bradford-on-Avon, Wiltshire BA15 1QN

Tel (01225) 866842
Fax (01225) 866648
e-mail
csh@bradfordoldwindmill.co.uk
website
www.bradfordoldwindmill.co.uk

Nearby Bath; Kennet and Avon Canal; Longleat.
Location just N of town centre; with cottage garden and parking for 3 small cars
Food breakfast, dinner (Mon, Wed, Thur, Sat only)
Price ££
Rooms 3; 2 double, 1 family suite, all with bath; all rooms have TV
Facilities sitting room, dining room; terrace **Credit cards** MC, V
Children welcome over 6
Disabled access difficult
Pets not accepted
Closed Nov to Mar
Proprietors Peter and Priscilla Roberts

Bradford Old Windmill

Town guesthouse

Peter and Priscilla Roberts' extraordinary home, an old windmill, continues to provide guests with a unique experience. Built in 1807, the windmill functioned for only 20 years but left a memorable building in its stead. It boasts a 4-storey Cotswold stone tower, conical roof, pointed Gothic windows and restored sail galley.

The rooms, with curved walls and oddly-angled corners, offer excellent views over old Bradford and beyond. The suite includes a minstrel gallery and the smallest room has a waterbed. Each room contains curiosities and guidebooks from the Roberts' extensive travels. Bathrooms have been updated.

Breakfast and dinner are occasionally served, weather permitting, on the pretty terrace that also overlooks old Bradford. You get breakfast at a communal table, but special provision is made for honeymoon couples booking the 'celebration special break' who wish to eat late and alone.

Priscilla will cook dinner (always vegetarian) if given notice. Recent menus include Caribbean, Thai and Nepalese food. The breakfast menu is extensive and includes free-range bacon. Ingredients are 90 per cent organic. This is a very different kind of guesthouse, and one with great character. See also our other windmill, Cley Mill (page 249)..

Bradford-on-Avon, Wiltshire

Newtown, Bradford-on-Avon,
Wiltshire BA15 1NQ

Tel (01225) 862230
Fax (01225) 866248
e-mail priorysteps@clara.co.uk
website www.priorysteps.co.uk

Nearby Barton Tithe Barn; Bath.
Location off A363 on N side of town; in 0.5 acre garden, with car parking
Food breakfast, dinner (to order)
Price ££
Rooms 5 double and twin, all with bath; 1 self-catering apartment in the Coach House; all rooms have TV
Facilities sitting room, dining room; terrace, garden
Credit cards MC, V
Children accepted
Disabled access difficult
Pets not accepted
Closed occasionally
Proprietors Carey and Diana Chapman

Priory Steps

Town guesthouse

High above the lovely little wool town of Bradford-on-Avon, Carey and Diana Chapman's converted row of weavers' cottages look out over the predominantly Georgian houses interspersed with a smattering of Saxon and medieval buildings. Although only a three minute walk from the centre, Priory Steps is not easy to find. It is so discreetly signposted that it looks like a private home – which it is for the Chapmans and their (now grown-up) children. As a result, the pictures and pieces that decorate the house have family connections and the atmosphere is informal and easy-going, especially in the book-lined sitting room.

Each of the bedrooms has a theme – Indian, Chinese and so on. In spite of the cottage architecture, there is nothing cramped about them: they are light and airy, with wonderful views. Beautifully decorated, each is furnished mainly with antiques. This is a well-maintained place with a continuing refurbishment programme.

Diana is a keen cook and dinner is served either at a communal table in the elegant dining room or, on fine days, out on the terrace of the garden looking down over the town. Dinners are three courses, with no choice, but special requirements are happily met, given notice. You will be made to feel like a house guest in a particularly well-run home.

Branscombe, Devon

Branscombe, Devon
EX12 3DJ

Tel (01297) 680300
Fax (01297) 680500
e-mail reception@masonsarms.co.uk
website www.masonsarms.co.uk

Nearby South Devon coastal path; Sidmouth.
Location in village 8 miles (11 km) S of Honiton, off A3052 between Sidmouth and Seaton; with ample car parking
Food breakfast, lunch, dinner
Price ££-£££
Rooms 21; 7 in the main inn; 14 cottage rooms; all rooms have phone, TV, hairdryer
Facilities sitting room, bar, restaurant; terrace, garden **Credit cards** MC, V **Children** welcome
Disabled access not possible
Pets accepted **Closed** never
Proprietors St Austell Brewery Company Ltd
Managers Simon and Alison Ede

Masons Arms

Seaside village inn

Branscombe is a picturesque little Devon village, at the end of a winding lane, surrounded by steep, wooded hillsides and overlooking the sea. The National Trust owns most of the land around, and the South Devon Coastal Path passes through it. In other words, this village is a hive of activity, inspiring visits from walkers in winter and beachcomers in summer, many of whom pitch up at the Masons Arms. Welcoming, yes; popular, certainly. It's what a village pub should be, although its success has led to expansion: what was a simple inn, converted from four cottages, now has a restaurant and a bar serving food, a large function room, plus 21 rooms spread out between the main inn and cottage rooms.

In 2010 The Masons Arms was taken over by St Austell Brewery Company Ltd, who wanted to make improvements while preserving the character of the place. They have refurbished the cottage rooms and restaurant, and all rooms now have their own bath.

The bedrooms have a cottagey feel, with pretty fabrics, beamed ceilings and sloping floors. The recently upgraded cottage rooms are modern and stylish. The bathrooms are mainly a smart slate grey. The food is several notches above pub fare, with the restaurant and bar offering the same menu.

28 High St, Bruton, Somerset BA10 0AE

Tel 01749 814070
e-mail mail@atthechapel.co.uk
website atthechapel.co.uk

Nearby Bath
Location central Bruton
Food breakfast, lunch, dinner
Price ££
Rooms 8 double, all with wi-fi, iPod docking station, TV, safe, tea/coffee facilities
Facilities sitting room, dining room, bar, brasserie, gun lockers
Credit cards AE, MC, V
Children welcome
Disabled access to the restaurant
Pets not accepted
Closed Christmas Day
Proprietors Catherine Butler & Ahmed Sidki

At the Chapel

Town guesthouse

This handsome 19thC congregational chapel has been brilliantly transformed. Catherine Butler, the inspired owner, along with her partner Ahmed, spent eight years restoring it, and rapidly established it as an indispensable meeting place ("it's the town piazza" a regular tells us) – a hub for the community, just as it was when it was first built.

You wake in a bedroom dominated by floor-to-ceiling stained-glass and stone-framed windows: what an estate agent would call the the wow factor. Freshly-baked croissants are delivered from the in-house bakery to your room at seven each morning. The smell wafts temptingly through the door (handmade by Ahmed, like all the doors, much of the furniture and the stone bread oven in the bakery).

Things just happen here. The walls are decorated with modern art on loan from celebrated gallery Hauser & Wirth; Sergei Polunin and other Royal Ballet stars have danced here; the night we stayed, there was a showing of local boy Julian Temple's film *London: The Modern Babylon* downstairs in the 'club room' ... and on it goes. "People just suggest things," says Catherine. "The building has the right chemistry; I believe it always did."

Bude, Devon

Summerleaze Crescent, Bude, Devon EX23 8HJ

Tel 01288 389800 **Fax** 01288 389820 **e-mail** enquiries@the-beachatbude.co.uk
website www.thebeachatbude.co.uk

Nearby Bude heritage centre and museum, the National Coastal Path, surfing and seawater swimming pool available on the beach, Boscastly village, the ruins of King Arthur's Castle in Tintagel **Location** Bude, some car-parking available
Food breakfast **Price** ££-££££
Rooms 16; all with flat-screen TV, Blu-Ray player, iPod docking station, direct-dial telephone, hairdryer, fridge, safe, hospitality tray.
Facilities conservatory, dining room, sun terrace, bar, treatment room, wi-fi **Credit cards** AE, MC
Children accepted, extra bed £30 per night
Disabled no disabled access, but there is a lift to all floors, and 1 ground-floor room **Closed** over Christmas
Manager Sarah Whiteman

The Beach

Coastal hotel

Reopened in May 2011 after 18 months of renovations, The Beach can claim to be one of the hottest places on the north Cornwall coast. The old Victorian building has kept its character, with rooms of different shapes and sizes, but a modern feel has been added by thoughtful, contemporary redecoration.

Guests especially enjoy the bedrooms, describing them as comfortable and homely. All the rooms are decorated in cool colours – in the New England seaside style – with fashionable design features and accessories, particularly in the bathrooms. It is the combination of the views over Summerleaze Beach and the stylish decoration that make them so appealing – most have views that also extend over the spectacular Cornish scenery surrounding Bude, including the Downs at Efford and the Bude canal.

With enough style and taste to be a 'proper' hotel, the owners have decided against adding a restaurant for the time being, and instead encourage guests to explore the interesting town of Bude with its many local restaurants. Definitely a place for more than one night's stay.

Chettle, Dorset

Chettle, near Blandford Forum,
Dorset, DT11 8DB

Tel (01258) 830096
Fax (01258) 830051
e-mail
enquiry@castlemanhotel.co.uk
website www.castlemanhotel.co.uk

Nearby Kingston Lacy House; Cranborne Chase; Salisbury.
Location in village, signposted off A354, 6 miles (9 km) NE of Blandford; ample car parking
Food breakfast, Sunday lunch, dinner **Price** ££
Rooms 8 doubles, all with bath; all rooms have phone, TV, hairdryer
Facilities dining room, 2 sitting rooms, bar; garden
Credit cards MC, V
Children welcome
Disabled access difficult
Pets not accepted in house; 2 stables available for guests' horses and dogs
Closed Feb
Proprietor Barbara Garnsworthy

Castleman

Country house hotel

Chettle is one of those rare estate villages that has hardly changed in the 150 years it has been in the benign ownership of one family, who live in the fine Queen Anne manor house, open to the public during summer months. Teddy Bourke, one of the family, took on the decrepit ex-dower house ('locals all thought it was haunted') in 1996, together with his partner, Barbara Garnsworthy, transforming it into a charmingly eccentric and very reasonably priced hotel and restaurant. Part of the building dates back 400 years, but it was much altered in Victorian times when it was tricked out with a galleried hall; a richly carved oak Jacobean fireplace was also installed in one of the reception rooms (the other is Regency style) with bookcases to match. Upstairs, the elegant proportions of the rooms have been left intact, and bedrooms are just right: comfortable and in good taste, but without room service or unnecessary frills so as to keep prices sensible; several of the bathrooms have Victorian roll-top baths. The 'large' rooms are enormous, one with a huge bay window overlooking the fields, whilst the smaller ones are still spacious. The Castleman's restaurant – a long, rather plain room at the rear – serves straightforward traditional and modern British dishes, and the bill is not indigestible. 'Superb value', say regular guests.

Coverack, Cornwall

Coverack, Nr Helston, Cornwall, TR12 6TF

Tel 01326 280464
e-mail enquiries@thebayhotel.co.uk
website www.thebayhotel.co.uk

Nearby Lizard Peninsula, the Eden project, Trebah gardens, Iron-Age fort, open-air theatre, St Michael's Mount, Falmouth, Helston, Penzance, Truro, St Ives
Location M5 Motorway: junction 31 onto A30 into Cornwall, then onto Broads.
Food breakfast, lunch, dinner
Price £-££ **Rooms** 13 double and twin; hairdryers, tea and coffee making facilities **Facilities** restaurant, terrace, wi-fi, flatscreen televisions, private parking **Credit cards** MC, V **Children** not under 8 **Disabled** some ground floor rooms **Pets** small and medium dogs welcome but not in public rooms; £8 valeting charge per dog per day; pet food arrangeable. **Closed** Dec-Feb **Proprietors** House Family

The Bay Hotel

Seaside hotel

Peace and quiet. One visitor remarked that during her whole time here, she saw "no more than fifty people on the entire beach." Nestling in the fishing village of Coverack, the hotel is a second's walk from miles of unspoilt coastline.

Inside, proprietors the House family have gone to great lengths to create a peaceful and calming atmosphere. Rooms are decorated in mellow, coastal tones, which perfectly complement the sea views most visitors will have. Some are smallish, but all are well furnished with more than enough storage space. You can really switch off here: none of the rooms have a phone, and the area itself has no mobile reception. There is, however, free wi-fi.

The hotel has a terrace and a superbly decorated conservatory restaurant, which looks out across the sea. Guests should expect to sit down to top food – chef and proprietor Ric House has a reputation for creating excellent dishes. Ingredients are all local, and, of course, all fish is freshly caught. Service is excellent in the restaurant, as it is throughout the rest of the hotel. The House family have more than 30 years of experience within the hotel business, and the welcoming atmosphere crops up continually in guests' comments.

Crudwell, Wiltshire

Crudwell, Malmesbury
Wiltshire SN16 9EP

Tel (01666) 577194
e-mail info@therectoryhotel.co.uk
website www.therectoryhotel.com

Nearby Cotswolds
Location village of Crudwell on the edge of the Cotswolds with car parking **Food** breakfast, lunch, dinner
Price ££-£££
Rooms 12 doubles, all with bath and shower, radio, iPod docking station, TV/DVD players, skincare products
Facilities bar/sitting room, Victorian walled garden, table tennis, helipad, outer heated swimming pool
Credit cards AE, MC, V
Children welcome
Disabled not suitable
Pets dogs accepted
Closed never
Proprietors Jonathan Barry, Julian Muggridge

The Rectory

Village hotel

A real find: this hotel is as soothing as it is professional. Assured, and stylishly simple, devoid of gimmicks, it's unaffected but excellent. Recently refurbished and reopened in 2008 by its young and savvy new owners, The Rectory stands on the edge of the Cotswolds in the village of Crudwell.The entrance hall-reception area is homely as well as contemporary, with an arresting pair of lamp stands and tall, unadorned, half-shuttered windows.

Jonathan Barry trained with the Hotel du Vin group; Julian Muggridge had an art gallery and antiques business: a happy combination if ever there was one.The reception area opens on to a wide, light, flagstoned corridor, prettily decorated with side tables and mirrors. Opening off it are a lovely panelled dining room, elegant in its simplicity, and a warmly, eclectically decorated bar/sitting room. The dining room offers a short, interesting menu, or if you prefer to eat out, try The Potting Shed Pub in Crudwell village, which produces great pub fare with some interesting twists.

The 12 bedrooms could have been furnished and decorated just for this guide. Named after hills along the Cotswold Way, they are all different, attractive without being fancy, sensibly priced homes from home in which it's a pleasure to spend time.

Dittisham, Devon

Old Coombe Manor Farm, Dittisham, near Dartmouth, Devon Q6 OJA

Tel (01803) 722398
Fax (01803) 722401
e-mail richard@fingals.co.uk
website www.fingals.co.uk

Nearby Dartmouth Castle.
Location 7 miles (6 km) N of Dartmouth, 1 mile (1.5 km) from village; with garden and car parking
Food breakfast, dinner
Price ££-££££
Rooms 3-4 doubles, 5 self-catering for 2-6 people, all with bath or shower; all rooms have phone, some have TV
Facilities dining room, bar, library, TV room, jacuzzi, sauna, snooker, cinema; swimming pool, croquet, tennis, table-tennis; rowing boat
Credit cards AE, MC, V
Children accepted
Disabled access difficult
Pets accepted in bedrooms
Closed after New Year to before Easter **Proprietor** Richard Johnston

Fingals

Manor house hotel

Fingals is different, and those who love it will really love it – which sums up why we remain enthusiastic about this manor farmhouse in a secluded valley close to the River Dart. Owner Richard Johnston calls it a 'hotel and restaurant', but in practice, Fingals comes much closer to the 'country house party' type of guesthouse, where it is normal (though not obligatory) for guests to share a table in the wood-panelled dining room at mealtimes.

The 17thC house, with Queen Anne front additions, has plenty of charm. Inside, new and old furniture, pine and oak blend stylishly. In 2014 the owner will reduce the number of bedrooms to three or four, and there will be five self-catering properties for families or for those who want extra space and privacy while still being able to use the hotel's facilities.

Fingals is an exceptionally relaxed place – you pour your own drinks, eat breakfast until 11 in the morning – and those who insist on everything being just so are likely to be disappointed. The three-course dinners, chosen from a short menu, are modern in style, competent in execution, and ample in quantity. A laid-back place with a laid-back yet thoroughly professional proprietor.

East Chelborough, Dorset

East Chelborough, near Dorchester, Dorset DT2 0QA

Tel 01935 83362
e-mail relax@woodencabbage.co.uk
website www.woodencabbage.co.uk

Nearby Lyme Regis, Charmouth, Lulworth Cove, Abbotsbury and Cerne Abbas, Bridport, Beaminster.
Location 12 miles north of Bridport and Dorchester, 10 miles west of Sherborne
Food breakfast, dinner on request
Price ££
Rooms 3; 2 double rooms and 1 twin all with en-suite; all rooms have flat screen TV, wi-fi, hairdryers and tea trays
Facilities garden room with cosy sitting room area, TV and wi-fi, hall, garden and terraces, tea/coffee facilities; private parking (under cover if necessary) **Credit cards** via Paypal **Children** normally over 3/4 years **Disabled** no access **Pets** not accepted in the house **Closed** during winter months please enquire **Proprietors** Susie and Martyn Lee

Wooden Cabbage

Village guesthouse

'Wooden cabbage' is the local jargon for the many small oak trees that grow around here and this house named after them is superbly sited on a gently sloping hill with satisfyingly long views over gentle unspoilt Dorset countryside. It's a former keeper's cottage that has been enlarged to quite gracious proportions – there's an airy feeling of space in the main rooms and it's furnishings are elegant – owners Martyn and Susie Lee's family heirlooms are everywhere, some of them fine pieces, but with homely touches such as family photos.

Bedrooms are like the rooms you would find in a cared-for family home – stylish without being over the top. Service is exceptionally good for an operation such as this – professional but relaxed. Our series editor Fiona Duncan says that if Oscars were awarded for guesthouses, Martyn and Susie would get one.

There's breakfast, and dinner is served on request – Susie's food is more than competent, flavourful home cooking. The wines and canapés, are included in the dinner price. Prices are very fair. Martyn's vegetable garden will make amateur kitchen gardeners want to go home and give up: it's not only functional but a key feature of the garden at one end of the house.

Fonthill Gifford, Wiltshire

Fonthill Gifford, Tisbury, Wiltshire, SP3 6PX

Tel 01747 870385
e-mail info@beckfordarms.com
website www.beckfordarms.com

Nearby Fonthill Estate; Tisbury station (5 minute drive); Rushmore Golf Club
Location just off the Fonthill Estate, near Tisbury
Food breakfast, lunch, dinner
Price ££
Rooms 10; 8 rooms above the pub and 2 private lodges a short walk away; all with own bath or shower, TV with DVD player and internet radio
Facilities traditional pub bar, large garden; terrace
Credit cards DC, MC, V
Children welcome
Disabled only to downstairs rooms
Pets welcome (except in the lodges)
Closed never
Proprietors Dan Brod and Charlie Luxton

The Beckford Arms

Country pub

Although a night-time fire threatened to destroy the Beckford Arms a few years ago, new owners Charlie Luxton and Dan Brod have taken this event in their stride and used it to create something exceptional.

Our series editor Fiona Duncan notes that it's a bit of a hybrid – traditional country pub, restaurant and charming place to stay all in one. You can either eat at the bar, where mulled wine and cider are warmed over an open fire during winter, the elegant private dining room, the laid back conservatory, or even the sitting room if you like. The food can't be faulted.

After dinner, you can retire to one of their ten small but well-appointed bedrooms, where a range of comforts await you: Siberian goose-down duvets, vintage Welsh blankets and woolly hot-water bottles. We particularly enjoyed the quirky drawings by local artist Zebedee Helm.

Outside, the garden rambles towards a professional *boules* court. There are hammocks, a games area for entertaining children, even a dog bath. On the Fonthill Estate, opposite The Beckford, there are two beautiful private lodges. Arrive to a fully-stocked fridge and cook yourself breakfast in the morning, or saunter over to The Beckford for their famous eggs benedict.

Fowey, Cornwall

28 Fore Street, Fowey, Cornwall
PL23 1AQ

Tel (01726) 833302
Fax (01726) 833668
e-mail info@theoldquayhouse.com
website www.theoldquayhouse.com

Nearby The Eden Project; The Lost Gardens of Heligan; Lanhydrock; coastal walks
Location on main street; no hotel car park but in summer low-cost permits available for car park 800 yards away
Food breakfast, lunch, dinner
Price £££
Rooms 11 double, all with shower, some with bath; all have phone, TV, video player, wi-fi
Facilities restaurant, sitting areas, bar, riverfront terrace
Credit Cards AE, DC, MC, V
Children not under 12
Disabled not suitable
Pets guide dogs only
Closed never
Proprietors Jane and Roy Carson
Manager Anthony Chapman

Old Quay House

Seaside hotel

Location, location, location. This is a long, thin building jutting out over the wonderful Fowey River in the heart of charming Fowey, loved by yachties and the rest, and it is rightly geared around the endless amusement you'll get from the comings and goings on the river, not to mention the prettiness of it all.

You can eat or just sit with a drink on the terrace right over the water watching it all go by, or, when cold, move just inside to a sitting area. Most of the bedrooms have the view, the best being corner rooms and the (£325) top-floor suite. The interior design is cool, uncluttered, contemporary, to attract a core market of 30s-50s: grey paint, pine floors, perspex tables. The long, thin, downstairs combined bar, restaurant and sitting area has recently been redecorated. Food was fairly priced at around £30 for three courses when we visited; the list of wines by the glass has been extended since then.

They aim for a personal welcome and with 11 bedrooms, and the current competent, friendly management, that's a reasonable claim. However, with so many non-residents coming in to eat, it's not especially strong on the private, unique character we appreciate. It's a 'hotel and restaurant' formula, one that can work well, but in different hands might be merely formulaic.

Gillingham, Dorset

Gillingham, Dorset, SP8 5NR

Tel (01747) 823626
Fax (01747) 825628
e-mail
reception@stockhillhouse.co.uk
website www.stockhillhouse.co.uk

Nearby Shaftesbury; Stourhead House and Gardens.
Location 5 miles (8 km) NW of Shaftesbury on B3081; in 11-acre grounds with ample car parking
Food breakfast, lunch, dinner
Price ££££
Rooms 9 double, 8 with bath, 1 with shower; all rooms have TV, phone, hairdryer
Facilities sitting room, dining room, breakfast room, parkland, kitchen garden, tennis court, croquet, putting green, helipad
Credit cards MC, V
Children welcome over 7
Disabled not suitable
Pets not accepted
Closed never
Proprietors Peter and Nita Hauser

Stock Hill House

Country house hotel

This restored Victorian manor house, reached up a long drive through wooded grounds, has been immaculately furnished and decorated in indivual, opulent and somewhat heavy turn-of-the-century style by its hands-on owners, the Hausers, who have been at the helm for 30 years. Bedrooms are luxurious, and although the atmosphere is definitely formal, one is relieved to discover that it is also genuinely warm and friendly. Three of the bedrooms are in a separate coach house, and are more contemporary in style.

Peter Hauser and Lorna Connor do all the cooking and produce superb results. Peter's Austrian roots are reflected in the varied, generous menu, which changes daily. Fruit and vegetables come from his impressive walled kitchen garden. While he works away in the kitchen, guests are apt to pop in for a chat or to see what he is planning for dinner that evening. Many of the hotel's staff are recruited from across Europe and they are attentive and friendly.

The extensive grounds include formal gardens and a tennis court. More reports would be appreciated.

Gittisham, Devon

Gittisham, Honiton, Devon
EX14 3AD

Tel (01404) 540 400
Fax 01404 46004
e-mail stay@combehousedevon.com
website
www.combehousedevon.com

Nearby Gittisham village, Honiton antique trail, Dartmoor National Park, Jurassic Coast, Ottery St Mary
Location set in 3,500 acres of grounds, 2 miles from A30 and Honiton with ample car parking
Food breakfast, lunch, dinner
Price ££££
Rooms 16 including cottage, Combe Thatch House; all en suite with plasma TV, phone, hairdryers; most rooms have wi-fi internet
Facilities two bar/lounge rooms, two dining rooms, Georgian kitchen, extensive parkland, helipad; fishing, shooting and riding all nearby
Credit Cards MC, V **Children** welcome **Disabled** access to restaurant only **Pets** well behaved dogs, £7 per night **Closed** never
Proprietors Ken and Ruth Hunt

Combe House

Country hotel

Through delightful, unspoiled Gittisham village, up a long drive, past wild flower meadows you find this large Elizabethan manor house. Perhaps it's not as mellow as some photos make it look, but you're definitely in the isolated world of an old country estate.

Inside, old and new rub shoulders amusingly, perhaps eccentrically. In the hall, the main public space downstairs, gay splashes of colour contrast effectively with magnificent dark, heavy old panelling. Antique wallpaper has been preserved in a little reception room off the hall and the dining room walls are charmingly hand painted by former owners. It's full of quirky corners and surprises (including an outdoor bath house) to keep you amused. You'll see the odd imperfection downstairs, which could not matter less, because this is far from being a haphazard operation.

Ruth and Ken Hunter are natural but astute hoteliers who have built up Combe House's reputation from nothing over a decade of hands-on hard work. Now, all the basics are right: award-winning food; upstairs, fresh, imaginative rooms, some traditional, some more contemporary, some pretty, at a useful range of prices. For a treat, book the Linen Suite with its copper bath tub. People of most ages can feel comfortable here.

Gulworthy, Devon

Gulworthy, Tavistock,
Devon PL19 8JD

Tel (01822) 832528
website www.thehornofplenty.co.uk

Nearby Cotehele House, Dartmoor, Plymouth.
Location 3 miles (5 km) W of Tavistock on A390; with ample car parking
Food breakfast, lunch, dinner
Price ££-£££
Rooms 10; 4 in main house, rest in converted barn; 8 double and twin, all have bath/shower; all rooms have phone, TV, DVD, minibar, hairdryer, tea/coffee facilities
Facilities sitting room, bar, restaurant; terrace, garden
Credit cards MC, V
Children accepted
Disabled 2 suitable bedrooms
Pets not allowed in the main house
Closed never
Proprietors Julie Leivers and Damien Pease

The Horn of Plenty

Country hotel

The Horn of Plenty has long featured in this guide, despite some changes of ownership which it has undergone in recent years. On a recent visit we found that a major reinvestment was now complete, with all the rooms a high standard, including one imaginatively done in mauve: this goes for those in the main house and those in the coach house (the Garden Rooms), overlooking the charming walled garden. By spring 2014 there will be an additional six Garden Rooms.

Built in 1830 by the Marquess of Tavistock, the secluded house is approached down a short drive and has a splendid location overlooking the Tamar Valley, a view shared by the bedrooms, some of which have small terraces.

The Horn of Plenty is no longer primarily a restaurant. However, under head chef Scott Paton the menus are constantly changing in accordance with seasonal produce. Your food is served in front of picture windows in the two-part dining room.

It's not especially cheap (although prices have gone down with the new owners), but we reckon you get what you pay for here – a view backed up by a guest we overheard expressing his satisfaction. Competent, friendly manager.

Hinton St George, Somerset

High Street, Hinton St George
Somerset, TA17 8SE

Tel (01460) 73149
e-mail steveandmichelle@lord-poulettarms.com
website www.lordpoulettarms.com

Nearby local cider makers; Montacute House, Sherborne Castle, Forde Abbey; Jurassic coast, Blackdown Hills.
Location in village street, plenty of free car parking; own small private car park.
Food breakfast, lunch, dinner
Price ££ **Rooms** 4; 2 with bath in the room, two with separate private bathroom across corridor; all rooms except one have WC, radio, flat screen TV on request (except one room where no signal), leaf tea and coffee making **Facilities** bar, garden, boule area **Credit cards** MC **Disabled** not suitable **Children** one room can be converted to family room **Closed** Christmas Day and Boxing Day **Proprietors** Steve Hill and Michelle Paynton

The Lord Poulett Arms

Country inn

We reacted with pleasure to this country inn from the moment we were through the door. First, the arresting birdcage pattern wallpaper in the passage. Then the pleasant atmosphere in the bar – actually divided into three areas. A cheery local was installed in his favourite spot. Two mothers with babies were meeting for a tomato juice. Steve and Michelle, the proprietors, who took over in 2002 with no previous experience of the business, say they wanted to create a country get-away for visitors and a meeting place for locals – and they have. Tables and chairs are a mellow jumble of different antique country types. Food was the best we can remember in a pub. Upstairs, the bedroom corridor was decorated with a bold, striped wallpaper reminding us of a French inn, and the four simple, pretty but not over-feminine, homely bedrooms were charming, individual, again relying on unusual wallpapers rather than contemporary sludge-colours. Prices are fair.

At the back are two gardens for eating out in fine weather, one a herb garden, the other grassy, with an old *pelota* or fives wall at the end.

A pub that's got it just right, thanks to the owners' natural taste and emphasis on quality and things that matter.

Holsworthy, Devon

Clawton, Holsworthy,
Devon EX22 6PS

Tel (01409) 271219
e-mail courtbarnhotel@talk21.com
website www.hotels-devon.com

Nearby Bude; Boscastle; Tintagel; Hartland Abbey; Dartmoor.
Location on A388 from Launceston to Holsworthy, at Clawton; ample car parking
Food breakfast, dinner
Price ££
Rooms 7; 6 double and twin, 1 single, all with bath; all rooms have phone, TV, hairdryer, books, wi-fi
Facilities restaurant, breakfast room, 2 sitting rooms, bar, garden, croquet, badminton, 4-hole pitch and putt
Credit cards AE, DC, MC, V
Children accepted
Disabled access difficult
Pets dogs accepted by arrangement (£5 per night per dog)
Closed early Jan
Proprietors Robert and Susan Wood

Court Barn

Country house hotel

Court Barn lacks any trace of stuffiness or pretentiousness, and it has an abundance of easy-going warmth. It is a four-square house, dating from the 16th century but partly rebuilt in 1853, where antiques, souvenirs, books and games jostle with sometimes unusual furnishings in a carefree medley of patterns. The result is reassuring: this home-like environment spells comfort far beyond the meretricious harmony of hotels colour-matched by designers. And its owners, Susan and Robert Wood, spare no effort to make you feel at home and welcome.

Downstairs, there is a sitting room with open log fire and views over the garden, a breakfast room which looks out on to the croquet lawn, and an elegant restaurant which is candle-lit in the evenings. The food, on our most recent visit, was satisfying, accompanied by an extensive wine list.

Beautifully kept park-like grounds surround the house; croquet hoops, putting holes and badminton offer plenty to do outside. Beyond are gently rolling hills; and Court Barn is perfectly placed for exploring Devon and Cornwall.

Church Hill, Kingswear,
Dartmouth, Devon TQ6 0BX

Tel (01803) 752829
Fax (01803) 752357
e-mail enquiries@nonsuch-house.co.uk
website www.nonsuch-house.co.uk

Nearby Dartmouth; Totnes; Dartmoor; Torquay.
Location from Dartmouth ferry to Kingswear, take Fore Street, then turn sharp right after 100 yards on to Church Hill; street car parking
Food breakfast, dinner (Sun, Mon, Thu, Fri)
Price £££
Rooms 4 doubles, 2 with shower, 2 with bath/shower; all rooms have TV, CD player, wi-fi
Facilities sitting room, dining room, conservatory; terrace, garden
Credit cards MC, V
Children accepted over 10
Disabled 1 room suitable **Pets** not accepted **Closed** never
Proprietors Kit and Penny Noble

Nonsuch House

Riverside village guesthouse

The Noble family are old friends of this guide, having for many years run Langshott Manor near Horley in Surrey with great warmth and professionalism. They moved to Nonsuch House in Devon 16 years ago, and for 11 years it has been run by their son Kit and his wife Penny.

Nonsuch House is a tall, slim building which stands, rather unprepossessingly, on a hairpin bend in a one-way system high above the Dartmouth ferry at Kingswear. The views, looking across the river towards Dartmouth and out to sea, are superb, and can be had from all the windows. Bedrooms are named after shipping forecasts and are smart, comfortable and well-equipped – certainly a cut above the normal guesthouse. All of the rooms have now been refurbished and have their own bathrooms. The sitting room is decorated in rich, warm colours and furnished with large, comfy sofas and an open fire. Food is served in the modern conservatory that also has stunning views over the river to the sea. This in turn leads down the hill to a lovely little garden for residents to use.

Kit's cooking is simple yet delicious, with fresh seafood every day and an award-winning breakfast. The family will organise any of the varied activities around Dartmouth, such as sailing, river trips, or bracing walks.

Lewdown, Devon

Lewdown, near Okehampton,
Devon EX20 4PN

Tel (01566) 783222
e-mail info@lewtrenchard.co.uk
website www.lewtrenchard.co.uk

Nearby Dartmoor; Tintagel; Exeter; Boscastle.
Location from old A30 at Lewdown, take road signposted Lewtrenchard; in 11-acre grounds with ample car parking
Food breakfast, lunch, dinner, afternoon tea
Price £££–££££
Rooms 14; all double and 9 can be twin, all have bath/shower; all rooms have phone, TV, hairdryer
Facilities drawing room, bar lounge, restaurant, breakfast room, ballroom; garden, croquet
Credit cards AE, DC, MC, V
Children accepted
Disabled ramp, 1 room with disabled facilities, disabled loo, chairlift
Pets accepted
Closed never
Proprietors Murray family

Lewtrenchard Manor

Manor house hotel

Driving east down the narrow road from Lewdown, on the edge of Dartmoor, nothing quite prepares you for the first sight of Lewtrenchard Manor, a magnificent 16thC stone manor house, with some Victorian additions, approached by an avenue of beech trees and set in stunningly beautiful grounds which lead down to a lake studded with swans.

The interior is equally impressive. The massive reception rooms are rich in ornate ceilings, oak panelling, carvings and large open fireplaces. Despite its size, however, the hotel has the warm, hospitable atmosphere of a much humbler building, engendered in great part by its hostess, Sue Murray. The drawing room invites you to curl up with a good book.

On the first floor, a splendid long gallery, full of family paintings and portraits, leads to the spacious bedrooms, all of which have extensive views through leaded windows and over the Devon countryside.

A former owner of Lewtrenchard was the Reverend Sabine Baring Gould (who wrote, amongst others, the hymn *Onward, Christian Soldiers*). Mercifully, he largely resisted the Victorian habit of embellishing an already beautiful building.

The Murray family took over in 2012 and we would love to hear how they are getting on.

Lifton, Devon

Lifton, Devon, PL16 0AA

Tel (01566) 784666
Fax (01566) 784494
e-mail
reservations@arundellarms.com
website www.arundellarms.com

Nearby Dartmoor; Tintagel; Boscastle; Port Isaac; Exeter.
Location 3 miles (5 km) E of Launceston, just off A30 in Lifton; with ample car parking
Food breakfast, lunch, dinner
Price £££
Rooms 21; 18 double and twin, 3 single, all with bath; all rooms have phone, TV, hairdrier, fax/modem points **Facilities** 2 restaurants, 2 bars, games room, drying room; garden, salmon and trout fishing, fishing lake, fly fishing lessons, organised shooting parties
Credit cards AE, DC, MC, V
Children accepted
Disabled access possible
Pets dogs accepted
Closed 3 nights at Christmas
Proprietor Adam Fox-Edwards

The Arundell Arms

Fishing inn

A 200-year-old coaching inn, on a site that dates back to Saxon times, which is famous – indeed an institution – for fishing and for food. Traditional country pursuits are taken seriously here: the Arundell Arms has been one of England's premier fishing hotels for more than half a century. Anglers have 20 miles of private fishing and a 90-feet-deep lake at their disposal (containing some very large, wily trout). When autumn comes, the fisherman go, shooting parties arrive with spaniels and labradors, and talk at the bar is of high birds and driven snipe. Lifton is surrounded by some of the loveliest countryside in England. Fishing arrangements are flexible – don't be shy of visiting if you're a beginner.

Then there's the food. Head Chef Steven Pidgeon has the accolade of being a Master Chef of Great Britain – one of only 80. His food is meticulously prepared and beautifully presented, complemented by good wines and attentive, friendly service.

From the sitting room you can see the garden and the 250-year-old former cockpit, now a tackle room. There are two rather grand interconnecting dining rooms and a friendly bar. Bedrooms are homely, pretty and fresh. Home-made chocolates are placed in the sitting room for guests after dinner and there are vases of fresh flowers. A unique place.

Lizard, Cornwall

Church Cove, Lizard, Cornwall
TR12 7PQ

Tel 01326 290877
e-mail luxurybandb@landewednack-house.com
website
www.landewednackhouse.com

Nearby The Lizard peninsula; St Ives; Isles of Scilly.
Location from Helston take A3083 to Lizard; before entering village turn left to Church Cove, then left towards lifeboat station
Food breakfast, dinner
Price ££–££££
Rooms 3 double and twin, 1 with bath, 2 with shower; all beds kingsize or bigger, all rooms have phone, digital or satalite TV, hairdryer
Facilities dining room, drawing room, breakfast room; garden, swimming pool, bowls and wi-fi
Credit cards MC, V **Children** accepted **Disabled** access difficult
Pets accepted by arrangement
Closed never **Proprietors** Mrs S. M. Thorbeck

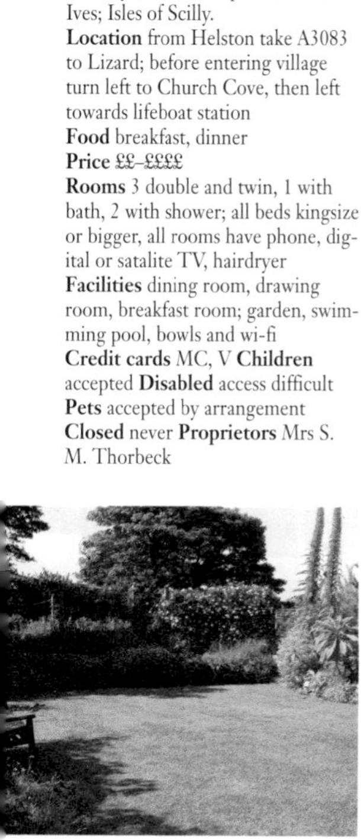

Landewednack House

Country house

This beautiful 17thC former rectory, taken over and updated by Mr and Mrs Thorbeck in 2004, is a warm and elegant private home where all guests are made very welcome.The parish of Landewednack, at the end of the Lizard peninsula, is the most southerly in England and is fortunate enough to have a climate mild enough for most of the year to encourage a wide variety of trees and plants to flourish.The gardens are a delight.

Inside, the house is equally enchanting. Leading off the flagstoned hall is the dining room with a beamed ceiling and massive granite fireplace where guests can dine by candlelight in front of a crackling log fire. Breakfast is taken in a separate, smaller room. The resident chef, Anthony, is proud of his work here, which has earned him a mention in the Michelin guide (though not a star, since Landewednack caters only for its guests).

House guests can relax in the elegant drawing room at any time of the day, or in the evening for pre-dinner drinks. The three bedrooms are all different, and all charming. The best view is from the Big Bedroom, with a mahogany half-tester. Through its large bay window you can see across the garden to the church and the sea beyond – a wonderful sight at sunset.

Lovington, Castle Cary, Somerset
BA7 7PT

Tel 01963 240600
e-mail jools@thepilgrimsatlovington.co.uk
website www.thepilgrimsatlovington.co.uk

Nearby Glastonbury, Wells, Bath & West Showground, Wincanton Races, Fleet Air Arm Museum, Bath, Jurassic Coast
Location in Lovington on B3153, 3 miles west of Castle Cary and 1 mile east of A37 Fosse Way at Lydford-on-Fosse **Food** breakfast, lunch, dinner, Sunday lunch (last Sunday of the month) **Price** £-££ **Rooms** 5; 4 double and 1 twin, all en suite; double rooms have bath and wet-room showers, twin has wet-room shower; all have TV, hairdryer, wi-fi, tea/coffee **Facilities** bar, restaurant, wi-fi **Credit cards** MC, V **Children** accepted over 14 **Disabled** access possible **Pets** not accepted in bedrooms **Closed** rarely **Proprietors** Sally & Jools Mitchison

The Pilgrims Restaurant

Restaurant-with-rooms

We especially like places that evolve over time under the same hands-on owner managers. Julian (Jools) and Sally bought the place in 1997 as a dead-beat village pub. Into the nothing-special building they inserted a rather good restaurant and set about persuading not just the pub-supporting locals but people further afield that it was worth driving some way for the rather special food. People came, and the restaurant prospered – but the place was still an awkward hybrid – a restaurant in a pub building with no accommodation.Then on the back of the restaurant's success, they added five rooms. So then they had a restaurant-with-rooms, and suddenly their operation was fully in its skin.

The ground-level bedrooms (step straight in from outside) are in a clean, modern style. Basics are right: quality beds, good linen. Details such as wind-up torches in bedside drawers get good feedback. You're on a B road with lightish traffic at times, not audible in bedrooms, which are steps away from the restaurant entrance.

The food is again the product of spadework and inspiration. Jools worked hard at finding top, local ingredients and maintain relationships with the suppliers. He triesto let the ingredients speak for themselves – "not to do too much to them".

Mells, Somerset

Mells, Somerset BA11 3PN

Tel 01373 812254
e-mail info@talbotinn.com
website www.talbotinn.com

Nearby Longleat Estate; Shepton Mallet; Wells; Farrington Golf Course.
Location the estate village of Mells
Food breakfast, lunch, dinner
Price ££-£££
Rooms 8; all with king- or emperor-sized beds, own bath or shower, Smart TVs, internet radio and wi-fi
Facilities pub bar, coach house grill room, garden, cobbled courtyard, in-room massage
Credit cards DC, MC, V
Children accepted, 1 family room
Disabled no special access
Pets not accepted
Closed never
Proprietors Dan Brod and Charlie Luxton

The Talbot Inn

Country inn

Our series editor Fiona Duncan visited this off-the-beaten track inn recently and rated it highly. Owners Charlie and Dan, proprietors of the Beckford Arms (see page 45) bought the lease from the present Earl of Asquith and Oxford and reopened in 2013. Their new venture is up there with the Beckford Arms because they know how to combine style, value for money and character.

The Talbot gets a head start with the charm of its location, the pretty Somerset village of Mells, and this is reinforced as you approach through the unevenly surfaced, cobbled courtyard. Inside there is a choice of cosy dining areas, a sitting room across the courtyard in a barn dating from the 1500s, and the Grill Room housed in the old coach house. The speciality here is meat and fish cooked over an open fire. When it's busy at weekends the atmosphere is bustling and jolly.

There are eight stylish but unpretentious bedrooms which are very fairly priced. We especially like spacious no 6: relax in a deep freestanding bath, have a rain shower or chill out in the sitting room with two sofas. Witness the sawn logs stacked in the fireplace, the woolly hot water bottle covers and pegs with hangars doing the work of wardrobes.

Milton Abbot, Devon

Milton Abbot, Tavistock, Devon
PL19 0PQ

Tel (01822) 870000
Fax (01822) 870578
e-mail mail@hotelendsleigh.com
website www.hotelendsleigh.com

Nearby Tavistock market, Tamar Valley, Plymouth historic dockyards, Exeter cathedral
Location 15 minutes from Tavistock down mile long drive in own extensive grounds; ample car parking
Food breakfast, lunch and dinner
Price ££££
Rooms 16; all have bath and shower; all have phone, TV, DVD player, internet access
Facilities dining room, sitting room, garden, terrace, library, helipad, use of local country club (swimming, golf, spa) **Credit Cards** AE, MC, V
Children accepted
Disabled good access, 1 ground floor suite with private garden
Pets accepted, dog beds provided
Closed 2 weeks in Mid Jan
Proprietors Alex and Olga Polizzi

Hotel Endsleigh

Country house hotel

Endsleigh, on the edge of Dartmoor, and sister hotel of Olga Polizzi's Tresanton in Cornwall (page 73), was one of the most talked about new British hotels when it opened eight years ago. Our reporter found it 'effortlessly elegant and – crucially – unpretentious, unlike many of its try-hard, oh-so-hip rivals.'

It's down a mile-long private drive in 'one of the loveliest locations I've seen in 20 years of writing about hotels.' The sixth Duke of Bedford built the 16-bedroom fishing and shooting lodge as a retreat, in the cottage *orné* style. The gardens are by Humphry Repton.

Olga Polizzi has decorated it in her cool, inimitable style, but the spirit of the old house remains intact – old pull-down maps of Devon in the hall, the family crests in the dining room, the floor made of sheeps' knuckles on the veranda. Bedrooms are lovely: stylish and unfussy, with original baths and basins and a welcome lack of puzzling technology. You'll get a TV and DVD player, but you are more likely to spend time pouring over the absorbing collection of books in the library. Apart from that, there's little to do, other than to fish, walk or picnic in the grounds, a fantasy of dells and grottoes. The food is good, but not quite as good as at its sister hotel, though prices are similar.

The Parade, Mousehole, Penzance, Cornwall TR19 6PR

Tel 01736 731222
e-mail restaurant@oldcoastguardhotel.co.uk
website
www.oldcoastguardhotel.co.uk

Nearby by the sea; 1 hour away from Newquay
Location situated above the harbour wall of Mousehole; St Clement's Isle in front
Food breakfast buffet, lunch, dinner
Price ££-£££
Rooms 15 double and twin; all rooms have bathroom with either shower or bath, all have sea view and some have a balcony, radio, books, tea and coffee
Facilities sub-tropical garden, seating area, dining room, bar, private access to beach **Credit cards** DC, MC, V **Children** welcome
Disabled not suitable **Pets** welcome
Closed 1 week a year, usually in Dec
Proprietors Edmund and Charles Inkin

The Old Coastguard

Seaside hotel

Not everyone likes the style of the Inkins' hotels, writes our series editor, Fiona Duncan, but if you agree with the *Charming Small Hotel Guide* attitude that a jar of fresh flowers and a stylish old radio are as good as a large flat screen TV in the bedroom, then you'll get the point of The Old Coastguard.

It was a boring Victorian seaside hotel until its recent makeover, but the Inkins have avoided formulaic designer dodges to bring it up to date. They have spent money instead on the basics – the beds are soundly comfortable, there are thick towels, and properly served, not over-ambitious food. Try the rich beef stew.

The downstairs sitting area is the hotel's ace card: full of sunlight. You relax on deep armchairs and sofas looking out over the harbour and sea through a wall of big windows that capitalise on a view that will keep you stationary for hours.

The 14 bedrooms are gradually being made over to Charlie Inkin's taste for tongue-and-groove panelling behind the beds, mustard yellow paint and striped curtains in greens and blues. We like bedrooms 1, 2 and 3 the best (even with fixed toiletry dispensers), and 5 with its bath facing the sea. See the Inkins' other hotels: Gurnard's Head and The Felin Fach Griffin Inn on pages 84 and 180.

Nettleton, Wiltshire

Nettleton Shrub, Nettleton, near Chippenham, Wiltshsire SN14 7NJ

Tel (01249) 782286
Fax (01249) 783066
e-mail caroncooper@compuserve.com **web-site** www.fossefarmhouse.com

Nearby Castle Combe; Cotswolds.
Location in countryside off B4039, 6 miles (9.5 km) NW of Chippenham, in 1.5 acres of garden with car parking
Food breakfast, lunch, dinner
Price £££
Rooms 18; 1 double and 1 suite in main building; 2 doubles one twin in The Stables; 2 doubles and sofa bed in Garden House; one double and sofa bed in Dovecote
Facilities sitting room, dining room, tea room; terrace, garden
Credit cards MC, V **Children** accepted **Disabled** The Garden House only **Pets** dogs allowed in main building and Stables at £15/night **Closed** never **Proprietor** Caron Cooper

Fosse Farmhouse

Country bed-and-breakfast

Former cookery presenter Caron Cooper presides over a small corner of France in the Wiltshire countryside. She has decorated Fosse Farmhouse with style, bringing together English vintage and French brocante. Antiques, including many French pieces, fill the house and the adjoining cottages.

Since our last visit Caron has added two more self-catering cottages, The Dovecote and The Garden House – making three along with the converted Stables. All follow the style of the main building and can be hired individually or as a group.

Some more recent renovations mean the bedrooms in the main house feel homely and Caron has added some charming detail to each, with the bathrooms being finished to a high standard.

While Fosse Farmhouse claims it is only a bed-and-breakfast, two and three course dinners are available if booked in advance. Caron's food blends French with English influences. You might get rack of lamb with a mint and port wine sauce or chicken basquaise; dessert might be sticky toffee pudding or crème brûlée.

Heasley Mill, North Molton, Devon EX36 3LE

Tel 01598 740213
e-mail enquiries@heasley-house.co.uk **website** www.exmoor-hotel.co.uk

Nearby walking on Exmoor, RHS Gardens at Rosemoor, golf, surfing, riding.
Location Heasley Mill, Exmoor National Park
Food breakfast, lunch, dinner
Price ££-£££
Rooms 8, twins and doubles, all with free wi-fi, power showers, direct dial telephone, tea and coffee making facilities, flat screen television
Facilities free wi-fi, restaurant, bar
Credit cards MC, V
Children accepted
Disabled no special facilities
Pets accepted
Closed Christmas and Feb
Proprietors Miles and Mandy Platt

Heasley House
Country hotel

A traditional, calm country hotel, Heasley House is all English charm. Located in Exmoor National Park in the quiet hamlet of Heasley Mill, it is a great place to escape to and explore the surrounding countryside.

The decoration inside the hotel is natural and unpretentious. Muted colours complement the spacious rooms and solid furniture. Bedrooms likewise share this theme, but with the addition of colourful bedspreads and cushions. All bedrooms are styled slightly differently and have luxurious king size or superking size beds.

The restaurant is wonderful, with an ever-changing menu throughout the seasons. Many local ingredients are used, such as lamb from local Exmoor and fish and beef from Devon and Cornwall. The food is traditional, hearty and simple: complementing the hotel and the location perfectly.

The wine cellar is a prime attraction at Heasley House, with a collection growing each year from lesser-known wine areas from around the world. The mainstream selection from Bordeaux and Burgundy are popular and reasonably priced.

As we went to press, the Platts had just taken over. Reports on their progress welcome.

Oakford Bridge, Devon

Oakford Bridge, Near Bampton, Tiverton, Devon EX16 9HZ

Tel (01398) 351236
e-mail bark.house.hotel@btinter-net.com
website www.thebarkhouse.co.uk

Nearby Exmoor; Knightshayes House; Marwood and Rosemoor gardens
Location in own grounds, on A396 near Bampton; car parking
Food breakfast, Sunday lunch, dinner **Price** ££
Rooms 7; 4 double and 1 twin with bath or shower, 1 double and 1 twin in self-catering cottage; all rooms have phone, TV **Facilities** sitting room, dining room, bar; garden, garden, orchard, croquet
Credit cards not accepted
Children accepted **Disabled** access difficult **Pets** accepted
Closed occasionally
Proprietors Mr M French and Miss M McKnight

Bark House

Country guesthouse

Tucked away in the beautiful Exe Valley, this delightful guesthouse is about 200 years old and was originally used to store bark for tanning. It's everyone's idea of a Devon cottage, particularly in spring when the facade is smothered by a magnificent old wistaria. By day, you can explore the woodland paths and gardens behind the house and, opposite the building, a sitting area provides a sunny spot for afternoon tea. By night, the tiny hamlet of Oakford Bridge sparkles in the velvet-black valley while the only sounds are the trickling of a small cascade in the garden and the burbling River Exe. Alistair Kameen handed over Bark House to new owners in 2007, who are continuing to run it as a guesthouse along much the same lines.

Inside, the cosy and intimate sitting room, with an open fire, is the perfect place to relax and anticipate dinner. The new owners describe the food as more traditional than Alistair's cooking, and dinner might be a starter of potted salmon, roast shoulder of lamb, and a choice of home-made pavlovas and puddings.

The bedrooms reflect the essential simplicity of Bark House. In 2008 Mr French added a further two rooms in a self-catering cottage, 'without spoiling the unique exterior'.

Reports welcome.

Padstow, Cornwall

Riverside, Padstow,
Cornwall PL28 8BY

Tel (01841) 532700
Fax (01841) 532942
e-mail reservations@rickstein.com
website www.rickstein.com

Nearby surfing beaches; Trevose Head **Location** in village centre, 4 miles (6 km) NW off A39 between Wadebridge and St Columb; car parking
Food breakfast, lunch, dinner
Price ££
Rooms 35 doubles, (some can be twins) in 3 different buildings, most with bath, some with shower; all rooms have phone, TV, hairdryer; some have minibar **Facilities** 3 restaurants, bar, sitting room, conservatory **Credit cards** MC, V **Children** welcome in St Petroc's Hotel and the Café, over 3 in The Seafood Restaurant **Disabled** access possible **Pets** dogs accepted in selected rooms **Closed** Christmas; restaurants closed on 1st May **Proprietors** Rick and Jill Stein

The Seafood Restaurant & St Petroc's Hotel

Restaurant-with-rooms

Rick Stein's Padstow empire now extends to seven different places to stay, at varying prices, and five places to eat: his flagship Seafood Restaurant, the Bistro in St Petroc's Hotel, Rick Stein's Cafe, Stein's Fish & Chips and the pub in St Merryn, and The Cornish Arms.

If you are intent on eating at the quayside Seafood Restaurant (superb seafood, straight from the fishing boats, served in a lively dining room) then the bedrooms above make the best choice for a night's stay. They are spacious, and understated, with superb estuary views from Nos 5 and 6. What the place lacks in public rooms, it makes up for in laid-back atmosphere and its prime position on the quay. St Edmund's House, behind the restaurant, has six new pricey suites. Less expensive, but no less tasteful, are the rooms in St Petroc's Hotel just up the hill, a little removed from the bustle of the quayside. This is an attractive white-painted building with views across the older parts of town and the estuary. The place exudes a friendly ambience, not least in the Bistro, where a short, very reasonably priced menu features meat and vegetable dishes as well as seafood. There are three attractive rooms above the Café in Middle Street, and self-catering properties just outside of Padstow in Trevone.

Abbey Street, Penzance,
Cornwall TR18 4AR

Tel (01736) 366906
Fax (01736) 351163
e-mail hotel@theabbeyonline.co.uk
website www.theabbeyonline.co.uk

Nearby Tregwainton Garden; St Michael's Mount; Land's End.
Location in middle of town, overlooking harbour; parking for 6 cars in courtyard
Food breakfast, dinner; room service
Price £££-££££
Rooms 7; 4 double and twin, 1 suite, 2 single, 4 with bath, 3 with shower; all rooms have TV, hairdryer
Facilities sitting room, dining room; walled garden
Credit cards AE, MC , V **Children** accepted **Disabled** access difficult
Pets accepted in bedrooms only
Closed never **Proprietors** Jean and Michael Cox

The Abbey Hotel

Town hotel

After several years of management problems, we believe that things are changing at The Abbey, and that it is back on track to being one of the most exceptional places to stay in the West Country. Jean and Michael Cox took a house with character in the heart of old Penzance (it was built in the mid 17th century and given a Gothic façade in Regency times); decorated and furnished it with unstinting care, great flair and a considerable budget; and they call it a hotel. In reality, it is run much more as a private house by their son, Thaddeus, and visitors who expect to find hosts eager to satisfy their every whim may be disappointed.

For its fans, the absence of hovering flunkies is of course a key part of the appeal of The Abbey. But there are other attractions – the confident and original decoration, with abundant antiques and bric-a-brac, the spacious, individual bedrooms (one with an enormous pine-panelled bathroom); the welcoming, flowery drawing-room and elegant dining-room (both with log fires burning 'year-round'); the delightful walled garden behind the house. Dinner can be had at the restaurant next door. Front rooms overlook the harbour and the dry dock.

Penzance, Cornwall

Cornwall Terrace, Penzance,
Cornwall TR18 4HL

Tel (01736) 363744
Fax (01736) 360959
e-mail reception@summerhouse-cornwall.com
website www.summerhouse-cornwall.com

Nearby Trengwainton Garden; St Michael's Mount; Land's End; St Ives; Newlyn School art colony.
Location close to the harbour; drive alongside the harbour and turn right immediately after the Queen's Hotel; car parking
Food breakfast, light supper (Mon to Fri), dinner (weekends)
Price £££ **Rooms** 5; 4 double, 2 with bath, 2 with shower, 1 twin with shower **Facilities** sitting room, dining room; small walled garden
Credit cards MC, V
Children not accepted
Disabled access difficult
Pets not accepted
Closed Oct-Mar
Proprietors Ciro and Linda Zaino

Summer House

Town restaurant-with-rooms

Linda and Ciro Zaino moved to the tip of Cornwall from London, where Ciro had managed some of the capital's top restaurants, to open this restaurant-with-rooms in a Grade II listed Georgian house close to the sea front. They run it with great panache, reports our inspector, who considers it a 'great find'. He describes it as Mediterranean in colour and feel, quirky in style and breezy in atmosphere. Brighton meets the Neapolitan Riviera.

The former home of one of Cornwall's leading naïve artists, the house is still full of paintings, indiosycratic furniture and lush pot plants. Downstairs there is a little cosy sitting room as well as the most important room in the building, the restaurant. Here creams and yellows predominate in a room that spills out in to a small walled garden burgeoning with terracotta pots and palm trees. Ciro's sunny cooking, using fresh local ingredients, has become a great draw.

Upstairs, the five simple bedrooms are highly individual with a diverse mix of family pieces and collectables. Fresh flowers are everywhere. The bathrooms are decorated with limestone and have power showers. Linda is charming and her front-of-house presence is just right: enthusiastic, friendly and welcoming.

Rock, Cornwall

Rock, Wadebridge, Cornwall
PL27 6LA

Tel (01208) 863394
e-mail info@enodoc-hotel.co.uk
website www.enodoc-hotel.co.uk

Nearby Polzeath 2 miles; Padstow (by ferry).
Location overlooking the Camel Estuary, bordering St Enodoc golf course in Rock, 2 miles off B3314 from Wadebridge; car park
Food breakfast, lunch, dinner
Price £££
Rooms 20; 16 double, all with bath/shower, 4 suites; all rooms have phone, TV, radio, hairdryer, fan
Facilities sitting room, library, dining room, bar, billiard room, sauna; outdoor heated swimming pool
Credit cards AE, DC, MC, V
Children welcome
Disabled adapted WC on ground floor **Pets** not accepted
Closed Jan to mid Feb
Manager Kate Simms

St Enodoc

Seaside hotel

Well-heeled British families have flocked to Rock for their bucket-and-spade holidays for generations, but hotels which are both stylish and child-friendly have been thin on the ground hereabouts – until, that is, the emergence in 1998 of the old-established St Enodoc Hotel from a change of ownership and total makeover.

The imposing building is typical of the area: no beauty, but solid and purposeful, with pebbledash walls and slate roof.

Emily Todhunter's interior decoration suits its seaside location, with its bright colours (paint, fabrics, painted furniture, modern art), clean lines, and easy-going comfort. The restaurant is run by the Michelin-starred chef, Nathan Outlaw, who focuses on buying the freshest market fish. The restaurant has panoramic views, with a wide terrace for outdoor eating.

Bedrooms, with bright colours and quirky artwork on the walls, feel like bedrooms rather than hotel rooms, with marvellous views across the Camel Estuary.

With its child-friendly facilities, the hotel is particularly popular during holidays and half terms. Although the hotel has been recently been sold, the management and staff remain unchanged. More reports please.

Rosevine, South Cornwall

Rosevine, near Portscatho,
South Cornwall, TR2 5EW

Tel (01872) 580644
e-mail info@driftwoodhotel.co.uk
website www.driftwoodhotel.co.uk

Nearby Eden Project, Tate Gallery, the gardens of Heligan, Glendurgan and Trebah.
Location in countryside just off A3078, S of Truro; ample parking for cars and boats
Food breakfast, dinner
Price ££££
Rooms 14 double and 1 twin, 3 with bath, 1 with shower; rest with bath and shower, cabin with double and twin; all rooms have phone, TV, hairdryer **Facilities** sitting room, drawing room, TV room, dining room, bar; garden, beach
Credit cards AE, MC, V
Children welcome
Disabled access difficult
Pets not accepted
Closed mid Dec to mid Feb
Proprietors Paul and Fiona Robinson

Driftwood Hotel

Coastal hotel

'Situated on seven glorious acres of Cornwall's finest heritage coastline,' says the brochure – and Driftwood does indeed provide all you could want on a sea-side break. It's a clapboarded converted family house that has been refurbished and renovated into a stylish yet comfortable haven by interior designer Fiona and husband Paul. All fourteen bedrooms, including the cabin overlooking the beach, have a clean, fresh style that helps maximise the space, as do the cosy sitting and drawing rooms.

Those who love seafood will be happiest here, but the rest of the food is good too. The menu is concentrated on well prepared dishes with fresh local ingredients. The Michelin-starred restaurant has spectacular views of the rugged Cornish coastline and you can eat outside, weather permitting. For children there is a TV room with computer games and video library. If you fancy getting out and about there are numerous small pubs and restaurants nearby St Mawes; or hampers can be made up for lazing on the beach.

All around Driftwood there are varied activities that suit different tastes. Great walks and gardens such as Trelissick, the Eden Project, within a short drive; for art lovers, the Tate Gallery at St Ives; or for the energetic, watersports, riding, tennis and golf.

St Austell, Cornwall

Boscundle, St Austell, Cornwall PL25 3RL

Tel (01726) 813557
Fax (01726) 814997
e-mail reservations@boscundle-manor.co.uk **website** www.boscundlemanor.co.uk

Nearby Eden Project, Heligan Gardens, Lanhydrock House
Location 2.5 miles (4 km) E of St Austell, close to A390; in 5 acre woodland gardens; ample car parking
Food breakfast, dinner
Price £££ **Rooms** 14; 7 double and twin, 2 suites, all with bath; 1 single with shower, 1 garden room, 1 cottage with 3 doubles; all rooms have phone, TV, safe, fridge **Facilities** sitting room, bar, restaurant; heated indoor pool; hot tub; spa treatment room; garden, croquet, woodland walks, civil wedding licence **Credit cards** MC, V **Children** welcome **Disabled** access difficult **Pets** in selected rooms **Closed** never **Proprietors** David and Sharon Parker

Boscundle Manor

Country house hotel

David and Sharon Parker took over Boscundle Manor a while ago, in 2002. It's been a mainstay of the guide for many years, and last time we looked was becoming tired and frayed around the edges. The Parkers stepped in, however, with a full-scale refurbishment plan, which is now complete. The previous owners took most of the antiques with them, so new furniture, mainly oriental mahogany, features throughout. Carpets and curtains have been replaced, fresh coats of paint brighten the walls and the bathrooms and bedrooms sparkle.

The grounds are now five acres of terraced gardens and woodland, with several pleasant walks through the woods. There are ponds and old tin mine remains.

Since our last visit the brasserie has closed, but the restaurant offers four different, daily-changing menus using Cornish produce whenever available. The butter on the table comes from hand-milked, West Country cows and is hand-packed at the local dairy. Chef Jenny Reed looks after the cooking and David eagerly seeks guests' reactions to new dishes.

St Blazey, Cornwall

Prideaux Road, Luxulyan Valley, near St Blazey, Cornwall PL24 2SR

Tel (01726) 814488
e-mail keith@nanscawen.com
website www.nanscawen.com

Nearby Fowey; Lanhydrock House; the Eden Project; Polperro; Looe.
Location in countryside, 0.5 mile (1 km) off A390, NW of St Blazey, 3 miles (5 km) NE of St Austell; in 5-acre grounds, with car parking
Food breakfast
Price ££
Rooms 4; 3 double and twin, 1 suite, all with bath; all rooms have phone, TV, hairdryer
Facilities drawing room, conservatory; terrace, garden, heated outdoor swimming pool, whirlpool spa
Credit cards MC, V
Children accepted over 12
Disabled access difficult
Pets not accepted
Closed never
Proprietors Keith and Sandra Martin

Nanscawen Manor House **Country guesthouse**

Dating from the 16th century, Nanscawen Manor has been carefully extended in recent years and sits amidst five acres of mature and very pretty gardens and grounds, with a 'wonderfully located' outdoor swimming pool. Its seclusion is enviable: approached by a fairly steep uphill track from the road, you can't see the house until you are almost upon it. As well as the pool, you can also sink into the whirlpool spa, and there is a terrace on which to sit in the sunshine amongst palm trees and hydrangeas. Reports confirm the Martin's family home is an excellent bed-and-breakfast guesthouse.

The entrance hall, with polished parquet floor, leads to a large, attractive sitting room with an honesty bar. Breakfast is taken in a sunny, cane-furnished conservatory; it's very good, and includes dishes such as locally-smoked salmon with scrambled eggs. A semi-spiral staircase takes you up to the three bedrooms, described by one reader as 'charming, but perhaps a touch too feminine for some tastes.' Rashleigh, in the newer part of the house, is vast, with a huge hand-carved four poster, while the two in the original wing have large beds, one a four-poster, and views of the garden to the south. With ongoing refurbishments, Keith told us they are "making things better as they go along".

St Hilary, Cornwall

St Hilary, Penzance, Cornwall
TR20 9BZ

Tel (01736) 740262
Fax (01736) 740055
e-mail ennys@ennys.co.uk
website www.ennys.co.uk

Nearby Lands End; Penzance; Lizard peninsula; St Michael's Mount; St Ives.
Location in gardens with car parking; from B3280 from Marazion turn left into Trewhella Lane, between St Hilary and Relubbus
Food breakfast **Price** ££
Rooms 5; 3 double, 2 with bath, 1 with shower, 2 suites, all with bath and shower; all rooms have TV, hairdryer, wi-fi **Facilities** breakfast room, sitting room; garden, grass tennis court, heated outdoor swimming pool
Credit cards MC, V
Children accepted over 14
Disabled access difficult **Pets** not accepted
Closed Nov 1 to Apr 1
Proprietor Gill Charlton

Ennys

Country bed-and-breakfast

Travel journalists don't often move over into the hospitality business themselves, but Gill Charlton is one who has, and she has brought her considerable knowledge of what makes an interesting place to stay to this excellent country guesthouse.

Ennys is a beautiful, creeper-clad 17thC Cornish manor house situated at the end of a long tree-lined drive in little St Hilary, a few miles from Penzance. The sheltered gardens are full of shrubs and flowers and include a swimming pool and grass tennis court. The fields stretch down to the River Hayle, along which you can walk and picnic.

Bedrooms in the main house are prettily decorated, furnished in country house style, and all have new bathrooms and window seats with garden or country views. Two recently renovated family suites are in an adjacent converted stone barn near which self-catering accommodation is also available. Proper cream teas are laid out in the rustic farmhouse-style kitchen. Afterwards, you can curl up in the large comfortable sitting room with open log fire. Gill is the perfect hostess, and a mine of information on the surrounding area.

St Mary's, Isles of Scilly

St Mary's, Isles of Scilly,
TR21 0TA

Tel (01720) 422317/423342
Fax (01720) 422343
e-mail info@star-castle.co.uk
website www.star-castle.co.uk

Nearby other Scilly islands including Tresco; bird watching; swimming with seals
Location in own grounds
Food breakfast, lunch, dinner
Price ££-£££
Rooms 38; 4 singles, 34 double or twin; all rooms have bath and shower, phone, TV
Facilities sitting room, bar, 2 restaurants, tennis, indoor swimming pool
Credit Cards AE, MC, V
Children accepted
Disabled difficult, but some ground level rooms
Pets accepted
Closed 3 days before Christmas, four weeks after New Year
Proprietor Robert Francis

Star Castle Hotel
Island hotel

There's only a handful of upmarket hotels in the Scillies, some of which strive to appeal to the mainland's chic set. They tend to lack heart, but this one decidedly does not. The welcome begins at the airport, or ferry, where Robert, his son James (the manager) or one of the staff meet guests.

Castles often make dismal hotels, but this one, inside its walls in the shape of an eight-pointed star, has something of the charm and intimacy of a Cotswold cottage. As well as the cosy bar, first floor sitting room and ground floor, stone-walled dining room, there are eight charming bedrooms in the castle itself, all recently redecorated.

Each morning at breakfast, Robert and James enquire from their guests what they feel like doing, making suggestions, arranging boat trips and providing packed lunches and maps for walkers. Many regulars simply say they are "going with Tim", a hugely popular local boatman who takes guests on trips to the off-islands.

The spacious bedrooms in the annexe have also been overhauled. An exotic garden is growing up between the two wings to detract from their somewhat Butlinesque appearance.

We could not fault the food, and there's an interesting personal wine list. This is not a chic hotel, but a very good one.

St Keyne, Nr Looe, Cornwall
PL14 4RN

Tel (01326) 270270
e-mail info@idlerocks.com
website www.idlerocks.com

Nearby St. Mawes, Trelissick, Glendurgan, Heligan and Trebah gardens; Truro; Eden Project; National Maritime Museum.
Location follow signs for the castle which will bring you down to the harbour side, allocated spaces in St Mawes Public Car Park
Food breakfast, lunch, dinner; afternoon tea, children's high tea at 5.30pm **Price** ££££
Rooms 20; 4 in separate annexe, all ensuite, with underfloor heating, some family rooms
Facilities bar, lounge, terrace, children's room, baby listening
Credit cards all major
Children welcome **Disabled** annexe has some disabled access **Pets** 1 dog-friendly room in the annexe **Closed** 3 weeks in Jan
Proprietors Mr and Mrs Richards

Idle Rocks

Seaside hotel

No surf here on the beautiful Roseland Peninsula, but there's 'harbour jumping' from St Mawes' harbour wall instead – a long-established St Mawes pastime at high tide. "We bet our friends to do it, and give the money to charity," says David Richards, owner of The Idle Rocks and the chairman of Aston Martin.

This is one of those seaside hotels so close to the water you can hear the waves from your bedroom window: magical. With 20 nigh-on faultless (though not large) bedrooms, kids' playroom, elegant dining room and stone-walled terrace where chilled music plays – it has much to recommend it to a generally younger clientèle. Everything is fresh, new and of the highest quality, predominantly white but liberally splashed with vibrant pattern and colour.

There are teething troubles at The Idle Rocks: it's a bit cramped for a fully-fledged hotel; the walls are thin between the rooms. However, we felt that the team (led by Josie and Amber) are striving for perfection, and would sort out problems as they go. The food is correctly pitched and reflects both ambience and location: we had 'roasted shells' with aioli to start; Josper-grilled sirloin and lemon sole to follow.

St Mawes, Cornwall

St Mawes, Cornwall
TR2 5DR

Tel (01326) 270055
Fax (01326) 270053
e-mail info@tresanton.com
website www.tresanton.com

Nearby Trelissick, Glendurgan, Heligan and Trebah gardens; Truro; Eden Project; National Maritime Museum.
Location in town, just below castle, 14 miles (22 km) S of Truro; car parking
Food breakfast, lunch, dinner; room service **Price** ££££
Rooms 30; 26 double and twin, 4 suites, all with bath; all rooms have phone, TV and DVD player, hairdryer, free wi-fi
Facilities sitting room, dining room, bar, cinema, terraces; 8-metre yacht
Credit cards AE, MC, V
Children welcome
Disabled not suitable
Pets accepted in 4 rooms **Closed** 2 weeks in Jan
Proprietor Olga Polizzi

Tresanton

Seaside town hotel

It's easy to drive past the hotel, as it has no obvious entrance, particularly for cars. Look closer and you will see a discreet sign and some steps next to a pair of white-painted garages. Stop, and within seconds someone will appear to welcome you, take your luggage and park your car. This is not any old seaside hotel.

Tresanton was opened in the summer of 1998 by Olga Polizzi, daughter of Lord Forte, and it is now well established as the West Country hotel for chic townies who prefer not to forego sophistication when by the seaside. Yet St Mawes is a happy-go-lucky holiday village, full in summer of chirpy families, bucket and spade in hand, and the two must rub along together. A whitewashed former sailing club and a cluster of cottages on the sea front make up the hotel, which was well known back in the 1960s, but had long lost its glamour before Olga Polizzi came across it. She set about redesigning it in minimalist, elegant style, using restful, muted tones of oatmeal and flax, accentuated by blues, greens, browns or yellows. Bedrooms are a study in understated luxury and have stunning sea views. The warm and comfortable sitting room and bar are more traditional.

Tresanton can claim to be one of the most sought-after hotels in the South West. The food is gaining many plaudits – restaurant extended in 2013.

Strete, Devon

Strete Barton House

Country bed-and-breakfast

Nestling in the peaceful coastal village of Strete, this smart B&B within reach of award-winning beaches and the Slapton Ley Nature Reserve will appeal to nature lovers with a taste for luxury.

The refurbished 16thC manor house has five smart bedrooms in a variety of eye-catching styles, with sea views, king-sized sleigh beds and flat-screen TVs. There's additional accommodation in the Cottage Suite, with its log-burning stove and inglenook fireplace. On arrival, the welcoming hosts will offer you a hot drink and a slice of home-made cake.

Strete is in the hilly area of south Devon known as the South Hams, with great walking and cycling, to give an extra dimension to the coastal scenery. If the weather's poor, book a massage appointment with the qualified therapist.

They make a serious effort with the buffet breakfast here, served in a pleasant room overlooking the large gardens. There's no lunch or dinner, but the hosts can recommend local restaurants.

According to one recent visitor, "hosts Stuart and Kevin deserve the highest of praise", while another termed Strete Barton "one of the most beautifully appointed guesthouses we have ever stayed in".

Totnes Road, Strete, Dartmouth, Devon TQ6 0RU

Tel 01803 770364 **Fax** 01803 771182
e-mail info@stretebarton.co.uk
website www.stretebarton.co.uk

Nearby Slapton Ley, Slapton Beach, South West Coast Path, Blackpool Sands, Greenway (NT), Coleton Fishacre (NT), Salcombe, Dartmouth, boating, golf **Location** access from A38 and A384, see website for full details **Food** breakfast; 2 restaurants serving lunch and dinner within a minute's walk **Price** ££-£££ **Rooms** 5 double and 1 cottage suite, with flat-screen television and DVD/CD player, wi-fi, fresh flowers, hairdryer, magazine selection **Facilities** drawing room, dining room, garden, massage treatments available **Children** 8 years and over **Disabled** no access **Pets** welcome in the Cottage Suite only – additional £7/pet/night **Closed** rarely **Proprietor/Manager** Stuart Litster & Kevin Hooper

Sturminster Newton, Dorset

Hazelbury Bryan Road, Sturminster Newton, Dorset DT10 2AF

Tel (01258) 472507
Fax (01258) 473370
e-mail book@plumbermanor.com
website www.plumbermanor.com

Nearby Thomas Hardy country; Shaftesbury; Sherborne.
Location 2 miles (3 km) SW of Sturminster Newton; private car parking
Food breakfast, Sun lunch, dinner
Price ££-£££
Rooms 16; 14 double, all with bath, 2 small doubles with bath; all rooms have phone, TV
Facilities dining room, sitting room, bar; garden, croquet, tennis court
Credit cards AE, DC, MC, V
Children welcome
Disabled easy access to barn bedrooms and dining room **Pets** accepted by arrangement **Closed** Feb
Proprietor Richard Prideaux-Brune

Plumber Manor

Manor house hotel

This is a handsome Jacobean manor house, 'modernized' in the early 20th century, that has been in the Prideaux-Brune family for well over 300 years. Since 1973, brothers Richard, Tim and Brian have been running it as an elegant but relaxed restaurant with comfortable bedrooms. Richard Prideaux-Brune is much in evidence front-of-house, as is his brother Tim. Together with Brian, who is responsible for the highly-regarded food, they draw in restaurant customers from far and wide – expect plenty of bustle on Friday and Saturday evenings, and non-residents in the dining room.

The brothers make charming hosts, and have created a very relaxed and welcoming atmosphere. Old family portraits hang in the house; labradors lounge in the bar; the decoration is homely and comfortable rather than smart. The large bar area might detract from the feeling of a family home, but it helps the Prideaux-Brunes' operation in a practical way (shooting parties are a feature in winter).

Bedrooms are divided between those in the main house (which lead off a gallery hung with portraits) and those in a converted stone barn and courtyard building which overlook the extensive gardens and stream. They are all spacious and comfortable.

Teffont Evias, Wiltshire

Teffont Evias, Salisbury,
Wiltshire SP3 5RJ

Tel (01722) 716392
Fax (01722) 716820
e-mail enq@howardshousehotel.com
website www.howardshousehotel.com

Nearby Salisbury Cathedral; Wilton House; Stonehenge; Old Sarum, Longleat.
Location in village, off B3089 (sign-posted from Teffont Magna), 10 miles (16 km) W of Salisbury; car parking
Food breakfast, lunch, dinner
Price ££-£££
Rooms 9; 8 double and twin, 1 family, all with bath; all rooms have phone, TV, hairdryer
Facilities dining room, sitting room; terrace, garden, croquet
Credit cards AE, MC, V
Children welcome
Disabled not suitable
Pets accepted
Closed never
Proprietor Noële Thompson

Howard's House

Village restaurant-with-rooms

Teffont Evias, in the Nadder valley, has been owned by the same family, father to son, since 1692. It is picturesque and has great charm without being twee. In the grounds stands Howard's House, opposite a marvellously knotty topiary hedge, and embellished by a Swiss gabled roof in the early 19th century – its then owner had fallen for all things Swiss on the Grand Tour. It is surrounded by two acres of pretty garden.

Its *raison d'être* is the food, created by chef Nick Wentworth. Dishes might include seared scallops with *sauce vierge* and crab mayonnaise, rack of lamb with onion puree and tomato and olive salsa, followed by summer berry jelly and elderflower ice cream. The smallish dining room, recently refurbished, is a soft cream and off-balanced by some deliberately striking artwork, as is the decoration in the cosy sitting room. The bedrooms: pastel-coloured walls, floral fabrics, oak furnishings. The four-poster room is the prettiest; rooms 1 and 2 look out over the garden.

Breakfast here is well above average: excellent coffee, warm croissants and toast wrapped in a white napkin, and the mouthwatering orange juice. You might choose a boiled egg, or something more sophisticated such as poached egg tartlet with Hollandaise sauce.

Tollard Royal, Wiltshire

Tollard Royal, Wiltshire SP5 5PS

Tel 01725 516207
e-mail info@kingjohninn.co.uk
website www.kingjohninn.co.uk

Nearby Thomas Hardy country; Shaftesbury; Salisbury, Rushmore Golf Club, Todber Manor Fisheries, Cranborne Chase.
Location village of Tollard Royal on Wiltshire/Dorset border
Food breakfast, lunch, dinner
Price £££-££££
Rooms 8; 5 in the inn, 3 in the coach house opposite (with self-catering facilities); all doubles and all have bath/shower, all have TV, telephone, wi-fi **Facilities** pub, restaurant, terraced garden and outdoor kitchen **Credit cards** DC, MC, V
Children welcome at lunch, can stay from 2 years **Disabled** one room in coach house with disabled facilities
Pets by prior arrangement
Closed Christmas Day and New Year's Eve
Proprietors Alex and Gretchen Boon

King John Inn

Village inn

At weekends the recently refurbished King John is jammed with urban couples, though locals come here too – it has a strong feel of village pub turned weekend hang-out. The charming new 'outdoor kitchen', with a cosmopolitan seafood bar under a Victorian-style pavilion, is popular in the summer. In the evening, don't be surprised to find a lively throng on the terrace outside, keeping warm from the wood-burning braziers.

Up the steep, hessian-carpeted stairs are the five bedrooms (there are also three in a converted coach house). They are decorated with an eye for the past as well as the present, and have a choice of fabrics that makes them refreshingly different from others of their ilk. Ours had a bay window dressed in a beautiful woven fabric and a great feeling of space. The bathroom was a little dark, but had both free-standing bath and shower.

Downstairs, the simple wooden tables quickly fill up and the noise levels can climb. We thought the pork and mustard pies 'good pub fare', and the snails, crab on toast and fish from Poole Harbour better than expected. The home-made bread and fudge are great.

Tresco, Isles of Scilly

Tresco Estate, Isles of Scilly, TR24 0QQ

Tel (01720) 422849
e-mail contactus@tresco.co.uk
website www.tresco.co.uk

Nearby Tresco's sub-tropical Abbey Garden; boat trips to other Scilly Isles; ferry to Bryher.
Location Tresco island.
Food breakfast, lunch, dinner
Price very variable, see website
Rooms 16; 7 self-catering, 9 self-catering with hotel services (eg daily clean), for 2-10 people. See website for details of individual cottages
Facilities restaurants and pubs (eg New Inn in New Grimsby), swimming pool, gym, spa, bike hire, golf buggies **Credit cards** DC, MC, V
Children welcome
Disabled no special access (golf buggies available for people with reduced mobility)
Pets not accepted
Closed Dec-Feb (although self-catering cottages run all year)
Proprietor Tresco Estate

Sea Garden Cottages

Self-catering cottages

The whole of Tresco is in effect a multi-faceted holiday destination, unique in Britain. The Island Hotel has disappeared, to leave a mix of timeshare and rental accommodation dotted all over the island. The Sea Garden Cottages – built from sympathetic wood and stone – comprise seven self-catering cottages and nine cottages that have certain hotel facilities as part of the package.

Our cottage suite was faultless: comfortable, well-equipped kitchen and garden, seaside-fresh decoration. It also had some interesting modern art, much of it from the collection of Tresco's proprietors, Robert and Lucy Dorrien-Smith.

There's an indoor pool and tennis court by the cottages. Guests can also eat in the stylish restaurant at the Flying Boat Club at New Grimsby or in the new restaurant, The Ruin. This shares the same electrifying sea views as the rooms, and does tasty food – although we preferred the surf'n'turf at The New Inn at New Grimsby, its menu was tantalising and made choosing difficult.

Accommodation on Tresco is expensive. However, it's a no-car, protected environment and under blue skies the archipelago dances in the sunlight. If you want the full hotel experience think about Hell Bay Hotel (http://www.hellbay.co.uk/), on Bryher, also owned by the Dorrien-Smiths.

Wareham, Dorset

Church Green, Wareham,
Dorset BH20 4ND

Tel (01929) 551666
Fax (01929) 554519
e-mail reservations@theprioryhotel.co.uk **website** www.theprioryhotel.co.uk

Nearby Poole Harbour; Swanage; Lulworth Cove.
Location in town near market square; in 4.5 acre gardens with ample car parking
Food breakfast, lunch, dinner
Price ££££
Rooms 18; 13 double, 5 suites, all have bath/shower; all rooms have phone, TV, hairdryer, minibar
Facilities sitting room, bar, restaurant; terrace, garden, croquet, pontoon, organise gold and fishing outings **Credit cards** DC, MC, V
Children accepted over 8 **Disabled** access difficult **Pets** guide dogs only
Closed never **Proprietor** Turner family

The Priory

Country town hotel

Hidden behind the church, this 16thC Priory is the perfect retreat for anyone who appreciates a sense of history, as well as peace, comfort and good food. It has been run for the last thirty years by the Turner family, and is currently under the guiding hand of Jeremy, who is ensuring that everything, from the excellent antiques to the pretty fabrics in the bedrooms, has been done with taste and in keeping.

The bedrooms are all that should be expected from a 16thC priory: beams, sloping ceilings and floors, as well as being supremely comfortable and well-equipped with books (no *Reader's Digest* here) and attractive toiletries in the bathrooms. To keep up with the demand for rooms the boathouse has been converted to provide four extra bedrooms, or rather suites, equipped with luxury baths and French windows opening on to the River Frome. Indeed, by boat is the best way to arrive at the Priory: moorings are available and, after a quick walk through the stunning gardens (from which Mrs Turner gathers flowers for the arrangements) you can relax with a pre-dinner drink on the terrace. The food is richly sastisfying, with a mainland European flavour emanating from the menu.

Wheddon Cross, Somerset

Wheddon Cross, Exmoor National Park, Somerset TA24 7DU

Tel 01643 841432
e-mail info@exmoorhotel.co.uk
website www.exmoorhotel.co.uk

Nearby Exmoor national park, Dunkery Beacon, Holnicote Estate, fishing, golf, country sports
Location Wheddon Cross, at junction of A396 and B3224, in centre of village
Food breakfast, lunch (pre-booked), dinner **Price** £
Rooms 5; 3 twin/doubles, 1 double, 1 family room (double and 2 singles), all have hairdryers, tea/coffee, hot water bottles
Facilities sitting room, dining room, bar, terrace
Credit cards MC, V
Children accepted, 1 family room
Disabled difficult for wheelchair users **Pets** not accepted
Closed only house parties over Christmas and New Year
Proprietors Frank Velander and Rosi Davis

Exmoor House

Town bed-and-breakfast

Exmoor House has an unusual history – it was built in Edwardian times for a local tailor and what is now the dining room, with its views of Dunkery Beacon, was orginally the tailor's shop. While the guests' sitting room was at one time the cutting room, it has also now doubled up as the village library. The rooms still have their original wooden panelling, and this gives them a cosy, homely feel.

In winter there's a crackling log fire in the sitting room – perfect for relaxing after a day on the moors with, perhaps, a warming glass of whisky from the bar. In summer, it's great to take your drinks out on to the terrace and soak up the sun or, if it's a warm evening, admire Exmoor's amazingly vivid night skies.

Food is one of the hotel's real highlights and the chef uses plenty of locally-sourced produce to create what the co-proprietor, Rosi Davis, descibes as 'traditional food with a twist' and 'a major part of the Exmoor House experience'. The menu changes day by day and can be tailored specifically to guests' requirements. Guests rave about Exmoor House's homely yet luxurious feel.

Wincanton, Somerset

Wincanton, Somerset BA9 8BS

Tel 01963 824466
Fax 01963 32681
e-mail
enquiries@holbrookhouse.co.uk
website www.holbrookhouse.co.uk

Nearby Wincanton Race Course; many National Trust attractions; Bath; Longleat Safari Park
Location 1 mile from Wincanton, Somerset; from M3 south, exit at junction 8 onto the A303, then take the A371 sign-posted to Wincanton and Castle Cary.
Food breakfast, lunch, dinner
Price £-££
Rooms 21; all double, 14 can be twin, 4 suites, all with bath; all rooms have phone, hairdryer
Facilities Health Club, Spa, 4 sitting rooms, cafe **Credit Cards** all accepted **Children** welcome **Disabled** 1 room with disabled facilities **Pets** accepted **Closed** never
Proprietors John & Patricia McGinley

Holbrook House

Country house hotel

John and Pat McGinley bought Holbrook House in 1998 on a whim. Passing by, they popped in for a cup of tea and found it was for sale. The current manager, Darren (the McGinleys' son) was a successful DJ before he took over – as we arrived we listened to a cool compilation of background music, mixed by Darren himself.

The place seems to defy time, what with Darren's music – he hopes, too, that performers at Glastonbury might stay here. The McGinleys completely redecorated when they took over, but you wouldn't know it, so quietly old-fashioned are the furnishings. We particularly liked the feel of the main hall.

In the 20 acres of grounds that surround the house there is a grass tennis court – a rarity these days – plus an enormous old cedar tree and a steep drop to a deep gully that eventually reaches the River Cale.

Value for money is exceptional. As we went to press, two people could pay as little as £100 on a weekday: for this they get for a huge room, beautiful grounds, use of the hotel's spa and pool and tennis court (rackets provided) and breakfast and dinner. In summer, many weekends are given over to weddings.

Winsford, Exmoor National Park, Somerset TA24 7JE

Tel 01643 851455
e-mail enquiries@royaloakexmoor.co.uk
website www.royaloakexmoor.co.uk

Nearby Exmoor Pony Centre; Dunster Castle; Tarr Steps; Caracatus Stone; Stone Age Burial Site **Location** in centre of village on B road, 1.5miles from junction with A396, ample parking in hotel car park and on street
Food breakfast, lunch, dinner
Price £££
Rooms 12; 6 doubles under the thatch (5 with four poster beds), 2 twins, 2 doubles in annexe; all rooms have bath/shower, telephone, TV, hairdryers, tea/coffee making facilities **Facilities** residents lounge, dining room, bar, wi-fi, garden
Credit Cards all major **Children** welcome **Disabled** access possible to annexe rooms **Pets** accepted in bedrooms **Closed** never **Proprietors** Henry family

The Royal Oak

Village inn

This Exmoor institution has been improving steadily since the Henrys took over in 2011. Locals popping in for a drink feel relaxed because their custom is valued and they have their own bar area. Hotel guests have a peaceful refuge at the far end of the building – a large sitting room replete with Victorian-style deep-buttoned chairs and sofas. Along with the rest of the public areas and bedrooms, it's conservatively rather than imaginatively decorated – 30 and 40-somethings won't like it as much as their parents – but it's appropriate to Exmoor.

There's room in the dining area for the shooting parties not to swamp the regular guests. Several menus, including a family one, and a long wine list, offer the wide choice needed to satisfy these different groups. We liked the chunky, brown-stained tongue-and-groove panelling throughout the ground floor – quite smart and pleasing because it pulls it all together in an unpretentious way. Ceilings are low, beams are everywhere and because of the thatch overhang, the ground floor is darkish. We also liked the spacious bedrooms, with conventional repro and antique furnishings and adequate, plain white bathrooms. No 4, at £140, is especially roomy. No 3, the smallest, is roomy by comparison with what other similar places offer for £120.

Barwick, near Yeovil, Somerset
BA22 9TD

Tel (01935) 423902
Fax (01935) 420908
e-mail
reservations@barwick7.fsnet.co.uk
website
www.littlebarwickhouse.co.uk

Nearby Brympton d'Evercy; Montacute House.
Location 2 miles (3 km) S of Yeovil off A37; car parking
Food breakfast, lunch, dinner
Price ££
Rooms 6 double and twin, all with bath or shower; all rooms have TV, hairdryer, phone, iPod dock, radio, wi-fi
Facilities sitting room, dining room, bar/private dining room; garden
Credit cards MC, V
Children welcome over 5
Disabled access difficult
Pets accepted
Closed 2 weeks Jan
Proprietors Emma and Tim Ford

Little Barwick House

Restaurant-with-rooms

Emma and Tim Ford have built up a reputation for fine food at this restaurant with rooms in Somerset. Tim is one of Britain's finest chefs: he trained at Sharrow Bay and spent time in several top hotels refining his art. Previously he was head chef at Summer Lodge in Evershot, but he and his wife Emma, who was front-of-house there, have now been running Little Barwick for 14 years.

Locally-sourced meat, game and fish provide the cornerstone of Tim's cooking (our inspector enjoyed pink roasted rump of Dorset lamb with aubergine caviar and black olive sauce), while the lunch menu is a simpler variation of the dinner menu.The wine list is extensive, including many wines by the glass or half bottle.

Little Barwick has featured in these pages for years, recommended for its friendly informality, and this has remained the case through changes of ownership. The Fords have completed a programme of redecoration that has freshened up both the interior and exterior of this lovely listed Georgian dower house.The dining room has recently been redecorated with a Farrow and Ball stripe wallpaper. Bedrooms remain cheerful with fresh flowers, real coffee in cafetières and home-made shortbreads.

Zennor, Cornwall

Treen, Zennor, Cornwall
TR26 3DE

Tel (01736) 796928
e-mail
enquiries@gurnardshead.co.uk
website www.gurnardshead.co.uk

Nearby Tate Galley at St Ives; South West Coast Path; Trengwainton
Location on the B3306 between St Ives and Land's End; ample car parking
Food breakfast, lunch, dinner
Price £££
Rooms 7; 4 double, 3 twin, all with shower; phone, TV and hairdryer available on request
Facilities bar, dining room; garden
Credit cards MC, V
Children welcome
Disabled no special facilities
Pets dogs welcome
Closed Christmas; 1 week Jan
Proprietors Charles and Edmund Inkin; they also own The Old Coastguard (page 59) and Felin Fach Griffin (page 180) in Wales

The Gurnard's Head

Seaside inn

An early 17th century coaching inn near Zennor, standing like a beacon on the windswept coastal road that runs between St Ives and Land's End. Brothers Charles and Edmund Inkin's motto is 'the simple things in life done well' and they reckon on applying this to all aspects of The Gunard's Head, as also to their other establishments.

The stunning location and views of the Atlantic make this inn popular with walkers, tourists and city dwellers looking for tranquility, although the sounds and smells from the neighbouring farm may not be for urban-outdoor types. The bedrooms are simple and tastefully decorated, with hand-made beds and good linen. Each room is lined with old books and local pictures and maps – you might be staying with friends.

With the Atlantic 500 metres away, locally caught fish is a highlight of the seasonal menu. The lunch menus suit most guests, from the hungry walker to those who want to settle in for a fixed-price menu with a carafe of wine. In the evening, the menu is short and delicious, changing daily according to what suppliers bring through the back door. Drink from a choice of well-chosen and affordable wines or local real ales and cider. Too good to be true? Our reporter, food writer Mark Taylor's, reply: 'Except for the quibble about the farmyard smells, it really is that good.'

Bath

Newbridge Hill,
Bath BA1 3PT

Tel (01225) 336966
Fax (01225) 425462
e-mail info@apsley-house.co.uk
website www.apsley-house.co.uk
Food breakfast, light supper in quieter times **Price** ££
Closed Christmas **Proprietors** Claire and Nicholas Potts

Apsley House

Town hotel

Once upon a time this was a grand house with huge grounds leading down to the River Avon. The grounds were sold off long ago to make way for the houses which now surround Apsley House, leaving enough garden to ensure privacy for the occupants.

There is a large, comfortable drawing room, with a grand piano for guests' use, as well as a licensed bar.

Owners Claire and Nicholas Potts have updated the bedrooms and bathrooms, and generally set about making the place "a lot cleaner". Since the last edition the Potts have opened up three further bedrooms in the hotel, complete with four-poster beds.

Claire does some of the cooking and is rightly proud of her breakfasts.

Bradford-on-Avon, Wiltshire

1 Church Street, Bradford-on-Avon,
Wiltshire, BA15 1LN

Tel (01225) 868686
Fax (01225) 868681
e-mail stay@theswanbradford.co.uk
website www.theswanbradford.co.uk
Food breakfast, lunch, dinner
Price £££ **Closed** never
Proprietors James

The Swan Inn

Town inn

In 2007 this 600-year-old Bradford-on-Avon institution got a new lease of life – a complete makeover. However, the listed building was hard to renovate, and the result lacks finesse. This shouldn't stop you staying here, if you want what it offers: a mixture of small town hotel, pub and informal restaurant. Locals and residents enjoy the bar and the (good) food; prices are fair. It's a serious alternative to lodging in Bath, where hotel prices are now higher than in London.

Lack of finesse? The interior design relies too much on predictable 'contemporary' colours, carpets and curtains. The sitting room near the main entrance is underwhelming; the bed creaked; there was some traffic noise. That said, rooms 8 and 12 are spacious and good value.

Bristol

Hotel du Vin

Town house hotel

Since our last edition, the Hotel du Vin chain has been taken over by Malmaison, a large group. However, this is probably still the most interesting and stylish place to stay in Bristol.

Converted from a collection of derelict 18thC sugar warehouses, the hotel's gracious Queen Anne frontage belies the wizardry behind. Open brickwork, painted girders and sweeping stairs with a curving steel bannister combine industrial elements with contemporary style to great effect.

The huge bedrooms contain custom-made beds, alongside equally huge bathrooms with showers and free-standing baths. The aptly-named Sugar Bar has whitewashed walls, wood flooring and rugs that contribute to the unhurried, plantation house feel.

The Sugar House,
Narrow Lewins Mead,
Bristol, Avon BS1 2NU

Tel 0117 9255577
Fax 0117 9251199
website www.hotelduvin.com
Food breakfast, lunch, dinner
Price £££
Closed never
Proprietors Lorraine Jarvie

Buckhorn Weston, Dorset

The Stapleton Arms

Village inn

In deepest Dorset lies this new-wave village inn, the type you might describe as 'urban-chic with a country twist'. With pillared portico and elegant proportions, it looks more like a gentleman's residence than a long-established hostelry. Step inside, and the scene is contemporary: open-plan, leather sofas and chunky tables.

The bedrooms are great, especially for the price: airy and well-proportioned. We had a lovely bathroom, with large, free-standing tub and generous toiletries.

Dinner, contrary to reports, was a little disappointing: we called more than once for missing cutlery and water. However, when the place is humming, as it often is, it makes a great stop-off en route to the West Country.

Church Hill, Buckhorn Weston,
Gillingham, Dorset SP8 5HS

Tel 01963 370396
e-mail relax@thestapletonarms.com
website www.thestapletonarms.com
Food breakfast, lunch, dinner
Price ££
Closed 24th/25th Dec
Proprietor Victoria Reeves

Exford, Somerset

Exford, Somerset TA24 7PP

Tel 01643 831554
Fax 01643 831665
e-mail info@crownhotelexmoor.co.uk **website** www.crownhotelexmoor.co.uk
Food breakfast, lunch, dinner
Price ££-££££ **Closed** never
Proprietors Sarah and Dan Whittaker

The Crown Hotel

Country inn

A reliable, unpretentious, friendly Exmoor base. Lancastrian Sarah Whittaker is front of house while husband Dan does the above-average (for the price) bar and restaurant food. Furnishings are traditional, not imaginative or modern – but then a contemporary designer hotel would seem unnatural on Exmoor. There's enough room to accommodate locals, hotel guests and shooting parties at the same time – they don't always mix. The eating areas in the bar are pleasantly informal. All the basics are right, including properly warm bedrooms and bathrooms, and fair prices.

Fontmell Magna, Dorset

Fontmell Magna, Shaftesbury, Dorset SP7 0PA

Tel 01747 811441
e-mail info@thefontmell.com
website www.thefontmell.com
Food breakfast, lunch, dinner
Price £-££
Closed never
Proprietor Robert Clark

The Fontmell

Village inn

'It's a boutique hotel with beer taps' says Tom Shaw, chef and manager at The Fontmell. A formerly run-down village inn that's been done up in contemporary country style (Farrow & Ball, mismatched antique dining chairs). It's more boutique hotel than rural drinking spot, but while we reclined in front of a wood-burning stove before dinner, six gents dropped in to prop up the bar and exchange the day's news. The stair carpet is grubby, but the rooms are all different – imaginative with comfortable beds. There are glitches – thin walls, nowhere for shower gel, missing soap. But the dining room is attractive; the food 'enjoyable, not outstanding', and we liked that the village stream ran between the bar area and the dining room extension.

Frome, Somerset

Babington House
Country house hotel

Babington was the idea of Nick Jones, owner of the trendy Soho Club in London, and bought as a country retreat for club members. In practice anyone can stay here, although it might be better if you were young, or at least young at heart. Having said that, everyone is made to feel welcome, in a laid-back yet professional, atmosphere. It's a contemporary hotel set in an elegant country house that offers metropolitan and unpretentious luxury. Bedrooms are wonderful, with huge bottles of complimentary lotions in the bathrooms. You can have any number of beauty treatments in the Cowshed, where there is also an indoor pool and a gym. Small children are kept occupied in the well-equipped crêche.

Babington, near Frome,
Somerset BA11 3RW

Tel (01373) 812266
e-mail reception@babingtonhouse.co.uk
website www.babingtonhouse.co.uk
Food breakfast, lunch, dinner, room service **Price** ££££
Closed never
Proprietors Nick Jones

Lifton, Devon

Tor Cottage
Country bed-and-breakfast

Tor Cottage is described as a hideaway on the edge of Dartmoor and it is true that if you make the trip to this remote hotel, you will find a pleasant hotel full of little touches that give Tor Cottage an edge over other similar hotels: for example, a jug of sparkling wine awaits your arrival, as do champagne truffles, fresh fruit and flowers in your bedroom and the bonus of access to a heated outdoor swimming pool for those guests interested in taking a late-night dip under the brilliantly clear skies of Dartmoor.

Maureen prides herself on good service and genuinely enjoys pampering her visitors. As a result, Tor Cottage has picked up a large amount of awards and guests claim to leave suitably rejuvenated.

Chillaton, nr Lifton, Devon PL16 0JE

Tel 01822 860248
Fax 01822 860126
e-mail info@torcottage.co.uk
website www.torcottage.co.uk
Food breakfast
Price ££-£££
Closed mid-Dec to mid-Jan
Proprietors Maureen Rowlatt

Mevagissey, Cornwall

School-Hill, Mevagissey, South Cornwall PL26 6TH

Tel (01726) 842468
Fax (01726) 844 482
e-mail stay@trevalsa-hotel.co.uk
website www.trevalsa-hotel.co.uk
Food breakfast, lunch, dinner
Price ££
Closed Dec-Jan
Proprietors John and Sue Gladwin

Trevalsa Court

Seaside hotel

This is a cliff-top hotel with spectacular views, courteous staff, a simple but refreshingly different style – and an interesting history. It was built in the 1930s as a private, cliff-top home with breathtaking sea views and a Daphne du Maurier character: oak-panelled walls and stone-framed mullion windows.

The bedrooms and bathrooms vary in size, and though decorated mostly neutrally, the bigger ones have eclectic wallpaper, art and solid wooden furniture.

Trevalsa isn't isolated: houses have grown up around it. We don't rate this as ideal for a beach holiday, but it's a great base for the local sights. The coastal path is literally at the bottom of the garden, reached by a vertiginous metal stairway.

Newquay, Cornwall

Fistral Beach, Newquay, Cornwall TR7 1EW

Tel 01637 872211 **e-mail** reception@headlandhotel.co.uk **website** www.headlandhotel.co.uk/accommodation/cottages **Food** breakfast, lunch, dinner **Price** £££-££££ **Closed** never **Proprietors** Mr and Mrs Armstrong

The Headland Cottages

Self-catering cottages

Talk about a Victorian pile. The Headland Hotel's outward appearance is so frightening it was the setting for the 1990 film adaptation of Roald Dahl's *The Witches*.

The 39 one- to three-bedroom self-catering cottages make an attractive alternative to staying at the hotel – indeed any hotel – with all the benefits of hotel facilities close by. They are built in Cornish village style with rough stone and granite walls. Ours was airy and freshly painted in seaside colours, and had an excellent kitchen and gas log fire too.

You can mix self-catering with meals in the hotel. The Headland also has a fully equipped new spa, to which cottage guests have full access. The cottages, food and spa are worth seeking out.

Virginstow, Devon

Percy's Country Hotel
Country hotel and restaurant

Percy's Country Hotel was originally bought as a retirement home by the Bricknell-Webbs, who ran a restaurant in London called Percy's. The bedrooms, in an adjacent converted barn, are spacious and (after recent refurbishment) smart in an understated way: the showers are power showers, the beds are king-size, and the real coffee comes in cafetieres. Two rooms, with stripped wood floors, flowers and a wood-burning stove make up the intimate and calming restaurant – residents only. Tina cooks in the modern English style, with almost all ingredients, such as salad, eggs and venison, coming from the estate. Fish features strongly, and it is very good. The wine list is equally good, and almost all wines are available by the glass.

Coombeshead Estate, Virginstow, Devon EX21 5EA

Tel 01409 211236
e-mail info@percys.co.uk
website www.percys.co.u
Food breakfast, lunch, dinner
Price £££
Closed never
Proprietors Tony and Tina Bricknell-Webb

Wedmore, Somerset

The Swan
Country inn

Another dead-beat country pub restored and converted (2011) into a comfortable up-to-date haven. New owner Rob Greacen has kept faith with the place's inherited country pub ambience by going for wooden floors, log burners and a choice of real ales. The food, served all day, is hearty country fare – chef Tom Blake was at Hugh Fearnley-Whittingstall's River Cottage. Rare-breed pork is a speciality.

The bedrooms are striking: quality beds and linen, some charming furniture and interesting auction room finds here and there.

Cheddar Road, Wedmore, Somerset BS28 4EQ

Tel 01934 710337 **e-mail** info@theswanwedmore.com **website** www.theswanwedmore.com **Food** breakfast, lunch, dinner, afternoon tea, snacks, Sunday lunch **Price** ££ **Closed** no dinner on Sunday evenings, Christmas Day drinks only **Proprietor** Rob Greacen

Alton (Lower Froyle), Hampshire

Lower Froyle, Alton, Hampshire
GU34 4NA

Tel 01420 23261
e-mail info@anchorinnatlower-froyle.co.uk
website www.anchorinnatlower-froyle.co.uk

Nearby Hampshire.
Location 1.8 miles from Bentley, just off the A31
Food breakfast, lunch, dinner
Price £££
Rooms 5; all with shower
Facilities 2 bar areas, dining room, private dining rooms, courtyard
Credit cards AE, DC, MC, V
Children welcome
Disabled access to the dining rooms, not to the bedrooms **Pets** dogs allowed in the bedrooms and bar area **Closed** Christmas Day
Proprietors Tracey & Ashley Levett

The Anchor Inn

Country Inn

As a pleasant place to stay, it works well. You might even ask yourself, why spend more in a hotel when you can stay just as comfortably here? Our room felt spacious, with French doors on to a balcony rising to a high apex, and room for a sofa and table. All the extras of a fully-fledged hotel are in place: a choice of teas and coffees; Bush radio; antique-style sleigh bed; Egyptian cotton linen. The decoration is fashionable yet full of character, with oriental carpets on sisal, pale sage walls covered in pictures and shelves of books.

The night we stayed we were chilly in the wood-panelled dining room, but that was probably a one off. We got used to the low beams in the bar and kept our heads, but it's good sport watching new arrivals lose theirs. The 'simple, honest', properly English food from chef Kevin Chandler is enjoyable. Breakfast is cracking, and the staff friendly.

Arundel, West Sussex

The Street, Burpham, Arundel, West Sussex BN18 9RJ

Tel 01903 882160
e-mail info@burphamcountry-house.com **website** www.burpham-countryhouse.com

Nearby South Downs National Park, Parham, Petworth, Anglo-Saxon fort, Arundel's Wildfowl and Wetlands trust, **Location** Burpham village, small car park available **Food** breakfast, dinner **Price** ££-£££ **Rooms** 9; all doubles, 4 can be twin, all have bath/shower, all have TV, desk, wi-fi, clock radio, tea/coffee, hairdryer, phone **Facilities** sitting room, 2 dining rooms, conservatory, gardens, croquet lawn **Credit cards** MC, V **Children** children under 10 only allowed in the ground floor room, extra bed/breakfast £25 **Disabled** no special facilities, and some steps into public rooms **Pets** dogs in the ground-floor room, £10 per night **Closed** Sunday and Monday evenings **Proprietors** Steve and Jackie Penticost

Burpham Country House **Country house**

Burpham is a village that defies time – flint-walled houses, century old cricket pitch and picturesque pub – on a road that winds up from the water meadows of the River Arun to the sunny chalk grasslands of the South Downs.

The house was originally an 18thC hunting lodge and later a rectory, which explains the wooden veranda and ecclesiastical entrance porch. The dining room leads off the elegant hall, and there are two guest sitting rooms. We loved the lack of pretension, despite the beautiful setting: chickens peck on the lawn and the cat, Lucy, plonks herself wherever she may.

The nine bedrooms are comfortable – all decorated in mild, but not overstated, country house style, with an assortment of furniture, fabrics and ornaments.

Steve Penticost, whose family have lived in the area for more than 400 years, is the chef, and his food is much liked – he specialises in game and provides hearty dishes such as stuffed partridge breast with Serrano ham. We were, however, disappointed by the mini-pots of jam and butter at breakfast.

Jackie told us that many of their guests live nearby, and seek out Burpham to relax within arm's reach of their home – possible because Burpham is a fine country house without the prices you'd expect.

Baughurst, Hampshire

Baughurst Road, Baughurst,
Hampshire RG26 5LP

Tel 0118 9820110
e-mail
hello@thewellingtonarms.com **website** www.thewellingtonarms.com

Nearby Highclere Castle, The Vyne, Silchester, Bishopswood Golf Course
Location on Baughurst Road, leading south from Baughurst
Food breakfast, lunch, dinner
Price £££-££££
Rooms 3 doubles; all with shower, heated floors, wi-fi, TV and mini bar
Facilities bar, restaurant, large garden **Credit cards** DC, MC, V
Children welcome, no special facilities **Disabled** wheelchair access possible **Pets** dogs accepted
Closed never **Proprietor** Jason King and Simon Page

The Wellington Arms

Pub restaurant-with-rooms

Our series editor, Fiona Duncan, writes: 'The Wellington Arms is a dining pub with three rooms so immaculate that even in plutocratic north Hampshire, it stands out like a supermodel in a street market – oak furniture, Hungarian goose down bedding and slate flagstones with underfloor heating are just some of the features that set it apart. Partners Simon and Aussie-born Jason have owned, run and gently expanded this pretty former shooting lodge of the Duke of Wellington for eight years and it looks and feels special.

'Just an hour's drive from central London yet set in peaceful countryside, it ticks all the boxes for urbanites seeking rural idyll; immaculate, fulsome flower- and vegetable-gardens, which the owners and kitchen staff tend themselves; orchards; they even keep rescue hens – not to mention the beehives, pet lamb and Tamworth pigs. They have tea cosies knitted by Simon's mum using undyed wool from their own sheep, and fabric hens dangling from the room keys.

'Jason's cooking takes pub dining to its highest level: home made, locally sourced and tasty, with a state of the art cheese soufflé. After lunch, take the footpath from the door of the Wellington Arms, which leads through woods and fields, or perhaps head for Watership Down, site of Richard Adam's famous book of the same name'.

Bepton, West Sussex

Bepton, Near Midhurst,
West Sussex GU29 0JB

Tel (01730) 819000
Fax (01730) 819099
e-mail reservations@parkhousehotel.com **website** www.parkhousehotel.com

Nearby Petworth; Goodwood; Cowdray Park; Chichester. **Location** on the B2226 just N of Bepton village; ample car-parking **Food** breakfast, lunch, dinner; room service **Price** £££ **Rooms** 21 doubles, inc 2 family rooms in main building and 2 in the South Down Cottage, all with bath; 3 cottages; all rooms have phone, TV, wi-fi and iMac monitors, hairdryer **Facilities** dining, drawing room, conservatory, bar; gardens, outdoor swimming pool, tennis courts, croquet lawn, bowls green, golf, spa and treatment rooms **Credit cards** MC, V **Children** welcome **Disabled** adapted ground-floor bedroom, South Down Cottage has lift **Pets** by arrangement **Closed** rarely **Proprietor** Seamus O'Brien

Park House

Country hotel

Park House has been in the O'Brien family for more than 50 years, and has always retained the atmosphere of a private country house thanks first to the careful attention of Ioné O'Brien,and now to Seamus. A 16thC farmhouse with Victorian additions with its cream-painted roughcast walls, at first it looks rather suburban.

Inside, however, the elegant public rooms strike a very different note. The honesty bar, festooned with mementoes and photographs of polo players (Cowdray Park is close at hand) is admirably well-stocked, while the drawing room, particularly appealing at night, gleams with polished parquet floor, velvet-backed alcoves filled with books and china, yellow walls, and table lamps which cast a golden glow.

Bedrooms are traditional; best are the two in the annexe, one of which has a private patio. The dinner menu has been expanded (it used to be quite limited) and features traditional English food. Lunch can be as simple as sausage and mash or oxtail pie. Comments on the food welcome.

To add to existing facilities including a swimming pool, tennis courts and six-hole golf course, recent innovations have seen the creation of the Park House spa, a luxurious area with an indoor pool, gym and fitness suite, saunas, steam rooms and a Jacuzzi.

Brockenhurst, Hampshire

Beaulieu Road, Brockenhurst, Hampshire SO42 7QL

Tel 01590 622354
e-mail info@thepighotel.com
website www.pighotel.com

Nearby Beaulieu National Motor Museum, Bucklers Hard; Lymington; New Forest wildlife centres. **Location** in own extensive grounds, in the heart of the New Forest, close to Brockenhurst; ample private car-parking **Food** breakfast, lunch, dinner **Price** ££–£££ **Rooms** 26; 16 in main house, 10 in stable yard; all with monsoon showers. Most have larder cabinet, television, DVD player. Family rooms have a log burner or a freestanding bath. **Facilities** restaurant, lounge, bar, spa treatments, vegetable garden, guided walks, cycling, tennis courts, pigsty with pigs **Credit cards** AE, DC, MC, V **Children** welcome **Disabled** no special access **Pets** one dog-friendly room **Closed** never **Proprietor** Robin Hutson

THE PIG

Country house hotel

In its earlier incarnations, we thought of this place as a benchmark for the sort of establishment we didn't want in the guide – it was one of hundreds of nothing-special country house hotels. But now that Robin Hutson, creator of the Hotel du Vin chain and one of Britain's most inspired hoteliers, has practised his magic on the place, the result is hard to ignore.

Robin's wife Judy did the interior. It's quite a contrast to the controlled, Georgian exterior: a set piece of shabby-chic with touches of anarchy. The conservatory-dining room is the big draw: an imaginative, light-filled space with a wonderful tiled floor, pots of herbs on wooden boxes lining the outside windows and on every table. Over the corridor in the drawing room shabby-chic reasserts itself emphatically. The floor boards are distressed, and 'damaged' plasterwork on the walls reveals areas of brickwork beneath – only it's not damaged, it's *trompe l'oeil*. The bedrooms are truly comfortable.

Don't leave without a stroll through the walled kitchen garden, where they grow some of what's eaten in the dining room.

See also our other PIG – THE PIG-in the wall, Southampton. A third and fourth PIG will be opening at Studland and near Bath in 2014. Their website: www.thepighotel.com

Bucklers Hard, Hampshire

Bucklers Hard, Beaulieu,
Hampshire SO42 7XB

Tel (01590) 616253
Fax (01590) 616297
e-mail enquiries@themasterbuilders.co.uk **website** www.themasterbuilders.co.uk

Nearby New Forest; Beaulieu; Lymington.
Location overlooking Beaulieu river at Bucklers Hard, 2 miles (3 km) SE of Beaulieu, 9 miles (14 km) SE of Lyndhurst; ample car parking
Food breakfast, lunch, dinner
Price £££ **Rooms** 26 double, 18 can be twin, all with bath; all rooms have phone, TV, hairdryer, wi-fi, tea/coffee facilities, complimentary Godminster vodka **Facilities** sitting room, dining room, yachtsman's bar; terrace, garden, pontoon available
Credit cards MC, V **Children** welcome **Disabled** access difficult
Pets 7 dog-friendly rooms
Closed never
Proprietors Hillbrooke Hotels

The Master Builder's

Riverside hotel

This superbly sited hotel has long been ripe for a carefully judged overhaul, and when its lease from Lord Montagu of Beaulieu came up some years ago for renewal, Hillbrooke Hotels stepped in. The location really is special, and historic, at the bottom end of a row of 18thC shipwrights' cottages, looking down on to the Beaulieu River. It contains a bar that's popular with visiting yachtsmen, and nearby is a maritime museum.

The 18thC house was lumbered some years back with an unsympathetic modern annexe, the Henry Adams Wing. Even the designer's best efforts cannot give the bedrooms here the character they lack, and although they are now comfortable and attractive, given their size, we feel they are somewhat ambitiously priced. But thanks to the new managers, the bedrooms in the main building have much more character. The sophisticated reception area is an improvement on the old, and in the smart dining room, with views down to the river, 'modern classical' dishes are served.

Hillbrooke Hotels specialise in hotels and inns on country estates. In this edition of the guide we also feature their places to stay in Stamford (page 241).

Camber, East Sussex

New Lydd Road, Camber, Rye, East Sussex TN31 7RB

Tel 01797 225 057
e-mail enquiries@thegallivanthotel.com
website www.thegallivanthotel.com

Nearby Camber Sands, Romney Salt Marshes, Dungeness, Rye.
Location 90 minutes from central London, 5 minutes from Rye, car park opposite
Food breakfast, dinner
Price £££–££££
Rooms 18 doubles; cottages also available for larger parties; rooms have wi-fi, telephone, DVD player, flat-screen television, hairdryer, tea and coffee
Facilities 2 function rooms, bistro
Credit cards MC, V
Children welcome
Disabled access possible and all rooms are ground floor
Pets dogs welcome
Closed sometimes for a week in Jan
Manager Tudor Hopkins

The Gallivant Hotel

Beach hotel

The Gallivant started in the Sixties as the Blue Dolphin Motel, when no doubt it saw its fair share of gallivants and their girls. It's still immediately identifiable as a motel, but it's also buzzy, inexpensive and in a great location: Camber Sands is over the road, and Rye is five minutes by car.

The food in the sunny Beach Bistro, with bleached wood bar, simple tables and chairs, is spot on. Every afternoon chef Trevor Hambley goes down to Rye Harbour to choose from the catch. On a predominantly piscatorial menu, we enjoyed a pungent fish soup and plump scallops, but also salt marsh lamb and a crunchy apple *tarte tatin*. The wine list has a useful choice of English whites.

The bedrooms are motel rooms given a makeover – compact, with beach shack-style furniture, but we thought that the taupe walls and curtains were blank and dull. And, no waste basket, no complimentary water, and mini toiletries for one when we were two.

We'll like it more when co-owner Tudor Hopkins has completed the next phase of his refurbishment. There need to be quirky, retro touches. Something a little raffish, that befits the name.

Cranbrook, Kent

Cranbrook, Kent TN17 3NR

Tel (01580) 712220
Fax (01580) 712220
e-mail clothhalloast@aol.com

Nearby Sissinghurst; Scotney Castle Gardens.
Location in countryside 1 mile (1.5 km) E of Cranbrook on road to Tenterden, before cemetery; in grounds of 5 acres; ample car-parking
Food breakfast, dinner by arrangement
Price ££
Rooms 3 double, 2 with bath, 1 with shower; all rooms have TV and hairdrier
Facilities sitting room, dining room; 2 terraces, garden, heated outdoor swimming pool, summer house, croquet
Credit cards not accepted
Children accepted by arrangement
Disabled access difficult
Pets not accepted
Closed Christmas
Proprietor Katherine Morgan

Cloth Hall Oast

Manor house guesthouse

Lovers of Mrs Morgan's old guesthouse will be happy to know that, although no longer running our long-time favourite Old Cloth Hall, she simply moved to the nearby Cloth Hall Oast a few years ago. With 20 years of experience to support her new venture, Mrs Morgan describes it as "just as nice as the other – if not better".

The house is situated on a 5-acre estate that is hidden from the road, slightly isolated and very quiet. A large pond with fish and a pretty tree in the middle provides a lovely view from lawn chairs on the half-moon shaped decking. For sunny summer days, you can enjoy a swim in the heated pool or simply relax in the nearby summer house. Two terraces with outdoor patio furniture, a superb croquet lawn and a pergola in the garden complete the picture.

The interior of Cloth Hall Oast is just as special as her previous place. The dining room, open to three galleried floors that include a grand piano, showcases a stunning custom-made chandelier. The bedrooms feel light and warm and one has a whirlpool bath. The sitting room has a fireplace that's perfect for curling up beside on a cool evening.

Ockenden Lane, Cuckfield, West Sussex RH17 5LD

Tel (01444) 416111
Fax (01444) 415549
e-mail reservations@ockenden-manor.co.uk
website www.hshotels.co.uk

Nearby Nyman's; Sissinghurst; Wakehurst Place; Gatwick; Brighton.
Location 2 miles (3 km) W of Haywards Heath close to middle of village, off A272; in 9-acre grounds, with ample car parking
Food breakfast, lunch, dinner
Price £££
Rooms 28 double, 2 single, all with bath; all rooms have phone, TV, hairdryer
Facilities sitting room, bar, dining room; terrace, garden, spa
Credit cards AE, DC, MC, V
Children welcome
Disabled no special facilities **Pets** not accepted
Closed never **Proprietors** Sandy and Pontus and Miranda Goodman

Ockenden Manor

Manor house hotel

Anne Goodman made many changes for the better here after taking over this attractive 16th/17thC manor house. Now, Sandy Goodman and his daughter own the hotel and continue to keep up her high standards.

Bedrooms are spacious and individual (and crammed with giveaways); a superb master suite with sombre panelling relies on reds and greens to give a feeling of brightness. Several of the bathrooms are notably spacious, and they are well-equipped. The main sitting room, though lavishly furnished, has a personal feel. Staff are friendly and obliging. (A notice in the hotel states that whatever a hotel's character and charm, it is only as good as its staff.)

Dinner, which is served in the new dining room with sweeping views towards the Souths Down National Park, is another highlight. Food is based on local produce, with vegetables and herbs from the garden.

Although Ockenden Manor is popular with business people, it is a human, comfortable hotel. 'Hidden away behind trees and a high wall; quiet; good value', says our reporter.

East Chisenbury, Wiltshire

East Chisenbury, Pewsey, Wiltshire
SN9 6AQ

Tel 01980 671124
e-mail troutbeck@redlionfree-house.com

Nearby Area of Natural Outstanding Beauty; Salisbury Cathederal & Magna Carta; Stonehenge; Longleat House & Gardens; Safari Park; Avebury; White Horse Trail. **Location** East Chisenbury village
Food breakfast, lunch, dinner; lunch hampers on request
Price £££ **Rooms** 5 doubles, 1 can also be twin, all rooms have riverside views & private decking, wi-fi, TV, tea & coffee, outdoor weather kit, organic handmade toiletries
Facilities dining room, pub, bar; garden, private fishing
Credit cards MC, V **Children** welcome in pub **Disabled** 1 room with wheelchair access **Pets** dogs welcome in pub and The Manser Room
Closed one week in Jan **Proprietors** Brittany & Guy Manning

Red Lion Freehouse

Village inn

The Red Lion is a quintessential English village pub – *à la mode.* As we went to press, it had recently retained its Michelin star, unveiled glamorous new bedrooms and been named Pub of the Year 2014 by the Good Food Guide. The delightful chef/patron, Guy Manning, runs the pub with his equally charming and hard-working wife and general manager, Brittany.

There's everything you could wish for in a thatched pub: a log burner, beams, blackboards and assorted wooden tables and chairs. However, we missed comfy sofas – their absence made it feel static.

The food was superb for an inn, but perhaps quite expensive compared with other similar establishments. But the care that Guy and his close-knit team put into what is essentially home cooking is of the highest order.

The five bedrooms are in a converted bungalow, Troutbeck, along the lane. They are a bit glitzy: silvery furniture and fake fur throws, but the standard is high, and they are an exhilarating contrast to the inn. Thoughtful extras include well-stocked minibar; a list of items you may have forgotten, which Brittany can then provide for you; and especially the views of the Hampshire Avon, running through the garden.

East End, Hampshire

Lymington Road, Hampshire SO41 5SY

Tel 01590 626223
website www.eastendarms.co.uk

Nearby Exbury Gardens, Cowes, New Forest, Buckler's Hard, Motor Museum, Beaulieu.
Location on Lymington Road, half way between Beaulieu and Lymington, close to Solent shore
Food breakfast, lunch, dinner (not Sunday night)
Price ££
Rooms 5 double/twin, all have bath/shower, all with TV, wi-fi, gun safe, tea/coffee facilities
Facilities bar, restaurant, terrace
Credit cards DC, MC, V
Children accepted
Disabled only to ground floor
Pets dogs in bar but not restaurant or bedrooms
Closed 3-6 o'clock Monday to Friday **Proprietor** John Illsley

East End Arms

Country inn

An honest, affordable base on the southern edge of the New Forest in a backwater between Beaulieu and Lymington. It's part of the renaissance since 2005 in New Forest places to stay, joining the quite recently refurbished Master Builder's (page 96) and THE PIG (page 95).

When owner John Illsley (the former bass guitarist of Dire Straits) bought the pub in the mid 1990s he got a letter from the regulars: 'Hands off our bar' – they wouldn't even let him repair the hole in the ceiling. Most new owners of old pubs would have turned the whole of the lower floor into a gastropub eating area, but Illsley had the sense to keep the old public bar intact. If you want posh food turn left after the front door; if you want a plain, bare floored room, with coal in the grate and murmuring locals, real ale and a chatty bar maid, turn right.

Upstairs, John's wife Steph has created five truly charming bedrooms: crisp sheets, king-sized beds, OKA furniture, Mulberry fabrics, walls decorated with John's paintings. The result is a country pub that is an up to date, comfortable place to stay yet retains its integrity and sense of identity. The food is mostly reliable, sometimes imaginative, above average for the price.

East Grinstead, West Sussex

Vowels Lane, near East Grinstead, West Sussex RH19 4LJ

Tel (01342) 810567
Fax (10342) 810080
e-mail info@gravetyemanor.co.uk
website www.gravetyemanor.co.uk

Nearby Wakehurst; Nyman's Gardens; Glyndebourne
Location 4.5 miles (7 km) SW of East Grinstead by B2110 at Gravetye; in 35 acre grounds with ample car parking
Food breakfast, lunch, dinner, room service **Price** ££££
Rooms 17; 16 double, 1 single, all with bath; all rooms have phone, TV, hairdrier, iPod dock, wi-fi; 8 rooms have air conditioning
Facilities 2 sitting rooms, bar, dining room; terrace, garden, croquet, trout fishing
Credit cards AE, MC, V **Children** welcome over 7 **Disabled** ramp access but no adapted rooms **Pets** not accepted (1 mile from kennel)
Closed never **Proprietors** Jeremy and Elizabeth Hosking

Gravetye Manor Hotel & Restaurant **Country hotel**

The country house hotel, now so much a part of the tourist scene in Britain, scarcely existed when Peter Herbert opened the doors of this serene Elizabethan house over 50 years ago. Under new ownership since February 2010, it's had a multi-million pound refurbishment, and standards in every department remain unflaggingly high. Service consistently achieves the elusive aim of attentiveness without intrusion, while the food can still claim to be among the best in the county. A recent visitor, who had known the hotel for 30 years, remained as impressed as ever: 'A sleek operation that doesn't compromise.' However, another commented on 'lots of wealthy-looking people in sunglasses and strange-looking jogging suits'.

The pioneering gardener William Robinson lived in the house for half a century until his death in 1935. Great care is taken to maintain the various gardens he created; Robinson was also responsible for many features of the house as it is seen today – the mellow oak panelling and grand fireplaces in the calm, gracious sitting rooms, for example. Bedrooms – all immaculate – vary in size from the adequate to the enormous, and prices range accordingly.

East Hoathly, East Sussex

East Hoathly, Sussex BN8 6EL

Tel (01825) 840216
Fax (01825) 840738
website www.oldwhyly.co.uk

Nearby Glyndebourne, Charleston Farm House, East Sussex National Golf Course, Batemans.
Location just off A22 S of Uckfield on road to Halland, ample car parking
Food breakfast, dinner
Price ££
Rooms 3 double and twin, 2 with bath, 1 with shower
Facilities sitting room, dining room; terrace, garden, croquet, hard top tennis court, heated swimming pool, lake, walking paths
Credit cards not accepted
Children welcome
Disabled access difficult
Pets by arrangement
Closed never
Proprietor Sarah Burgoyne

Old Whyly

Country house guesthouse

Driving up to Old Whyly in the springtime is magical; owner Sarah Burgoyne has planted 4,000 tulip bulbs and at the right season, the lawn is ablaze with colour. Set in 40-acre grounds, with a duck-dotted lake, well-maintained gardens and walks that take in the nearby 600-acre stud farm, this Grade II listed 18thC manor has an enviable setting

Once you cross the well-gravelled drive and climb the front steps, you will be welcomed in Sarah's (and her dog, Noodle's) antique-filled home. The impressive family painting collection lines the walls, including a full-length portrait of Sarah herself. The sitting room has a roaring fire with inviting furniture – perfect for admiring the china collection or just reading a book. Bedrooms are spacious and comfortable. However, one of the best reasons to stay at Old Whyly is the food. Sarah, a passionate cook who trained in Paris, prepares excellent dishes and, although many of her customers tend to eat at Glyndebourne, Sarah is more than happy to provide dinner.

Breakfast includes honey from Sarah's bees kept in the orchard and eggs from the hens that wander about on the lawn.

East Lavant, West Sussex

Pook Lane, East Lavant, West Sussex PO18 0AX

Tel 01243 527434
e-mail rooms@royaloakeastlavant.co.uk
website www.royaloakeastlavant.co.uk

Nearby Chichester, Littlehampton.
Location turn off A3 at Milford Junction onto the A286 via Haslemere and Midhurst. On entering Lavant take the left turn signposted East Lavant. Royal Oak is just past hump-back bridge
Food breakfast, lunch, dinner
Price ££-£££
Rooms 6 doubles, all have bath/shower. 2 additional self-catering cottages
Facilities bar, restaurant, terrace, garden **Credit cards** AE, MC, V
Children welcome
Disabled not suitable **Pets** allowed in bar area
Closed Christmas Day and New Year's Day **Proprietor** Charles Ullmann

The Royal Oak

Country inn

The Royal Oak is in beautiful Goodwood country just two miles from Chichester. With a widespread reputation for its food – the restaurant serves a combination of French, Mediterranean and New English cuisine with wines to match – the Inn is always busy at night, and a stay in one of six well-appointed rooms makes for an encapsulating short break.

Each room is lavishly furnished and with all mod-cons, including flat-screen TV and a DVD player. The exposed beams and brick work offer a pleasant old-and-new style we particularly liked.

Rooms in the Sussex Barn and Deluxe Flint Cottage however, just a few short steps from your dinner table, are universally acclaimed. A touch small, perhaps, but greatly prepared and provided for and with every angle and idea covered (including cots for children and complimentary morning papers for those with a little more time on their hands). Staff are always on hand and obliging and the buffet breakfast is top-notch.

Emsworth, Hampshire

47 South Street, Emsworth,
Hampshire PO10 7EG

Tel 01243 375592
Fax 01243 372257
website www.36onthequay.co.uk

Nearby Hayling Island, Portsmouth, Chichester, South Downs National Park, Portsmouth ferries 10 minutes
Location Emsworth is on A259 between Havant and Chichester
Food breakfast, lunch, dinner
Price £££-££££
Rooms 7; 5 doubles with bath/shower and 2 cottages; rooms have TV, phone, tea/coffee facilities, iPod docking station, wi-fi
Facilities restaurant, bar
Credit cards DC, MC, V
Children accepted
Disabled access to restaurant only
Pets dogs accepted in the cottages
Closed 2 weeks in Jan, one week in May and 1 week in Oct/Nov
Proprietors Raymon and Karen Farthing

36 on the Quay

Village restaurant-with-rooms

Chef Ramon Farthing got his Michelin star in 1997, but Restaurant 36 on the Quay only became a place to stay recently. He and wife Karen (front of house) developed the accommodation cautiously , achieving five doubles plus two cottages over several years.

In fact the operation feels like a wise balance of form with content. The food, served in an appropriately smart (but not flashy or unrelaxing) dining room overlooking Emsworth Quay and Bay, is consistently delicious and imaginative. Ramon's training was French classical, he migrated to modern British and has now added a Scandinavian influence – fresh, clean flavours, ingredients that speak out. One pudding, peanut parfait, could be unique.

The reasonably priced, comfortable rooms have quirky corners (the house is listed). Saffron is an apartment with kitchenette, useful for a family; Nutmeg has a great harbour view; Vanilla, the top room, has a lovely bay window seat, again with the harbour view. Neutral, off whites and variations on vanilla predominate.

There's nothing like this in the area – the waterfront location is charming and endlessly interesting. It would make a great weekend break, or a spoiling stopover before an early ferry from Portsmouth.

Fletching, East Sussex

Fletching, near Uckfield,
East Sussex TN22 3SS

Tel (01825) 722890
Fax (01825) 722810
e-mail info@thegriffininn.co.uk
website www.thegriffininn.co.uk

Nearby Sheffield Park; Glyndebourne; Ashdown Forest.
Location in village 1 mile (1.5 km) E of A275; with car parking
Food breakfast, lunch, dinner
Price ££
Rooms 12 double and 1 twin, 6 with bath, 7 with shower; all rooms have TV, hairdryer
Facilities bars, restaurant, bar billiards; terrace, patio, garden
Credit cards AE, DC, MC, V
Children welcome **Disabled** 2 rooms on ground floor
Pets accepted in bar, but not in bedrooms or restaurant
Closed Christmas Day
Manager James Pullan

The Griffin Inn

Village inn

On our latest visit to the Griffin Inn, the pub was packed, the dining room was almost full and the kitchen was bustling. Successful? Evidently. But still welcoming and cosy? Definitely.

This 16thC village inn has been owned by the Pullan family for 20 years and it maintains its winning combination of good food (it can claim to be Britain's first gastro-pub) and pretty bedrooms with beams, low ceilings and four-poster beds. Everything is a bit uneven, quaint, on a small scale – but endearing rather than cramped. Beds are inviting and bathrooms are in an attractive Victorian style, with funky porthole mirrors. That said, some of the rooms were looking a little tired on our last visit; but we imagine that re-investment is on the way.

The pub has more beams, panelling, open fires and hunting prints, while the old public bar has been turned into the 'Club Room', with sofas, armchairs and a backgammon board. Good food is always at hand either in the pub or in the restaurant, which uses fresh seasonal ingredients and local organic vegetables. Both menus change daily. The wine list has over 100 wines, many of which are priced at under £25 per bottle.

You can take your drink out to the garden overlooking Sheffield Park and enjoy live jazz at the weekends. In summer, there's a full-scale BBQ serving Pacific Rim dishes.

1 Hill Street, Hastings, East Sussex
TN34 3HU

Tel 01424 430014
email res@swanhousehastings.co.uk
website
www.swanhousehastings.co.uk

Nearby town centre, 1066 country, Rye, Camber Sands
Location in town centre, just behind East Parade which runs along seafront
Food breakfast
Price ££-£££
Rooms 4 doubles with TV, DVD
Facilities sitting room, telephone, wi-fi, outdoor patio
Credit cards AE, MC, V
Children accepted
Disabled 1 ground-floor bedroom
Pets not accepted
Closed Christmas
Proprietors Brendan McDonagh and Lionel Copley

Swan House

Town house guesthouse

In its building dating from the 14th century, Swan House, Hastings, could hardly lack old world charm. Aged timbers surface everywhere, while each of the four bedrooms has its own antique theme. The Garden Room uses dark wood and heavy curtains; the Renaissance Room is lighter, with lace curtains and hand-painted walls, while the Artisan Room is full of light and bright dashes of colour. Homely charm threads the whole interior. They are proud of breakfast here, using local produce in a choice of traditional cooked dishes.

Swan House is in the middle of Hastings, so parking can be a problem, but owners Brendan and Lionel can often help. Some reporters mention noise from adjoining rooms and passages, a natural hazard in buildings this old, but for most visitors this would be a quibble: this place offers a nice combination of charm and careful management.

Littlestone, Kent

Coast Road, Littlestone,
New Romney, Kent TN28 8QY

Tel (01797) 364747
Fax (01797) 367156

Nearby Rye; Dungeness Lighthouse; Sandwich.
Location in New Romney, take Station Road to sea front, turn left, and follow hotel signs for 1 mile; car parking
Food breakfast, weekday sandwich lunch, weekend light lunch, dinner
Price ££-£££
Rooms 10 double and twin, all with bath or shower; all rooms have TV, hairdryer
Facilities sitting room, dining room, look-out room, tea room; terrace, garden, croquet, boules, beach adjacent to golf course
Credit cards AE, MC, V
Children accepted over 14
Disabled access difficult
Pets not accepted
Closed Christmas
Proprietors Clinton and Lisa Lovell

Romney Bay House

Seaside hotel

The approach through sprawling Littlestone is unpromising, particularly in the dark when you don't know where you're heading. But this dignified 1920s house, built by Clough Williams Ellis for American columnist Hedda Hopper, has a superb position between the sea and Romney Marsh. Clinton and Lisa Lovell took over Romney Bay House in 2003, and have kept the style of the interior much the same, while upgrading the bathrooms. The interiors are reminiscent of a small hotel in Provence, with plenty of French furniture and fabrics. This is a thoroughly relaxed place: the cosy bar; the warm, fire-lit sitting room packed with groups of comfortable, inviting chairs; breakfasts in the pretty conservatory; drinks or cream teas on the terrace in fine weather. Dinner is a non-choice four-course menu, planned around the diners each evening and made with local produce.

An upstairs 'look-out' room has the feel of a beach house, with piles of towels for swimming, wicker chairs and sea shells. Bedrooms have creamy cottons, fresh white bedlinen, bright checks, and antiques; those on the first floor have full length windows, allowing uninterrupted views out to sea.

London

66 Turnmill Street, London, EC1M 5RR

Tel 0207 244 2000
e-mail enquiries@blueprintlivingapartments.com
website www.blueprintlivingapartments.com/66-turnmill-street

Nearby 1 min from Farringdon Rail Station. St Pancreas Rail Station, Hatton Garden (jewelry quarter) St Paul's Cathedral, Smithfield and the Barbican. Parking nearby. **Location** Clerkenwell **Food** self-catered apartments; restaurants near by **Price** ££££ **Rooms** 14 apartments with bedroom, bathroom, living room and kitchen; all with air-conditioning, iPod dock, direct dial phone, safe, television, kitchen utensils) **Facilities** wi-fi, air-conditioning, maid service, CCTV, luggage storage, lift **Credit cards** AE, MC, V **Children** welcome- cots and high chairs available on request **Disabled** lift to all floors, rooms accessible **Pets** not allowed **Closed** never **Properietor** Blueprint Living Apartments

66 Turnmill Street

Self-catering apartments

The entrance to 66 Turnmill Street is down an insignificant side street close to Farringdon Station, but once inside the atmosphere is stylish and sophisticated. We think these apartments will suit a wide range of tastes and needs, and they offer a winning combination of homely comfort with professional style.

When we visited soon after opening, most of the apartments were already booked. Each is similar in size and style: only colour scheme and layout differed a little in each. Heavy wooden panelling, grey fabrics and solid, comfortable furniture are key elements. A bit of colour is added in the kitchen units and the quirky cushions on the sofa, but overall the effect is muted and calm. Apartments on the higher floors are the best: they have more light and views of the historical buildings surrounding Turnmill Street. Bathrooms are white, bright and modern.

499 Old York Road, Wandsworth
SW18 1TF

Tel 020 8870 2537
email alma@youngs.co.uk
website www.almawandsworth,com

Nearby Wandsworth Common, Wimbledon Common, Battersea Park, Kew Gardens
Location Waterloo 15 minutes by train, on-street parking available
Food breakfast, lunch, dinner
Price ££-£££
Rooms 23; 13 doubles, 3 double/twin, 6 twin; all have bath/shower, with TV, iPod, phone, tea/coffee facilities, hairdryer, ironing board
Facilities bar, restaurant, wi-fi, luggage storage
Credit cards AE, MC, V
Children accepted
Disabled 2 easy access rooms
Pets not accepted
Closed never
Proprietors Young's

The Alma

Town restaurant-with-rooms

Built in 1866 and named to commemorate the Crimean Battle of Alma in 1854, shiny green tiles and a domed roof mark this place out as an example of the London pub boom of the 19th century.

Now it has a new lease of life. Young's the brewer landlord have turned four pokey ground-floor rooms into one impressive one, with a circular bar in the centre. A fine white plasterwork frieze was revealed during conversion, as were the solid mahogany staircase, woodwork and *fin de siècle* mosaics.

Despite claiming to be 'a friendly, local pub' on its website, The Alma is more than that now, with a restaurant as well, adjacent to the bar. You'll find all sorts: chaps in pinstripes propping up the bar, blokes in overalls arguing on the pavement after watching the football on a screen. Food is served in the dining room by busy waitresses from a kitchen open to view and a country-style pine table that doubles as a work station. Bar and dining spaces interact well; in either room everyone is happy.

The 23 bedrooms are well equipped, with armchairs, desks and the latest technology. The decoration is lively, and some have floor to ceiling windows. A laidback option for those who don't want the prices or chic formality of central London.

50 Great Cumberland Place, Marble Arch, London W1H 7FD

Tel 0207 724 4700
e-mail info@thearchlondon.com
website www.thearchlondon.com
Nearby Hyde Park, Oxford Street, the City
Location north-east corner of Hyde Park, short walk from Marble Arch tube
Food breakfast, lunch, dinner in Hunter 486 restaurant, 24 hour room service
Price ££££
Rooms 82; all have bath/shower, with TV, wi-fi, internet radio, DVD player, iPod docking station, Nespresso machine
Facilities restaurant, bar, Le Salon de Champagne, 3 conference rooms
Credit Cards all major
Children accepted
Disabled ramp, disabled rooms on ground floor
Pets accepted
Closed never
Properietor Mr Bejerano

The Arch

City hotel

This hotel spreads itself through seven town houses and two mews houses, but it feels smaller and more intimate than that. This place may be luxurious, but it's not grand – one of the new breed of city hotels for people who take the latest gadgets in their rooms for granted and who want to feel relaxed in their surroundings.

The striking bedrooms are more designed than homely, but with welcome extras such as complimentary soft drinks, Nespresso machines and bedside digital radios. We liked the common theme in the rooms and suites of a single wall decorated with individual, retro wallpaper.

The hotel's cleverest concept is the cocktail lounge that flows into a zinc-topped bar area and on into a dining space with an open-to-view kitchen. This is the heart of the operation, and you can dine and breakfast anywhere you like in these three areas. Laurence Glayzer's dishes are well-executed (the menu has a pizza section, and also focusses on grilled meats), and it makes for a buzzing experience now the locals have cottoned on. From a tiny kitchen Laurence also produces the hotel's jams, chocolates, breads and speciality éclairs for afternoon tea – impressive for a hardworking, value-for-money London hotel just off Oxford Street.

33 Beaufort Gardens, London
SW3 1PP

Tel (020) 7584 5252
Fax (020) 7589 2834
e-mail enquiries@thebeaufort.co.uk
website www.thebeaufort.co.uk

Nearby Harrods; Victoria and Albert Museum.
Location off Brompton Road, just W of Harrods; pay and display parking in street
Food breakfast; room service
Price ££££
Rooms 29; 18 double and twin, 7 suites and 4 single, all with bath or shower; all rooms have phone, TV, Sky, CD player, air-conditioning, fax/modem points, hairdryer; wi-fi, fax/answering machines on request
Facilities sitting room, bar **Credit cards** AE, DC, MC, V
Children accepted
Disabled access difficult
Pets not accepted
Closed never **Proprietors** Ahmed and Sarah Jajbhay

The Beaufort

Town bed-and-breakfast

Three Harrods doormen in a row gave our inspector unerring directions for the hundred-yard walk to The Beaufort, part of a Victorian terrace overlooking a quiet Knightsbridge cul-de-sac. Taken over by Ahmed and Sarah Jajbhay, this is still one of the few hotels in the world which surprises you with what doesn't appear later on your bill. Feel like a glass of champagne? No charge. Soft drink? Cream tea? The answer's still no charge. And, just when you have been made to feel so good that you want to give a tip, you fall victim to a no-tipping policy.

All the rooms are different, some decorated in muted pastels, others following in the cheerful footsteps of the public areas. Each room has a CD player and portable stereo and, for those who need added protection from the English weather, there are also chocolates, shortbread, brandy and umbrellas. And then there are the flowers. Plenty of them. Many are real, but most are hanging on the walls as part of the enormous collection of English floral watercolours. Noted for the friendliness of its staff, the Beaufort has many faithful regulars.

London

61-63 Petersham Road, Richmond Upon Thames, London TW10 6UT

Tel (020) 8940 0902
e-mail info@thebingham.co.uk
website www.thebingham.co.uk

Nearby Thames, Hampton Court Palace, Royal Botanic Gardens at Kew, Syon House, Ham House
Location 20 mins from Heathrow on A307, 8 min walk from Richmond station
Food breakfast, lunch, afternoon tea, dinner
Price ££££
Rooms 15 double and twin; air-conditioning, TV, DVD player, radio, iPod dock, wi-fi, shower
Facilities dining room, 2 conference rooms, bar
Credit cards AE, DC, MC, V
Children welcome
Disabled lift access to event rooms, access to restaurant
Pets guide dogs only
Closed never
Proprietor Samantha Trinder

The Bingham

Riverside restaurant-with-rooms

Here's a good example of an 'amateur' London hotel keeper competing with the 'professionals' – ie corporate hotel groups – and being every bit as good if not better.

The Bingham is slick and glamorous, and could be, almost, part of a hotel group: its contemporary, interior designed look is one you often see. It seemed, at first glance, 'professional' rather than 'amateur'. But you soon realize that it isn't: because of the warmth of the staff; the pristine way the place is kept; and the cohesive atmosphere which makes people feel at home.

In 1984, the Trinders bought the two Georgian town houses and turned them into a B&B. In 2001, their daughter Samantha joined and turned it into what it is today – a lovely place to dine and stay.

The rooms are smart, if a bit dull. But they are also soothing, spotless and well equipped, with comfortable beds. You wake to the river at the end of the garden, with the towpath and rowing boats beyond. A balcony runs the length of the restaurant – this is a subtly opulent room that is successful by anyone's standards.

Chef Shay Cooper's immaculate dishes are the equal of their surroundings. Professionalism, mixed with the pride of an independent 'amateur' owner, is at work here.

London

22 Basil Street, London SW3 1AT

Tel 0207 589 5171 **Fax** 0207 225 0011 **email** reservations@capitalhotel.co.uk **website** www.capitalhotel.co.uk

Nearby Harrods, Harvey Nichols, Sloane Street, Brompton Arcade, Hyde Park, South Kensington Museums **Location** Knightsbridge, close to Harrods and Harvey Nichols **Food** breakfast, lunch, dinner, afternoon tea **Price** ££££ **Rooms** 50; 1 Two Bedroom Suite, 8 suites and 7 doubles. All rooms have air-conditioning, radio, television, TV, emails and films on demand, hairdryer, mini-bar **Facilities** Outlaw's restaurant, 2 function rooms, wi-fi, laundry/dry cleaning, international newspapers, cot, babysitting, private car-parking, 24 hour room service, The Peak health club and gym **Credit cards** all major **Children** welcome **Disabled** access unavailable **Pets** guide/small dogs **Closed** never **Proprietor** David Levin **Manager** Kate Levin

The Capital

City hotel

A firm favourite of our series editor Fiona Duncan, The Capital's outstanding reputation has been long established and remains unfaltering. Scottish proprietor David Levin created it in 1971, and it remains faithful to its original concept, to be a family-run hotel in the busy and popular heart of Knightsbridge. Guests can be near Harrods, Harvey Nichols and Hyde Park and get relief from the bustle back within the hotel's luxurious, comfortable atmosphere.

Staff are notoriously brilliant: Clive, the head concierge, can claim to be London's finest, and always goes beyond expectations. He will even take guests jogging around Hyde Park. Likewise in the cosy bar, César the barman holds cocktail master classes for guests, promising a wonderfully fun evening. Nathan Outlaw runs the Michelin-starred, seafood restaurant Outlaw's, and does masterclasses as well.

In each bedroom the decoration is typically English, with tasteful colour schemes and traditional furniture. Luxury, handmade mattresses and Egyptian cotton sheets add to the comfort.

Bathrooms are marble and beautiful, with the attention to detail of bathrobes and toiletries that we like.

Camberwell Church Street,
London SE5 8TR

Tel (020) 7703 5984
Fax (020) 7385 4110
e-mail info@churchstreethotel.com
website www.churchstreethotel.com

Location in busy high street near Camberwell Green; parking in nearby residential street with permits (£5) from reception.
Nearby South London Gallery, Oval cricket ground, clubs, London Eye 20 minutes by bus, also County Hall (Saatchi Gallery); leisure centres
Food breakfast, dinner **Price** ££
Rooms 31; 25 double, 6 single; all doubles except 3 have own bath, 3 have shared bathroom; all rooms have TV, hairdryer; most have flat-screen TV, DVD, air-con **Facilities** breakfast 24-hour room-bar, with honesty bar; tapas restaurant
Cards AE, MC, V **Disabled** not suitable **Children** welcome; under six, free in parents' room **Closed** never **Proprietors** Jose and Mel Raido

The Church Street Hotel

City hotel

The conventional name and restrained exterior give no hint of what's inside. In reception, a gold painted altar for the desk; colourful ikons on the walls; French tiles on the floor. Swirly patterned carpets lead you upstairs; lurid religious paintings hang in the passages; custom-made brown bedroom doors have iron studs. The signals are a little confusing, but hip-60s-Latin-American with a contemporary twist more or less sums it up. Your bedroom is likely to burst with colour: our reporter's was cobalt blue with a comfortable hand-made wrought-iron bed, painted crucifixes in high alcoves and hand-painted Mexican tiles in the bathroom.

Spanish-Greek brothers José and Mel Raido created this place, wanting to do something refreshing and affordable – and they have. Their success is borne out by the generally youthful, cool crowd from all over the world that you'll meet in the walnut-panelled breakfast room/bar. The Angels and Gypsies restaurant, downstairs, is a delight. It's tapas, done well – fine local ingredients; relaxed and highly-skilled staff. A cocktail bar called 'Communion' has recently opened in the basement – otherwise it lacks a separate public sitting area. Located in noisy, multi-ethnic Camberwell, just along from the Green, but Oval tube, with fast access to the centre, is just around the corner. Nothing like this anywhere else in Britain.

2 Warrington Crescent, Little Venice, London W9 1ER

Tel (020) 7286 1052
e-mail reservations@colonnadehotel.co.uk
website www.colonnadehotel.co.uk

Nearby Little Venice.
Location 1-minute walk from Warwick Avenue tube, 3 car parking spaces in garage, £15 per night, must be pre-booked
Food breakfast, lunch, dinner, 24 hr room service
Price £££
Rooms 43; 35 double, 5 twin, 3 single, most with shower, some with bath; all rooms have TV, stereo, phone, minibar, safe, hairdryer, trouser press, iron
Facilities sitting room, restaurant with terrace, bar
Credit cards AE, DC, MC, V
Children welcome
Disabled not suitable
Pets not accepted
Closed never
Manager Shahar Rothschild

The Colonnade

Town house hotel

Set in Little Venice, with its canals and bridges, The Colonnade manages to overcome the trappings of a large hotel to provide a private place to stay. The building itself occupies two Victorian town houses that were built in 1865 as private residences. In the late 1800s, it was used as a girls' school and, in the early 1900s, it became a maternity hospital. Alan Turing, creator of the first computer and the man who solved the Enigma code, was born here, and you'll find a suite named after him. When the building later became a hotel, Sigmund Freud stayed here while waiting for his house in Hampstead to be finished. In his suite, a bed sits in a gallery above a sitting room with enormous floor-to-ceiling windows. In the JFK Suite, you can sleep in the four-poster bed built for President Kennedy's state visit in 1962. The rest of the bedrooms are done out in three smart colour schemes: black and gold, green and gold or red and gold. In the sitting room, comfy sofas, attractive stripy chairs, an open coal fire and complimentary sherry, port and lollipops offset the strange artificial topiary.

In the basement, the achingly hip bar and restaurant serves Mediterranean fare. Much of the downstairs is due for refurbishment, and we would welcome reports on the results.

10 Monmouth Street, London
WC2H 9HB

Tel (020) 7806 1000
Fax (020) 7806 1100
e-mail covent@firmdale.com
website www.firmdale.com

Nearby Covent Garden; Royal Opera House; West End theatres.
Location in fairly quiet street between Shaftesbury Avenue and St Martin's Lane; metered parking or public car park nearby
Food breakfast, lunch, dinner; room service
Price ££££ **Rooms** 58; 52 double and twin, 6 suites; 6 single, all with bath; all rooms have phone, TV, video, CD player, fax/modem point, air-conditioning, minibar, hairdryer
Facilities drawing room, restaurant, bar, library, work-out room, beauty treatment room, screening room, meeting rooms **Credit cards** AE, MC, V **Children** accepted **Disabled** access possible, lift/elevator
Pets not accepted **Closed** never
Proprietors Tim and Kit Kemp

Covent Garden Hotel

Town hotel

The group of seductive London hotels owned by Tim and Kit Kemp includes seven sprinkled across London and one in New York. They began with Dorset Square and then opened several more similar town house hotels, before becoming more expansive here in Covent Garden, but without losing any of their previous assurance. The latest addition is Ham Yard Hotel opening in 2014.

Monmouth Street is an attractive, quiet street ideally placed for theatre and medialand. The building was formerly a French hospital, which Tim and Kit (she is responsible for all the decoration) have transformed into a hotel that at once feels glamorous, yet welcoming and not in the least intimidating. A stunning drawing room and library stretches across the first floor, with a well-stocked honesty bar at one end, where guests can help themselves. On the gound floor is a bar and restaurant, serving tasty, simply cooked dishes; or you can order from the well-balanced room service menu.

Bedrooms all look different, although each possesses a matching fabric-covered mannequin, and they all have superb granite bathrooms. One bedroom has a memorable four-poster bed. The cosy attic rooms are also delightful.

Fleet River Bakery

City rooms

71 Lincoln's Inn Fields, London
WC2A 3JF

Tel (020) 7691 1457
e-mail info@fleetriverbakery.com
website www.fleetriverbakery.com

Nearby Lincoln's Inn Fields, central London.
Location 5-minute walk from Holborn tube, no car-parking available **Food** breakfast (cafe serves lunch, cake, wine, coffee)
Price £££
Rooms 4; 1 double with sofa bed, 2 king with sofa bed, 1 king
Facilities bakery available for private hire **Credit cards** AE, MC, V
Children welcome
Disabled no specific arrangement
Pets not accepted
Closed Christmas and New Year
Manager Lucy Clapp and Amy Peak

Checking in at this unusual hotel involves a long look at a carrot cake, some just-baked muffins and the cups of bespoke, barista-made coffee. 'Would you like full cream or skimmed milk?' asks the receptionist. You are in a café, but the milk is for your fridge, and you trot down a side passage at the corner of Lincoln's Inn Fields to the Bakery's three rooms (a fourth is coming soon), milk jug in hand.

You don't just get a high-ceilinged bedroom, but a well-equipped kitchen too. There's a double and a sofa bed; a wooden, rug-covered floor, wall-mounted television, radio and shower room complete the picture. We would have liked a desk, and a chest of drawers had we stayed longer. The style is practical, contemporary, loft-like. The price is amazing for decent, characterful accommodation in central London. It's also remarkably quiet.

For breakfast, we ate scrambled eggs on sourdough and marvelled at the Bakery's young owners throwing in breakfast – as much as you want – with the already generous cost of the room.

Fox and Grapes

Restaurant-with-rooms

9 Camp Road, Wimbledon Common, London SW19 4UN

Tel (020) 8619 1300
e-mail reservations@foxandgrapeswimbledon.co.uk
website www.foxandgrapeswimbledon.co.uk

Nearby Wimbledon village, central London
Location Camp Road, short drive from Wimbledon train and underground station
Food breakfast, lunch, dinner
Price ££
Rooms 3 doubles, all have bath/shower, all with TV and tea/coffee facilities **Facilities** restaurant, wi-fi
Credit cards AE, DC, MC, V
Children accepted but no extra beds for children over 2
Disabled access possible to restaurant and pub, but not to rooms
Pets not accepted in bedrooms
Closed never
Proprietor Jolly Fine Pubs

It's not a bad idea, staying in this modest pub on Wimbledon Common instead of an expensive central hotel. Kensington is 40 minutes away, yet the feel of the Fox and Grapes is that of a country inn, especially at weekends, when it is jammed with muddy dogs and their owners.

Or rather, according to *les frères français*, the Bosis, who started the place, an English version of something peculiarly French – a *bouchon* – a neighbourhood bar where the food is hearty, and the owner is key.

Chef Patrick Leano serves robust dishes that echo meat-heavy *bouchon* fare. Quality cuts of steak, braised ox cheek – eaten at plain deal tables quickly laid with cutlery when you are ready to begin.

The building itself is unusual – one huge room, a beamed village-hall-style extension, with a stylish bar and a kitchen open to view. The atmosphere is certainly convivial (though noisy when busy).

The bedrooms are quite well decorated and equipped, but small, with nowhere to put a sponge bag in our tiny bathroom. Breakfast is taken in the pub, somewhat desolate in the early morning and smelling of beer. Nevertheless, the Fox and Grapes is *très sympa*, as the French say.

190 Queen's Gate, London
SW7 5EX

Tel (020) 7584 6601
Fax (020) 7589 8127
e-mail reservations@gorehotel.com
website www.gorehotel.com

Nearby Kensington Gardens; Hyde Park; Royal Albert Hall; Harrods.
Location on Queen's Gate; metered parking and public car park nearby
Food breakfast, lunch, dinner
Price ££££
Rooms 50; 44 double, 6 single or twin, all with bath or shower; all rooms have phone,TV, DVD, mini-bar, hairdryer, safe, wi-fi, 24 hr concierge
Facilities library/sitting room, bar, restaurant
Credit cards AE, MC, V
Children welcome
Disabled access possible, lift/elevator
Pets not accepted
Closed never
Proprietor Con Ring

The Gore

Town house hotel

In 1990 the team who opened Hazlitt's (see opposite) bought this Victorian town house (long established as a hotel) set in a wide tree-lined street near Kensington Gardens and Hyde Park, and gave it the Hazlitt treatment: bedrooms furnished with period antiques, walls enlivened with pictures, and they recruited a young and friendly staff, trained to give efficient but informal service.

It has character by the bucketload; walls whose every square inch is covered with prints and oil paintings; bedrooms furnished with antiques, each with its own style – a gallery in one room, Judy Garland's bed in another. There is also an impressive dossier in each room describing what to do locally – 'put together with verve and a feel for what the guest might really want'. The panelled bar on the ground floor is a popular rendezvous for non-residents as well as guests. Across the hallway is Bistro 190 (same owners, same style) which opens from 7.30 am to 11.30 pm and, and as well as breakfast, offers lighthearted modern dishes with an international spin. The place is stylish, with rosewood panels and red chairs.

Since our last edition it has changed hands, so reports would be welcome.

6 Frith Street, Soho Square, London W1D 3JA

Tel (020) 7434 1771
Fax (020) 7439 1524
e-mail reservations@hazlitts.co.uk
website www.hazlittshotel.com

Nearby Oxford Street; Piccadilly Circus; Covent Garden; theatres.
Location in Soho, between Oxford Street and Shaftesbury Avenue; public car parks nearby
Food breakfast; room service
Price ££££
Rooms 30; 24 doubles, 3 suites, 3 singles; all with bath; all rooms have phone, TV, fax/modem point, hairdryer, safe, minibars
Facilities sitting room, library with honesty bar, meeting room
Credit cards AE, DC, MC, V
Children welcome
Disabled not suitable
Pets not accepted
Closed never
Proprietors Peter McKay and Douglas Blaine

Hazlitt's

Town house hotel

There is no quarter of central London with more character than Soho; and there are few places to stay with more character than Hazlitt's, formed from three Georgian terraced houses off Soho Square. The sloping, creaking floorboards have been retained (it can be an uphill walk to your bed), and the rooms decorated with suitable antiques, busts and prints. Restoration work has revealed original fireplaces and Georgian panelling that's 300 years old. The bedrooms, named after some of the people who visited or stayed in the house where the eponymous essayist himself lived, are delightfully different from most London hotel rooms, some with intricately carved wood headboards, one with a delightful four-poster, all with free-standing bath tubs and Victorian fittings in the bathrooms.

As befits an establishment with such literary connections, Hazlitt's is particularly popular with visiting authors, who leave signed copies of their works when they depart. Sadly, the dresser in the little sitting room in which they are kept is now locked to protect the books, which had a habit of going missing. Continental breakfast is served in the bedrooms, as well as light dishes such as pasta and filled baguettes. A hotel for people who like their comforts authentic, yet stylish.

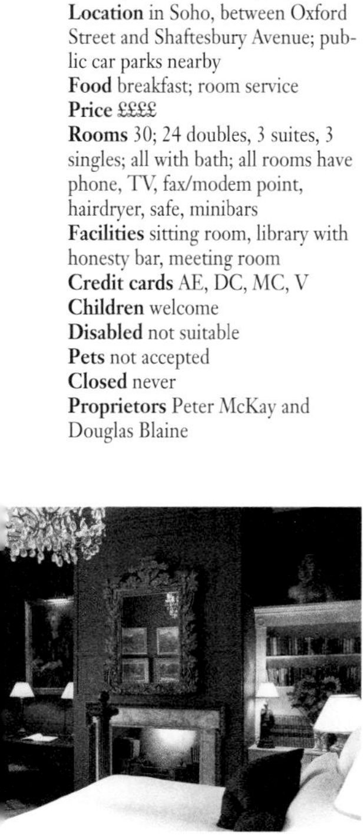

London

162 Chiswick High Road, London
W4 1PR

Tel (020) 8742 1717
Fax (020) 8987 8762
e-mail reservations@highroad-house.co.uk
website www.highroadhouse.co.uk

Nearby Hampton Court Palace, Twickenham, Richmond, Kew Gardens
Location on Chiswick High Rd (A315) with no parking but hotel can feed your meter. Nearest tube Turnham Green
Food breakfast, lunch, dinner, room service **Price** £££
Rooms 14; 13 standard doubles, 1 superior; all have showers, superior has bath; all rooms have phone TV/DVD player, wi-fi, phone, hairdryer **Facilities** dining room, bar, games room, tv plasma room, brasserie **Credit cards** AE, DC, MC, V **Children** accepted **Disabled** 1 adapted room **Pets** not accepted **Closed** never **Proprietor** Nick Jones

High Road House

City hotel

You can hope that a hotel owned by Nick Jones (proprietor of Soho House and Babington House) is going to be interesting and this doesn't disappoint. The decoration is city chic but doesn't feel cold: the colours bring the place to life and add an air of cosiness. The bar and dining room are buzzy, with masses of light and are not so cramped that you think that your next door neighbour can hear your thoughts. The food is traditional English with French twists, but nothing too pretentious.

Downstairs in the basement is a fantastic space painted in deep red with retro furniture which can be a nightclub; a place for meetings; a place for private sports parties (big plasma screen); a children's activity area or a place for chilling out and playing pool or mini football.

The bedrooms are, as you would expect, very cool (maybe a bit too white) with comfy beds, delicious Cowshed toiletries in the bathrooms and very quiet. All the windows are triple glazed, which is just as well as there is a very busy yet fun, trendy road outside.

This a great hotel for all ages; and it is especially popular with mothers and children – activities for the latter are supervised by minders on Sundays, while parents have some time off.

55 Hanger Lane, London
W5 3HL

Tel (020) 8991 4450
Fax (020) 8991 4451
email info@hotel55-london.com
website www.hotel55-london.com

Nearby Heathrow (20 mins), Ealing Common, Central London (20 mins), North Ealing Tube
Location on A406 Hanger Lane, parking for 5 cars, ample space behind hotel in NCP
Food breakfast, lunch, dinner
Price ££
Rooms 26; all double, all with shower, 5 with bath and shower; all rooms have phone, TV, hairdryer, air-con, wi-fi, safe, tea/coffee facilities
Facilities restaurant, bar lounge, bar, garden, garden room
Credit cards AE, MC, V
Children welcome (but no extra beds provided)
Disabled 2 suitable rooms
Pets not accepted
Closed never
Proprietor Sanjay Tohani

Hotel 55

City hotel

This young hotel had only been open a year when we went to press. It's well placed for Heathrow: the Piccadilly line (North Ealing) is right behind the hotel, and takes you in without a change.

Sri, the charming and helpful manager, greets you as you step through the automatic doors. Straight through the ground floor and you are in the chic bar area, with walls clad in leather, low seating and a plasma screen. But the real joy of this place is the garden room leading on to a landscaped garden – rare in London. It's surprisingly quiet, considering the hotel is on a busy road and the tube is so close. You can have your continental breakfast in the garden room, read the papers or have a light lunch. The restaurant is now operated by Momo Japanese Restaurant.

The bedrooms and bathrooms are small, but nicely done, and with some interesting furniture in the bigger ones. They too are refreshingly quiet (double glazing): the ones overlooking the garden are particularly peaceful. If climbing stairs is an effort, (there's no lift) then flop on to the orthopaedic mattress (in every room) while sipping your environmentally friendly water. Plenty of business people here – which does affect the atmosphere.

28 Basil Street, London SW3 1AS

Tel (020) 7589 6286
email
reservations@thelevinhotel.co.uk
website www.thelevinhotel.co.uk

Nearby Knightsbridge; Hyde Park; Buckingham Palace.
Location between Sloane Street and Harrods; public car park opposite and at Capital Hotel, if available
Food breakfast, lunch, dinner; afternoon tea
Price ££££
Rooms 12; 8 std/exec doubles, 3 deluxe, 1 suite; all with bath and shower; all rooms have phone, flat screenTV, wi-fi, digital radio, minibar, safe, air-con **Facilities** lounge, The Metro Bar & Bistro, honesty bar **Credit cards** AE, DC, MC, V
Children welcome
Disabled access difficult (steps), but has 1 ground floor room and lift/elevator **Pets** accepted by arrangement
Closed restaurant only, Sun lunch and dinner **Proprietor** David Levin
Manager Harald Duttine

The Levin

City hotel

This impressively-situated hotel, in the heart of Knightsbridge, opened in late 2007. Owner David Levin has renewed its appeal with a multi-million pound renovation.

The stylishness strikes you as you walk in – everything is 'designer' and top quality – hand-blown ice-blue crystal chandeliers by Refer and Star, George Smith chairs, a green pony skin love seat by Christopher Guy. Whether or not the names matter to you, the effect is impressive and everything is immaculate. Bedrooms are beautifully designed, with contrasting colours and textures. Fabric-covered back-lit headboards give the rooms a cosy feel. The non-uniform room shapes of this old building have been imaginatively put to use, with sofas built into large bay windows. Original fireplaces add further character. Bathrooms are a fair size, with Italian marble and under-floor heating: stylish and spotlessly clean.

Attention to detail is superb, with all the technical wizardry you could want and also – uniquely, we believe – a mini-champagne-cocktail-bar in each room, with champagnes, mixers and a book of cocktail recipes.

Despite its design credentials, The Levin has a friendly atmosphere and manages to avoid pretentiousness. It is hard to find fault with the place – though equestrians may bridle at the pony skin love seat.

London

25 Courtfield Gardens, London
SW5 0PG

Tel (020) 7244 2255
Fax (020) 7244 2256
email
kensington.info@thenadler.com
website www.thenadler.com

Nearby Royal Albert Hall, Hyde Park, Earl's Court, Natural History Museum, V&A Museum, Science Museum, Kensington Palace
Location Courtfield Gardens, walking distance from Earl's Court tube, private parking spaces
Food breakfast
Price ££-££££
Rooms 65; all have bath/shower, with TV, wi-fi, phone, hairdryer, safe, ironing board, kitchenette,
Facilities lounge reception area
Credit cards AE, MC, V
Children welcome
Disabled lift access, 1 room with disabled access
Pets not accepted
Closed never
Proprietor Robert Nadler

The Nadler, Kensington

Self-catering hotel

The Nadler is not the sort of place we usually recommend – with 65 standardised rooms, at first sight it looks like an upmarket stopover for travelling businessmen. Rooms are neutrally decorated, the only colour comes from a couple of pictures – the same in every room.

But it has some useful features that break the mould. We like the (fairly original) concept of a self-catering hotel. However apart from a Nespresso machine in each compact kitchenette, guests are offered just sink, fridge and microwave – not ideal for cooking. Breakfast can be delivered to your room. Soft carpets warm up otherwise sterile corridors; two rooms have recently been sacrificed to make a reception area furnished with antiquarian books and sofas – a shame there's no separate sitting room for guests. For families, the hotel offers flexibility: there are pull-out beds (a dingy brown) in bigger doubles and rooms with bunk-beds.

For their size, the rooms are value for money (as we went to press, a standard double was from £169) The friendly staff will provide you with the names of local restaurants and cafes that offer discounts to guests. Their sister hotel in Soho has been booked up since it opened in June, and there's a branch in Liverpool (all on www.base2stay.com).

Doughty Street, London WC1N 2PL

Tel 020 7244 2000
e-mail enquiries@blueprintlivingapartments.com
website www.blueprintlivingapartments.com/no-5-doughty-street

Nearby Great Ormond Street Hospital, Charles Dickens Museum, Gray's Inn Fields, West End theatres, restaurants and bars **Location** literary district of Bloomsbury, close to the Financial District
Food self-catering
Price £££-££££
Rooms 11 serviced apartments; all with fully-equipped kitchen, shower room, flat screen television, free wi-fi, direct dial telephone, radio, CD player and iPod dock **Facilities** wi-fi, safe deposit box, laundry room, DVD library, babysitting services
Credit cards AE, MC, V
Children welcome
Disabled no lift **Pets** no
Closed never **Proprietor** Marldon

No. 5 Doughty Street

Self-catering apartments

Tucked away in the heart of London's literary district, yards from The Charles Dickens Museum and Gray's Inn Fields, lies Doughty Street, one of the most picturesque Georgian streets in London. These 11 luxury, serviced apartments in a Grade II listed building offer spacious comfort and value for money. While other serviced apartments tend to have stale, corporate decoration, No.5 Doughty street has the tasteful interior design of a modern boutique hotel, with all the contemporary trimmings, while remaining faithful to the period architecture of the building.

A range of studio, one-bedroom and two-bedroom apartments is on offer. Each has a fully-equipped kitchen, free wi-fi, flat screen television, direct dial telephone and iPod dock. Due to the building's listed status, a lift could not be fitted, but the stairs up to the fifth floor apartment are well lit with a large airy skylight. Once inside this top-floor apartment, admire the great view down the Georgian street below. Room service is limited to a linen change and clean once a week (a tip can be given to the staff for extra attendance). The location, mid-way between the West End and The City and wealth of nearby sights and restaurants, could hardly be better.

16 Sumner Place, London
SW7 3EG

Tel (020) 7589 5232
Fax (020) 7584 8615
e-mail reservations@numbersixteenhotel.co.uk
website www.numbersixteenhotel.co.uk

Nearby South Kensington museums; Knightsbridge; Kings Road.
Location off Old Brompton Road; no private car parking
Food breakfast; room service
Price ££££
Rooms 41 double, all with bath/shower; all rooms have phone, TV, iPod dock, minibar, hairdrier, safe, umbrellas, wi-fi
Facilities sitting room, bar, conservatory; small garden
Credit cards AE, DC, MC, V
Children accepted
Disabled access possible, lift/elevator **Pets** not accepted
Closed never
Manager Kate McWhirter

Number Sixteen

Town bed-and-breakfast

Number Sixteen is one of London's most characterful luxury bed-and-breakfast establishments. The original building has spread along its early Victorian South Kensington terrace, to encompass four adjoining houses – all extensively refurbished a few years ago.

Public rooms and bedrooms alike are brimful of pictures, including a huge eye-catching abstract in the reception room. Downstairs there are always big bowls of fresh flowers – sweet peas or roses perhaps – and the large rear patio garden is well kept and full of colour. Inside, the decoration is richly traditional and harmonious. A series of small sitting rooms with Victorian moulded ceilings, polished antiques and luxurious drapes, lead to an award-winning conservatory, from where, on summer days, you can sit and admire the profusion of flowers outside.

Bedrooms are generously proportioned, comfortable and stylish, largely furnished with period or contemporary pieces; some have French windows opening on to the garden. Breakfast is served in your room or in the drawing room, library, conservatory or garden. The hotel has no dining room but there are plenty of restaurants on the Old Brompton Road nearby.

37 Pimlico Road, London SW1W 8NE

Tel 020 7881 9844
e-mail reservations@theorange.co.uk
website www.theorange.co.uk

Nearby Victoria station, Ranelagh Gardens, Kings Road, Saatchi Gallery, Tate Britain
Location Pimlico Road, walking distance from Sloane Square station and Belgravia, Victoria station short drive away
Food breakfast, lunch, dinner, room service
Price ££-££££
Rooms 4 doubles, all have bath/shower, all have air-conditioning, wi-fi, iPod docking station, TV
Facilities restaurant, bar
Credit cards all major
Children accepted
Disabled disabled toilets
Pets not accepted
Closed never
Proprietor Cubitt House

The Orange

Town house hotel

This place was once evidently a public house, and the ground-floor bar still acts as a meeting and drinking spot for locals, albeit noisy, well-heeled ones – it stands opposite Daylesford Organics, on Pimlico Road. They love its wooden floors, country furniture and shabby-chic atmosphere and decoration. But 'restaurant-with-rooms' would be a more accurate description, as there are no other guest facilities.

As we went to press, a standard room was £205 – not dissimilar to rates in fully-fledged hotels – but without the same comfort. At the bar there was nowhere to sit, and we had to produce a room key to prove we were guests.

Of the four rooms, two are compact, two a decent size. The best is Pimlico, charming with original floorboards, lofty ceiling criss-crossed with rafters and pine panelling. There was a desk, a whitewashed wardrobe and a bedside radio.

There are tables on the first floor and downstairs. The starter of smoked salmon tartare was enjoyable, as was the main course of slow-cooked beef cheeks. Breakfast was beautifully presented, but is not included in the room rate. Despite these reservations, The Orange makes a useful, informal London stopover.

181-183 Cromwell Road, London SW5 0SF

Tel (020)7 244 2000
e-mail enquiries@therockwell.com
website www.therockwell.com

Nearby Kensington High Street, Earl's Court, South Kensington, Heathrow (30 minutes on underground) **Location** on Cromwell Road. Pay parking behind hotel 8.30 am to 6.30 pm and (usually) free spaces after 6.30. NCP car park in Holiday Inn – details from reception. **Food** breakfast, lunch, dinner **Price** £££ **Rooms** 40; 27 double, 13 single, all with shower only, air conditioning, telephone, voicemail, flat screen satellite TV, free broadband, safe, minibar **Facilities** bar, dining room, garden, reception sitting area, conference room, laundry service, 24-hour room service **Credit cards** AE, DC, MC, V **Children** welcome **Disabled** no specially adapted rooms but some rooms on ground floor; lift/elevator **Pets** not accepted **Closed** never **Proprietor** Marldon

The rockwell

Town hotel

We must declare an interest: one of the backers of The rockwell, a new London hotel opened in 2006, is architect Michael Squire, neighbour and sailing cronie of the guide's publisher. How to write about it without bias? Some years ago, Squire and his partners acquired two large, adjoining houses at the impersonal west end of the Cromwell Road, opposite the Cromwell Hospital, and first thought of making them rooming houses for students. Then, unexpectedly, they got permission for change of use. Overcoming their worries about the location, they spent serious money turning it into a contemporary hotel.The bedrooms, though created out of a variety of spaces, and very comfortable, seemed at first a little too much like conventional city hotel rooms for this guide. But, staying the night, they grew on us, with their beautiful oak fittings and large beds with fine sheets. Most are far from being boxes. Fairly priced, too. And we found the corridors and connecting parts unusually well lit and congenial. But the essential charm we seek came home when we had drinks in the attractive garden followed by dinner in the cosy but coolly decorated little dining room. Imaginative, carefully prepared food, relaxed but friendly service and again, fair prices. Londoners could do a lot worse than eat out here (see above left for tips on parking).

Peter's Lane, Cowcross Street,
London EC1M 6DS

Tel (020) 7336 0931
Fax (020) 7336 0932
e-mail reservations@rookery.co.uk
website www.rookeryhotel.com

Nearby The City; St Paul's; Smithfield; Farringdon tube station.
Location in pedestrian street in Clerkenwell, near Smithfield and City; parking in nearby public car park
Food breakfast, 24 hour room service **Price** ££££
Rooms 33; 27 double, 3 single, 3 suite, all with bath; all rooms have phone, TV, minibar, hairdryer, safe, wi-fi
Facilities conservatory, honesty bar; terrace
Credit cards AE, DC, MC, V
Children accepted
Disabled 2 bedrooms on ground floor **Pets** not accepted
Closed never
Proprietors Peter McKay and Douglas Blaine

The Rookery

Town hotel

Opened by the owners of the imaginative Hazlitt's and the Gore (see pages 120 and 121), this homely little hotel full of old curiosities and flights of fancy is in a traffic-free alleyway among the restaurants of fashionable Clerkenwell. Created from a row of converted listed Georgian cottages, it is packed with character and 'time-warp' detail: wood panelling; period shutters; open fires; flagged floors; even a special creaky sound put into the treads of the new stairs to make them seem old. Pretty bedrooms have little half-shutters, fresh Egyptian cotton sheets, summer and winter duvets. Minibars and 'workstations' are discreetly hidden behind antique doors. Bathrooms are delightful, with Victorian fittings, exposed copper pipes and wainscotting. One suite, on two floors, has a rococo French bed, attendant blackamoor and an Edwardian bathing machine; an electronically controlled panel shuts off the upper floor for business meetings.

A conservatory, with open fire and leather chairs, serves as a day room, opening on to a tiny terrace garden. Breakfast, continental, is on trays: fresh orange juice, coffee and croissants prepared and baked by the hotel's own pâtissier. We visited recently and enjoyed the vaguely Dickensian atmosphere as much as ever. Try nearby Portal restaurant in St John Street – good Portuguese food.

9-11 Sydney Street, London, SW3 6PU

Tel (020) 7376 7711
e-mail info@sydneyhousechelsea.com
website www.sydneyhousechelsea.com

Nearby Harrods, Victoria & Albert Museum, Natural History Museum **Location** between Fulham Road and Kings Road; no parking but two NCP car parks nearby (corner of Sydney St & Kings Road, Sloane Avenue) **Food** breakfast, 24 hour room service (limited after 10pm)
Price ££££
Rooms 21 double, plus 'room at the top'; all have shower, 11 have baths. All have telephone, flat-screen TV, DVD player, hairdryer, combination safe and internet access **Facilities** sitting room, bar, breakfast room **Credit cards** AE, DC, MC, V **Children** welcome **Disabled** not suitable **Pets** not accepted **Closed** never **Proprietor** Andrew Brownsword

Sydney House Chelsea

Town guesthouse

On a handsome residential street, announced only by a subtle nameplate, Sydney House could be a private residence – clearly a draw for its many regular guests, some of whom stay weekly while in London on business.

Andrew Brownsword, owner of Gidleigh Park and Bath Priory, bought this elegant grade II listed Georgian town house in 2002, totally refurbishing it. Original features are found alongside sophisticated, modern decoration and furnishings. Neutral colours dominate the reception/sitting area, where a large palm, modern tapestries and matching cushions in the suede-covered chairs add splashes of colour.

Bedrooms are smart and fresh, with clean, light bathrooms. The 'room at the top', set on the fifth floor, is perhaps surprisingly small, but leads out on to its own generously-sized private terrace, with wooden table and chairs and an area heater – so you can take in the impressive views over London year-round.

The staff at Sydney House are immaculately presented, professional and courteous but seemed to be feeling the strain of too many visitors. We wondered whether the high volume of guests might take its toll on the interior, or on the service. Reports welcome.

St Johns Square, 86-88 Clerkenwell Road, London, EC1M 5RJ

Tel (020) 7324 4444
Fax (020) 7324 4445
e-mail info@thezetter.com
website www.thezetter.com

Nearby Farringdon tube, Barbican, Old Spitalfields Market, Liverpool St Station **Location** Location: off A5201 Clerkenwell road; NCP parking around the corner (residents at hotel get discount) **Food** breakfast, lunch, dinner **Price** £££-££££ **Rooms** 59; all doubles with shower; all rooms have phone, TV, CD/DVD players, hairdryers, safe, air-con, wifi, rooms on 5th floor have tea/coffee facilities **Facilities** restaurant, sitting room, terrace with tables, 2 board rooms with private kitchen **Credit cards** MC, V **Children** accepted **Disabled** 2 rooms **Pets** not accepted **Closed** hotel: never; restaurant closed over Christmas and New Year **Proprietors** Mark Sainsbury and Michael Benyan

The Zetter

Town hotel

This is one of the new breed of eco-friendly hotels gaining popularity in London. Water is pumped from its own bore hole, supplying the rooms and air-conditioning. When it gets too hot, the sky-lights in the glass atrium pop open for ventilation; the room keys control the lights, so no energy is wasted when you leave.

The bar, restaurant and terrace are all done out in kitsch, retro style which manages, thankfully, not to be garish. The restaurant is wonderfully light thanks to the floor-to-ceiling windows. The food is best described as 'modern Mediterranean'; note the selection of cocktails.

The bedrooms are stacked over 4/5 storeys, clustered around the central atrium: quite a dizzying sight from the ground floor. Their colours might not be to everyone's taste: neon pinks, greens and blues – but they are all of a fairish size and peaceful. Complimentary hot water bottles. The seven roof-top suites have great views from their private balconies.

The Zetter room service has two options: food and drinks can either be brought up to your room, or located near the bedrooms on each floor are vending machines. Swipe your room card, and they give you tea, coffee, wine and snacks, adding the cost to the bill.

Margate, Kent

31 Hawley Square, Margate, Kent
CT9 1PH

Tel 01843 225166
e-mail
info@thereadingroomsmargate.co.uk
website www.thereadingroomsmargate.co.uk

Nearby Shell Grotto, Powell Cotton Museum, Turner Contemporary Art Centre, outdoor activites
Location Hawley Square in Margate old town, 5 minutes from beach and Old Town Quarter
Food breakfast
Price £££
Rooms 3; all double and all have bath/shower
Facilities room service
Credit cards all major, not AE
Children not accepted
Disabled no lift
Pets not accepted
Closed never
Proprietors Louise Oldfield and Liam Nabb

The Reading Rooms

Town bed-and-breakfast

There are two big reasons to make a special visit to has-been Margate: the new Turner Contemporary Art Centre, and this luxury B&B on a Georgian square five minutes from the seafront, with restricted views to the sea from some of the rooms. It's a little unconventional: each of the three large rooms occupies its own floor, and there is no guest sitting room or dining room, so your room, though large, is your world. Breakfast is delivered to the bedroom – and is unusually good. Bathrooms are huge and glitteringly luxurious.

There's no lift – rooms on the top floors mean climbing the staircase, but the hosts will offer to carry your bags. As we went to press, rooms cost from £150 a night, which might seem high for a place with no facilities except the rooms. But you'll be happy to pay this if you are, for example, a moderately sophisticated metropolitan type who values quality, style and bespoke service, and does not want to interact with other guests or the hosts. The rooms are indeed beautiful and gracious, one with floor-to-ceiling windows.

Midhurst, West Sussex

Church Hill, Midhurst, West Sussex GU29 9NX

Tel 01730 812990
mobile 07875 971368
website www.churchhousemid-hurst.com

Nearby South Downs National Park, Petersfield, Cowdray Park, Goodwood, Langham Brewery
Location central Midhurst, unlimited free parking on Church Hill
Food breakfast, dinner (minimum 6 people)
Price £££
Rooms 5; all doubles, 3 suites
Facilities sitting room, dining room, conservatory, garden
Credit cards MC, V
Children welcome
Disabled access possible to Dali suite **Pets** not accepted
Closed Christmas Eve, Christmas Day, Boxing Day
Proprietors Fina and Jaque Jurado

The Church House

Town bed-amd-breakfast

You think you're about to enter the modest hall of a small town house in a Midhurst side street... in fact you step into a huge, beautifully designed ground floor space stretching into the distance. The scale could be that of a stately home, but the laid-back country house ambience, the antiques to be used, not revered, the use of colour are something else. Fina Jurado, who is Spanish, fashioned her highly original B&B out of four town houses in 2011, having run Gaudis, a well known restaurant here for years. She lives two doors away – guests have the run of it – and is a characterful, naturally friendly hostess.

The bedrooms (some huge, such as the master suite, Silver) combine English country house and European style elements. Comfortable, not staid, each is stylishly individual but homely in its way.

You start asking yourself, why stay in a hotel when this is so much more interesting – a place where you can be yourself. The ground floor, resolving into several sitting areas, plus the garden, is big enough for three or four guest groups to co-exist privately. Dinners are cooked to order; tea is with home-made cakes; help yourself to a drink – singles are free; or buy a bottle.

Romsey, Hampshire

Market Place, Romsey, Hampshire
SO51 8ZJ

Tel 01794 512431
Fax 01794 517 485
e-mail
thewhitehorse@silkshotels.com
website
www.thewhitehorseromsey.co.uk

Nearby Broadlands; Romsey Abbey; Romsey Rapids; Southampton.
Location Romsey, a market town in Hampshire's Test Valley **Food** breakfast, lunch, dinner; afternoon tea, tapas
Price ££–£££
Rooms 31; all with shower, TV and wi-fi **Facilities** brasserie, private dining area, 2 sitting rooms, 24-hour room service, conference facilities
Credit cards MC, V
Children welcome
Disabled access to restaurant but not to rooms
Pets accepted
Closed never
Proprietors The Bereweeke Trust

The White Horse

Town inn

Our series editor Fiona Duncan writes: 'The White Horse's brasserie is one of my favourite eating places in Hampshire – and that's not an idle compliment because I know that in recent years the competition has warmed up.

'If you need a bed for the night, it offers 31 recently redone rooms, all my idea of comfy, charming and fairly priced. Some of the doubles are quite cottage-like – snug and intimate; at the other end of the scale is an enormous penthouse in the main building. Don't overlook the rooms in the coach house with its pretty shutters.

'The main building is just what you'd expect of a coaching inn with its roots in the Middle Ages. It's somewhat rambling, levels change unpredictably, and the layout seems illogical. The private dining area is on the street, there are sitting rooms in the middle of the ground floor and then a corridor takes you to the brasserie at the rear. This is the part that works best: it has tall windows that let you look out on to the internal courtyard and the feeling is of well-designed, restrained elegance. There are often special offers here.

'There's a 'horse' theme throughout – witness the the Lewis and Wood wallpaper in reception, and the bedrooms each get a famous racehorse's name.'

Rushlake Green, East Sussex

Rushlake Green, Heathfield,
East Sussex TN21 9QJ

Tel (01435) 830553
Fax (01435) 830726
website
www.stonehousesussex.co.uk

Nearby Battle; Glyndebourne.
Location just off village green 3 miles (4.5 km) SE of Heathfield, in large grounds with ample car parking
Food breakfast, lunch by arrangement (summer only), dinner
Price £££ (special offers in spring and autumn)
Rooms 7 double and twin, all with bath; all rooms have phone, TV, hairdryer, wi-fi
Facilities sitting room, library, dining room; billiards, snooker; gardens, croquet, fishing, shooting
Credit cards MC, V
Children welcome over 9
Disabled access difficult **Pets** accepted in bedrooms only
Closed Christmas to 6 Jan
Proprietors Peter and Jane Dunn

Stone House

Country house hotel

Our latest reporter enthusiastically agrees with everything we have said about Stone House in the past. It is Peter and Jane Dunn's ancestral family home, a glorious 16thC manor house. The delightful Jane ('old world and lovely manners') does what she enjoys most – cooking, and looking after her guests individually. Her relaxed and friendly demeanour belies a very sure touch, and Stone House is run with great competence – which means it's much in demand for Glyndebourne visitors (luxury wicker picnic hampers can be prepared), shooting weekends, house parties and even small executive conferences. A few years ago they created a Victorian walled vegetable garden and an 18thC-style rose garden. Wine has become a hobby for Peter and Jane, and they are justly proud of their wine list.

Bedooms are beautifully decorated; two have fine antique four-posters and are particularly spacious (the bathrooms can double as sitting rooms). An excellent place in which to sample authentic English country living at its most gracious – log fires and billiards, woodland walks and croquet – together with the atmosphere of a home. A favourite of the guide for many years, we have had consistently good feedback.

Rye, East Sussex

98 High Street, Rye, East Sussex
TN31 7JT

Tel (01797) 222114
Fax (01797) 224065
e-mail stay@thegeorgeinrye.com
website www.thegeorgeinrye.com

Nearby Camber Sands, Great Dixter Gardens, Bodiam castle, Hastings Old Town, Sissinghurst castle gardens
Location off A259 in centre of town; no car parking
Food breakfast, lunch, dinner
Price ££££
Rooms 6 junior suites, 28 doubles, all with bath and shower; all rooms have phone, TV, CD, DVD, hairdryer, wi-fi
Facilities ballroom, restaurant, private dining room, bar; courtyard garden
Credit cards MC, V
Children accepted
Disabled access difficult
Pets not accepted
Closed never
Proprietors Alex and Katie Clarke

The George in Rye

Seaside hotel

The George is a Rye institution enjoying a new life. In 2005 it was bought by Katie Clarke and her husband Alex. They lived with swirly carpets and partition walls for a year "to get the feel of the place" then attacked, closing for eight months and reopening with stunning results.

At one end of the entrance hall, panelled walls and a huge hearth create a cosy sitting area, while the other side shows the hotel's contemporary face, with psychedelic portraits of the Beatles adding warm splashes of colour. By contrast, the sprawling bar at the back is somehow less inviting – the panelled sitting room perhaps has a better ambience for pre-dinner drinks.

Katie, a set designer, is responsible for the 34 delicious bedrooms, designing much of the furniture herself. A warren of stairs and corridors leads to the rooms, each different, demonstrating her confident eye for colour as well as comfort.

The dining room, though elegant, doesn't have quite the allure of the bedrooms or lobby. However, The George Grill's food is memorable. If the 2003 Pinot Noir from Sandhurst Vineyard in Kent is on the winelist, try it. They're making every effort to provide quality at affordable prices here – long may it last.

Mermaid Street, Rye, East Sussex
TN31 7ET

Tel (01797) 222828
e-mail jeakeshouse@btinternet.com
website www.jeakeshouse.com

Nearby Great Dixter; Ellen Terry Museum, 1066 country.
Location in centre of Rye; private car parking nearby (3 minute walk)
Food breakfast
Price ££
Rooms 11; 8 double and twin, 2 family rooms, 1 suite; 9 rooms with bath, 1 with private bath across hall; all rooms have TV, phone, wi-fi
Facilities dining room, sitting room, bar, wi-fi
Credit cards MC, V
Children accepted over 8
Disabled access difficult
Pets by arrangement
Closed never
Proprietor Jenny Hadfield

Jeake's House

Town house bed-and-breakfast

This splendid 16thC house – or rather three houses turned into one – has been lovingly restored to make a delightful small hotel: a verdict confirmed by many readers, who return time after time. It is the domaine of Jenny Hadfield, who used to be an operatic soprano, and although the place is essentially a charming small hotel, she has lent it a certain theatrical quality. Originally built as a wool store in 1689, it later became a Baptist school and, earlier this century, the home of American writer Conrad Potter Aiken, when it played host to many of the leading artistic and literary figures of the time.

The beamed bedrooms, which come in various shapes and sizes, overlook either the old roof-tops of Rye or Romney Marsh. Bedsteads are either brass or mahogany (some are four-poster), bedspreads lace, furniture antique. There are plenty of thoughtful extras in the rooms. Downstairs, a galleried ex-chapel makes the grandest of breakfast rooms. A roaring fire greets guests on cold mornings, and Jenny will serve you either a traditional breakfast or a vegetarian alternative. There is a comfortable parlour with a piano and a bar, with books and pictures lining the walls. 'Situated on *the* street in Rye (the cobbled Mermaid Street) within walking distance of all the sights,' says our reporter. This will suit our older readers.

Taynards Lane, Winchelsea, Rye, East Sussex TN36 4JT

Tel 01797 226276
email info@thestrandhouse.co.uk
website www.thestrandhouse.co.uk

Nearby Rye, Romney Marsh churches and miniature railway, Hastings battle site, National Trust properties and gardens.
Location in own grounds, with off-road car-parking
Food breakfast, dinner; afternoon tea **Price** ££-£££
Rooms 13; 12 double and 1 twin; all rooms except 1 have bath or shower, TV, free wi-fi, DVD player
Facilities sitting room, honesty bar, garden **Credit cards** DC, MC, V
Children accepted, but not especially suitable (steep stairs, open fires, pond) **Disabled** access difficult
Pets welcome by arrangement
Closed weekdays in winter
Proprietor Mary Sullivan and Hugh Davie

Strand House

Country house hotel

Is it an upscale B&B? Or is it a small hotel? We like places which occupy the grey area between these types, especially when run by dedicated on-the-spot owner-managers. Mary Sullivan and Hugh Davie are just that – she mainly in the kitchen, and he front of house. They are just as happy with guests who treat the place as a B&B, keeping themselves to themselves, as with those who eat Mary's dinners (good, daily changing menu with choices) in the intimate dining room and engage with other guests and the hosts. Which is only a start.

The thing here is the building: mainly Tudor, with some medieval elements and as quirkily charming as they come. We rarely see such low ceilings (one door way is five foot five in height) or so many blackened old beams. The country cottage interior decoration is in keeping. Bathrooms tend to be smallish, carved out of corners, as you'd expect in a building of this age. To appreciate Strand House you need to be happy stooping for the low ceilings, and to 'get' what Mary and Hugh do (essentially, to provide a home from home). Three contemporary bedrooms (with normal-height ceilings) are available in a cottage in the garden.

St Leonards-on-Sea, East Sussex

9 Eversfield Place,
St-Leonards-on-Sea, East Sussex
TN37 6BY

Tel (01424) 460109
e-mail info@zanzibarhotel.co.uk
website www.zanzibarhotel.co.uk

Nearby Hastings old town, Hastings Fort
Location on seafront near Warrior Square, just off A21; permit parking at the front of the hotel
Food breakfast
Price £££-££££
Rooms 8 double, all with shower/bath; all rooms have flatscreen TV with freeview, DVD, hairdryer, ironing board, iron, tea and coffee making facilities, fridge with milk/water
Facilities restaurant, sitting room, garden, honesty bar
Credit cards DC, MC, V
Children welcome
Disabled access difficult
Pets small dogs only
Closed never
Proprietor Max O'Rourke

Zanzibar

Seaside town house hotel

The somewhat run-down seaside town of St Leonards-on-Sea is not overwhelmed with hotels worth writing about, but this stylish and relaxed place stands out. Zanzibar occupies a Victorian seafront town house which has been restored and modernised by its enthusiastic and hands-on owner, Max O'Rourke. On arrival, along with your complimentary glass of champagne you are given a parking permit, a key, and advice on where to go if you want to explore. The ethos here is very much 'make yourself at home', though the friendly staff are always on hand.

Zanzibar's eight rooms are individually themed around a region of the world and the decoration and furniture subtly reflect this, adding a unique character to each without going over the top. Every bathroom has a special feature – in 'Antarctica' where our inspector stayed, it was a combined shower/sauna. Breakfast is ordered the previous evening and delivered hot to your room, or the grand salon. Choices include kippers, poached eggs, smoked salmon and a 'full English' – all fresh and delicious.

Max says: "the best thing about Hastings and St Leonards is that there isn't that much to do", and the steady stream of (mostly) Londoners coming to Zanzibar for a refreshingly calm, relaxing break, seem to agree.

Seaview, Isle of Wight

Priory Drive, Seaview, Isle of Wight
PO34 5BU

Tel (01983) 613146
Fax (01983) 616539
e-mail enquiries@priorybay.co.uk
website www.priorybay.co.uk

Nearby Osborne House; Bembridge Maritime Museum; Cowes.
Location in own grounds with private beach, on B3330 S of Seaview between Nettlestone and St Helens; ample car-parking; with satnav, use postcode PO33 1YA
Food breakfast, lunch, dinner
Price £££-££££ **Rooms** 18 double and twin, all with bath; all rooms have phone, TV, hairdryer; also 10 self-catering cottages and 3 yurts
Facilities drawing room, sitting room, bar, 2 dining rooms; garden, 6-hole golf course, tennis, swimming pool, private beach, sailing, fishing, windsurfing **Credit cards** AE, MC, V **Children** welcome **Disabled** access possible **Pets** not accepted **Closed** never **Proprietors** Andrew and James Palmer

Priory Bay Hotel

Seaside hotel

When Andrew Palmer's motorboat broke down on the sweeping private beach of Priory Bay, he stumbled on an old-fashioned hotel with extensive grounds that he never knew existed, despite a lifetime of holidaying in the area. He bought it, and with the help of a talented friend, Annabel Claridge, effected a stunning transformation, opening in summer 1998. Bedrooms are decorated with charm and freshness, each different, some seaside simple, others more dramatic. The house itself has a colourful history and a quirky hotch-potch of styles with a Tudor farmhouse at its core and a Norman tithe barn in the grounds. Memorable details include the Gothic church porch brought from France in the 1930s, the Tudor fireplace depicting the Sacrifice of Isaac, and the delightful Georgian murals of pastoral island scenes in the dining room. Less lovely are the grounds – or so we thought last time we visited – and the scattered oubuildings, some barrack-like, which have appeared since the last edition. But the highlight is the wonderful sweep of beach where children can be kept happy for hours (this is an extremely child-friendly hotel). Dinner, on our visit, was very good.

Sidlesham, West Sussex

Mill Lane, Sidlesham
West Sussex, PO20 7NB

Tel (01243) 641233
e-mail enquiries@crab-lobster.co.uk
website www.crab-lobster.co.uk

Nearby Chichester, Selsey Bill, Bosham, Pagham harbour walk and nature reserve
Location on B1245 south of Chichester
Food breakfast, lunch, dinner
Price £££
Rooms 4 double; 1 with shower only, 3 with bath; 2-bed self-catering cottage
Facilities bar, dining room, terrace, garden; internet connection
Credit cards AE, MC, V
Children accepted
Disabled access possible to restaurant only
Pets not accepted
Closed never
Proprietor Sam and Janet Bakose

The Crab and Lobster

Restaurant-with-rooms

The landscape surrounding The Crab and Lobster is enchanting: salt marsh and woodland interlaced with watery creeks stretching across Pagham Harbour to the distant sea. Despite its spanking new interior, this 350-year-old building offers, with its slate floors, cream painted or bare brick walls and open fire, sophisticated charm.

There are four attractive bedrooms – all stylishly decorated with pastel or beige walls, and fresh flowers – in the main building, plus a delightful two-bedroom cottage for self-catering next door. We stayed in a deluxe room under the eaves, a cosy hideaway with binoculars for a closer look at that wonderful view – a thoughful touch. The elegant bathroom had a velvet *chaise longue* (great touch), but was lacking in shelf space.

The Crab and Lobster is a stylish waterside hideaway, with slate floors, exposed brick walls and an open fire in the dining room and bar downstairs, and what's more the food is excellent. Dinner was a great success: local crab from Selsey and lobster, superbly dressed, plus a wild sea bass that had been brought to the door that day by a local fisherman, and a bottle of Sancerre – perfect. The Halfway Bridge in nearby Petworth is under the same ownership (page 165).

Southampton

8 Western Esplanade, Southampton, Hampshire SO14 2AZ

Tel 0845 0779494
website www.pighotel.com

Nearby Southampton Docks, historic Southampton, museums and the city's modern high street and shopping centre are within walking distance.
Location within Southampton's historic medieval walls, near cruise terminal and city centre
Food breakfast, snacks, dinner at THE PIG (free shuttle service)
Price £££
Rooms 12; most with shower only, 3 with bath, some rooms have larders full of snacks and drinks, TV and DVD player
Facilities deli, wi-fi throughout
Credit cards AE, DC, MC, V
Children welcome, cot and additional bed available
Disabled no special facilities **Pets** not accepted
Closed never
Proprietor Robin Hutson

THE PIG-in the wall

Town house hotel

This is the latest venture – opened October 2012 – of Robin Hutson, his wife Judy and backer Jim Radcliffe. They are the same team that created THE PIG at Brockenhurst (page 95) – one of the most acclaimed of recent new hotels. Its description – a 'Boutique B&B' – might tempt you to suspect it's a triumph of form over content – but it's not.

They've made this pleasing Georgian house in the medieval walls of Southampton near Town Quay feel as if it's always been a happy place to stay. You step off the wide pavement through the front door straight into the downstairs public space – a long sitting room, bar and bistro dining area. It smells pleasantly of wood smoke and herbs, which are grown in pots as table decorations and for the kitchen. At both ends are log fires with guests relaxing in chairs upholstered in smart fabrics that could be in your home. Warm, friendly, relaxed.

Simply decorated connecting corridors lead to the bedrooms. The cheapest room is artfully shoehorned into the attic. Mid-price and superior rooms are spacious enough – perhaps not especially so, but this is a town house. Colours are soothing browns, whites, greys with splashes of purple velvet. New PIGs were due to open in 2014-5 after we went to press.

Stockbridge, Hampshire

31 High Street, Stockbridge,
Hampshire SO20 6EY

Tel 01264 810833
website www.thegreyhoundon-thetest.co.uk

Nearby Mottisfont Abbey, Winchester Cathedral, Salisbury Cathedral, Stonehenge, New Forest, Beaulieu Motor Museum
Location on village High Street in Stockbridge, ample car-parking at rear of building
Food breakfast, dinner
Price ££-£££
Rooms 7; 6 doubles 3 can be twin, 1 single, all have bath/shower, all with TV, tea/coffee facilities
Facilities restaurant, pub, honesty bar, fly fishing
Credit Cards all major
Children accepted
Disabled no special access
Pets well-behaved dogs welcome
Closed no set period
Proprietor Lucy Townsend

The Greyhound

Country inn

An atmospheric Hampshire pub run by Lucy Townsend, who used to be at The Peat Spade (see opposite) and The Anchor at Lower Froyle (page 91). She bought this new venture in 2011 with an investment partner, runs it hands-on, and plainly wants it to succeed.

The seven first-floor rooms are better than similar country offerings in the area at the same price. They are all different styles, enhanced by painted panelling in Farrow & Ball colours; upholstered bedheads; pretty fabrics; chaises longues; country furniture, big mirrors and colourful paintings. In ours, there wasn't much room for a laptop, and we would have liked fuller information on what to do and see in the area. Six of the rooms have a shower only, but at £110 as we went to press, in the heart of plutocratic Hampshire, they are fair value.

Downstairs, the dining room, with OKA chairs at rustic tables set with prettily coloured glassware, offers top-end pub fare. The Test is right at the back – ask about fishing deals, and barbecues in the fishing hut.

Stockbridge, Hampshire

Village Street, Longstock,
Stockbridge, Hampshire SO20 6DR

Tel (01264) 810612
Fax (01264) 811078
e-mail info@peatspadeinn.co.uk
website www.peatspadeinn.co.uk

Nearby Stockbridge, Romsey, Winchester, Test Valley fishing and fisheries
Location in sleepy village centre with off road car parking
Food breakfast, lunch, dinner
Price ££
Rooms 8 doubles, 2 can be twin, all with bath shower; all rooms have phone, TV and DVD player, hairdryer, wi-fi, minibar, tea/coffee facilities
Facilities bar, dining room, courtyard, terrace, in-house sporting agents
Credit cards MC, V
Children over 10
Disabled access difficult
Pets not accepted
Closed Christmas Day
Manager Ben Maybury

Peat Spade Inn

Village inn

'A charming mix of traditional and new, rustic and efficient' says our reporter.

The bar-dining area is one long room, and is rustic-smart. It has warm red walls until you reach The Rod Room, which opens on to the garden. With green walls, the decoration is more faithful to its status as a fishing inn, and features cane fly rods, mounted trout, reels, gilt-framed mirrors, period shooting and fishing prints. There are clean white napkins on scrubbed pine tables; the food OK – ambitious but given the prices perhaps in some respects not quite there. The Mayfly Mess upstairs accommodates private lunch and dinner parties.

Our reporter's room – restful browns and greens and wide oak floor boards in the bathroom, excellent cotton sheets on a thoroughly comfortable bed – homely, comfortable. Ask about their fishing weekends for novices and experts, individuals and companies. Ghillies and tutors to order.

Ventnor, Isle of Wight

151 Mitchell Avenue, Ventnor, Isle of Wight PO38 1DR

Tel 01983 852271
e-mail mail@hillsideventnor.co.uk
website www.hillsideventnor.co.uk

Nearby St Boniface Down, Ventnor beach, botanical gardens, Roman villa
Location on Mitchell Avenue, just off the B3327 towards Ventnor
Food breakfast; lunch and dinner at nearby bistro
Price ££-££££
Rooms 12; 7 doubles, 1 can be twin, 2 twins, 2 singles; 2 apartments sleeping up to 4 in each
Facilities restaurant, terrace, sitting room, bistro
Credit cards MC, V
Children welcome over 12
Disabled no special facilities
Pets not accepted, kennels nearby
Closed never
Manager Gert

Hillside

Country hotel

Gert has recently re-invented the imposing 18thC house at Ventnor on the south coast of the Isle of Wight. The exterior remains unchanged – thatched roof and stone walls – but inside it's now contemporary, mostly white, and with a distinctly Scandinavian feel. The colour scheme – or lack of – initially feels impersonal, but Gert is a friendly host who knows how to create a relaxing, welcoming environment.

Downstairs, the public areas are large and furnished with Scandinavian pieces, while colourful modern paintings adorn most walls. The bedrooms, although rather uniform, are stylish, comfortable and provide everything you need.

Recent developments include two apartments, Hillside Stables and Hillside 30PS with similar decoration and furnishings. The Stables are adjacent to Hillside whereas 30PS is a self-catering Victorian house 50 metres from the sea in downtown Ventnor. The restaurant is now open seven days a week (not just for dinner), and there's a 'continental' bistro a five-minute walk away.

St Boniface Down – the highest point of the Isle of Wight – has tremendous views over the island and is a brisk walk away. The Boniface cliffs give Ventnor its sheltered, mild maritime climate.

West Hoathly, West Sussex

Queen's Square, West Hoathly, West Sussex RH19 4PP

Tel 01342 810369
e-mail thecatinn@googlemail.com
website www.catinn.co.uk

Nearby The Priest House, Standen, Penshurst, Hever Castle, Bluebell Railway, golf courses, wine tasting, walking
Location West Hoathly village, parking at the inn and in the village
Food breakfast, lunch, dinner
Price £££
Rooms 4 doubles, all have bath/shower and TV, wi-fi, tea/coffee facilities
Facilities pub, dining room
Credit cards MC, V
Children over 7 in pub, no special rooms **Disabled** ramp to pub, but no access to rooms
Pets not accepted
Closed Sunday nights
Proprietor Andrew Russell

The Cat Inn

Village freehouse

Andrew Russell, formerly general manager of nearby Gravetye Manor, recently took on this formerly run-down pub. His management skills, concentrated on a more compact operation, are achieving almost everything we look for. Step into the bar, and it's comfortable and genuine, buzzing with locals; try the food, and it's simple but better than you would expect; go to your bedroom and you find it instantly comfortable, unflashy but pretty. A balance of form and content.

Back downstairs, we noticed how he has cleverly combined airy and cosy dining areas, and made an old-fashioned bar with huge inglenook fireplace work alongside other, gently upmarket modern features. Breakfast is well above average. West Hoathly is an interesting, historic village with views – if you can, spend time strolling the sites.

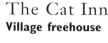

14 Southgate Street, Winchester,
Hampshire S023 9EF

Tel 0844 748 9267
website www.hotelduvin.com

Nearby Cathedral; Venta Roman Museum; Winchester College.
Location in the town centre, a minute's walk from the cathedral; limited car-parking onsite
Food breakfast, lunch, dinner; room service
Price £££
Rooms 24; 23 double and twin,1 suite, all with bath; all rooms have phone, TV, CD player, minibar, hairdryer
Facilities sitting room, dining room/breakfast room, private dining room, bar, wine-tasting cellar; garden, boules
Credit cards AE, DC, MC, V
Children welcome
Disabled several bedrooms on ground floor
Pets not accepted
Closed never
Manager Grant Callaghan

Hotel du Vin

Town house hotel

There is still an alluring buzz in the air at this stylish, affordable Georgian town house, once the flagship of the Hotel du Vin mini-chain – even though it's now been taken over by Malmaison, a large hotel group. This was the original Hotel du Vin and it's got panache. The wood-floored, hop-garlanded Bistro sets the tone: staffed by a charming bunch of mainly French youngsters, it has the intimate, slightly chaotic yet professional air of the genuine article. Start with a bucket of champagne in the voluptuous mirrored and muralled bar, then choose a bottle from the inventive, kindly priced wine list to go with the inventive, sunny, Modern English food.

The bedrooms and bathrooms are every bit as appealing, with fresh Egyptian cotton bedlinen, CD players, capacious baths and huge showers. For maximum quiet, ask for a Garden Room, or splash out on one of the principal suites (see top picture), with hardwood floors, roll-top baths and panoramic floor-to-ceiling windows. 'Breakfast in Bed' is available as part of the room service.

We also recommend the Hotel du Vins in Bristol (page 86) and Brighton (page 160). There are also Hotels du Vin in Harrogate and Tunbridge Wells (pages 271 and 26) – see www.hotelduvin.com.

Yarmouth, Isle of Wight

Quay Street, Yarmouth, Isle of Wight PO41 OPE

Tel (01983) 760331
Fax (01983) 760425
e-mail res@thegeorge.co.uk **website** www.thegeorge.co.uk

Nearby Yarmouth Castle (adjacent); Newport 12 miles; ferry terminal.
Location in town, close to ferry port overlooking Solent; long stay car park 3-min walk
Food breakfast, lunch, dinner; room service
Price £££
Rooms 17; 13 double and twin, 2 suites, 2 single, all with bath; all rooms have phone, TV, hairdryer
Facilities sitting room, restaurant, brasserie; garden, private beach, 36 ft motor yacht available for charter
Credit cards AE, MC, V
Children welcome over 8
Disabled 1 disabled room downstairs **Pets** not accepted
Closed never
Proprietors Jeremy Willcock and John Illsley

The George Hotel & Restaurant **Seaside town hotel**

In many ways the George is a perfect hotel: an atmospheric building in the centre of a breezy and historic harbour town, with welcoming rooms, a buzzing brasserie with tables spilling across the waterfront garden, and a quieter, more formal restaurant where good, inventive food is served. When they took over the peeling and faded 17thC former govenor's residence, owners John Illsley (former bass guitarist of Dire Straits) and Jeremy Willcock took great care to restore and renovate with sympathy. A panelled and elegantly proportioned hall sets the scene, leading to a cosy wood-panelled sitting room with thick velvet drapes at the windows, an amusing mid-Victorian evocation of the George above the fireplace and a roaring log fire in winter. Across the hall is the dark red dining room, and beyond the central stairs, the Brasserie and garden, where you can eat in fine weather.

Upstairs, the bedrooms are all inviting and all different: one has a four-poster; another is a light and pretty corner room; two have wonderful teak-decked balconies with views across the Solent. (The hotel has its own motor yacht for outings.) 'It's a sheer pleasure,' writes a satisfied reader, 'to hop on the ferry at Lymington, alight at Yarmouth, and settle in to the George for two or three days.'

Braye, Alderney

Braye Street, Alderney, GY9 3XT

Tel 0800 2800550
Fax 01481 824301
email holiday@brayebeach.com
website www.brayebeach.com

Nearby St Anne's Church, 'The Cathedral of the Channel Islands', Mannez Lighthouse at Quesnard Point.
Location Alderney island
Food breakfast, lunch, dinner
Price ££ **Rooms** 27; all with wi-fi, bathrobes, refrigerator, flat screen television, choice of classic films on in-room box office, hairdryer, complimentary decanter of sherry, tea and coffee making facilities, personal safe, fresh seasonal fruit on arrival
Facilities free wi-fi throughout, computer room with internet access, cinema, restaurant
Credit cards AE, MC, V
Children welcome
Disabled 1 specially adapted room
Pets dogs in bar but not in rooms
Closed never
Manager Richard Proctor

Braye Beach

Beach hotel

Much needed renovation has breathed new life into Braye Beach Hotel. Thoughtfully and tastefully redesigned, it is a welcome retreat for guests, and a great base from which to explore the little island of Alderney.

The old public areas have been opened up to create a big open space, including an award-winning restaurant and bar. Outside, the wraparound terrace gives plenty of outdoor seating, and allows you to follow the sun. There's a little cinema for rainy days.

The bedrooms are comfortable and cosy, and exceptional value for money. Bright patterned covers and cushions give a homely, welcome feel and offset neutral walls and furniture. There are rooms with views and rooms without, but the ones with views on to the beach are the best, and are available on a first come first serve basis. However, our reporter did comment that the windows needed cleaning – sea salt spray obscured the view – but this was after a storm and we are assured that they are normally cleaned regularly.

Deserted and charming, Braye Beach itself is ideal. Located on the edge of the beach, the hotel has great views across the bay and beyond the harbour.

Kings Mills, Castel, Guernsey GY5 7JT

Tel (01481) 257996
Fax (01481) 256834
e-mail info@fleurdujardin.com
website www.fleurdujardin.com

Nearby Vazon and Richmond beaches for surfing and sea fishing trips.
Location Castel
Food breakfast, lunch, dinner
Prices ££-£££
Rooms 15; all rooms have phone, TV, hairdryer
Facilities restaurant, bar, health suite; outdoor solar-heated swimming pool, car and bike hire
Credit cards all major
Children welcome
Disabled not suitable
Pets not accepted
Closed never
Proprietors Ian and Amanda Walker

Fleur du Jardin

Village hotel

A voluptuous bouquet of flowers greets you in reception, teetering on a table next to a vintage suitcase. Thus, the tone is set for Fleur du Jardin – it is a quirky, eccentric and comfortable place that welcomes all guests as if they are returning travellers.

Throughout the hotel we were met with jokey signs ('duck or grouse' over a low ceiling), beautiful furniture and lovely decoration in each room – a mixture of natural elegance and seaside charm. Owners Ian and Amanda Walker were keen to combine design influences seen on their own travels around the world, as well as ensuring Fleur du Jardin's Guernsey heritage.

The award-winning restaurant is charming and homely, and uses as much locally bred beef, pork and fresh fish as possible. Real effort has been spent on thoughtful decoration – a dainty vase of fresh flowers is placed on each table – making the dining room one of the most charming and relaxing places to be in the whole hotel. The adjoining bar is also award-winning, and has a changing selection of real ales.

The bedrooms are spacious and charming, decorated in a seaside theme. Big white lampshades, fluffy bedding and rustic walls make them feel cosy and peaceful.

St Peter Port, Guernsey

Fermain Lane, St. Peter Port,
Guernsey GY1 1ZZ

Tel 0800 316 0314
e-mail
reservations@fermainvalley.com
website www.fermainvalley.com

Nearby St. Peter Port.
Location close to St Peter Port town centre, Guernsey
Food breakfast, lunch, dinner
Price £££-££££
Rooms 43; all with free wi-fi, bathrobes, refrigerator, flat screen TV, hairdryer, personal safe
Facilities computer room with internet access, indoor heated swimming pool and sauna, poolside terrace, cinema with 3D, 2 lounges, 2 restaurants, gardens
Credit cards all major
Children welcome
Disabled lifts, 1 fully-equipped room
Pets not accepted
Closed never
Proprietors Derek Coates

Fermain Valley

Seaside town hotel

It's larger than our preferred size, but Fermain Valley's focus on individuality and unique design give it charm and originality. Situated high over popular Fermain Bay, its views over the surrounding Channel Islands and, on clear days, as far as France, are spectacular.

The style and ambience is modern, with neutral colours that will appeal to a wide cross-section of people. However, it is the thoughtful little touches that we like the most, such as fresh flowers and seasonal fruit in the bedrooms to make you feel at home. Bedrooms are all individually designed, many with sea or garden views, and thoughtful touches such as matching headboard cushions or curtain covers and chunky bedspreads give a lovely greeting.

The facilities you find here are typical of most large-scale, successful hotels. The Valley Restaurant and The Rock Garden Restaurant, private cinema and indoor swimming pool have all helped this place to achieve its four stars, but we especially value the hard work that goes into providing a calm and relaxing atmosphere. One guest commented that it was a 'relaxed atmosphere for such a plush place'.

The hotel is justifiably proud of its landscaped gardens, which won the Floral Guernsey Horticultural Award for Horticultural Excellence in 2008.

St Saviour, Guernsey

Sous L'Eglise, St Saviour, Guernsey GY7 9FX

Tel (01481) 263862
Fax (01481) 264835
e-mail bookings@aubergedu-valguernsey.com
website www.aubergedu-valguernsey.com

Nearby Guernsey Woodcarvers, St Apolline's Chapel, Castle Cornet, Hauteville House, Saumarez Manor, local beaches
Location St Saviour, near Guernsey airport
Food breakfast, lunch, dinner
Price ££
Rooms 9; 2 family, 4 double, 3 twin, all en-suite with central heating, television, telephone, tea and coffee making facilities
Facilities restaurant, bar, 3 acre gardens **Credit cards** MC, V
Children welcome
Disabled no special facilities
Pets not accepted
Closed Feb
Proprietor Fernando

Auberge du Val

Town bed-and-breakfast

A friendly, quaint establishment in St Saviour, Auberge du Val is a 150-year-old converted farmhouse. Manager Fernando has been there for 12 years and has retained the busy-but-cosy feel of a traditional farmhouse.

Our room was clean and comfortable, with wonky walls and little bay windows sympathetic to the old-fashioned building.

The grounds are impressive – three acres of lush countryside complete with a trout stream and woodland valley. In keeping with its farmhouse heritage, the garden supplements the local supplies of vegetables and herbs for the restaurant.

The focal point of this little hotel, however, is the award-winning restaurant. Reminiscent of a homely hunting lodge, it is wonderfully cosy and hearty. The menu is chalked erratically on blackboards in the bar, and the locally caught fish on the 'Specials' is always changing. It was busy when we were there, full of guests and non-residents, who grew noisier and happier with each excellent dish; the wine is reasonably priced. A rustic retreat.

La Grande Maison Road, Vale, Guernsey GY6 8LP

Tel 07781 440438
e-mail shelley@maisondebasvilla.co.uk
website www.maisondebasvilla.co.uk

Nearby beaches and many restaurants catering for families, wildlife
Location inland from Guernsey's north-west coast
Food breakfast
Price £-££
Rooms 4; king to twin in size, all with en-suite wet rooms (toiletries and towels provided), flat screen and FreeSat television, wi-fi, tea/coffee making facilities, wine glasses and a corkscrew, hairdryer, iron and ironing board available **Facilities** wi-fi, tennis court, extensive grounds
Credit cards not accepted
Children accepted
Disabled access unavailable
Pets not accepted
Closed never
Proprietors Shelley

Maison de Bas Villa

Country guesthouse

Owner Shelley brought up her large family in Guernsey, living in this grand Victorian house for 20 years before deciding to turn it into a guesthouse. The homely, welcoming feel still prevails – Shelley treats every guest like family. When we arrived we were greeted with a tray of home-made cupcakes in our room, and a personal letter from Shelley.

The bedrooms are homely and spacious – a mixture of traditional and modern design. The neutral, calm decoration in the rooms matches this homely feel. Two bookcases with what seemed like the family's stock of novels lined the walls, and made it feel as if we were staying in a spacious spare room. Adjoining wet rooms provide the modern twist, with sensor-lighting in the bathroom mirror and a special effort made with the natural toiletries. Everything was clean and well designed.

Breakfast is served in the grand Victorian dining room. It was above average, with inventive home-made jams, tasty eggs from Shelley's own hens, and charming mismatching tableware.

The grounds are extensive, great to walk around on a lovely day, and complete with a tennis court and Shelley's many dogs and cats. Maison de Bas Villa recently received a 'Silver Award' from the Guernsey Tourist Board.

Herm, near Guernsey GY1 3HR

Tel (01481) 750075
Fax (01481) 710066
e-mail hotel@herm.com
website www.herm.com

Nearby Shell Beach (200 yds/180 m); wildlife: puffins, dolphins and seals; coastal walks.
Location Herm island
Food breakfast, lunch, dinner
Prices ££-£££
Rooms 40; 18 in cottages, some on ground floor
Facilities 3 sitting rooms, 2 restaurants, 2 bars, conference room; garden, tennis, croquet, solar-heated swimming pool; beach
Credit cards DC, MC, V
Children welcome; over 9 only in restaurant for dinner
Disabled not suitable
Pets dogs accepted in 1 room
Closed Oct to Mar
Proprietors John and Julia Singer

The White House

Village hotel

Herm is 'an enchanting, self-sufficient time warp' says Fiona Duncan, our series editor. Its sole hotel, The White House, is like a step back in time. There are no televisions, clocks or telephones in the hotel, as they have been deemed inappropriate to the atmosphere of the island – Herm is car-free. You will hear the occasional tractor or the piping of oystercatchers but not much else.

The hotel has a great sea view, and is in a prime location. When the tide goes out over nearby Shell Beach, it really goes out, leaving a vast and fascinating waterless expanse of sand. Coastal walks in this area are lovely. If visiting from May to July keep an eye out for puffins.

The interior of the hotel is essentially an extended inn, but with attractive staircases and light, spacious rooms. There's a beautiful conservatory with a swimming pool surrounded by palms.

John and Julia Singer took over recently, so we're interested in reports. When Fiona visited the decoration was old-fashioned, and the place had something of a boarding-house atmosphere, that could have been improved, not with a complete overhaul, but with some artful updating.

Gorey Village, Jersey

Gorey Village, Jersey JE3 9FX

Tel (01534) 854285
Fax (01534) 854725
e-mail
reception@oldbankhousejersey.com
website
www.oldbankhousejersey.com

Nearby Grouville Bay – watersports; Royal Golf Club; Gorey Castle.
Location Gorey villages, close to Mont Orgueil
Food breakfast, afternoon tea
Prices £–££
Rooms 18 rooms; 4 twins, 11 doubles, 3 family rooms
Facilities bar, tea garden
Credit cards DC, MC, V
Children accepted
Disabled not suitable
Pets not accepted
Closed mid-Oct to mid-Apr
Manager June Lawlor
Proprietor Paul MacCallum

Old Bank House

Village guesthouse

On the fringe of picturesque Gorey Village, Old Bank House is steeped in history, taking its name from the merchant banking business run from the house when Gorey Harbour was one of Jersey's main trading centres. Gorey Village is lovely and quaint: we were held up in a traffic jam just outside at a 'ducks crossing' zone.

The best feature of Old Bank House is the secluded tea garden, which serves Jersey cream teas all day. This is a lovely outdoor area, surrounded by lush greenery and white sun umbrellas, which on the glorious day we visited, seemed Mediterranean, and very romantic.

The rooms are small – white in colour – but comfortable, and most have views. The family room at the top of the hotel is the best; it is a lot more spacious, brighter and has lovely sloped ceilings.

Old Bank House is within easy walking distance of several interesting sights, including the famous Mont Orgueil – Mount Pride – which was once the military headquarters of Jersey, and housed Sir Walter Raleigh when he was governor. There are also plenty of restaurants and bars within walking distance.

St Aubin, Jersey

Clifden 1, Mont Les Vaux, St Aubin
JE3 8AF

Tel 01534 741350
email clifden@hotmail.co.uk
website
www.jerseyyurtholidays.com

Nearby St. Aubin village: bank, post office, supermarket, beauticians, taxi hire, bike hire, art and craft shops, restaurants; the Railway Walk, beaches.
Location situated on terraced cotils, overlooking St Aubin's bay
Food self-catering – condiments available to buy **Price** ££ **Rooms** 3 yurts, 1 double bed, 2 with king sized beds, all with wood-burning stove, BBQ, picnic table, sunloungers
Facilities bathroom has 3 showers – one for each yurt – a toilet and 2 wash basins; hairdryer and natural toiletries available, books, games and toys to borrow, hot tub
Credit cards not accepted **Children** welcome **Disabled** unsuitable **Pets** not accepted **Closed** never
Managers Cath and Andy Mesch

Clifden Yurts

Beach yurts

'Glamping' is the new camping – appealing to young and old alike – and these yurts are one of many local visitor attractions that show how wrong it is to think of the Channel Islands as old-fashioned.

Set into the hill opposite St Aubin these three luxury yurts bring hotel comfort to lovers of the outdoors. The circular tents are comfortable and cosy, with double beds, furniture and a log-burning stove for chilly nights. Each one, and its fittings, is designed to be eco-friendly, making the whole experience as 'green' as possible.

Matching their names, Ship Ahoy, Forest Green and Harbour Retreat, the yurts are kitted out with vintage and home-made accessories. Decorations such as handmade lavender bags adorn the walls, apple crates become bedside tables, ladders are turned into towel rails and potato boxes make quirky mirror frames.

The lavatory and shower block is thoughtfully designed, and gleaming clean, as is the communal kitchen 'The Lookout', which has home-grown ingredients to purchase, and a panoramic window with views of the sea. There is an eco-friendly but romantic hot tub installed at the top of the site, again with views over St Aubin.

Many guests are often avid walkers and cyclists, as Clifden is situated perfectly for exploring Jersey's amazing coastline.

St Brelade, Jersey

Le Boulevard, St Aubin's Harbour, St Brelade, Jersey JE3 8AB

Tel (01534) 741585
Fax (01534) 499460
e-mail
wakeup@harbourviewjersey.com
website
www.harbourviewjersey.com

Nearby Railway Walk to Corbiere Lighthouse; airport (10 mins); St Helier (15 mins).
Location overlooking St Aubins Harbour; 10 minute drive from airport **Food** breakfast, lunch, dinner
Prices £-££
Rooms 16; 12 double/twin, 2 singles, 2 suites for up to 5; all rooms have central heating, satellite TV, hairdryer, most have harbour views
Facilities breakfast room, wi-fi; sun terrace
Credit cards AE, DC, MC, V
Children accepted
Disabled not suitable
Pets well-behaved dogs accepted
Closed never
Proprietor Kelly Keadell

Harbour View

Harbourside guesthouse

Modest prices, plus the view of St Aubin's Harbour basin and, beyond, the expansive bay, combine to make this possibly Jersey's most charming budget place. From the long, thin garden out front, you can watch the rise and fall of the tide and the comings and goings of the boats. The garden is eclectically – perhaps eccentrically – planted and furnished by owner Kelly, who is not just a people-person, but a bit of a character. Through an unassuming entrance you find a similarly unassuming reception area, which is unlike any hotel, B&B or anything else we can think of. Adjacent is Danny's restaurant, and up a dark and uninviting staircase (which Kelly plans to improve) are the rooms, under an ongoing refurbishment plan. They offer fair space and comfort for the price charged, with cheery stripped bedspreads.

Danny's restaurant focuses on flavour. Danny the chef works hard to be imaginative with his bistro-style food and the place was buzzing when we visited. One jolly celebration continued with squeals of laughter until some time after eleven – not a problem for residents, we were assured, because diners are always eased out before midnight. Of course, this place comes into its own during warm summer weather, when you can loll in the garden.

St Brelade, Jersey

La Neuve Route, St Brelade, Jersey
JE3 8BS

Tel (01534) 741426
Fax (01534) 745501
e-mail
lahaulemanor@jerseymail.co.uk
website www.lahaulemanor.com

Nearby La Lande d'Ouest; Portelet Common; St Catherine's Wood; Jersey War Tunnels.
Location St Aubin's Bay, close to airport and Elizabeth ferry terminal
Food breakfast
Prices ££-£££
Rooms 16; all rooms have TV, hairdryer, wi-fi, most have views; 1 self-catering apartment
Facilities outdoor swimming pool, Jacuzzi, hot tub
Credit cards AE, MC, V
Children accepted
Disabled no special facilities
Pets not accepted
Closed Nov to mid-Mar
Manager Craig Dickson
Proprietor Michael Cushion

La Haule Manor

Village manor hotel

A grand, sturdy exterior combined with a romantic, stylish interior gives La Haule its special charm. Overlooking St Aubin's Bay and Fort and originally dating back to the early 15th century, it was restored once in 1796 and again a few years ago. The owners have succeeded in combining the traditional manor with typically French style and decoration. The mood is romantic and relaxing, and, unsurprisingly, La Haule is popular with honeymooners.

The spacious bedrooms have high ceilings and are decorated in neutral colours, with ornate vintage furniture. We liked the mirrors in the bathrooms, the elegant baths and the impressive chandeliers. All bedrooms are different and most have sea views. The recently refurbished dining room is modern, with an award-winning breakfast bar that caters to all appetites.

There's a lovely, lush sunken garden, where guests can play games or just relax and enjoy the view. Each day there are guided walks around the island. A peaceful, spacious place.

Bray, Berkshire

The Waterside Inn

Riverside restaurant-with-rooms

The world-famous cuisine of Alain Roux is the thing at this elegant Thames-side restaurant, these days run by Alain's son Michel – so much so that people tend to overlook the existence of 13 superb bedrooms upstairs and in cottages nearby. They are individually designed, in a French style, feminine and elegant rather than glitzy. Midweek package prices for a room and dinner are, relatively speaking, value for money, given the quality. This is a half-page entry only because super-luxury dining is a little, but only a little, outside our usual territory. It would be easy to fill several pages describing the charm, the service, and of course the sublime food.

Ferry Road, Bray, Berkshire SL6 2AT

Tel 01628 620691
e-mail reservations@waterside-inn.co.uk **website** www.waterside-inn.co.uk **Food** lunch, dinner
Price £££ **Closed** Monday, Tuesday; from 26th Dec for 4 weeks
Proprietor Alain Roux (Chef Patron)

Brighton, East Sussex

Hotel du Vin

Town hotel

Down a narrow cobbled street, tucked back from the seafront, a collection of part-gothic-styled buildings make up this member of the stylish du Vin micro-chain. In the main building, bizarre gargoyles watch over a double-height hall and a heavily carved staircase. Through glass windows and doors, you can see the Bistro, done out in wine-related pictures, floor-to-ceiling windows and bunches of dried hops. Bedrooms facing the central courtyard have chalky blue-green wood siding, a beach-house style, and inside, are decorated in soft blue and sand tones. In the bathrooms, scroll top baths are mounted in driftwood and old railway sleepers.

Ship Street, Brighton, East Sussex BN1 1AD

Tel (01273) 718588
Fax (01273) 718599
website www.hotelduvin.com
Food breakfast, lunch, dinner
Price £££
Closed never
Manager Simon Maguire

Faversham, Kent

Read's

Restaurant-with-rooms

We felt relaxed and content as we pulled up in front of this elegant Georgian house. At the door, bags are taken and you are ushered immediately to your room.

Ours was large, elegant and traditional with graceful bay windows, but we thought the decanter of cream sherry and the repro Sheraton furniture somewhat old-fashioned. The bar/sitting room, where guests gather for drinks before dinner, could also do with judicious updating.

However, Read's has integrity. Rona and David Pitchford bought the house 11 years ago and David, the chef, has had a Michelin star for 20 years. Consistent quality and attention to detail: a well-run place.

Macknade Manor, Canterbury Road, Faversham, Kent ME13 8XE

Tel 01795 535344 **Fax** 01795 591200 **e-mail** enquiries@reads.com **website** www.reads.com **Food** breakfast, lunch, dinner **Price** £££ **Closed** 2 weeks in Sept, Christmas/Boxing Day, a week in Jan **Proprietors** Rona and David Pitchford

Gurnard, Isle of Wight

The Little Gloster

Restaurant-with-rooms

Gurnard is curious: suburban roads; contemporary houses and Edwardian villas; seaside chalets and beach huts. In among them, right on the sea, next to the sailing club, is The Little Gloster – quite a new venture (opened 2010). Chef-proprietor Ben Cooke's grandfather once owned The Gloster in Cowes.

The modern, purpose-designed building is based around the restaurant with Ben hands-on in the kitchen. It's an open, clean white space, with large windows maximising views over the Solent. The menu focuses on fresh, local fish. Holly, front of house, creates a friendly atmosphere.

In an annexe with a separate entrance are three immaculate white bedrooms, done in seaside-chic style.

31 Marsh Road, Gurnard, Isle of Wight PO31 8JQ

Tel 01983 200299
e-mail info@thelittlegloster.com
website www.thelittlegloster.com
Food breakfast, lunch, dinner
Price £££
Closed 1st Jan – 12th Feb
Proprietors Cooke family

Herstmonceux, Sussex

Wartling, Herstmonceux, East Sussex BN27 1RY

Tel 01323 832590
email accom@wartlingplace.prestel.co.uk
Food breakfast, dinner by prior arrangement
Price ££ **Closed** never
Proprietors Barry and Rowena Gittoes

Wartling Place Country House **Country guesthouse**

Rowena and Barry Gittoes run their upmarket B&B in a substantial former eight-bedroom rectory – room for guests and hosts to be separate – guests have the first floor, and their own drawing room and dining room, and there's a 3-acre garden. Tasteful country house decoration and furnishing, including some genuine antiques. This is solid, unflashy quality, with personal but not intrusive attention, backed by 17 years of experience as we went to press. Wartling is a small, peaceful village on the edge of the Pevensey Levels nature reserve and there's much else of interest nearby – this is '1066 country'.

Kintbury, Berkshire

53 Station Road, Kintbury, Berkshire RG17 9UT

Tel 01488 658263
e-mail info@dundasarms.co.uk
website www.dundasarms.co.uk
Food breakfast, snack lunch, dinner
Price ££
Closed never
Proprietor Tom Moran

The Dundas Arms
Village inn

At first, we were distinctly underwhelmed by our awkwardly shaped room, its sombre furnishings and clock that told the wrong time. In the cramped bathroom, the basin was so shallow that water bounced off the porcelain and on to the floor. But next morning we were charmed by the sunshine on our private terrace bordering the River Kennet .

Much of the emphasis is on the food, served in two comfortable dining rooms, but it's still the quirky original bar that acts as the focal point – this is an upgraded pub that can still bring in the locals. The Dundas Arms is not perfect, but the team is cheerful, and its heart is definitely in the right place. At £75 per night, pretty fair value.

London

The Mayflower Hotel

City hotel

Trudging past the dire Earl's Court budget hotels en route to The Mayflower, you will feel relief at the sight of its smart, freshly painted façade. No disappointment, either, once inside: to the left, an airy bar/sitting room; to the right, a spacious, calm, sophisticated reception area.

Our reporter's room was tiny, but perfectly formed. In a clever move that makes this budget address feel both hip and characterful, the rooms have been enlivened with Oriental artefacts, carved wooden cupboards and mirrored bedheads, silk cushions and velvet bedspreads, plus attractive wooden blinds and sweeping curtains.

Our reporter reflected that the Mayflower stands out 'like an Aladdin's lamp in a junk shop amongst budget central London hotels.'

26-28 Trebovir Road, London SW5 9NJ

Tel 020 7370 0991
Fax 020 7370 0994
e-mail info@mayflower-group.co.uk
website www.themayflowerhotel.co.uk
Food breakfast **Price** ££-££££
Closed never
Manager Frank Davies

London

The Sumner

City hotel

The previous owners, the Palgan family, completed renovations of this Georgian town house in 2006, when it opened as The Sumner. The results of their £1.5m investment are impressive – the place is immaculate and stylishly done.

The sitting room is particularly striking – its high Georgian ceilings and original cornicing are complemented by a beautiful wooden floor, chunky dark wood furniture and inviting, deep sofas.

Bedrooms are generously proportioned, particularly those on the ground and first floors, which have very high ceilings. Bathrooms are spotless: white-tiled, with a block of turquoise colour.

This hotel is now under new management, and we would welcome reports.

54 Upper Berkeley Street, Marble Arch, London W1H 7QR

Tel (020) 7723 2244
Fax (0870) 705 8767
e-mail reservataions@thesumner.com
website www.thesumner.com
Food breakfast **Price** £££
Closed never
Manager Rohit

London

Twenty Nevern Square, London
SW5 9PD

Tel (020) 7565 9555
Fax (020) 7565 9444
e-mail
hotel@twentynevernsquare.co.uk
website www.20nevernsquare.co.uk
Food breakfast, 24 hour room service **Price** ££ **Closed** never
Manager Sulaiman Saloojee

Twenty Nevern Square

Town house hotel

Peace and tranquility aren't two words usually associated with London but, just around the corner from bustling Earl's Court, Twenty Nevern Square is suprisingly calm and cosy.

Decorated in a combination of colonial and Italian influences, rooms have a feeling of understated luxury. Natural fabrics have been used throughout; silk curtains, wooden floors and hessian carpets blend nicely with smart patterned bedspreads. One hundred metres of silk has been used in decorating the Chinese room, with oriental-print cushions and floor-to-ceiling white and navy drapes. Bathrooms are brick, smart and done out entirely in marble.

Breakfast is served downstairs in the conservatory-style restaurant.

Lymington, Hampshire

14-15 High Street, Lymington,
Hampshire, SO41 9AA

Tel (01590) 677123 **Fax** (01590) 677756 **e-mail** enquiries@stanwellhousehotel.co.uk **website** www.stanwellhousehotel.co.uk **Food** breakfast, brunch, lunch, afternoon tea, dinner **Price** £££ **Closed** never **Proprietors** Robert Milton and Victoria Crowe

Stanwell House

Town hotel

On Lymington's attractive High Street, an Italianate stone-flagged courtyard stretches the length of this building, affording inviting views from the street of a glass-roofed sitting room; on one side of the entrance is a country clothing shop, on the other a seafood restaurant in 17thC style.

This quite stylish hotel has been run by Robert Milton and Victoria Crowe for five years. When they took over in 2008, they redecorated, designing the suites individually and adding two new suites with roof terraces.

The candle-lit seafood restaurant and the bedrooms in the main house are theatrical. Dramatic walls, rich hangings and piles of colourful cushions vie for attention. The place attracts a youngish clientèle.

Petersfield, Hampshire

20 Dragon Street, Petersfield, Hampshire GU31 4JJ

Tel 01730 262030
email jsw.restaurant@btconnect.com
website www.jswrestaurant.com
Food breakfast, lunch, dinner
Price ££
Closed 2 weeks in Jan, 2 weeks in Jun
Proprietor Jake Watkins

JSW

Restaurant-with-rooms

An award-winning restaurant in a bustling Hampshire town, JSW also has four double rooms which follow the kitchen's 'stylish yet simple' mantra. Rooms are comfortable with character, both light enough to be attractive in summer and cosily well-heated in winter. The Egyptian cotton sheets and towels are a treat.

After the high point of dinner, breakfast is a simple continental affair served in your room, with an emphasis on fresh fruit and breads, as well as pastries from the renowned Rungis Market in Paris.

Petworth, West Sussex

Lodsworth, Petworth, West Sussex, GU28 9BP

Tel (01798) 861281
website www.halfwaybridge.co.uk
Food breakfast, lunch, dinner
Prices £££
Closed never
Proprietors Sam and Janet Bakose

The Halfway Bridge

Restaurant-with-rooms

Sam and Janet Bakose hit the spot with the Crab and Lobster at Sidlesham (page 142) and have done it again with this reinvented restaurant-with-rooms between Petworth and Midhurst. It's ideal for a South Downs walking weekend, for browsing the antique shops in Petworth, or for visiting Cowdray Park.

The pleasing 17thC coaching inn has been immaculately restored by Sam and Janet, making it contemporary-stylish but relaxed. The six bedrooms, all different, are smart, comfortable and spacious. There are quirky design features such as a row of old beams upended to form panelling.

When we visited, the food was as expected for the price: local fish and game alongside Mediterranean dishes.

Petworth, West Sussex

The Old Railway Station Bed-and-breakfast

If you've ever dreamed about stepping back in time and taking a great rail journey, now you can do just that – in West Sussex. The Old Railway Station provides unique accommodation in either the original Petworth Railway Station building or in one of four Pullman carriages.

The station building, Grade II listed, is impressive and welcoming. The former waiting-room now contains the breakfast room and sitting-room, and has vaulted ceilings and original ticket office windows

Bedrooms and bathrooms are narrow, but very long. Original furnishings, marquetry in the walls and antique luggage and clocks all add to the charm.

Inside the main building the bedrooms are spacious and well-fitted out.

Petworth, West Sussex GU28 0JF

Tel (01798) 342346
email info@old-station.co.uk
website www.old-station.co.uk
Food breakfast, afternoon tea
Prices ££-£££
Closed Christmas
Proprietors Gudmund Olafsson and Catherine Stormont

Seaview, Isle of Wight

Seaview Hotel

Seaside hotel

If you like breezy, old-fashioned English seaside resorts, you will love sailing-mad Seaview. The Seaview was bought by Brian Gardener in 2003. Since then a whole new wing has been built, adding a further seven rooms, and greatly improving disabled facilities. The whole hotel has been thoroughly refurbished and redecorated.

There are two public bars, and two restaurants, both serving the same menu. One, called the Sunshine Room, but actually painted blue, is an airy room with a contemporary feel. The other is more formal, and contains The Naval Bar and terrace. We would welcome comments on the food and on whether the high standards and personal service enjoyed here previously are being maintained.

High Street, Seaview, Isle of Wight PO34 5EX

Tel (01983) 612711
Fax (01983) 613729
e-mail reception@seaviewhotel.co.uk
website www.seaviewhotel.co.uk
Food breakfast, lunch, dinner; room service **Price** ££ **Closed** never
Proprietor Brian Gardener

Totford, Hampshire

The Woolpack

Village inn

It stands in the smallest hamlet in Hampshire, possibly in England, in the Candover Valley. Built around 1880, the Grade I-listed brick-and-flint building is simple but full of character.

Inside, it's as appealing as outside, with room for armchairs and a pool table in the spacious bar. Next to it is a dining room with a raised open fire. Or you can choose to eat in the extension that cleverly encases the exterior walls of the pub and is designed to look like stables.

The rooms, found at the back of the inn in converted outbuildings, could be improved. In ours, Snipe, the exposed brick-and-flint walls also included swathes of ugly concrete and the furniture was basic.

Totford, near Northington, Alresford, Hampshire SO24 9TJ

Tel 0845 2938066/01962 734184 **Fax** 0845 2938055 **email** info@thewoolpackinn.co.uk **website** www.thewoolpackinn.co.uk **Food** breakfast, lunch, dinner; bar snacks, picnic hampers, Sunday lunch **Price** £££ **Closed** evening of Christmas Day **Proprietor** Andrew Cooper

Ventnor, Isle of Wight

The Hambrough Hotel

Seaside hotel

Ventnor is a pretty Victorian cliff-top town with winter gardens, an esplanade, a sandy beach and a shack selling crab and lobster. The Hambrough stands between the High Street and the seafront, overlooking the Cascade Gardens and the harbour. It has seven spacious bedrooms, a restaurant and a bar. It doesn't aim to do too much, but what it does, it hopes to do well and, by and large, it succeeds.

The restaurant continues to make waves locally and the five-course, tasting menu comes with well-chosen wines. A serious kitchen opens off an all-white dining room.

Our inspector had absolute quiet in her spacious room. Her only quibbles: the service lacked warmth; and the overall feel is stylish rather than characterful.

Hambrough Road, Ventnor, Isle of Wight, PO38 1SQ

Tel (01983) 856333
e-mail info@thehambrough.com
website www.thehambrough.com
Food breakfast, lunch, dinner
Price £££-££££ **Closed** never; restaurant only, 2 weeks Nov, 3 weeks Jan, 2 weeks Apr **Manager** Johanna Rogers

Wickham, Hampshire

Old House

Village hotel

The Old House possesses much that we look for: an interesting setting – at a corner of the main square of one of the finest villages in Hampshire; a superb building; a delightful garden; an immaculately kept interior; an intimate bar; and attractive dining rooms, created from the original timber-framed outhouse and stables.

Bedrooms vary – some palatial, others with magnificent beams, many with original features, one or two rather cramped – but again a mood of civilized comfort prevails. Times are changing for the Old House, and it has changed hands several times in recent years. The decorations, the ambience and the British/Mediterranean menu have happily stayed largely the same and so, it seems, does the warmth of welcome.

The Square, Wickham, Hampshire
PO17 5JG

Tel (01329) 835870
Fax (01329) 835139
e-mail enquiries@oldhousehotel.co.uk
website www.oldhousehotel.co.uk
Food breakfast, lunch, dinner
Prices ££-£££ **Closed** never
Proprietor James Guess

Winchester, Hampshire

The Wykeham Arms

Town pub-with-rooms

'Enormously charming; tons of personality,' confirms our latest reporter. Tucked away in the oldest part of the city, with Winchester College yards away and the Cathedral close by, this is a well-frequented pub, and it's first-rate: 250 years old with four bars furnished with old school desks. Quirky character runs to the bedrooms, which are small and low-ceilinged, but each furnished in its own style, and accommodating all the usual facilities.

Breakfast is served upstairs, over the pub, in a pleasant, straightforward English country breakfast room with Windsor chairs and a fine collection of silver tankards. Hearty food at lunch time and an *à la carte* menu in the evenings; real ales and an impressive list of over 100 wines, changed regularly.

75 Kingsgate Street, Winchester,
Hampshire SO23 9PE

Tel (01962) 853834
email wykehamarms@fullers.co.uk
website www.wykehamarmswinchester.co.uk
Food breakfast, lunch, dinner
Price ££
Closed Christmas Day
Managers Jon Howard

Winkfield, Berkshire

The Winning Post

Country inn

During the week, this pub attracts people on business, but the majority of people drinking at the bar or dining are to do with the worlds of polo and racing – this is polo heartland, with major polo clubs and Ascot racecourse close at hand.

From the outside, the pub looks like a modest cottage but its interior is surprisingly spacious, cosy and characterful. Bedrooms are in a purpose-built nineties addition at the back of the building, and need to be more alluring to justify their price, their dated fittings and dull fabrics.

Staff are friendly and local. Food arrived swiftly and was a cut above the norm for such a place. Cooked breakfast (continental is included in the room price) is an extra £4.

Winkfield Street, Winkfield, Windsor, Berkshire SL4 4SW

Tel 01344 882242
email manager@winningpostwinkfield.co.uk
website www.winningpostwinkfield.co.uk **Food** breakfast, light lunch, lunch, dinner **Price** £££
Closed never
Proprietor Upham Pub Brewery

Yattendon, Berkshire

The Royal Oak

Village hotel

The Royal Oak is easy to find in the centre of the village of Yattendon.

Lest you mistake it for a mere pub, the sign on the front of this cottagey, mellow red-brick inn announces Hotel and Restaurant. Certainly, the Royal Oak is no longer a common-or-garden local (as it was when Oliver Cromwell reportedly ate there). Its two restaurants have a style and elegance not usually associated with ale and darts. But there is still a small bar where residents and non-residents alike can enjoy a choice of real ales.

Bedrooms are prettily decorated and equipped with every conceivable extra. Another attraction is the walled garden, full of colour and a delight during the summer.

The Square, Yattendon, Berkshire RG18 0UF

Tel 01635 201325
e-mail info@royaloakyattendon.com **website** www.royaloakyattendon.co.uk
Food breakfast, lunch, dinner
Price ££
Closed New Year's Eve
Proprietors Rob McGill

St Peter Port, Guernsey

Sunnycroft Hotel

Town guesthouse

This little hotel is well positioned in the heart of busy St Peter Port, close to shops and visitor attractions. It's a two-star hotel, so the smallish bedrooms are not unexpected. They are very clean and comfortable, ideal as a base from which to explore the local sights. Bright, cheery accessories are thoughtful and neutral walls lend a feeling of extra space – overall, they're relaxing and cosy. The balcony rooms have views over the garden and St Peter Port beyond.

Downstairs there are plenty of places in which to relax: on clear days the conservatory has views reaching as far as Herm and Sark. The bar area is friendly and welcoming. Guests say that for the price and location it's one of the best deals in town. You reach it by a climb up a large flight of stone steps.

5 Constitution Steps, St Peter Port,
Guernsey GY1 2PN

Tel (01481) 723008
Fax (01481) 712 225
e-mail sunnycroft@cwgsy.net
website www.sunnycrofthotel.com
Food breakfast
Price ££
Closed never
Proprietor Vista Hotels

St Peter Port, Guernsey

The Yacht Inn

Seaside town hotel

In a great location for exploring busy St Peter Port, overlooking the Albert Marina. Inside, it's cosy and informal, decorated well in a contemporary style. The dining room has (tasteful) brown leather chairs and – like the rest of the hotel – a distinctly pleasant nautical feel.

Clean, contemporary bedrooms – again with brown leather and light walls – have all the latest fittings. Sea-facing rooms are more expensive, but worth it.

The downstairs bar is the highlight, appealing to young business people who like its relaxed feel and the in-house DJ. Recently re-styled, the tables are curvy, and a copper bar compliments the nautical theme. The restaurant is popular with non-residents.

South Esplanade, St Peter Port,
Guernsey GY1 1AN

Tel 01481 715488
e-mail info@theyacht.gg
website www.theyacht.gg
Food breakfast, dinner
Price £-££
Closed Christmas Day, Boxing Day
Proprietor Andy

Area introduction

The ancient kingdom of Wales, the Midlands industrial heartland and the mostly flat counties of Cambridgeshire, Norfolk and Suffolk are the main ingredients of this section. It also includes the fashionable counties of Gloucestershire and Oxfordshire, and the home countries to the west and north of London (Buckinghamshire, Hertfordshire, Essex and so on). Wales and East Anglia have always been important tourist regions, as are Oxfordshire and Gloucestershire because they contain Oxford and the Cotswolds. But imaginative tourist developments in Midland industrial cities (for example, Birmingham) and historic centres such as Ironbridge Gorge in Shropshire now also means that the Midlands, far from being tourist deserts, are increasingly important. Our selection of special places to stay in all of these has grown accordingly since the last edition.

Below are some useful back-up places to try if our main selections are fully booked:

Wales

The Bear Hotel
Country hotel, Crickhowell
Tel 01873 810408
www.bearhotel.co.uk
Comfortable hotel in the heart of the Brecon Beacons.

Fairyhill
Restaurant-with-rooms, Reynoldston Tel 01792 390139 www.fairyhill.net
Peaceful retreat with award-winning restaurant.

England

The Riverside Inn
Country inn, Cound
Tel 01952 510900
www.theriversideinn.net
Charming inn with great views of the River Severn.

Barnsdale Lodge
Farmhouse hotel, Exton
Tel 01572 724678
www.barnsdalelodge.co.uk
Extended farmhouse on the shore of Rutland Water.

The Five Alls
Restaurant-with-rooms, Filkins Tel 01367 860875
www.thefiveallsfilkins.co.uk
Picturesque Cotswold restaurant-with-rooms.

Old Swan & Minster Mill Town hotel, Minster Lovell Tel 01993 774441
www.oldswanandminster-mill.com Traditional and contemporary rooms.

Lion + Pheasant
Townhouse hotel, Shrewsbury Tel 01743 770345 www.lionandpheas-ant.co.uk
Historic inn.

Crazy Bear
Village hotel, Stadhampton
Tel 01865 890714
www.crazybeargroup.co.uk/stadhampton
Off the wall.

Godwick Hall
Town hotel, Godwick
Tel 01328 701948
www.godwickhall.co.uk
Country house with The Great Barn for events.

Bruisyard Hall
Country house, Saxmundham
Tel 01728 639000
www.bruisyardhall.co.uk
Countryside bed-and-breakfast, perfect for events.

Linden House
Restaurant-with-rooms, Stansted Tel 01279 813003
www.lindenhousestansted.co.uk
Smart, trendy restaurant and stylish rooms.

Aberaeron, Ceredigion

Pen Cei, Aberaeron, Ceredigion
SA46 0BA

Tel (01545) 570 755
Fax (01545) 570 762
e-mail info@harbour-master.com
website www.harbour-master.com

Location off A487 in centre of town on the quay; with ample car parking
Food breakfast, lunch, dinner
Price ££
Rooms 13; 1 suite, 10 double, 2 can be twin, 2 single all with bath and shower (1 with hand held); all rooms have TV, DVD player, hairdryer, some have phone and wi-fi, others have broadband
Facilities dining room, bar, bikes
Credit cards MC, V
Children accepted in the cottage
Disabled 1 room is adapted, and 3 others acessible by lift
Pets not accepted
Closed Christmas day
Proprietors Menna and Glyn Heulyn

Harbourmaster

Seaside inn

Back in the 1950s, an eccentric resident of Aberaeron decided to give each of her five properties a different brightly coloured coat of paint.The idea caught on, and today the purpose-built Regency harbour town is an uplifting riot of colour, where The Harbourmaster Hotel makes a splash all its own with a brilliant cobalt blue external livery. Opened in 2005, it is, as you would expect, a former harbourmaster's residence.

The ground floor is given over to eating and drinking, with a curving bar, informal dining room and inventive menu featuring local produce, including the day's catch, Welsh black beef and tapas. At breakfast, freshly baked bread or Welsh laverbread.

The light, tasteful interior decoration manages to be contemporary 'cool' as well as homely; an eyecatching feature is the listed spiral staircase. Upstairs there are seven bright, modern bedrooms, fine for a stopover. Best is the one at the top, from where the harbourmaster once kept an eye on all three harbours under his control in Cardigan Bay. No children under five.

Bontnewydd, Gwynedd

Bontnewydd, Caernarfon, Gwynedd
LL54 7YF

Tel (01286) 830214
e-mail info@plasdinas.co.uk
website www.plasdinas.co.uk

Nearby Caernarfon Castle; Portmeirion; Welsh Highland Railway; Snowdon.
Location 2.5 miles from Caernarfon, ample parking
Food breakfast, dinner (Tue to Sat only – book in advance)
Price £££
Rooms 9 double/twin, all with bath/shower; all rooms have TV, wi-fi **Facilities** dining room, sitting room, bar, fireplace; gardens
Credit cards MC, V
Children not accepted
Disabled 1 ground-floor room
Pets dogs accepted in Buckley or South rooms
Closed Christmas to New Year
Proprietors Neil and Marco

Plas Dinas

Country house hotel

It could easily be overbearing, but this elegant, Regency-style gentleman's house (though some parts date back 400 years) is the kind of place where you can be yourself. As we went to press new owner-hosts had just taken over from Andy and Julian. We guess that they will welcome guests in the same friendly, but not intrusive way.

Downstairs, the highlights are the drawing room and the atmospheric Gun Room (private dining for small groups) with its royal memorabilia. Upstairs, the mostly spacious bedrooms are decorated in either traditional country house style, or modern 'boutique' style, with bold wallpaper. All combine antiques with contemporary comforts. Each has its own character, with the kind of individual touch we look for, including the amusingly masculine Bachelor Room. Views are of the 15 acres of grounds to the Menai Strait, or over the unspoilt countryside.

The house, down a 100-m long drive, once belonged to the Armstrong-Joneses, the family of Lord Snowdon, who married the Queen's late sister, Princess Margaret. She stayed here, and Prince William has visited for a private lunch in the Gun Room.

Brechfa, Carmarthenshire

Brechfa, Carmarthenshire
SA32 7RA

Tel (01267) 202332
Fax (01267) 202437
e-mail info@wales-country-hotel.co.uk **website** www.wales-country-hotel.co.uk

Nearby Kidwelly Castle; Llansteffan Castle; Brecon Beacons, National Botanical Gardens of Wales.
Location 10 miles (16 km) NE of Carmarthen, on B4310, in village; with ample car parking
Food breakfast, dinner
Price ££
Rooms 5; 3 double, 1 twin, 1 4-poster, all with bath; all rooms have TV, DVD, minibar, hairdryer
Facilities sitting room, dining room, restaurant, 2 bars, microbrewery; garden
Credit cards MC, V
Children welcome over 12
Disabled not suitable
Pets by arrangement
Closed rarely
Proprietors Stephen and Annabel Thomas

Ty Mawr

Country hotel

Firmly at right angles to the main street of this tiny village on the fringe of Brechfa Forest, and by the River Marlais, Ty Mawr has a pretty garden and fine views of the surrounding wooded hillsides. It was bought in 2004 by Stephen and Annabel Thomas, who completely refurbished it while preserving the oak beams, stone walls and tiled floors that proclaim the building's three and a bit centuries' tenure of this glorious spot.

The public rooms are cosy and cheerful and include an immaculate bar with smart pine fittings, and a comfy sitting room with an open log fire. The long slate-floored restaurant looks out on to the garden and, candle-lit in the evenings, is where the chef's skill in the kitchen shows in earnest: fresh, usually Welsh, ingredients are assembled without undue fuss but with plenty of imagination. The wines are well-chosen and offered at eminently reasonable prices.

Upstairs, the bedrooms are bright, comfortable and pleasantly rustic, and breakfast in the morning answers to appetites ranging from the merely peckish to the downright ravenous. The flowers in the garden tubs are quite impressive, but it's worth remembering that the National Botanical Garden of Wales is nearby.

Builth Wells, Powys

Cwmbach, Newbridge-on-Wye
Builth Wells, Powys, LD2 3RT

Tel (01982) 552493
e-mail post@the-drawing-room.co.uk
website www.the-drawing-room.co.uk

Nearby Elan Valley walks; Brecon Beacons; Cambrian and Black Mountains
Location off A470 in Builth Wells with ample car parking
Food breakfast, dinner
Price ££££
Rooms 3 doubles, 2 with bath, 1 with shower; all rooms have TV/DVD player, internet
Facilities dining room, 2 sitting rooms, garden
Credit cards MC, V
Children not accepted
Disabled not suitable
Pets not accepted
Closed Sun, Mon except bank holidays – best to ring and check
Proprietors Colin and Melanie Dawson

The Drawing Room

Restaurant-with-rooms

This is one of Wales's growing group of exceptional restaurants with rooms, where commitment and attention to detail are second to none. Colin and Melanie Dawson have converted a Georgian house into a small restaurant, two sitting rooms and three guest bedrooms named after Colin's grandchildren Phoebe, Otis and Oliver. The bedrooms are contemporary in style, one decorated bright red and quite masculine, the other two more feminine. They are not large, but perfectly formed and whilst lounging in the bath (one of them is a slipper bath) you can watch the hill sheep grazing opposite.

Colin and Melanie have decorated this property beautifully and with great attention to detail. Although the sitting rooms are small you don't mind because they are immaculately furnished with comfy sofas, chairs, roaring fires and interesting objets d'art. However, the emphasis here is on the food – pleasant as it is to get good bedrooms too. Both Colin and Melanie are chefs, and their food wins many plaudits. When we visited the menu included a ragout of sea bass, salmon and black bream with langoustine, fennel and leeks as well as a fillet of local Welsh beef. Make sure you book well in advance as this place gets booked up quickly.

Capel Garmon, Conwy

Capel Garmon, near Betws-y-Coed, Llanrwst, Conwy LL26 0RE

Tel 01690 710507
Fax 01690 710 681
e-mail enquiries@tyfhotel.co.uk
website www.tyfhotel.co.uk

Nearby Conwy Castle; Caernarfon Castle; Bodnant Gardens; Llanberis
Location just off the A5, head towards Capel Garmon/Nebo, 1.5 miles (2.5 km) up the hill, Tan-y-Foel is on the left
Food breakfast, dinner
Price ££
Rooms 6 doubles all with bath and shower; all rooms have TV, hairdrier, phone
Facilities sitting room, dining room; garden
Credit cards MC, V
Children welcome over 7
Disabled not suitable
Pets not accepted
Closed Dec and Jan
Proprietors Mr and Mrs Pitman

Tan-y-Foel

Country guesthouse

Parts date back to the 16thC; parts are highly contemporary and it pulls it off remarkably well. The interior is a riot of vibrant colours cleverly kept in check with beautiful furnishings and distressed paint work.

The intimate reception rooms are decorated in peaceful earth tones, for relaxing in with a drink before dinner. The gardens are secluded and well looked after, but not too manicured, perfectly in keeping with the ruggedness of the country beyond.

All the rooms are individually decorated, comfortable, out of the ordinary. Interesting objets d'art are placed on shelves or hang on the walls making you feel as if you should be somewhere more exotic, certainly farther afield than Wales. The food is adventurous and has earned many awards.

Mediterranean influences contrast with traditional Welsh dishes and classic French ones. A highly original hotel for people who want something out of the ordinary in Wales.

Crickhowell, Powys

Crickhowell, Powys, NP8 1RH

Tel (01874) 730371
Fax (01874) 730463
e-mail calls@gliffaeshotel.com
website www.gliffaeshotel.com

Nearby Brecon Beacons National Park, River Usk, Abergavenny
Location off A40 in own large grounds with ample parking
Food breakfast, lunch, dinner, afternoon tea,
Price £££
Rooms 23; all doubles, 5 can be twin, all rooms have shower, some have bath, all rooms have phone, TV, hairdryer, some have DVD player **Facilities** dining room, sitting room, drawing room, conference room, conservatory garden, terrace, fishing
Credit Cards MC, V
Children accepted
Disabled no special facilities
Pets accepted
Closed Jan
Proprietors James and Susie Suter, and Peta Brabner

Gliffaes

Country house hotel

We've known about Gliffaes for many years and hesitated to put it in the guide despite its fine reputation because it seemed a little large (23 bedrooms), a little imposing (quite a grand Victorian-Italianate country pile); but above all not especially relaxed or personal. Then we dropped in by chance one day and changed our minds.

It's a superb example of a family-run (now third generation) country house hotel: a stunning location; caring, hands-on management; unpretentious yet with high standards. You will probably take away memories of the lovely views from the terrace, grounds falling steeply to the rushing Usk; and of the large grounds with exotic plantings. You might also catch a fish: the hotel has a mile and a half of highly regarded salmon and trout fishing on the Usk.

The decoration is traditional yet stylish. Most of the homely-smart country house style bedrooms are spacious, and one has a four-poster bed. Dinner is a smartish occasion – guests change, but into 'country casual' clothes, not black tie. The food is good, much of it from local suppliers. Tea is the most lavish spread you are likely to see for a while.

Denbigh, Denbighshire

Llandyrnog, Denbigh LL16 4LA

Tel 01824 790732
e-mail info@pentremawrcountry-house.co.uk **website** www.pentremawrcountryhouse.co.uk

Nearby Denbigh castle; Horseshoe Pass; Chester; Snowdonia.
Location from Denbigh take Llandyrnog turn-off. Exit for Bodari at roundabout, then take lane on left after 50 yds. **Food** breakfast, dinner
Price £-£££ **Rooms** 5 doubles and twins; all with TV, DVD player, iPod dock, hairdryer, 1 with private patio and hot tub, 5 outdoor luxury tents with private hot tub terraces, bathrooms, underfloor heating
Facilities restaurant, drawing room, study, conservatory, swimming pool, hot tubs, fishing, parking, DVD library **Credit cards** MC, V
Children accepted over 12 **Disabled** wide-doored rooms in lodges
Pets welcome, owners have dogs
Closed Christmas
Proprietors Bre and Graham Carrington-Sykes

Pentre Mawr Country House **Country house**

Pentre Mawr offers a great mix of two things we love: old-fashioned, excellent service and individual character. It's an elegant white house which has been in the family for over 400 years, surrounded by 200 acres of woodland and meadows. Owners Bre and Graham greet every arrival with Buck's Fizz and afternoon tea: providing a mere hint at how 'spoilt rotten' you'll feel after a stay here.

The place has a feeling of being tirelessly worked at. Bedrooms vary in size, but all doubles have king-size beds. More modern, minimalist styles can be found in a few of the rooms, but the attention to detail is impressive everywhere.

Outside, there's an ultra-fashionable 'glamping' option: five tents which look military from the outside, but are truly opulent within, with king-size beds, underfloor heating, tiled bathrooms, en-suite hot tubs: the works. A Michelin-graded dinner is served either at a huge grand dining table or in the more private conservatory. A full Welsh breakfast 'to die for' is served in the pretty morning room.

Despite all of this perfection, the atmosphere at Pentre Mawr is friendly, not formal. A guest describes it as a 'home from home' and the personalities of Bre and Graham shine through: they are thoughtful, welcoming and overall excellent hosts.

Eglwysfach, Powys

Eglwysfach, Machynlleth, Powys
SY20 8TA

Tel (01654) 781209
Fax (01654) 781366
e-mail info@ynyshir-hall.co.uk
website www.ynyshir-hall.co.uk

Nearby Llyfnant valley; Aberystwyth.
Location 11 miles (18 km) NE of Aberystwyth, just off A487; ample car parking
Food breakfast, lunch, dinner
Price ££££
Rooms 10; 5 doubles, 5 suites, all with bath and shower; all rooms have phone, TV, hairdryer
Facilities sitting room, dining room, bar, conservatory in 1 room
Credit cards AE, DC, MC, V
Children accepted
Disabled 1 ground-floor room
Pets accepted in 1 bedroom
Closed Jan
Proprietors Rob and Joan Reen; partners John & Jen Talbot

Ynyshir Hall

Country house hotel

The Reens have been at Ynyshir Hall for some 25 years now and, happily, seem to know what they are about. Since regaining ownership two years ago, the Reens have completely refurbished the house, inside and out. Both are ex-teachers, Joan of geography, Rob of design and art – and his paintings now decorate the walls of the whole house. Given Rob's background, you might well expect the decoration of the hotel to be rather special, too – and you would not be disappointed. The colour schemes are adventurous, the patterns bold, the use of fabrics opulent, the attention to detail striking. The bedrooms are named after famous artists, which is paralleled in the colour schemes. There are two new suites, Miro and Chagall, which are comfortable, with ultra-modern bathrooms. Both have uninterrupted views across the gardens to the Cambrian Mountains.

The white-painted house dates from the 16th century, but is predominantly Georgian and Victorian. It stands in 12 glorious acres of landscaped gardens next to the Dovey estuary. The food is adventurous – modern British – and based on fresh local ingredients, especially fish, game, shellfish and Welsh lamb.

Felin Fach, Powys

Felin Fach, Brecon, Powys
LD3 0UB

Tel (01874) 620111
e-mail enquiries@eatdrinksleep.ltd.uk
website www.eatdrinksleep.ltd.uk

Nearby Hay Bluff; Pen y Fan; Brecon Beacons and Black Mountains; Brecon; Hay-on-Wye; Llangorse Lake (sailing and wind-surfing).
Location edge of village with off-road car parking
Food breakfast, lunch, dinner
Price ££-£££
Rooms 7 double and twin; all rooms have bath, phone, some have TV
Facilities bar, dining area; grassed outdoor drinks area, croquet
Credit cards MC, V
Children accepted
Disabled no special facilities
Pets accepted
Closed Christmas Day
Proprietors Charles and Edmund Inkin

The Felin Fach Griffin

Country inn

The location is uninteresting, beside a busy-ish road, and you might think this is any old Welsh pub. But there's a clue it may be something different: the exterior is painted a mellow ochre, the colour seen all over Tuscany. Inside, you'll be struck by the layout: right by the bar is a pair of squashy leather sofas where you flop with the papers. A log fire is raised above floor level, radiating heat in two directions, into the bar and the adjacent dining room. Tongue-and-groove panelling is painted a brilliant blue. Nooks and crannies are filled with books: we spied *Debrett* and *Who's Who*. Upstairs are seven fresh, but perhaps boxey bed-rooms with homey decoration, again using bright colours. Some have four-poster beds and all have extra beds for children.

The food is distinctly above average for the price. Home-made soda bread arrives on a simple wooden board. There's a large choice of interesting wines by the glass, including *prosecco*. The Griffin can claim to be Wales's original gastropub. Off the main dining room there's another smaller one with two tables seating eight (great for a party) in front of the AGA, where the day's fresh stocks simmer.

The Inkins also run The Gurnard's Head (page 84) and The Old Coastguard (page 59).

Ganllwyd, Gwynedd

Ganllwyd, Dolgellau, Snowdonia, Gwynedd LL40 2HP

Tel 01341 440273
Fax 01341 440640
e-mail info@dolly-hotel.co.uk
website www.dolly-hotel.co.uk

Nearby Cymer Abbey; Snowdonia; Lake Vyrnwy. **Location** in countryside, on A470 5 miles (8 km) N of Dolgellau; ample car-parking
Food breakfast, lunch by arrangement, dinner **Price** ££
Rooms 10; 9 double, 1 single, all with bath; all rooms have phone, TV, hairdrier
Facilities sitting room, dining room, breakfast room, conservatory bar; garden, fishing **Credit cards** AE, DC, MC, V
Children welcome over 8
Disabled not suitable
Pets accepted in 2 bedrooms
Closed Nov to Mar
Proprietors Alan and Julie Pulman

Plas Domelynllyn

Country hotel

Alan and Julie Pulman took the reigns at Plas Domelynllyn in 2008 and run it with considerable style. Parts of it are more than half a millennium old but there was still work going on when we visited. It sits in on its own terrace above Ganllywd, near Dolgellau, taking in the beautiful views across the valley, and, in the principally Victorian interior, antiques mingle equally comfortably with more modern furnishings to create a warm, friendly atmosphere. China and crystal twinkle on all sides. The drawing room is elegant but the dining room is obviously where the team gets down to real business. Visitors mention the quality and choice of breakfast in the breakfast room, which dates back to the ninth century and has stained glass windows. Locally sourced meats are used for dinner, and there are homemade pâtés and sausages on offer.

Bedrooms are named after local rivers and individually furnished and decorated. There is excellent walking from the door and all guests have access to that essential room in a Welsh hotel – the drying room. This a passionately non-smoking hotel.

Llanarmon Dyffryn-Ceiriog, Wrexham

Llanarmon Dyffryn-Ceiriog
Nr Llangollen, Wrexham
LL20 7LD

Tel (01691) 600 665
Fax (01691) 600 622
e-mail gowestarms@aol.com
website www.thewestarms.co.uk

Nearby Chirk Castle, Ceiriog Valley, Rhaeadr waterfall, Erdigg Hall, Llangollen
Location on B4500, 7 miles SW of Llangollen situated in centre of hamlet, surrounded by countryside with ample car parking at the rear
Food breakfast, lunch, dinner
Price ££-£££
Rooms 15; 2 suites, 1 four poster, 11 doubles, 1 twin, all with bath, some with shower; all rooms have phone, flat-screen TV, hairdryers, wi-fi
Facilities dining room, bar; garden
Credit cards MC, V
Children welcome
Disabled 1 accessible room
Pets accepted **Closed** never
Proprietors Geoff and Gill Leigh-Ford

The West Arms

Country inn

A traditional, unspoilt inn with above average food and simple but comfortable bedrooms (try one of the character rooms which have pretty brass or four poster beds.) They are perhaps a little feminine, but decorated in a comfortable, unpretentious country style. You should get a warm welcome, and the mood will be helped along by flagstones and roaring inglenook fires surrounded by old blackened beams with traditional brasses on display. Our inspector found the dining room quite lacking in atmosphere, however the bar seemed the place to be for informal eating and drinking with the locals or alternatively the beer garden which has truly spectacular views over the Welsh hills and valleys.

Heartening food comes from the reputable head chef Grant Williams, who had been there 20 years as we went to press – a long time in this business, so there's probably a happy team here. The inn has a rosette and has been in the Good Food Guide for three consecutive years.

The West Arms is located in a natural spot for an inn, where three cattle drovers' tracks converge on the way to the markets at Oswestry, Chirk and Wrexham. Wonderful walking in the Berwyn Hills or Ceiriog Valley is a must if staying here.

Llanbrynmair, Powys

Llanbrynmair, Powys SY19 7DY

Tel 01650 521479
Fax 01650 511414
e-mail barlbarn@zetnet.co.uk
website www.barlbarn.zetnet.co.uk

Nearby Snowdonia; Aberdovey beach
Location 2 miles (3 km) NE of Llanbrynmair at end of private lane off road to Pandy; with ample car parking
Food self-catering
Price ££-£££
Rooms barn sleeps between 14-16 people
Facilities garden, indoor swimming pool, squash, table tennis, sauna, sunbed, wi-fi
Credit cards not accepted
Children welcome
Disabled 2 ground-floor rooms
Pets accepted by arrangement
Closed never
Proprietors Terry and Felicity Margolis

Barlings Barn

Self-catering barns

The only sounds to disturb the peace in this corner of Powys come from the sheep on the surrounding hillsides, and from the nearby brook. Barlings Barn is a rural idyll in Llanbrynmair, in the heart of Wales, with a garden full of roses and honeysuckle: a picturesque setting for the outdoor activities, such as walking, bird-watching, fishing and golf, that you can enjoy in the surrounding Powys countryside.

It is, in fact, the perfect peace of the place that keeps in the guide despite the move a few years ago towards a self-catering set-up. Home-made biscuits await your arrival in the secluded barns adjacent to Felicity and Terrys Welsh farmhouse, one with an oak-beamed stone fireplace and wood-burning stove. Their latest project has been to enclose the spring-fed, heated swimming-pool in a stunning new building, so guests can now make use of it all through the year.

The barns are well-equipped with fridge/freezers, microwaves and barbecues even a dishwasher. Though its basically self-catering, the local baker will deliver delicious warm bread to the door. There's a colourful market every Wednesday in Machynlleth.

Llandrillo, Denbighshire

Llandrillo, near Corwen,
Denbighshire LL21 0ST

Tel (01490) 440264
Fax (01490) 440414
e-mail tyddynllan@compuserve.com
website www.tyddynllan.co.uk

Nearby Bala Lake and Railway; Snowdonia.
Location 5 miles (8 km) SW of Corwen off B4401; with ample car parking
Food breakfast, lunch, dinner
Price ££££ (half board)
Rooms 12 double and twin, 10 with bath, 2 with shower; all rooms have phone, TV, radio
Facilities sitting room, bar, restaurant; croquet, fishing
Credit cards MC, V **Children** welcome **Disabled** 1 suite suitable
Pets accepted in bedrooms by arrangement **Closed** never
Proprietors Bryan and Susan Webb

Tyddyn Llan

Restaurant-with-rooms

A firm favourite with readers since our first edition, this Georgian stone house near Llandrillo is decorated with elegant flair, period antiques and fine paintings, creating a serene ambience. Tyddyn Llan is very much a home, despite the number of guests it can accommodate. There is a major extension to the building, cleverly complementary to the original, using slate, stone and cast-iron.

A reader writes: 'No intrusive reception desk; spacious sitting rooms furnished with style; dining room shows great flair; bedrooms well equipped with original pieces of furniture; small but modern and very pleasing bathrooms; peaceful, comfortable stay, warm atmosphere provided by attentive hosts'. When Fiona Duncan, our series editor, visited a few years ago, she felt that Bryan deserved a Michelin star 'for his instinctive cooking' and we were delighted to hear that he was awarded one not long after, in 2011.

Bryan and his wife Susan offer diners with a new angle on Welsh country house food with inventive and well-planned small menus using quality local ingredients, plus an impressive wine list.

The place is surrounded by large, beautiful grounds.

Llandudno, Conwy

Promenade, 17 North Parade, Llandudno, Conwy LL30 2LP

Tel (01492) 860330
e-mail sales@osbornehouse.co.uk
website www.osbornehouse.co.uk

Nearby dry ski slope; Conwy Castle; Bodnant Gardens; Snowdonia
Location on seafront opposite pier and promenade gardens; off-road car parking
Food breakfast (in room), lunch, dinner
Price £££
Rooms 7 suites (1 family room), all with phone, bath, walk-in shower, TV, DVD, fridge, wi-fi
Facilities bar, 'bistro' restaurant, cafe area, sitting area in reception, terrace
Credit cards AE, DC, MC, V
Children welcome, but no children's menu
Disabled access via a ramp
Pets not accepted
Closed one week at Christmas
Proprietors Maddocks family

Osborne House

Town hotel

There's virtually no mobile signal in the charmingly old-fashioned resort of Llandudno, but that's part of its appeal. Between the unspoilt beaches and the backdrop of mountains, life goes at a gentle pace. Summer here means strolling along the Promenade with an ice-cream cornet, pausing to watch Punch and Judy. In a plum position on the Prom, Osborne House fits its surroundings perfectly.

The Maddocks family have lavished attention on it. The public rooms are glamorous enough, but it's the seven gorgeous suites, six with sea views and private parking spaces, that really impress, and are kindly priced considering the wealth of antiques, pictures and porcelain in each one, and the marble bathrooms with splendid roll top baths. Some might find it all a bit over the top, certainly very Victorian, but downstairs the public spaces have plenty of modern touches including a sleek bar with two large plasma TV screens competing for attention. 'The Café,' a bistro-café, reckons on serving good food in a rather grand Victorian surroundings, but in an informal style – no set hours, okay to have just one course, and eat at the bar, a table or on a sofa.

Osborne House will suit younger readers better than our other Llandudno entry, St Tudno, page 186.

Llandudno, Conwy

Promenade, Llandudno, Conwy, LL30 2LP

Tel (01492) 874411
Fax (01492) 860407
e-mail sttudnohotel@btinternet.com
website www.st-tudno.co.uk

Nearby dry ski slope; Conwy Castle; Bodnant Gardens; Snowdonia.
Location on seafront opposite pier and promenade gardens; garage parking for 12 cars and unrestricted street parking
Food breakfast, lunch, dinner
Price £££
Rooms 19; 12 double/twin, 4 family, 2 suites, 1 single, all with bath or shower; all rooms have phone, TV, fridge, hairdryer
Facilities 2 sitting rooms, dining room, bar, indoor swimming pool; garden
Credit cards AE, DC, MC, V
Children welcome
Disabled not suitable, lift/elevator
Pets by arrangement
Closed never
Proprietor Martin Bland

St Tudno

Seaside hotel

Martin Bland is meticulous in attending to every detail of this award-winning seafront hotel, which he has been improving for almost 42 years now. He could not, however, improve on its location: right on Llandudno's attractive promenade, opposite the carefully restored Victorian pier and sheltered from inclement weather by the Great Orme headland. Each of the nineteen rooms have been individually decorated in bright, cheerful colours with matching fabrics and furnishings: many have spectacular views of the sea. The two sitting rooms facing the Promenade are delightfully Victorian yet surprisingly light and spacious, perfect for reading or indulging in afternoon tea.

The air-conditioned Terrace Restaurant is light and inviting, and is decorated with murals of Lake Como. The seasonal menu with daily changing carte, based on the best local ingredients, deserves serious study in the comfortable bar, as does the wine list, and – though it's not cheap – the cooking is right on target. If you over-indulge, you can try to recover your figure by pounding up and down the lovely covered pool, decorated with murals. All of this would be difficult to resist even without the bonus of the hotel's young and helpful staff.

Llanthony, Gwent

Llanthony, Abergavenny, Gwent NP7 7NN

Tel (01873) 890487
website www.llanthonyprioryhotel.co.uk

Nearby Offa's Dyke; Brecon Beacons; Hay-on-Wye.
Location off A465 from Abergavenny to Hereford, take mountain road heading N at Llanfihangel Crucorney; with ample car parking
Food breakfast, lunch, dinner
Price £
Rooms 4 double and twin
Facilities dining room, bar; garden
Credit cards not accepted
Children accepted over 10 in the hotel
Disabled access not possible
Pets not accepted
Closed Oct to Easter (open week-ends) **Proprietor** Geoffrey Neil

Llanthony Priory

Country inn

Far into the Black Mountains, on the west bank of the Afon Honddu and over-looked by Offa's Dyke to the east, Llanthony Priory lies high and remote in the Vale of Ewyas. The most spectacular approach is southwards from the sloping streets and busy bookshops of Hay-on-Wye.

One of the earliest Augustinian houses in Britain, it was endowed by the de Lacy family, but by the time of Henry VIII's dis-solution of the monasteries had fallen into disuse. The Prior's quarters survived amongst the ruins and are now used as the hotel. Gothic horror enthusiasts will be delighted not only by the setting but also when they learn that the highest of the bedrooms can only be reached by climbing more than 60 spiral steps up into the south tower.

This is not a hotel for the fastidious or the faint-hearted: it is a long way from any-where and much used by walkers attracted to the stunning country that surrounds it. Unless you plan to arrive on foot yourself, you should remember that your fellow guests may have had their appetites sharp-ened by fresh air and their critical faculties dulled by fatigue. However, the chance to sleep in this unique piece of history (with a four-poster and half-tester available) and to wake up to the view from the tower also comes with a very modest price tag.

Nant Gwynant, Gwynedd

Nant Gwynant, Gwynedd,
LL55 4NT

Tel (01286) 870211
email escape@pyg.co.uk
website www.pyg.co.uk

Nearby Bodnant Gardens; Caernarfon, Beaumaris and Harlech Castles; Isle of Anglesey; Blackrock Sands. **Location** take the A5 to Holyhead, as you enter Capel Curig, turn left on to the A4086. 4 miles (6 km) on the hotel is on a T junction with the lake in front of it
Food breakfast, lunch, dinner, tea
Price £ **Rooms** 15 double and twin, 1 single; 5 with private bathroom, 1 ground floor annexe room with bathroom, 5 public bathrooms
Facilities sitting room, dining room, smoke room, bar, sauna, natural swimming pool, games room, fishing
Credit cards MC, V **Children** welcome **Disabled** 1 ground-floor room
Pets by arrangement **Closed** Nov to Dec and mid week until the 1st of March **Proprietors** Jane and Brian Pullee

Pen-y-Gwryd Hotel
Climbing hostel

A pilgrimage place for climbers: this is the home of British Mountaineering, where Edmund Hillary and his team set up their training base before the assault on Everest in 1953. Still in the same friendly family after 58 years, the charming old coach inn, set high in the desolate heart of Snowdonia, is just the sort of place you dream of returning to after a day outdoors: simple, unsophisticated, warm and welcoming, with good plain home cooking, including wickedly calorific puddings.

In keeping with the purpose of the place the bedrooms are simple with no frills, not all of them have private bathrooms, but they all have fluffy towels and warm embroidered bedding and linen; the best room is in the annexe and has a grand four-poster bed. One of the bathrooms houses a vintage Victorian bath that looks deep and inviting. For the less intrepid walkers there is still plenty to see in the vicinity, as it is littered with castles and gardens.

After a hard day on the hill you can soak your aching muscles in the natural pool in the garden or unwind in the sauna. For children (or playful adults) there is a games room with a dart board and table tennis.

The Pullee sons, Rupert and Nick, are mostly in charge now – they tell us that they are adding two new rooms with private sitting room. Reports welcome.

Narberth, Pembrokeshire

Molleston, Narberth,
Pembrokeshire SA67 8BX

Tel 01834 860915
email info@thegrove-narberth.co.uk
website www.thegrove-narberth.co.uk

Nearby walks through Cannaston Wood to the Blackpool Mill; Stackpole Estate Coastal Walk; Tenby; St David's; Porthgain; the Blue Lagooon; galleries; craft shops
Location Narbeth with shops, restaurants and boutiques, close to the beautiful Preseli Hills
Food breakfast, lunch, dinner
Price £££
Rooms 24; 20 rooms, 4 self-catering cottages away from the main house: all en-suite with cast iron bath and shower, rooms have flat-screen television and DVD player, fireplace
Facilities restaurant, sitting room, bar, kitchen garden **Credit cards** all major **Children** welcome **Disabled** accessible **Pets** only in selected rooms **Closed** never **Proprietors** Neil Kedward and Zoe Agar

The Grove

Country hotel and restaurant

Neil Kedward and his partner Zoe Agar acquired this place as a wreck and after nine months of blood, sweat and tears – they worked on a shoestring – got a beautiful result. The former somewhat quirky mansion is now a unique boutique hotel and restaurant that gets a big vote of confidence from our series editor, Fiona Duncan. Its magic worked on her as soon as she arrived. The exterior is unusual, with two facades: one tall and Georgian, painted brilliant white, the other with gables and Arts and Crafts elements that also crop up inside.

She could not fault her bedroom. The rooms are spread out across the house, a cottage and an old long house; there are also four self-catering cottages with good views – ideal for families, who are allowed to pick their own food from the nearby vegetable garden.

Inside the house public spaces include a relaxing library with chessboard, books and games. We especially like the light breakfast room. Chef Duncan Barnham uses local Welsh ingredients to memorable effect and has his sights on a Michelin star.

Penally, Pembrokeshire

Penally, near Tenby, South Pembrokeshire SA70 7PY

Tel (01834) 843033
e-mail info@penally-abbey.com
website www.penally-abbey.com

Nearby Tenby; Colby Woodland Garden; Upton Castle, Pembroke Castle
Location in village 1.5 miles (2.5 km) SW of Tenby; with ample car parking
Food breakfast, dinner
Price £££
Rooms 12 double and twin with bath; all rooms have phone, TV, fax/modem point, hairdryer
Facilities sitting room, billiards room, dining room, bar, indoor swimming pool; garden
Credit cards AE, MC, V
Children accepted
Disabled access possible to 2 ground-floor bedrooms
Pets not accepted
Closed never
Proprietors Steve and Elleen Warren

Penally Abbey

Country house hotel

Ever since the Middle Ages this has been recognized as one of the spots from which to appreciate the broad sweep of the Pembrokeshire coast and National Park from Tenby to Giltar Point. The links golf course wasn't there, but the ruins of the medieval chapel which gave this Gothic country house its name are still in the secluded and well-tended gardens. The windows and doors all have the characteristic double curve arches. There is a comfortable and well furnished drawing room with an open fire, a welcoming bar far from the world's woes and weather, and a tall, candle-lit dining room for the well planned and prepared dinners, which include a wide choice of fresh Welsh produce. The bedrooms are well equipped: some you could play cricket in and are furnished traditionally, some in quite a grand style. St Deiniol's Lodge now houses a further five rooms, decorated in more contemporary style. Steve and Elleen Warren have made a smart but easy and informal hotel that is child friendly (babysitting on tap). Children are welcome in the dining room for the (excellent) breakfasts, but an early supper sensibly makes this a child-free zone in the evening.

We revisited recently and enjoyed Steve's *bonhomie* and Elleen's food as much as ever.

Penmaenpool, Gwynedd

Penmaenpool, Dolgellau, Gwynedd LL40 1YB

Tel (01341) 422129
Fax (01341) 422787
e-mail relax@penhall.co.uk
website www.penhall.co.uk

Nearby Mawddach Estuary; Snowdonia; Lake Vyrnwy, Portmeirion.
Location off A493 Dolgellau-Tywyn road; with ample car parking
Food breakfast, lunch, dinner
Price £££
Rooms 14 double and twin with bath; all rooms have phone, TV, iPod dock, hairdryer, minibar, wi-fi
Facilities sitting rooms, library, 2 dining rooms, bar; garden, helipad, trout and salmon fishing
Credit cards DC, MC, V
Children babes-in-arms and children over 6 accepted
Disabled only restaurant accessible
Pets accepted in 1 room by arrangement
Closed 8 days in Dec, 10 days in Jan
Proprietors Mark Watson and Lorraine Fielding

Penmaenuchaf Hall

Country house hotel

Not far from the market town of Dolgellau, Penmaenuchaf Hall's drive winds steeply up a wooded hillside from the south bank of the Mawddach Estuary to this sturdy grey stone Victorian manor house. Set on terraces in 21 acres of grounds, the views across Snowdonia must have been top of the list of reasons that brought the original builder – a Lancashire mill owner – to this peaceful spot at the foot of Cader Idris. A rose garden and a water garden add a charm of their own to the beautiful setting.

Indoors, Mark Watson and Lorraine Fielding have saved but also softened the Victorian character of the house so that, from the imposing main hall you are drawn to the warmth and light of the ivory morning room, the sitting rooms and the library. The same sympathetic treatment carries through to the bedrooms – fine fabrics are married with fine furniture and only the beds are baronial. If you are not tempted by the excellent walking in the surrounding hills, you can doze in the sunny conservatory, or eat in the oak-panelled garden room restaurant, Llygad yr Haul.

Pwllheli, Gwynedd

Pwllheli, Gwynedd, North Wales
LL53 5TH

Tel (01758) 612363
email gunna@bodegroes.co.uk
website www.bodegroes.co.uk

Nearby National Trust walks, Snowdonia, Bodmant Gardens
Location 1 mile west of Pwllheli on the A497 Nefyn road; in own grounds with ample car parking
Food breakfast, dinner (lunch on Sundays)
Price ££
Rooms 10 doubles; all have bath and shower; all rooms have phone, tv, hairdryer
Facilities restaurant, garden
Credit cards MC, V
Children welcome
Disabled not suitable
Pets accepted
Closed Dec, Jan and Feb, and Mondays
Proprietors Chris and Gunna Chown

Plas Bodegroes

Restaurant-with-rooms

Plas Bodegroes means Rosehip Hall – a fittingly romantic name. It's a small Georgian manor with a delicate frill of a veranda, whose slim cast-iron columns are smothered in wisteria, roses and wild strawberry. The grounds feature a heart-shaped swathe of lawn and a 200-year-old avenue of beech trees. To one side, a long red-and-white Danish pennant on a tall flagpole flutters in the wind. Chef-proprietor Chris Chown's elegant wife, Gunna, who looks after front of house is Danish/Faroese.

Plas Bodegroes is emphatically a restaurant-with-rooms. The ten bedrooms are cosy and pretty, in Scandinavian style, all shapes and sizes. The dining room is romantic, too, with its clever use of mirrors, its elegant French doors on to the veranda and its beautifully lit duck-egg blue walls. Welsh lamb and Black beef feature prominently on the unpretentious menu, though equal emphasis is given to fresh fish. The wine list is interesting with gentle prices and breakfast is exceptional. Plas Bodegroes is off the beaten track on the Lleyn Peninsula, with mystical Bardsey Island at its tip, in almost completely unspoilt countryside. Food and a setting of this quality are hard to find at these prices.

Skenfrith, Monmouthshire

Skenfrith, Monmouthshire,
NP7 8UH

Tel (01600) 750235
Fax (01600) 750525
e-mail enquiries@skenfrith.co.uk
website www.skenfrith.co.uk

Nearby Brecon Beacons National Park; Ross-on-Wye; Hereford; Hay-on-Wye; Abergavenny; Monmouth.
Location beside river, off minor road on edge of village in own grounds; ample car parking
Food breakfast, lunch, dinner, afternoon tea
Price ££-££££
Rooms 11 double, all with bath; all rooms have phone, TV
Facilities bar, dining room, function room; terrace, garden
Credit cards MC, V
Children welcome, but not for evening meals unless over 10
Disabled disabled loo downstairs, upstairs not suitable
Pets accepted (supervised at all times; £5 per night) **Closed** Tue in winter **Proprietors** Janet and William Hutchings

The Bell at Skenfrith

Country inn

Though contemporary and cosy rarely coincide, this is one place that convincingly combines the two. Tucked into the fold of a hill in the Welsh Marches, it has all the ingredients for a winter break that metropolitans could wish for: a huge inglenook radiating heat, surrounded by sofa, settle and rocking chair; a candle-lit, flagstone dining room serving locally sourced modern British dishes – planned around vegetables and fruits grown in the kitchen garden – along with a well-organised wine list; and 11 delightful, simple-sophisticated bedrooms.

Converted in 2001 by Janet and William Hutchings, the formerly run-down inn stands on the Monnow River close to Skenfrith Castle in an unchanged village. There are wonderful walks from the door, including the 18-mile Three Castles Walk, which is demanding, but possible in a single day. When you get back, you could have a Jersey cream tea to ease your sore feet.

The Bell has regular special offers. As we went to press they were offering two nights dinner, bed and breakfast for two people from £340.

Tal-y-llyn, Gwynedd

Tal-y-llyn, Tywyn, Gwynedd LL36 9AJ

Tel 01654 761247
e-mail info@dolffanogfawr.co.uk
website www.dolffanogfawr.co.uk

Nearby Cadair Idris, Snowdonia National Park, sandy beaches at Aberdyfi, Tywyn and Barmouth, Coed y Brenin Forest, Tal-y-llyn railway, Ynys Hir RSPB reserve, Dyfi Osprey Project **Location** Tal-y-llyn Valley at the foot of Cadair Idris mountain and overlooking Tal-y-llyn lake. **Food** breakfast, dinner
Price £ **Rooms** 4; 3 double/twin, 1 double **Facilities** guest sitting room with log fire, dining room, garden, private off-road parking, hot tub, drying room, secure storage for mountain bikes or fishing tackle, fishing on over 13 miles of local rivers and a mountain lake.
Credit cards MC, V **Children** accepted over 7 **Disabled** no special facilities **Pets** by prior arrangement **Closed** Nov-mid Mar **Proprietors** Alex Yorke and Lorraine Hinkins

Dolffanog Fawr

Country guesthouse

Recommended by a trusted reporter, this unpretentious Welsh farmhouse, renovated in 2004, has four bedrooms done up in contemporary-traditional style, with restrained good taste. All the basics are spot on: Egyptian cotton sheets, best quality beds. Three of the rooms have window seats for pondering the views across the Tal-y-Llyn valley, with the superb Cadair Idris almost on the doorstep. A top-end, modern B&B, run by friendly Alex and Lorraine, who live in a separate wing. Guests can feel private in their own sitting room and dining room. The daily-changing dinner menu, with a useful choice of wines, was £25 for three courses as we went to press.

Think about coming here to enjoy the coast as well as the mountains – it's only half an hour from the sea. The scenery around here, north of the Dovey estuary, is exceptionally wild and beautiful, and less overrun than Snowdonia. While the main route up Cadair Idris starts from nearby Minfford, a non-standard route to the top begins within half an hour's walk of Dolffanog Fawr.

Three Cocks, near Brecon, Powys LD3 OSL

Tel (01497) 847215
Fax (01497) 847339
e-mail info@threecockshotel.com
website www.threecockshotel.com

Nearby Brecon Beacons; Hay-on-Wye; Hereford Cathedral; Black Mountains.
Location in village, 11 miles (18 km) NE of Brecon on A438; ample car parking
Food breakfast, lunch, dinner
Price ££
Rooms 7 double and twin, 6 with bath/shower, 1 with shower
Facilities sitting room, reception room with TV, dining room, breakfast room; large garden
Credit cards MC, V
Children welcome over age of 12
Disabled access difficult
Pets not accepted
Closed Jan
Proprietors Roy and Judith Duke

Three Cocks

Village inn

The building is a charming ivy-covered 15thC coaching inn in the Welsh hills, constructed around a tree (still in evidence in the kitchen) and with its cobbled forecourt on the most direct route from Hereford to Brecon. Inside, carved wood and stone walls continue the natural look of the exterior, with beams and eccentrically angled doorways serving as proof positive of antiquity. The charmingly friendly and enthusiastic Roy and Judith took over in 2006 and continue to draw people great distances to the warm welcome and roomy restaurant with its lace-covered tables. There are plenty of places where you can sit in peace, and residents have a drawing room of their own, in keeping with its public oak-panelled counterpart but with more light, stone and fabric in evidence. There is now also a coffee shop, leading on to the extensive gardens, serving refreshments and light lunches.

Bedrooms are modest but comfortable and well equipped, with dark oak furniture and pale fabrics. The food is honest, hearty British fayre, making full use of the wealth of local sources, including the Black Mountain Salmon Smokery, as well as local cheeses and meats. Roy uses local merchant Tanners as his wine cellar, importing an eclectic range of wines from around the world.

Abergavenny, Monmouthshire

15 Cross Street, Abergavenny,
Monmouthshire, Wales NP7 5EN

Tel 01873 857121
Fax 01873 858059
e-mail mail@angelabergavenny.com
website www.angelabergavenny.com
Food breakfast, brunch, lunch, dinner; afternoon tea
Price ££ **Closed** Christmas Day
Proprietors Caradog Hotels Ltd

The Angel Hotel/The Walnut Tree **Inn/restaurant**

The Angel Hotel and The Walnut Tree restaurant are closely associated – the Griffith family, owners of The Angel, also have an interest in The Walnut Tree, which is run by Shaun Hill. The two places mark out Abergavenny as a useful gourmet base for exploring the Black Mountains.

Inside The Angel there's plenty of stylish architecture and pristine white walls, with bars and sitting rooms that are contemporary but still welcoming. The bedrooms are calming, with cream walls, wooden furniture and smart bathrooms; for more privacy there are nearby cottages.

It's a ten-minute taxi ride from The Angel to The Walnut Tree restaurant (which has two cottages), where Shaun presents a menu of uncomplicated yet sublime dishes.

Abergavenny, Monmouthshire

Old Raglan Road, Abergavenny,
Monmouthshire NP7 9AA

Tel 01873 854220
e-mail info@thehardwick.co.uk
website www.thehardwick.co.uk
Food breakfast, lunch, dinner
Price £££-££££
Closed one week in Jan, Christmas Day
Proprietor Stephen Terry

The Hardwick
Restaurant-with-rooms

This is well-known chef Stephen Terry's latest venture, where rooms were added in 2010. His CV is as impressive as a chef's can be, including La Gavroche with Michel Roux and The Canteen at Chelsea Harbour (where he got his first Michelin star aged 25). The list is long, spanning Europe and America, and together with his grounding in classic French cooking adds up to quality and depth. Shame then that guests query the speed of service and value for money. We think it's worth the price when things are running smoothly, but perhaps the tough economics of the restaurant trade in places such as Abergavenny make it hard to afford enough hands to achieve consistency. The rooms are smart and modish, but some would say formulaic.

Dolydd, Gwynedd

Dolydd, Caernarfon, Gwynedd
LL54 7EF

Tel 01286 830942
Mobile 0770 8491234
e-mail john@ygoedeneirin.co.uk
website www.ygoedeneirin.co.uk
Food breakfast, dinner by arrangement **Price** £ **Closed** Christmas to New Year **Proprietors** John and Eluned Rowlands

Y Goeden Eirin

Country guesthouse

Set in what was originally a granite cow-shed, Y Goeden Eirin (The Plum Tree) is a cosy, charming guesthouse situated in the little hamlet of Dolydd in Gwynedd. Run by welcoming hosts Eluned and John Rowlands, the place offers a comforting blend of traditional and contemporary.

The well-designed bedrooms are attractive and homely, with slate floors and underfloor heating, and include all the necessary modern amenities to make for a supremely comfortable stay. The dining room (also with slate floor) is wonderfully traditional, with its wooden beams and exposed granite walls. The atmosphere is laidback and intimate. Food is home-cooked on the AGA and is locally sourced wherever possible.

Llyswen, Powys

Llyswen, Brecon, Powys, Wales LD3 0YP

Tel 01874 754525
Fax 01874 754545
e-mail enquiries@llangoedhall.com
website www.llangoedhall.co.uk
Food breakfast, lunch, dinner, afternoon tea
Price ££££ **Closed** never
Manager Calum Milne

Llangoed Hall

Country house hotel

With 23 bedrooms this (on the face of it) large and conventional country house hotel is a little outside the guide's territory, but our series editor Fiona Duncan rates it very highly. The house is imposing and beautifully restored by the late Sir Bernard Ashley, and wife Laura, of wallpaper and fabric fame. It houses his notable collection of 20thC British paintings.

Despite its formality, it's the type of place where guests are encouraged to be themselves – to curl up on the sofa, even play the piano.

The rooms are charmingly done with antiques and pictures, fine linen, new bathrooms – guests will want to linger.

The food by Nick Brodie (ex-Olive Tree in Bath) is imaginative yet sensible.

Milebrook, Powys

Milebrook, Knighton, Powys LD7 1LT

Tel 01547 528632
e-mail hotel@milebrookhouse.co.uk
website www.milebrookhouse.co.uk
Food breakfast, lunch, dinner
Price ££
Closed Sunday and Monday between Dec-Feb
Proprietors Marsden family

Milebrook House Hotel **Country house**

Inside it's homely and chintzy rather than 'boutique' and minimalist: curtains are floral, walls are lined with paintings and bunches of flowers spring from vases. Bedrooms however, are calmly uncluttered, with bright walls and white linen. Certain things here are to everyone's taste: the food and the service.

Owners the Marsden family have built up a loyal following thanks to the genial atmosphere and high standards: Beryl, Rodney and Joanne run the hotel.This is also open to non residents and serves breakfast, lunch and dinner. The quality of the food is a recurring theme of guests'comments.

In the grounds there's a wildlife pond and a riverbank; and wildlife enthusiast Rodney is on hand with advice about where to point binoculars.

Talsarnau, Gwynedd

Talsarnau, Gwynedd, Wales LL47 6YA

Tel (01766) 780200
Fax (01766) 780211
e-mail maes@neuadd.com
website www.neuadd.com
Food breakfast, lunch, dinner, room service **Price** £££ **Closed** never
Proprietors Lynn and Peter Jackson, Peter and Doreen Payne

Maes-y-Neuadd
Country hotel

You arrive outside a stone-built, slate-roofed manor, creeper-clad in parts. Look back across the water and you might see the sun set behind the Lleyn peninsula. It may be Snowdonia outside, but inside it is definitely deep-pile all the way. Chintzes in the drawing room, and in the pale and elegant dining room masterpieces from the kitchen of Peter Jackson (chef and co-owner) all combine to make this a seriously comfortable hotel.

Much of the fresh produce comes from Maes-y-Neuadd's own garden. The menu has choices for each of the possible five courses until pudding when you reach 'Diweddglo Mawreddog' (the grand finale): you get them all.The smart, variously-sized bedrooms are individually decorated.

Mappleton, Ashbourne, Derbyshire DE6 2AA

Tel (01335) 300900
Fax (01335) 300512
e-mail reservations@callowhall.co.uk **website** www.callowhall.co.uk

Nearby Chatsworth House; Haddon Hall; Hardwick Hall.
Location 0.75 mile (1 km) N of Ashbourne off A515; with ample car parking
Food breakfast, lunch Sun or on request, dinner **Price** £££ **Rooms** 16; 15 double and twin, 1 suite, all with bath or shower; all rooms have phone, TV, hairdryer
Facilities sitting room, dining rooms, bar; garden, fishing **Credit cards** AE, DC, MC, V **Children** welcome **Disabled** 1 specially adapted room **Pets** accepted by arrangement **Closed** Christmas Day, Boxing Day, New Year's Day
Proprietors Hardman Family

Callow Hall

Country house hotel

The legacy of old owners the Spencers (master bakers in Ashbourne) is that one of the highlights of staying at this fine Victorian country house hotel is its excellent dining room. As well as growing many of their own ingredients, the restaurant at Callow Hall also smokes and cures meat and fish themselves – arts that have been passed down over generations.

Set in extensive grounds at the entrance to the Peak District National Park, the hotel overlooks the stunning landscape of the Dove valley. Public rooms and bedrooms are done out in an appropriate and not too flamboyant country-house style. The walls of the entrance are guarded by stags' heads and the flag-stoned floor is scattered with Persian rugs. In winter an open fire crackles, while guests dine in the glow of the deep-red dining room, and in the drawing room, comfy sofas and chairs provide plenty of space for relaxing. Carved antiques and family heirlooms mingle with period repro furniture. Ask for a decent-sized room when you book: one or two are on the small side for the price. Staff are helpful yet unobtrusive.

Since the last edition Callow Hall has changed management, and we would welcome reports.

Ashford-in-the-Water, Derbyshire

Fennel Street, Ashford-in-the-Water, Bakewell, Derbyshire, DE4 1QF

Tel (01629) 814275
Fax (01629) 812873
e-mail riversidehouse@enta.net
website www.riversidehousehotel.co.uk

Nearby Chatsworth; Haddon Hall; Bakewell.
Location 2 miles (3 km) NW of Bakewell off A6, at top of village, next to Sheepwash Bridge; with ample car parking
Food breakfast, lunch, dinner
Price £££
Rooms 14; 1 executive suite, 13 double/twin, all with bath/shower; all rooms have phone, TV, hairdryer
Facilities 2 sitting rooms, conservatory, bar, 2 dining rooms; garden
Credit cards AE, DC, MC, V
Children welcome over 16
Disabled access possible to 4 rooms
Pets not accepted **Closed** never
Proprietor Penelope Thornton

Riverside House

Country hotel

Nestling in one of the Peak District's prettiest villages, this stone-built, ivy-clad house, has an idyllic setting in its own secluded grounds, bordered by the river Wye. The village is aptly named – on our inspector's visit during a spate of heavy rain, the river was threatening to encroach, but the hotel's manager was coping admirably, sandbags at the ready, with the possibility of a flood alert.

Penelope Thornton (of the Thornton chocolate family), who took over the hotel in 1997, has instituted a refreshingly plain style, entirely in keeping with the house's Georgian origins. A large plant-filled conservatory leads into a cosy snug with a recessed carved-oak mantelpiece and open fire. There is an elegant, comfortable sitting room and a variety of well-equipped bedrooms of different sizes. Rooms in the newer Garden wing overlook the river.

Crucial to Riverside is its reputation for fine food, which is served in two intimate dining rooms. Chef John Whelan creates imaginative dishes such as *mille-feuille* of marinated salmon with beetroot confit, and celery and wild mushroom strüdel; he also offers an intriguing selection of cheeses – Lincolnshire Poacher, Belineigh Blue and Gubbeen. Coffee is accompanied by a little box of locally made Thorntons chocolates.

Barnsley, Gloucestershire

Barnsley, Cirencester,
Gloucestershire GL7 5EF

Tel 01285 740421
e-mail info@thevillagepub.co.uk
website www.thevillagepub.co.uk

Nearby Cotswold Water Park, riding, Cirencester, Daylesford Organics
Location Burnley village with free parking
Food breakfast, lunch, dinner
Price £££
Rooms 6, all have bath/shower
Facilities restaurant, bar as well as access to spa and cinema at Barnsley House (across the road)
Credit cards AE, DC, MC, V
Children welcome
Disabled no special facilities
Pets welcome
Closed never
Proprietors Calcot Health & Leisure TA Calcot Hotels, MD Mr Richard Ball

The Village Pub

Country pub

Don't come here for authenticity or the laid-back village pub atmosphere. This is nearby Barnsley House's sister establishment, and you'll like it if you are after something of chic, contemporary Barnsley House's luxury and style at half the price. The bedrooms are not large, but have creamy, sophisticated good looks and top bathrooms. The cheapest cost from £125 – at Barnsley House they start at £275. Also come for the varied menu with imaginative variations on English classic dishes.

And you can buy into some of the benefits of Barnsley House. On Sunday, go over for a five-star afternoon tea, followed by a film in the private cinema, slumped in a pink leather armchair, plus free popcorn. After, you could eat in the hotel's all-white Potager dining room. A two-course dinner, tea and film cost £25 as we went to press – not bad for the overpriced Cotswolds.

Baslow, Derbyshire

Baslow, Derbyshire DE45 1SP

Tel (01246) 582311
Fax (01246) 582312
e-mail info@cavendish-hotel.net
website www.cavendish-hotel.net

Nearby Chatsworth; Haddon Hall; Peak District.
Location 10 miles (16 km) W of Chesterfield on A619; with ample car parking
Food breakfast, lunch, dinner
Price £££
Rooms 23 double with bath; all rooms have phone, TV, minibar, hairdryer
Facilities sitting room, dining room, bar, garden room, shop; garden, putting-green, fishing
Credit cards AE, DC, MC, V
Children welcome
Disabled access difficult
Pets not accepted
Closed never
Proprietor Eric Marsh

The Cavendish

Country house hotel

The Cavendish doesn't sound like a personal small hotel. But the smart name is not mere snobbery – it is the family name of the Duke of Devonshire, on whose glorious Chatsworth estate the hotel sits (and over which the bedrooms look). And neither the hotel's size nor its equipment interferes with its essential appeal as a polished but informal and enthusiastically run hotel – strictly speaking an inn, as Eric Marsh is careful to point out, but for practical purposes a country house.

Outside, the solid stone building is plain and unassuming. Inside, all is grace and good taste: the welcoming entrance hall sets the tone – striped sofas before an open fire, elegant antique tables standing on a brick-tile floor, while the walls act as a gallery for Eric Marsh's eclectic collection of more than 300 pictures. The whole ground floor has recently been remodelled, and a conservatory added. Bedrooms are consistently attractive and comfortable, but vary in size and character – older ones are more spacious.

The elegant, duck-egg blue restaurant claims to have a 'controversial' menu. It is certainly ambitious and highly priced, but it met the approval of recent guests who described the food as 'unsurpassed – we were spoilt to death!' The Garden Room is less formal.

Bishop's Castle, Shropshire

The Square, Bishop's Castle, Shropshire SY9 5BN

Tel 01588 638403
e-mail stay@thecastlehotelbishop-scastle.co.uk
website www.thecastlehotelbishop-scastle.co.uk

Nearby Ludlow, Shrewsbury, Clun, Welshpool, Welsh borders, Offa's Dyke, South Shropshire Hills, Bishop's Castle centre, arts and crafts shops
Location overlooking Bishop's Castle, around 30 mins away from Ludlow and Shrewsbury
Food breakfast, lunch, dinner
Price £
Rooms 10; double, single and twin, all with en-suite bath or shower, tea and coffee making facilities and TV
Facilities 3 bars, restaurant, garden, terrace
Credit cards MC, V **Children** welcome **Disabled** not suitable
Pets welcome
Closed never
Proprietors Henry Hunter and Rebecca Arthan

The Castle Hotel

Town hotel

Built in 1719 by Lord Carnarvon, on the site of an old motte and bailey, the Castle Hotel stands overlooking the town of Bishop's Castle, in the midst of the Shropshire countryside. They do things traditionally here: wooden panelling, roaring open fires, chalk board menus, bar billiards and a fine selection of real ales.

The ten rooms are simple, pretty and unpretentious, with wooden furniture, original features and views right over the gardens, town and countryside. Some have high, gabled ceilings. They're not ultra-modern, but are well equipped.

With Ludlow only down the road, the kitchen has a fine range of suppliers from which to choose, and makes good use of them. The menu has the same traditional feel as the hotel, but with a modern twist. Meals are hearty, healthy and fresh. Guests can dine in one of the three bustling bars or more serenely in the oak-panelled restaurant, The Oak Room. In the summer, many eat outside on the vine-covered terrace, overlooking the fishponds. At least five real ales are usually on tap, and a comprehensive wine list is also on hand.

Ludlow, Shrewsbury and mid-Wales are all within easy reach, and the South Shropshire hills offer some excellent walking. Bishop's Castle is a pretty little town with plenty of antique shops and tea rooms.

Bourton-on-the-Hill, Gloucestershire

Bourton-on-the-Hill, Moreton in Marsh, Gloucestershire GL56 9AQ

Tel 01386 700413
Fax 01386 700413
e-mail greenstocks@horseand-groom.info **website** www.horseand-groom.info

Nearby Chipping Campden, Daylesford, Stratford-upon-Avon.
Location follow A44 from Moreton-in-Marsh and Horse & Groom is at top of hill on left-hand side
Food breakfast (included in price of room), lunch, dinner
Price ££-£££
Rooms 5 doubles
Facilities TV, DVD, hairdryer, wi-fi, garden, restaurant
Credit cards MC, V
Children welcome **Disabled** no access **Pets** allowed in garden only
Closed 25 Dec, open lunch only Boxing Day, New Year's Eve, New Year's Day
Proprietors Will and Tom Greenstock

Horse & Groom

Restaurant-with-rooms

Run by two brothers (Will and Tom Greenstock) who come from a family of hoteliers, this restaurant-with-rooms in the small Cotswold village of Bourton-on-the-Hill is full of bright ideas and imagination.

The fun starts in the kitchen, where chef Will writes a new menu daily, with offerings often changing in the course of service as one successfully finished dish becomes replaced with a fresh alternative. Atmosphere in the dining room is laid-back and the service energetic and friendly.

Each of the five bedrooms is light and spacious and abounds with finesse and modern finery. While some may find the shapes and colours in the rooms a little too eclectic for their taste, many will think it's rather invigorating to offer chequered chairs in one room or vibrant metallics in another. A pristine view of the Cotswolds helps to compensate for some noise from the road and the downstairs pub that affects one or two rooms.

A hearty breakfast is served and, like dinner, offers fresh ingredients and local produce. Prices are very reasonable, and visitors come away saying the Horse & Groom is an 'imaginative' but 'unpretentious' place which won't stand still.

Bourton-on-the-Water, Gloucestershire

High Street, Bourton-on-the-Water, Gloucestershire, GL54 2AN

Tel (01451) 822 244
e-mail info@dialhousehotel.com
website www.dialhousehotel.com

Nearby Burford, Blenheim, Upper and Lower Slaughter
Location in the heart of the village with large hotel car park
Food breakfast, lunch, tea, dinner (Wed – Sat evenings)
Price £££-££££
Rooms 14 rooms, (2 twins)
Facilities bar, sitting-room, garden
Credit cards all major
Children over 12
Disabled a garden room is accessible by wheelchair, 5 ground floor rooms
Pets 2 rooms, £10 per pet
Closed one week in Jan
Proprietor Elaine Booth

Dial House

Country hotel

The Dial House attracts a certain type of client (the upwardly mobile *Daily Telegraph* reader) and that type of client will like it very much. This is a place to forget boardroom worries; and wives (or girl-friends) will enjoy being 'pampered'. In the summer, Bourton-on-the-Water can be crowded, so the neat garden behind the hotel gives guests a place to escape the hordes.

The place is spotless. Rooms are furnished comfortably with antiques and top-quality repro. The walls are hung with hand-blocked paper in handsome patterns. Bathrooms have roll-top free-standing baths, lots of Penhaligon's toiletries and piles of thick white towels. A small bar down-stairs caters for most tastes. A sitting-room for residents has a log fire in winter and brightly coloured modern chairs, for the owners are careful not to let this honey-coloured 17th century house become too old-fashioned. The two dining-rooms are likewise furnished in modern restaurant style and Paul Nicholson and his team serve dishes combining both French and English influences, and classical and modern techniques. Try the sea bass with Alsace bacon foam, or the poached and roast fillet of veal with Madeira glazed snails.

Broad Campden, Gloucestershire

Broad Campden, Chipping Campden, Gloucestershire GL55 6UU

Tel (01386) 840295
e-mail stay@thecotswoldmalt-house.com
website www.the cotswoldmalt-house.com

Nearby Hidcote Manor; Sezincote Garden; Snowshill Manor; Court Barn Museum; Stratford-upon-Avon; Cotswold villages; Cheltenham.
Location 1 mile (1.5 km) SE of Chipping Campden; with ample car parking **Food** breakfast **Price** ££ **Rooms** 7; 6 doubles, 1 suite, all with bath and shower; all rooms have TV, DVD, hairdryer, tea and coffee making facilities, wi-fi **Facilities** 2 sitting rooms, dining room; croquet **Credit cards** MC, V **Children** welcome if well behaved **Disabled** access difficult **Pets** not accepted **Closed** Christmas **Proprietor** June Denton

The Malt House

Country guesthouse

It is easy to miss this 17thC Cotswold house (in fact a conversion of two cottages and a malt house) in a tiny picture-postcard hamlet comprising little more than a cluster of thatched, wisteria-covered cottages, a church and a pub. Once found, the Malt House is delightful – with low-beamed ceilings, antique furniture and leaded windows overlooking a dream garden. 'Beautifully done out and a peaceful, charming atmosphere,' comments our latest reporter.

All of the bedrooms overlook the croquet lawn, gardens and paddock and orchard beyond. They are individually decorated in tasteful neutral shades (some with *toille de jouie*) and furnished with antiques and collections from the family. The public rooms are immensely comfortable, with log fires in winter. The accommodation includes a pleasantly laid out garden suite with a private sitting room and an entrance to the garden. Guests breakfast in the beamed dining room, with inglenook fireplace.

Dinner can be arranged for parties of 12 or more – usually if the whole house is taken exclusively.

In 2013 new owners took over and have refurbished the house. We would welcome reports.

99 High Street, Burford,
Oxfordshire OX18 4QA

Tel (01993) 823151
Fax (01993) 823240
e-mail stay@burfordhouse.co.uk
website www.burford-house.co.uk

Nearby Cotswold Wildlife Park; Blenheim Palace; Broadway.
Location middle of Burford High Street; parking in street or free car park nearby
Food breakfast, light lunch, dinner (Wednesday-Saturday)
Price ££
Rooms 8 doubles with bath and shower; all rooms have phone, satellite TV, DVD, wi-fi, hairdryer
Facilities 2 sitting rooms, dining room, courtyard garden
Credit cards AE, MC, V **Children** welcome
Disabled 1 ground-floor room
Pets not accepted
Closed never
Proprietors Ian Hawkins

Burford House

Town house hotel

Without disturbing its historical integrity, you'll find 21stC comforts in the 15thC Cotswold stone and black-and-white timbered house in the heart of Burford. The whole place positively gleams with personal care and attention, with fresh flowers, books and magazines in the smartly decorated, dark-beamed bedrooms, and their own belongings dotted amongst the public furniture. There are two comfortable and contrasting sitting rooms downstairs, one of which gives on to a walled and paved garden, as does the ground-floor bedroom. There is also that welcome reviver of the thirsty traveller, afternoon tea.

Upstairs there are six more bedrooms, three with four-posters and one of these also has a huge free-standing bath in it. Each thoughtfully organized room is full of character, and each has an immaculate bathroom. Breakfast (included in the price of the room) is an excellent production, taken in the dining room looking out on to the High Street. There's a monthly-changing dinner menu in the hotel now – dinner is served from Wednesday to Saturday. There are also plenty of restaurants and pubs within easy walking distance.

Burford, Oxfordshire

Sheep Street, Burford, Oxfordshire OX18 4LR

Tel (01993) 823155
Fax (01993) 822228
e-mail info@lambinn-burford.co.uk
website www.cotswold-inns-hotels.co.uk/lamb

Nearby Minster Lovell Hall; Cotswold villages; Blenheim Palace.
Location in village; with car parking
Food breakfast, lunch, dinner
Price £££
Rooms 17 double and twin with bath or shower; all have phone, TV, hairdryer, wi-fi
Facilities 3 sitting rooms, dining room, bar; garden
Credit cards AE, MC, V
Children welcome
Disabled 1 ground-floor bedrooms
Pets dogs in room by prior arrangement
Closed never
Proprietors Cotswold Inns and Hotels
Manager Bill Ramsay

The Lamb

Town inn

If you want some respite from Burford's summer throng, you won't do better than The Lamb, only a few yards behind the High Street, but a veritable haven of tranquillity – particularly in the pretty walled garden, a view endorsed by a recent inspection.

Inside the creeper-clad stone cottages, you won't be surprised to find traditional pub trappings (after all, The Lamb has been an inn since the 15th century), but you may be surprised to discover 17 spacious beamed bedrooms decorated with floral fabrics and antiques. All are different – 'Shepherds', for example, has a vast antique four-poster bed and a little attic-like bathroom, 'Malt' (in what was once the neighbouring brewery) has a smart brass bed and large stone mullion windows.

Head chef Sean Ducie produces the daily-changing meals. These are served in the dining room, looking on to the geranium-filled patio. Coffee can be taken in here, or one of the sitting rooms, both of which have comfortable chairs and sofas grouped around open fires

Since our last edition, the Lamb has been taken over by the Cotswold Inns and Hotels mini-chain. Reports welcome.

Chipping Norton, Oxfordshire

10 New Street, Chipping Norton, Oxfordshire OX7 5LJ

Tel 01608 645060
e-mail enquiries@wildthymerestaurant.co.uk
website www.wildthymerestaurant.co.uk

Nearby Oxford, Gloucester, Banbury.
Location Chipping Norton, in a row of terraced houses opposite Sainsburys car park
Food breakfast, lunch, dinner
Price £-££
Rooms 3 doubles, all have bath/shower, with TV, DVD players, radio alarms, hairdryers
Facilities restaurant, courtyard garden **Credit cards** DC, MC, V
Children welcome, the Pink room and Lilac room are ideal for families with older children
Disabled wheelchair access to restaurant, not for rooms
Pets not accepted
Closed no specific closing times
Proprietors Nick and Sally Pullen

Wild Thyme

Restaurant-with-rooms

Natural, honest and charming. This diminutive spot in Chipping Norton shows that the Cotswolds can do things simply and well, and isn't just there for the trendy and the rich.

It's owned by Nick Pullen, chef, and his wife Sally, front-of-house and in charge of rooms. Sally is a natural hostess who creates an easy-going ambience.The 400-year-old terraced house is as pretty (pale blue) on the outside as it is inside – the small, interconnecting dining rooms are painted white, with pink and silver wallpaper on one wall, oriental cushions scattered on banquette seats, plain wooden tables and white-painted chairs.

"I worried about lots of things when we decided to set up our own place," says Sally "but not about Nick's ability: he cooks from the heart." His food is essentially home-made, unaffected and moreish, and his menu changes with the advent of seasonal produce.

The rooms are as charming as the rest of Wild Thyme – pretty, cosy and well equipped. Gold, the largest, has gently sloping floors and walls and a small bath and shower. Pink and Lilac are snug, the latter with views of the countryside.

If you want a really good-value weekend away in the Cotswolds – and enjoyable food – this is the place.

Clipsham, Rutland

Main Street, Clipsham, Rutland
LE15 7SH

Tel (01780)410355
Fax (01780) 410000
e-mail info@theolivebranchpub.com
website
www.theolivebranchpub.com

Nearby Burghley, Belvoir Castle, Rutland Owl and Falconry Centre
Location in the centre of Clipsham
Food breakfast, lunch, dinner
Price ££-££££
Rooms 6 en-suite; all rooms have TV, radio, tea and coffee making facilities; most have DVD player, broadband
Facilities DVD/CD library, patio/gardens
Credit cards MC, V
Children welcome
Disabled fully wheelchair-accessible room **Pets** accepted in ground floor rooms **Closed** Christmas night, Boxing day, New Year's day
Proprietors Sean Hope and Ben Jones

Beech House

Bed-and-breakfast

The Beech House is where you sleep, but the Olive Branch began it all and the two, though divided by the road, are really indivisible. So good was the food in the pub (named to mark the end of a quarrel with a farmer; this is not an ordinary place) that rooms were needed to house those who had travelled to enjoy it. What looks like a pretty doll's-house was bought and six en-suite rooms were made, decorated with fashionable modern colours and furnished with a mix of rather striking antique and modern pieces. It is a thoughtful management that provides a fully wheelchair-accessible bathroom in the ground floor room and attention to the guests' needs and attention to detail are probably what won the combined establishments the Michelin Pub of the Year award in 2007. There are four types of tea in the bedrooms and fresh coffee for the cafetière; a Roberts digital radio (*de rigueur* in smart inns these days); DVDs and a choice of duvets or sheets and blankets. So far so homely. But the extra factor which this place seems to have in spades is what Michelin's men call 'star quality', the willing, informal, kind and efficient service you get from people who have put their hearts (and their savings) into a venture like this.

Corse Lawn, Gloucestershire

Corse Lawn, Gloucestershire,
GL19 4LZ

Tel (01452) 780771
Fax (01452) 780840
e-mail enquiries@corselawn.com
website www.corselawn.com

Nearby Tewkesbury Abbey; Malvern Hills.
Location 5 miles (8 km) W of Tewkesbury on B4211; ample car parking
Food breakfast, lunch, dinner
Price £££
Rooms 18; 16 double and twin, 2 suites, all with bath; all rooms have phone, TV, hairdrier
Facilities 3 sitting rooms, bar, restaurant, 2 meeting rooms; garden, croquet, tennis, indoor swimming pool
Credit cards AE, DC, MC, V
Children accepted if well-behaved
Disabled 5 ground-floor bedrooms
Pets accepted in bedrooms
Closed 24 to 26 Dec
Proprietor Baba Hine

Corse Lawn House

Country hotel

This tall, red-brick Queen Anne house, set back across common land from what is now a minor road, must have been one of the most refined coaching inns of its day. Should you arrive in traditional style, you could still drive your coach-and-four down the slipway into the large pond in front of the house, to cool the horses and wash the carriage.

Baba Hine has been here since the late 1970s, first running the house purely as a restaurant, later opening up four rooms and in recent years adding various extensions (carefully designed to blend with the original building) to provide more and more bedrooms as well as more space for drinking, eating and sitting. Baba Hine is now front of house, having handed over the kitchen to Martin Kinahan who, she says, produces dishes just as good as hers. The menu is an eclectic mix of English and French, modern and provincial dishes, all carefully prepared and served in substantial portions; there are fixed-price menus (with a vegetarian alternative) at both lunch and dinner as well as *a la carte*, all notably good value.

Bedrooms are large, with a mixture of antique and modern furnishings and the atmosphere of the house is calm and relaxing. Breakfasts are a home-made feast. A recent visitor was enchanted.

Faringdon, Oxfordshire

Faringdon, Oxfordshire SN7 8RF

Tel 01367 870382
e-mail info@trout-inn.co.uk
website www.trout-inn.co.uk

Nearby Vale of the White Horse; Kelmscott Manor; Chimney Nature Reserve; Blenheim Palace; 20 mins from Oxford town centre
Location on the River Thames in the Cotswolds
Food breakfast, lunch, dinner
Price ££
Rooms 6; all with TV, DVD player, radio
Facilities bar, dining room, garden
Credit cards DC, MC, V
Children welcome
Disabled 4 accessible rooms
Pets welcome **Closed** Christmas and Boxing Day **Proprietors** Gareth and Helen Pugh

The Trout at Tadpole Bridge **Bed-and-breakfast**

In this little-known, idyllic spot in Oxfordshire, the river flowing under Tadpole Bridge's diminutive span is, in fact, the Thames. Many customers arrive by boat, for a pint of ale or a night ashore. The Trout's garden runs down to the water, where there are moorings for patrons and The Trout's motorised punt (£40).

The old brick inn has the hallmarks of a modernised pub-with-rooms, but in owner Helen Pugh's hands they add up to an unpretentious, family-friendly whole. There are lovely bedrooms that make you stop in surprise, a clutch of faithful regulars propping up the bar; the owners' young sons catching crayfish in the river before proudly handing their haul (licensed of course) to the chef. Staff are local and cheerful.

At dinner we had tasty starters and there was an excellent wine list devised by Helen's husband, Gareth. But "is everything alright?" was asked too many times and the lamb cutlets were overcooked.

Still, The Trout, where the infant Thames is at its most peaceful, provides the most delightful base for a weekend away: downstream are the wildflower meadows and wading birds of the Chimney Nature Reserve; across the fields is Bampton, one of the oldest villages in the county; Blenheim Palace is within easy reach.

Great Rissington, Gloucestershire

Great Rissington, Gloucestershire
GL54 2LP

Tel (01451) 820388
e-mail enquiry@thelambinn.com
website www.thelambinn.com

Nearby The Slaughters; Stow-on-the-Wold; Burford; Sudeley Castle.
Location 4 miles (6 km) SE of Bourton-on-the-Water, 3 miles (5 km) N of A40; with ample car parking
Food breakfast, lunch, dinner
Price ££
Rooms 13; 4 suites in The Lamb Inn, 2 garden suites, 5 pub rooms, 2 stable rooms, all with bath or shower; all rooms have TV, wi-fi
Facilities sitting room, bar; garden
Credit cards AE, MC, V
Children welcome
Disabled not suitable
Pets accepted in bedrooms by arrangement
Closed Christmas Day
Proprietors Paul and Jacqueline Gabriel

The Lamb Inn

Country inn

If you follow the River Windrush as it rises westwards from Burford, and then roughly follow its curve from the north (where it has given Bourton-on-the-Water its name), you will arrive in Great Rissington, deep in the Cotswolds. Overlooking gently rolling farmland and built from the local stone, the original elements of this inn are 300 years old. Taken over in the year 2000 by Paul and Jackie Gabriel, The Lamb is still very much a pub, indeed it is enough of a pub to merit a recommendation in a national guide to good beer. But it also now has two elements that many other inns lack – good board and lodging. Board comes in the shape of a surprisingly large – and comfortingly busy – restaurant. It does a roaring trade in traditional dishes freshly prepared from the best of local produce, often with a modern twist.

The bedrooms are bright, fresh and individually designed, and more than half have space for sitting as well as sleeping. All bathrooms have recently been renovated.

Hambleden, Oxfordshire

Hambleden, Henley-on-Thames, Oxforshire RG9 6RP

Tel (01491) 571227
Fax (01491) 520810
e-mail enquiries@thestagandhuntsman.co.uk
website www.stagandhuntsman.com

Nearby Hell-fire caves, Clivedon, Henley-on-Thames, The Hughenden Manor
Location Hambleden village, just off Skirmett Road
Food breakfast, lunch, dinner
Price ££
Rooms 9 doubles with private bathrooms **Facilities** bar, restaurant, beer garden **Credit cards** all major
Children welcome
Disabled accessible, one disabled room.
Pets welcome in some rooms and all public areas apart from the restaurant **Closed** never
Manager Jaxon Keedwell
Proprietor Urs Schwarzenbach

The Stag & Huntsman

Village inn

The Stag and Huntsman, a Chilterns institution, recently reopened after a lavish makeover, paid for by its philanthropic owner, Urs Schwarzenbach, whose main aim was to create a welcoming hub for the community.

The makeover has succeeded, and the place thrives, even with a more sober appearance than other similar places. The handsome dark green livery may stray from contemporary colour palettes, but it's authentic and a refreshing change from the norm. It's said that architect Ptolemy Dean, who restored The Stag and Huntsman on behalf of the Culden Faw Estate, cried out "That's the colour!" as an innocent man strolled past in a dark green Barbour.

The whole place has echoes of elderly relatives – in a pleasing way – right down to the tessellated tile floors and the narrow staircase. But it has attitude – we were pleased to find a retro Roberts radio in our room.

The food is superior pub fare. The Stag and Huntsman has recently appointed a new manager, Jaxon Keedwell, who trained at the Savoy. We would welcome reports on how he's getting on.

Hambleton, Rutland

Hambleton, Oakham, Rutland
LE15 8TH

Tel (01572) 756991
e-mail hotel@hambletonhall.com
website www.hambletonhall.com

Nearby Burghley House; Rockingham Castle; Stamford, Belvoir Castle.
Location 2 miles (3 km) E of Oakham on peninsula jutting into Rutland Water; with ample car parking
Food breakfast, lunch, dinner
Price ££££
Rooms 17 double and twin with bath; all rooms have phone, TV, hairdryer
Facilities sitting rooms, 3 dining rooms, bar; garden, swimming pool, tennis, helipad; fishing, golf, sailing, riding all nearby **Credit cards** AE, DC, MC, V **Children** accepted **Disabled** access possible, lift/elevator **Pets** by arrangement **Closed** never **Proprietors** Tim and Stefa Hart

Hambleton Hall

Country house hotel

If you're planning a second honeymoon, a break from work or a weekend away from the kids, this Victorian former shooting lodge in the grand hotel tradition is a sybaritic paradise, from which only your wallet and your waistline will suffer. The location is unrivalled, standing in stately grandeur on a wooded hillock, surrounded by manicured lawns, surveying the expanse of Rutland Water. The interior is sumptuous. In her design of the rooms, Stefa Hart uses rich, heavy fabrics in some of the bedrooms, and showing a preference for delicate colours. The rooms still have their original mouldings and are furnished with fine antiques and paintings. Bedrooms with a view over the water are the most sought-after and expensive.

Many people are drawn here by the wizardry of Michelin-starred chef, Aaron Patterson. He works his magic on only the freshest of ingredients, whether Hambleton beef, sea bass or veal sweetbreads. One of the joys of staying here is that you can blow the cobwebs away with an exhilarating walk from the front door of the hotel as far as you want around Rutland Water, birdwatching as you go.

Some time ago the Harts opened a home bakery – Hambleton Bakery – that makes a variety of breads and cakes. We particularly like their Hambleton Sourdough loaf.

Hereford, Herefordshire

Castle Street, Hereford
HR1 2NW

Tel (01432) 356321
website www.castlehse.co.uk

Nearby Hereford Cathedral, chained library, Mappa Mundi, cider museum, Offa's Dyke
Location In Hereford city centre on Castle Street; valet parking
Food breakfast, lunch, dinner
Price £££-££££
Rooms 24; 17 suites, 3 doubles, 4 singles; all with bath; all rooms have TV, phone, video player, mini hi-fi, fridge, safe
Facilities lounge, dining room, bar, gardens, terrace
Credit cards AE, DC, MC, V
Children welcome
Disabled one adapted room
Pets not accepted
Closed never
Proprietor David Watkins

Castle House

Town house hotel

Life goes at a slower pace in this rural part of England and Hereford is the ideal county town: tight-knit, accessible and tranquil, yet with world-class attractions in its fine cathedral and Chained Library. Castle House is an elegant Grade II listed town mansion whose charming gardens overlook the old Castle moat. The cathedral and shops are nearby, yet there is absolute quiet: no traffic noise, just birdsong and the quack of ducks. We can think of few lovelier, or better sited, city hotels in Britain.

Past the pillared entrance, you find an impressive hall, with wooden central staircase and reception tucked neatly out of sight. To one side: a panelled bar; to the other, a spacious restaurant and sitting room whose doors lead to the garden. All the rooms are full of light. Upstairs are bedrooms of various shapes and sizes, some optimistically described as 'luxury suites' when 'spacious double' is more accurate.

The hotel was revamped in 2000 in a style that might be described as 'continental bijoux' or 'faux posh'. We felt this was at odds with the building and with Hereford itself, but Castle House is a very good hotel. The management is excellent and the food imaginative. A 'tasting menu' at £50 per person, however, reiterates the hotel' s pretentious side, in a city and a county that are among the least pretentious in England.

Hough-on-the-Hill, Lincolnshire

Hough-on-the-Hill, Grantham Road, Lincolnshire NG32 2AZ

Tel 01400 250234
e-mail armsinn@yahoo.co.uk
website www.thebrownlowarms.com

Nearby Belton House, Lincoln Cathedral, Lincoln Castle, Belvoir Castle, Tattershall Castle
Location 5-10 minutes from A1, village of Hough on the Hill
Food breakfast, dinner (Tues-Sat), Sunday lunch
Price £-££
Rooms 7; 3 in the barn conversion, 4 in the pub, all with en suite, TV, DVD players, hairdryers, wi-fi, phone **Facilities** bar, restaurant, terrace **Credit cards** MC, V
Children accepted over 8
Disabled 3 rooms on ground floor in barn conversion, but some steps into the pub
Pets not accepted
Closed Christmas Day and Boxing Day, 1-14th Jan
Proprietors Paul and Lorraine Willoughby

The Brownlow Arms

Restaurant-with-rooms

Lorraine Willoughby has worked at The Brownlow Arms since she was 17; she and Paul now own and run it together.

The rooms are stylishly decorated under the acute eye of Paul. We entered our room through a wide lobby, beyond which our room opened out. The dramatic focal point of the room was a white bed framed by a huge antique oak mantelpiece on the wall behind, padded in the middle to create a headboard, with a capacious red sofa at the end of the bed. The other rooms in the inn and house next door are decorated in fresh checks and stripes, and displayed an equally impressive attention to detail (not to mention well-equipped with television, radio, and ironing board). They work, although we didn't like the artificial flowers.

The restaurant makes a refreshing change from modern, wood-floored pub dining rooms – you get warm panelling, stone fireplace and high-backed, medieval-style tapestry pattern chairs. As we went to press, Paul and Lorraine had plans to renovate this area, and we can only imagine a positive result. We couldn't fault the food: all the dishes (such as bresaola with gazpacho jelly and parmesan crisp) were gracefully and swiftly presented.

This place gives value for money – the bedrooms could easily be in a luxury town house hotel at double the price.

Langar, Nottinghamshire

Langar, Nottinghamshire
NG13 9HG

Tel (01949) 860559
Fax (01949) 861045
e-mail info@langarhall.co.uk
website www.langarhall.com

Nearby Belton House; Chatsworth; Sherwood Forest; Lincoln Cathedral, Belvoir Castle, Nottingham.
Location in village behind church; with ample car parking
Food breakfast, lunch, dinner
Price £££
Rooms 12 doubles; 1 room has shower, all others have baths; all rooms have phone, TV, hairdryer
Facilities sitting rooms, dining rooms, bar; garden, croquet, fishing, helipad **Credit cards** MC, V
Children welcome
Disabled 1 ground-floor bedroom
Pets accepted by arrangement
Closed never
Proprietor Imogen Skirving

Langar Hall

Country house hotel

After the death of Imogen Skirving's father, she couldn't bear the thought of losing the house, nor could she afford to keep it on, except on the basis of sharing it with guests. Thus was born the concept of Langar Hall as a hotel and, despite burgeoning success, people who stay here feel more like guests in a beautiful Georgian stuccoed country house rather than customers in a hotel. The library appears to be totally unchanged, with hundreds of books available to leaf through with a drink or two before dinner. The food is superb and the wine list well judged.

The best bedrooms are airy, with furniture appropriate to the house that Imogen wanted to save, and enjoy glorious views of the Vale of Belvoir. For exercise, you can play croquet or stroll round the village church. Best of all is the friendliness of the hostess and her staff. Imogen wanders around the dining room, alighting at tables of single, bored businessmen and exchanging any sort of gossip, while nothing is too much trouble for the chef or staff. When our inspector realised, at 12.45 am, after an excellent dinner, that he had forgotten his sponge bag, an assortment of toothbrushes, toothpaste and razors was provided. We revisited recently and enjoyed the Imogen Skirving show as much as ever. Winner of *Food and Travel* magazine's best rural hotel award, 2013.

Little Malvern, Worcestershire

Little Malvern, near Malvern, Worcestershire WR13 6NA

Tel (01684) 310288
e-mail enquiries@holdfast-cottage.co.uk
website www.holdfast-cottage.co.uk

Nearby Eastnor Castle; Worcester; Hereford; Gloucester.
Location 4 miles (6.5 km) S of Great Malvern on A4104; with ample car parking
Food breakfast, lunch, bar meals, dinner
Price £££
Rooms 8; 5 doubles, 2 twins, 1 single all with bath or shower; all rooms have phone, TV, hairdryer
Facilities sitting room, bar, dining room, conservatory; croquet
Credit cards MC, V
Children welcome
Disabled access difficult
Pets not accepted
Closed never
Proprietors Steven and Julie Thompson

Holdfast Cottage

Country hotel

'Cottage' seems to be stretching things somewhat – and yet, despite its size, this Victorian farmhouse does have the cosy intimacy of a cottage, and Steven and Julie Thompson create an atmosphere of friendly informality.

Inside, low oak beams and a polished flagstone floor in the hall conform to cottage requirement; beyond, headroom improves – though flowery, Laura Ashley decoration emphasizes the cottage status. There's been a big refurbishment in the last 12 months – bedrooms are light and airy, with carefully co-ordinated fabrics and papers; some bathrooms are small. Outside, the veranda with its wistaria keeps the scale of the house relatively intimate. The garden – scarcely cottage-style – adds enormously to the overall appeal of the place, with its lawns, shrubberies, fruit trees and delightful 'wilderness'. Beyond are spectacular views of the Malvern Hills.

The daily-changing menu is based on continental as well as traditional English dishes, using the best local and seasonal produce, as well as freshly prepared home-baked rolls and hand-made ice cream. Herbs are gathered from the garden to compliment the English fare, which is sometimes found alongside more unusual dishes such as guinea fowl.

Malvern Wells, Worcestershire

Holywell Road, Malvern Wells, Worcestershire WR14 4LG

Tel (01684) 588860
Fax (01684) 560662
e-mail reception@cottageinthe-wood.co.uk
website www.cottageinthewood.co.uk

Nearby Malvern Hills; Eastnor Castle; Worcester Cathedral.
Location 2 miles (3 km) S of Great Malvern off A449; with ample car parking
Food breakfast, lunch, dinner
Price £££
Rooms 30 double and twin with bath or shower; all rooms have phone, TV, hairdryer; some have air-conditioning **Facilities** sitting room, dining room, bar; garden
Credit cards AE, MC, V
Children welcome
Disabled ground-floor rooms in annexe **Pets** accepted in ground-floor rooms, £9 per night
Closed never **Proprietors** John and Sue Pattin

The Cottage in the Wood **Country hotel**

Three buildings and a family form this glossy little hotel perched, very privately, in seven wooded acres, high above the Severn valley and with a superb vista across to the Cotswolds thirty-something miles away (binoculars provided). There are bedrooms in all three buildings, taking the hotel over our usual size for this guide; but the smartly furnished Georgian dower house at its heart is so intimate, calm and comfortable that we decided to relent.

A short stroll away is the rebuilt Coach House, known as the Pinnacles, where rooms are smaller but have the best views, and Beech Cottage with four cottage-style bedrooms. The family consists of John and Sue Pattin, their daughter Maria, son Dominic (head chef) and son in law Nick. Apart from its food, the restaurant (modern English cuisine) has two other substantial qualities: windows that let you see the view and a wine list that lets you roam the world. Walkers can get straight out on to a good stretch of the Malvern Hills and for tourers the Pattins provide leaflets giving concise notes on everything that's worth visiting for 50 miles (80 km) around. For the rest of us, there's a very well stocked bar and a free video library.

Norton, Shropshire

Bridgenorth Road, Norton, Near Shifnal, Telford, Shropshire, TF11 9EE

Tel (01952) 580240
e-mail reservations@hundred-house.co.uk **website** www.hundred-house.co.uk

Nearby Telford, Chester, Ironbridge Gorge Museum, Severn Valley steam way, The Long Mynd (walk).
Location just off the M54 from junction 4, on the A442 between Telford and Bridgnorth, with car-parking
Food breakfast, lunch, dinner
Price ££–£££ (min 2 night stay)
Rooms 9; 8 doubles, 1 single, all with bath; all have TV, phone, tea and coffee making facilities, hairdryer **Facilities** dining room, bar, brasserie; herb garden, beer garden
Credit cards AE, MC, V
Children welcome
Disabled some access in public rooms **Pets** well behaved dogs (£10 charge) **Closed** Christmas night
Proprietors Phillips family

Hundred House Hotel

Country hotel

"Quite extraordinary, a pleasant surprise around every corner" says one recent reporter. From the moment you pull in to the car park you don't quite know what to expect next. The building itself dates back to the 1500's, when it was the local court house, and the remains of the stocks and the whipping post can still be seen opposite. Push open the stained glass doors, and the atmosphere hits you: dim lighting, mellow wood floors, panelled walls, bouquets of dried herbs and flowers hanging from ceilings. The dining areas are spacious – the Hundred House caters for non-residential guests, but the tables are cosy and intimate, some in front of a large open fire, others tucked in various nooks. The menu is impressive and unusual, but cooked well with no corners cut. The bar is in the brasserie area and offers an impressive range of ales, with more little tables for a quick bite of lunch.

The bedrooms are, well, eccentric: swings in the 'superior' rooms; lively, floral decoration; and some very spacious bathrooms. The one single room in the house is a little cramped. The herb garden tended by Sylvia Phillips, is magical and is regularly used for marriage blessings. Elsewhere, you'll find relaxing sitting areas and a small pond. It is very much a family-run hotel, with parents and sons working together to create a memorable experience.

Oxford

92-94 High Street, Oxford
OX1 4BN

Tel (01865) 799599
e-mail info@oldbank-hotel.co.uk
website www.oldbank-hotel.co.uk

Nearby Oxford colleges; Botanical Gardens; Sheldonian Theatre.
Location in city centre, with ample car parking
Food breakfast, lunch, dinner; room service
Price £££-££££
Rooms 42; 41 double and twin, 1 suite; all rooms have phone, TV, CD player, air-conditioning, safe, hairdryer
Facilities restaurant, bar, courtyard
Credit cards AE, DC, MC, V
Children accepted
Disabled 1 room is specially adapted, most other rooms have lift/elevator access
Pets not accepted
Closed never
Proprietor Jeremy Mogford

Old Bank Hotel

Town hotel

Hardly a quintessential charming small hotel because of its size, but we still think Old Bank Hotel is a good central Oxford address. What was, until the 1990s, a venerable bank with a fine Georgian façade, is now a cool, sophisticated hotel with a buzzing brasserie. It has kept up its high standards since we last visited.

The building has much to recommend it. The best bedrooms are graced with floor-length windows or, in the Tudor part, beams and deep window seats under lattice windows – room 45, in this style (see above), is particularly charming. All the rooms – and the bathrooms – are impeccably decorated in an understated chic-rustic style (think taupe, think beige, think cream). Although elegant, they might feel dull if it weren't for Jeremy Mogford's punchy art collection that decorates rooms, corridors and brasserie. There were tea and coffee facilities in our room, but no milk – a shame. However, it can be found in the guest sitting rooms downstairs.

As well as a hotel, the Old Bank has become the 'in' place to eat in Oxford. The Quod Brasserie and Bar stretches across the former banking hall. Most guests will enjoy the buzz and bonhomie that emanates from this always packed meeting place (service can be slow), with a wide-ranging menu. Staff are welcoming, helpful and knowledgeable.

1 Banbury Road, Oxford OX2 6NN

Tel (01865) 310210
Fax (01865) 311262
e-mail info@oldparsonage-hotel.co.uk **website** www.oxford-hotels-restaurants.co.uk

Nearby Oxford colleges; Botanical Gardens; Sheldonian Theatre.
Location 5 minutes' walk from city centre, at N end of St Giles, close to junction of Woodstock and Banbury Roads; limited car parking
Food breakfast, lunch, dinner; room service and afternoon tea
Price £££ **Rooms** 35; 30 double and twin, 1 single, 4 suites, all with bath; all rooms have phone, TV, hairdryer, internet connection **Facilities** sitting room, dining room, bar, garden library; terrace, roof garden **Credit cards** AE, DC, MC, V **Children** welcome
Disabled access difficult **Pets** not accepted **Closed** never **Proprietor** Jeremy Mogford

Old Parsonage Hotel

Town hotel

Talk about contrast. The two best hotels in Oxford, Old Bank House (see opposite), and this one are in the same ownership – Jeremy Mogford.The Old Parsonage is much more typical of our guide, occupying a characterful, wistaria-clad house that has been owned by University College since 1320. Compared to its sleek, hip younger sibling, it seems at first quaint and old-fashioned, yet there is no themed olde worlde charm here, despite the great age of the building.

In early 2014, there were major renovations to the hotel. In addition to five new bedrooms, a garden library has been added for guests. The development of these new areas is in line with the rest of the hotel – wool, linen and velvet have been used in the rooms, and a colour scheme that centres on plum, deep red and grey. There is a brand new Old York stone floor downstairs.

We've had reports that the restaurant and bar area is to retain that intimate and Bohemian atmosphere that marked it out before, even with new furniture and decoration. We would welcome reports on the new look.

Painswick, Gloucestershire

Cardynham House

Village bed-and-breakfast

Built with money from wool and from pale gold stone out of a local quarry, Painswick is a classic Cotswold town perched rather precariously on (and over the brink of) a steep hillside. If you're not paying attention you might quite easily walk past Cardynham House – a discreet sign above the venerable front door of this Grade II-listed building, right on the street, is hardly enough to focus your attention when everything else around is so worth looking at. The real fun starts once you get inside. A cavernous open fireplace, flanked by a bread oven, warms a cosy drawing room which seems to metamorphose at some point into a conservatory.

Somehow, nine totally unique bedrooms have been created in this apparently modest-sized house, and each one is a triumphal exercise of imagination. Dotted with antiques and murals, each is decorated to a different theme and, even side by side in the same building, they all work unusually well. The most eccentric of all, air-conditioned because it hasn't a window to its name, has been got up like a desert pavilion. Another has its own private patio largely taken up with a covered plunge pool (heated, and with a powered current to swim against). Breakfast is taken in the restaurant that, on the evenings that it's open, serves Thai food.

Tibbiwell Street, Painswick, Gloucestershire GL6 6XX

Tel (01452) 814006
Fax (01452) 812321
e-mail info@cardynham.co.uk
website www.cardynham.co.uk

Nearby Cheltenham; Chedworth Roman Villa; Cirencester, Gloucester, Sudeley.
Location in village, 3 miles (5 km) N of Stroud; car parking on street
Food breakfast, Tues to Sat dinner and Sun lunch
Price ££-££££
Rooms 9; 6 double, 3 family, all with bath or shower; all rooms have phone, TV
Facilities sitting room, breakfast room
Credit cards AE, MC, V
Children accepted
Pets not accepted
Disabled not suitable
Closed restaurant only, Sun eve, Mon eve
Proprietor John Paterson

Rhydycroesau, Shropshire

Rhydycroesau, Near Oswestry, Shropshire, SY10 7JD

Tel (01691) 653700
e-mail stay@peny.co.uk **website** www.peny.co.uk

Nearby Erdigg; Llanrhaedar waterfall; Powys Castle; Pistyll Rhaedar waterfall
Location 3 miles (4.5 km) West of Oswestry on the B4580. Hotel is 3 miles (4.5 km)down on that road on the left
Food breakfast, dinner, light lunch on request
Price ££
Rooms 12 double; all with bath and shower; all rooms have TV, hairdryer, modem point, tea and coffee making facilities, phone
Facilities dining room, sitting room, bar, reading room; garden
Credit cards AE, MC, V
Children welcome
Disabled 1 ground-floor room
Closed 21st of Dec for 4 weeks
Pets by arrangement
Proprietors Mr and Mrs Hunter

Pen-y-Dyffryn

Country hotel

Driving through the windy lanes cutting through the Shropshire hills from Oswestry, you can easily miss this attractive Georgian House tucked away off the main road. It nestles serenely among trees and green fields and you will be taken aback by the views that stretch (on a clear day) to the Welsh mountains. The dining room and sitting areas are decorated in warm colours; open log fires for the chilly winter evenings are perfect. If you prefer to drink or dine outside, there's a delightful little patio stretching round the side of the hotel. Look closely and you'll see modern touches about the place, such as abstract art.

The bedrooms are large, spacious and comfortable, with large fluffy towels provided in all the en suite bathrooms (some with spa baths and Jacuzzis) and fresh flowers on arrival. Four of the bedrooms are in the coach house, which is ideal for guests with animals. They each have spectacular views and their own private little patio. Chef Dave Morris has been here for 15 years and his cooking is perfect for the place – we enjoyed goats' cheese and maple syrup mousse and rose veal with Madeira cream sauce. The small bar by the entrance is staffed by helpful staff who can advise you on sightseeing, walking, or shopping in Wales or Shropshire.

Rowsley, Derbyshire

Rowsley, Derbyshire DE4 2EB

Tel (01629) 733518
Fax (01629) 732671
e-mail reception@thepeacockatrowsley.com **website** www.thepeacockatrowsley.com

Nearby Haddon Hall, Chatsworth, rivers Wye and Derwent
Location beside A6, between Matlock and Bakewell
Food breakfast, lunch, dinner; room service
Price £££
Rooms 15; 14 doubles and 1 suite, 2 with four-poster, all en suite; all rooms have phone, TV, DVD player, tea and coffee making facilities, hairdryer **Facilities** bar, conference rooms, private dining and restaurant, fishing, golf nearby **Credit cards** AE, DC, MC, V **Children** accepted, but not on Friday or Saturday
Disabled not suitable **Pets** dogs £10 per night, not in public rooms
Closed 7th-24th Jan **Proprietor** Lord Edward Manners
Managers Ian and Jenni Mackenzie

The Peacock at Rowsley

Country hotel

Just inside the door of the Peacock is a bowl of water and a basket for your dog. This is a sportsman's hotel, though an aesthete would be just as happy here; the pictures are outstandingly good. The River Wye – the only water in the country where wild rainbow trout breed naturally – is what the sportsmen come for. It is said to be the finest dry fly trout fishing in the land and the Head River Keeper from Haddon Hall is on hand to help you enjoy it. The Hall (Thornfield in BBC TV's *Jane Eyre*) is a nearby outing for days when the fish won't bite.

The Peacock, built in the 17th century, was once Haddon's dower house. Now it has all the comforts and convenience (wi-fi, DVDs) that modern visitors expect. Furnished with a mixture of old pieces and comfortable modern upholstery, there is an aura of antique furniture wax and wood smoke. In the bedrooms, fresh flowers, mahogany dressing tables and top-notch beds will make you feel at home. Uniformed staff are attentive and friendly – occasionally a little too much so for old-fashioned tastes. A great ledger in the hall records the fishermen's daily successes and disappointments. Whatever their luck on the river bank, they will not be disappointed in this handsome, well-run hotel.

Stratford-upon-Avon, Warwickshire

58-59 Rother Street, Stratford-Upon-Avon, Warwickshire CV37 6LT

Tel (01789) 267309
e-mail CaterhamSoA@btconnect.com
website www.caterhamhousehotel.co.uk

Nearby Royal Shakespeare Theatre; Shakespeare's Birthplace.
Location in centre of town; with car parking
Food breakfast
Price ££
Rooms 10 double and twin, all with bath or shower; all rooms have TV
Facilities sitting room, breakfast room, bar
Credit cards MC, V **Children** accepted
Disabled not suitable
Pets not accepted
Closed Christmas Day
Proprietor David Young

Caterham House

Town bed-and-breakfast

Two Georgian houses have been knocked together to form this friendly B&B which, despite its central location – just a ten-minute walk from the Royal Shakespeare Theatre – has a surprisingly peaceful ambience. David Young took over ownership of Caterham House in 2003 from Dominique and Olive Maury, who had been here since the 1970s. He has since renovated the interior to a traditional English style, while making use of some of the furniture that was collected by his predecessors.

There is a small conservatory-style sitting room with an eclectic assortment of furniture, where generous teas and coffees are served each afternoon. Although there are no gardens, the sitting room opens out on to a small, colourful terrace.

You couldn't call the bedrooms huge, but all are spacious enough to accommodate a comfy chair, and each one is individually decorated. Breakfast is the only meal served, but guests can choose between a full English or continental with a variety of fruit compotes.

Reports would be welcome.

Tetbury, Gloucestershire

Near Tetbury, Gloucestershire
GL8 8YJ

Tel (01666) 890391
Fax (01666) 890394
e-mail reception@calcotmanor.co.uk
website www.calcotmanor.co.uk

Nearby Chavenage; Owlpen Manor; Westonbirt Arboretum.
Location 3 miles (5 km) W of Tetbury on A4135; with ample car parking
Food breakfast, lunch, dinner
Price ££££
Rooms 35; 22 double and twin, 7 family suites, 6 family rooms, all with bath or shower; all rooms have phone, TV, hairdryer **Facilities** 2 sitting rooms, dining room; garden, swimming pool, croquet, 2 all weather tennis courts; playroom, Spa
Credit cards AE, DC, MC, V
Children welcome (crèche)
Disabled 4 ground-floor bedrooms
Pets by arrangement
Closed never
Proprietor Richard Ball

Calcot Manor

Country house hotel

This 15thC Cotswold farmhouse has been functioning as a hotel since 1984. Richard Ball took over Calcot Manor from his parents when they retired, and with a team of dedicated staff continues to provide the highest standards of comfort and service while preserving a calm and relaxed atmosphere. The lovely old house itself was a sound choice – its rooms are spacious and elegant without being grand – and the setting amid lawns and old barns, surrounded by rolling countryside, is all you could ask for.

Furnishings and decorations are carefully harmonious, with rich fabrics and pastel colours throughout. A converted cottage provides seven family suites, designed specifically for parents travelling with young children. For their entertainment, there's an indoor playroom.

Michael Stenekes is head chef of both the Conservatory Restaurant and the adjoining Gumstool Inn, which is more informal and moderately priced. In the restaurant, you might dine on champagne poached halibut with sea vegetables and a mussel saffron nage, or Calcot organic beef with a *béarnaise* sauce, French beans and artichokes.

Titley, Herefordshire

Titley, Kington, Herefordshire HR5 3RL

Tel 01544 230221
e-mail reservations@thestagg.co.uk
website www.thestagg.co.uk

Nearby Offa's Dyke, The Mortimer Trail, Ludlow, Hay-on-Wye, Hereford.
Location Titley village on B4355
Food breakfast, lunch, dinner
Price ££-£££
Rooms 6; 3 in The Vicarage, 3 in the pub; all have bath/shower and wi-fi, tea/coffee facilities
Facilities bar, dining room, garden
Credit cards AE, MC, V
Children accepted, but no special facilities
Disabled not suitable
Pets dogs welcome to stay in the pub **Closed** Mondays and Tuesdays, Christmas and Boxing Day, 2 weeks in Nov, 1 week in Jan or Feb
Proprietors Stephen and Nicola Reynolds

The Stagg Inn

Country inn

This was the first gastropub to get a Michelin star, in 2001. Chef Steve Reynolds was recognized for his straightforward country dishes using locally sourced ingredients. He has held on to it since then, but the food, though good, is only part of the story. There are six rooms, three in the pub and three in the nearby Old Vicarage. The pub rooms are beamy and comfortable, but the vicarage ones are exceptional: large, with high ceilings, elegant shuttered windows, wooden floors and great bathrooms. The furniture is unpretentious and pleasing – in fact the whole effect is that of a well-loved family home. And, starting at £110, they are notable value.

Guests may use the garden and dine out of doors in the summer. Take children to The Vicarage garden down the road – it's Steve's pride and joy – to visit the resident chickens and ducks.

High Street, Winchcombe,
Gloucestershire, GL54 5LJ

Tel (01242) 602 366
Fax (01242) 604360
e-mail enquiries@wesleyhouse.co.uk
website www.wesleyhouse.co.uk

Nearby Sudeley Castle, Cheltenham race course, Hailes Abbey (NT)
Location in the centre of the town, parking in the street about 200m away
Food breakfast, lunch, dinner; afternoon tea
Price ££
Rooms 5 doubles, 1 can be twin, shower only; all with TV; one with a small roof terrace/balcony
Facilities wine bar and grill, restaurant **Credit cards** AE, MC, V
Children welcome
Disabled access not possible
Pets no dogs
Closed Boxing Day; restaurant is closed on Monday
Proprietor Matthew Brown

Wesley House

Restaurant-with-rooms

You don't go to Wesley House for spacious rooms, for fine antique furniture or for its facilities. There are no telephones or hairdryers in the bedrooms; no spas or conference rooms. It doesn't even have a place to park your car. As the smiling owner put it, "We were built before the internal combustion engine." And the five rooms, which are small and furnished with old (not antique) pieces, are squeezed into the old town house where the original Methodist once stayed. You go for the food, which is excellent. The restaurant serves a short fine-dining menu that would not disgrace a more pretentious London restaurant. Portions are generous, the price is modest (£35 for three courses), the kitchen is skilled and the wine list exemplary. Recorded music (Louis Armstrong, Edith Piaf) was slightly intrusive. Next door there is a grill for simpler meals. For breakfast there were outstanding croissants, a full English and good *cafetière* coffee. You will have slept well because the beds are comfortable and the town is quiet at night, but don't expect luxury. Our inspector's shower room, hardly larger than the loo on a train, was scented with Champagne and Roses from an aerosol. This is out of character (and smells disagreeable). The rooms are *vin ordinaire*, that is to say, inexpensive and fine for everyday, but not for an occasion.

Winteringham, North Lincolnshire

Winteringham, North Lincolnshire
DN15 9PF

Tel (01724) 733096
Fax (01724) 733898
e-mail enquiries@winteringham-fields.com **website** www.winteringhamfields.com

Nearby Normanby Hall; Thornton Abbey; Lincoln.
Location in centre of village on S bank of Humber, 4 miles (6 km) W from Humber bridge off A1077; with ample car parking
Food breakfast, lunch, dinner; room service **Price** £££ **Rooms** 11; 10 double, 1 suite, 7 with bath, 3 with shower; all rooms have phone, TV, hairdryer **Facilities** 2 sitting rooms, 2 dining rooms, conservatory; garden, helipad **Credit cards** AE, MC, V **Children** welcome **Disabled** restaurant and public rooms accessible but not bedrooms **Pets** accepted in courtyard and dovecote rooms **Closed** Christmas, 1 week in Jan, 3 weeks in Aug **Proprietors** Colin and Bex McGurran

Winteringham Fields

Manor house hotel

Halfway between Scunthorpe and the Humber bridge is one of Britain's gastronomic hotspots. Furthermore, you can sleep in great comfort no more than a few paces from the table. The hotel is in the middle of Winteringham, a quiet country village on the south bank of the Humber estuary. Colin and Bex McGurran are in charge, and Colin, the chef, is relishing the challenge of maintaining the very high culinary standards set by their predecessors, the Schwabs. Having lived and worked in such diverse places as Zambia, the UAE and France, Colin's influences are eclectic.

The rambling 16thC house is full of nooks and crannies and still has many original features such as exposed timbers and period fireplaces. These are set off by the warm colours of walls and fabrics and the antique furniture. The bedrooms are all uniquely decorated and have recently been renovated, and the bathrooms modernised. There are four in the main house (with not a single right-angle between them), three in the courtyard, one in a cottage round the corner, and two more made from a dovecote a couple of minutes away.

Woodstock, Oxfordshire

Market Street, Woodstock,
Oxfordshire OX20 1SX

Tel (01993) 812291
Fax (01993) 813158
e-mail enquiries@feathers.co.uk
website www.feathers.co.uk

Nearby Blenheim Palace; Oxford.
Location in middle of town; with limited car parking
Food breakfast, lunch, dinner; afternoon tea
Price £££
Rooms 21; 16 double and twin, 5 suites all with bath or shower (some have steam showers); all rooms have phone, TV
Facilities 2 sitting rooms, conservatory, bar, dining room, restaurant; courtyard garden
Credit cards AE, DC, V
Children welcome
Disabled access difficult
Pets accepted by arrangement
Closed never
Proprietor Dr Nunirr

The Feathers

Town hotel

The Feathers is an amalgam of four tall 17thC town houses of mellow red brick in Woodstock. It makes an exceptionally civilized town hotel: one visitor was full of praise for the way the staff managed to make a weekend entirely relaxing, 'without intruding in the way that hotel staff so often do.

The upstairs drawing room (with library) has the relaxed atmosphere of a well-kept English country home rather than a hotel, with antiques, an abundance of fresh flowers and a refreshing absence of the ubiquitous Olde Worlde.

There is also a cosy study for reading the papers or drinking tea. If you want fresh air, there is a pleasant courtyard garden and bar. Bedrooms are spacious (on the whole) and beautifully decorated, comfortable yet still with the understated elegance that pervades the whole hotel. Five further bedrooms are to be found in the building next door, renovated a few years ago. The elegant panelled dining room serves excellent food from Simon Tealy's contemporary menu. Recent visitors have been impressed by both the food and service in the lively restaurant.

Technically, this has all the trappings of a smart business hotel, but don't be put off it has character and a very home-like atmosphere.

Worfield, Shropshire

Worfield, near Bridgnorth, Shropshire WV15 5JZ

Tel (01746) 716497
e-mail admin@oldvicarageworfield.com
website www.oldvicarageworfield.com

Nearby Ludlow; Severn Valley Railway; Ironbridge Gorge Museum.
Location in village, 8 miles (12 km) W of Wolverhampton, 1 mile off A454 , 8 miles (12 km) S of junction 4 of M54; in own grounds with ample car parking
Food breakfast, lunch, dinner
Price ££
Rooms 14 double, 1 family, 2 rooms with shower, 1 room with bath only, all the rest have both; all rooms have phone, TV, minibar, hairdryer
Facilities 2 sitting rooms, 3 dining rooms, 1 with bar **Credit cards** AE, DC, MC, V **Children** welcome **Disabled** 1 specially adapted bedroom **Pets** accepted in bedrooms **Closed** never **Proprietors** David and Sarah Blakstad

Old Vicarage

Country house hotel

When this substantial red-brick vicarage was converted into a small hotel in 1981, every effort was made to retain the Edwardian character of the place – restoring original wood block floors, discreetly adding bathrooms to bedrooms, furnishing the rooms with handsome Victorian and Edwardian pieces, carefully converting the coach house to four 'luxury' bedrooms (one of which, 'Leighton', has been specially designed for disabled guests). Readers have praised the large, comfortable bedrooms, named after Shropshire villages and decorated in subtle colours, with matching bathrobes and soaps.

Attention to detail extends to the sitting rooms (one is the conservatory, with glorious views of the Worfe valley) and the three dining rooms. The award-winning food (a daily-changing menu with several choices and impressive cheeseboard) is English-based, ambitious and not cheap, served at polished tables by cheerful staff. There is a reasonably extensive wine cellar.

Biggin-by-Hartington, Derbyshire

Biggin Hall

Country house hotel

A gaggle of geese may follow you up the path to this friendly 17thC house. Popular with walkers, it's ideal to come back here after a day's trek: sink into a well-worn chair by a crackling fire and enjoy a drink in a relaxed, cosy atmosphere. Rooms are attractively decorated, with personal touches and stone mullioned, leaded windows. The roofs slope steeply. Breakfast is generous. Dinner (set menu with vegetarian options, changing daily) is excellent for the price – like home dining, but at the house of a very good cook.

Biggin-by-Hartington, Buxton, Derbyshire SK17 0DH

Tel 01298 84451
e-mail enquiries@bigginhall.co.uk
website www.bigginhall.co.uk
Food breakfast, lunch, dinner
Price ££-£££
Closed never
Proprietor James Moffett

Bledington, Oxfordshire

The King's Head Inn

Village inn

A revamped village pub, but special because its character has been correctly preserved. A warren of cosy rooms circle the central bar. It's popular at weekends, and almost all the public space is devoted to dining tables – we often wish there could be more flopping space (armchairs and sofas) in pubs-with-rooms. The bedrooms are simple and unpretentious, but well decorated, with some amusing junk shop finds, books, pictures, pretty fabrics and rugs.

The food is top-quality pub fare, locally raised beef a speciality. The location, on the village green, is unspoiled, with a stream nearby and swings for the children. Owners Archie and Nicola Orr-Ewing give a friendly welcome and have happy staff.

The Green, Bledington, Oxfordshire OX7 6XQ

Tel 01608 658365
Fax 01608 658902
e-mail info@kingsheadinn.net
website www.thekingsheadinn.net
Food breakfast, lunch, dinner
Price £££ **Closed** Christmas Day
Proprietors Archie and Nicola Orr-Ewing

Chipping Campden, Gloucestershire

Cotswold House Hotel & Spa **Town hotel**

Described by one reader as 'the place to stay' in Chipping Campden, Cotswold House can claim to be a very popular hotel. Set in a fine street, the building, dating from 1650, was renovated in 1999, with new rooms and the new coach house, where clean modern lines, gas log fireplaces and broad exposed beams definitely add to the place. In the main hotel, an impressive spiral staircase leads to well-appointed rooms, which are a similar standard to those in the coach house.

You have the choice of two restaurants: the relaxed brasserie and the formal dining room. Alongside the coach house, a Mediterranean-style garden, attractively lit in the evening, is perfect for an after-dinner stroll.

The Square, Chipping Campden, Gloucestershire GL55 6AN

Tel (01386) 840330
e-mail reservations@cotswold-house.com **website** www.bespokehotels.com/cotswoldhouse
Food breakfast, lunch, dinner; afternoon tea **Price** ££££
Closed never **Proprietors** Bespoke Hotels **Manager** Michael Obray

Dinham, Shropshire

Mr Underhill's at Dinham Weir **Restaurant-with-rooms**

As we approached this Michelin-starred restaurant-with-rooms at the end of the walk to Ludlow on the Mortimer Trail, we could almost have been reminded of many a similar place on the Lot or the Dordogne. The paved garden is a sun trap looking on to the weir that breaks the flow of the River Teme below Ludlow Castle's walls. Here you can have breakfast or tea, or a glass of wine before an impressive dinner. The no-choice menu might include a cone of dill-marinated smoked salmon; and slow roasted breast of Mullard duck.

The suites (upgraded since the last edition) are contemporary and stylish, if mostly compact, all with river views and cleverly shaped bathrooms. A great place, run on a personal scale.

Dinham, Ludlow, Shropshire, SY8 1EH

Tel (01584) 874431
Fax (01584) 874431
website www.mr-underhills.co.uk
Food breakfast, dinner
Price ££
Closed 2 weeks in June, 2 weeks in Oct
Proprietors Chris and Judy Bradley

Ilmington, Warwickshire

Lower Green, Ilmington,
Warwickshire CV36 4LT

Tel 01608 682226
email info@howardarms.com
website www.howardarms.com
Food breakfast, lunch, dinner
Price ££-£££
Closed never
Manager Grant Owen

The Howard Arms

Village inn

Equidistant between Stratford-upon-Avon and Moreton-in-Marsh, this is useful for Stratford and the Cotswolds.

It's laid back: locals drink at the bar and the place has an easy-going charm. But there's professionalism too: our bags were carried upstairs and when the television didn't work in our room, it was dealt with at once.

The food is exactly what one wants in a 400-year-old stone-built inn, with pretty arched windows, a mix of old furniture and giant polished flagstones. Expect comforting dishes such as steamed suet pudding and sticky toffee pudding – all at sensible prices.

There are two rooms above the pub and six in a low-key garden wing. They are excellent, if somewhat formulaic.

Ironbridge, Shropshire

Severn Bank, Ironbridge, Near
Telford, Shropshire TF8 7AN

Tel 01952 432299
e-mail info@libraryhouse.com
website www.libraryhouse.com
Food breakfast, lunch, dinner
Price ££
Closed never
Proprietors Sarah and Tim Davis

Library House

Townhouse hotel

Reliable B&B (rooms from £80) with high standards in the heart of the Ironbridge World Heritage Site, opposite the Ironbridge itself and centrally located for the shops, pubs and restaurants. Smart decoration and authentically Georgian features in the guest drawing room. Bedrooms are more homely, and properly equipped for the price. New hosts, Tim and Sarah Davis, took over in 2014 and will only make changes gradually, after a few months. They welcome guests personally, with a drink if it's that time of day, and are strong on advice on where to eat and what to see – ask for their Ironbridge walks. Free passes to the local car parks are a genuine bonus.

A church bell rings nearby, day and night, but it's a light sound which doesn't disturb.

Kingham, Oxfordshire

The Wild Rabbit

Country inn

Two endearing flop-eared topiary bunnies flank the entrance to this place – Lady Bamford's latest creation – fashioned from a former inn close to her Daylesford Organic farm shop, café and wellness retreat.

Our room, The Boar, was chilly. There were no free plugs for laptop and hairdryer, and the wi-fi didn't work. But it did have aromatic Bamford toiletries, attractive beams and scrubbed stone walls, a desk and a big bed.

Downstairs there's a big buzzing dining space and, adjacent, a generous bar area with comfy seating for those who simply want a drink at the bar. Carol Bamford was determined to make this a casual meeting place for locals, and she has succeeded.

We were underwhelmed by the food. Despite the negatives, a useful new address.

Church Street, Kingham, Oxfordshire OX7 6YA

Tel 01608 658389
e-mail theteam@thewildrabbit.co.uk
website www.thewildrabbit.co.uk
Food breakfast, lunch, dinner (no food served Sunday night and Monday) **Price** ££ **Closed** no specific dates **Proprietors** Lord and Lady Bamford

Leamington Spa, Warwickshire

The Lansdowne

Town house bed-and-breakfast

The Lansdowne is a creeper-covered Regency house in the heart of Leamington Spa – just as well there is double-glazing, says our reporter, who liked it not for its location but its food – though now only breakfast is served.

The public rooms are elegantly decorated in vibrant colours; the bedrooms, comfortable and cosy with pine furniture and pretty fabrics. Readers comment on the friendly atmosphere.

Leamington's heyday as a popular spa town might be over, but the Royal Pump Rooms were reopened to visitors in 1999 as a cultural complex, and there is still much to see in the neighbourhood. The Lansdowne makes an ideal base from which to explore Warwickshire sights. Reports welcome

87-89 Clarendon Street, Royal Leamington Spa, Warwickshire CV32 4PF

Tel 01926 450505
website www.thelansdowne.co.uk
Food breakfast
Price ££
Closed never
Proprietor Mr Ross

Leonard Stanley, Gloucestershire

The Grey Cottage

Village guesthouse

This Cotswold, stone-built cottage, run by Rosemary Reeves, dates from 1838 and is spotless and pleasingly furnished. The cottage is a very private guesthouse with a cosy, cottagey atmosphere.

Dinner is by arrangement; no choice, but food preferences are discussed. Generous home cooking includes such dishes as grilled avocado with bacon, mustard chicken with a tarragon cream sauce and *crème brûlée*, followed by tea or coffee.

The bedrooms and bathrooms have recently been refurbished: 'beautifully done', said a recent visitor. They are immensely cosy, with firm beds, reliable hot water and books.

Rosemary is capable, charming and dedicated – but not intrusive.

Bath Road, Leonard Stanley, Stonehouse, Gloucestershire GL10 3LU

Tel (01453) 822515
email rosemary.reeves@btopenworld.com
website www.grey-cottage.co.uk
Food breakfast, dinner by prior arrangement **Prices** £-££
Closed occasional holidays
Proprietor Rosemary Reeves

Ludlow, Shropshire

Bromley Court

Town bed-and-breakfast

Whether it's houses or horses that brought you to Ludlow, you'll find plenty of both – all thoroughbreds. The entire centre of Ludlow is listed Grade II (a bit too late for the castle, which is a ruin), and the racetrack brings people from far and wide. Another strong draw is the plethora of gourmet restaurants, several of them Michelin-starred, from which to choose.

In Lower Broad Street, Simon Berresford and James Edwards have taken over the running of Bromley Court, two tiny Tudor cottages further along the road, creating three suites, each on two levels and with a well-equipped breakfast bar. Each has its own front-down, with a communal courtyard where guests can chat after afternoon tea or pre-dinner drinks if they feel so inclined.

73-74 Lower Broad Street, Ludlow, Shropshire SY8 1PH

Tel (01584) 876996
e-mail bromleycourt@yahoo.com
website www.ludlowhotels.com/index.html
Food breakfast
Price ££ **Closed** never
Proprietors Simon Berresford and James Edwards

Nether Westcote, Oxfordshire

The Feathered Nest Country Inn **Country inn**

Another converted Cotswold inn, less formal but just as comfortable as some country house hotels.

Tony and Amanda Timmer's four bedrooms may be coyly named (eg Cuckoo's Nest, Cockerel's Roost), but they are a blend of the practical, the luxurious and the countrified.

The food in the homely but elegant dining room is as impressive as the bedrooms. The pub fare served in the bar (where the stools are fashioned from riding saddles) is also above average. The wine list features unsung 'boutique' growers from around the world.

The Feathered Nest wouldn't work everywhere, but in the Cotswolds it does.

Nether Westcote, Oxfordshire OX7 6SD

Tel 01993 833030 **e-mail** info@thefeatherednestinn.co.uk **website** www.thefeatherednestinn.co.uk **Food** breakfast, lunch, dinner, afternoon tea **Price** £££-££££ **Closed** Mondays, Christmas Day **Proprietor** Tony and Amanda Timmer

Northleach, Gloucestershire

The Wheatsheaf Inn
Country inn

Welcome to the Cotswolds: Chelsea tractors in the drive; leggy blondes in designer country-wear sipping martinis at the bar; landscaped gardens leading up to a Farrow & Ball-painted inn.

But we were won over by the owners, Sam and Georgie Pearman. They are down-to-earth, hard working, but with the talent to know what people want and how to deliver it. There are attractive dining areas, gleaming with polished wood; the relaxed Game Bar; the treatment room.

The location is not special, but the bedrooms are fabulous: imaginitive wallpapers and fabrics, zinc bath, comfortable bed.

The food from chef Anthony Ely doesn't miss a beat. Breakfast was superb, including wonderful devilled kidneys.

West End, Northleach, Gloucestershire GL54 3EZ

Tel 01451 860244 **e-mail** reservations@cotswoldswheatsheaf.com **website** www.cotswoldswheatsheaf.com **Food** breakfast, lunch, dinner **Price** £££-££££ **Closed** never **Proprietors** Sam and Georgina Pearman

Shipton-under-Wychwood, Oxfordshire

The Shaven Crown

Country house hotel

The Shaven Crown Hotel, as its name suggests, has monastic origins; it was built in 1384 as a hospice to nearby Bruern Abbey, and many of the original features remain intact – most impressively the medieval hall, with its beautiful double-collar braced roof and stone walls decorated with tapestries and wrought ironwork. The hall forms one side of the courtyard garden, which is decked with flowers and parasols, and on a sunny day is a lovely place in which to enjoy wholesome pub lunches. Some of the bedrooms overlook the courtyard, others are at the front of the house and suffer from road noise – though this is unlikely to be a problem at night.

Phil & Evelyn Roberts took over in 2013 with refurbishment – reports welcome.

High Street, Shipton-under-Wychwood, Oxfordshire OX7 6BA

Tel 01993 830500
e-mail relax@theshavencrown.co.uk
website www.theshavencrown.co.uk
Food breakfast, lunch, dinner
Price ££
Closed on occasion (check website)
Proprietors Phil and Evelyn Roberts

Shrewsbury, Shropshire

Brompton Farmhouse B&B

Bed-and-breakfast

This gentrified farmhouse in National Trust-owned Attingham Park offers an unusual package. The Bean family run both – B&B in the farmhouse and a cookery school in the smart farm buildings across the yard. Marcus Bean, who has appeared in several television cooking programmes, is an excellent chef and a good cookery teacher. He produces dinner to order in the farmhouse. When we stayed we enjoyed beautifully done scallops and tender lamb.

The bedrooms are comfortable and furnished with Edwardian antiques, but lacked personal touches; the reception area and sitting rooms are also a touch impersonal.

An ideal place for exploring nearby Shrewsbury and learning about everything from cupcakes to currymaking.

Brompton, Near Cross House, Shrewsbury, Shropshire SY5 6LE

Tel 01743 761629
e-mail info@bromptonfarmhouse.co.uk
website www.bromptonfarmhouse.co.uk
Food breakfast **Price** ££ **Closed** Christmas **Proprietors** Marcus and Jenny Bean

Stamford, Lincolnshire

The Bull and Swan

Town inn

Quaint is an over-used description for inns in old buildings, but here it really does fit. This historic inn on the High Street of Stamford's St Martins district is mainly 17thC and has been sympathetically made over in the usual quirky-luxurious style of the Hillbrooke mini chain, of which it is a part.

Well-chosen antiques rub shoulders with top-quality beds and pristine white linen in the seven bedrooms. Most of the rooms are a fair size.

Food is better-than-average country inn fare using local ingredients. A drinking club for a 17thC Earl of Exeter and friends was based here, and members' nicknames eg The Badger are used for the rooms. Burghley House can be reached on foot.

St Martins, Stamford, Lincolnshire
PE9 2LJ,

Tel 01780 767061
email
enquiries@thebullandswan.co.uk
website www.thebullandswan.co.uk
Food breakfast, lunch, dinner
Price ££ **Closed** never
Proprietors Hillbrooke
Manager Ben Larter

Stamford, Lincolnshire

The William Cecil

Town hotel

With 27 rooms this is somewhat outside our usual size, but the unstuffy staff make it feel like a smaller place. The atmosphere is relaxed but gracious, as you would expect from a house on this scale.

They've got the basics right here, including the quality beds, the Egyptian cotton linen and the intelligent use of space. Design and furnishings are nicely in keeping with the building, and the overall effect is perhaps more harmonious than other Hillbrooke hotels.

It's just along the road from The Bull & Swan (see above), and part of the same group. This guide doesn't normally favour chains, but the Hillbrooke philosophy shares much with ours: no managers in suits, no staff uniforms, no name badges.

St Martins, Stamford, Lincolnshire
PE9 2LJ

Tel 01780 750070
e-mail
enquiries@thewilliamcecil.co.uk
website www.thewilliamcecil.co.uk
Food breakfast, lunch, dinner
Price ££-£££ **Closed** never
Proprietors Hillbrooke
Manager Nick Jefford

Stokenchurch, Buckinghamshire

Park Lane, Stokenchurch, High Wycombe, Buckinghamshire HP14 3TQ

Tel 01494 482520
e-mail deborah@hallbottomfarm.co.uk
website www.hallbottomfarm.co.uk
Food breakfast
Price £ **Closed** Christmas
Proprietor Deborah Abbot

Hallbottom Farm

Country bed-and-breakfast

From Stokenchurch village you drive down a long private lane to find the farm in a wonderful position at the head of narrow, secluded valley. The garden, with its large pond, is laid out on the floor of the valley with green hillsides rising on either side.

This is a relaxed home, full of unpretentious, shabby-chic charm and character. The breakfast table faces the garden and valley. Bedrooms are homely and comfortable.

Bring walking shoes and treat yourself to lunch at The Sir Charles Napier Restaurant, a 40-minute walk down the valley and up through the woods. The food (Michelin star) is exceptional, but unfussy, as are the surroundings. Beyond the charming terraced eating area is the garden, featuring work by local sculptor Michael Cooper.

Aldeburgh, Suffolk

41 Park Road, Aldeburgh, Suffolk, IP15 5EN

Tel 01728 452486
e-mail dunanhouse@btinternet.com
website www.dunanhouse.co.uk

Nearby seaside, Aldeburgh Museum, RSPB reserve at Minsmere, Ipswich, Snape Maltings concert halls.
Food breakfast
Prices ££
Rooms 3; 2 doubles – 1 can be a twin, both have bath/shower, 1 family room sleeping up to 4
Facilities family room, garden
Credit cards MC, V
Children accepted
Disabled not suitable
Pets not accepted **Closed** Christmas Day and Boxing Day **Proprietors** Annie Lee and Simon Farr

Dunan House

Town guesthouse

Artistic touches flourish in this late 19thC building, down a private tree-lined road in Aldeburgh. Run by artists Annie Lee and Simon Farr, the three-bedroom guesthouse thrives on bright and distinct schemes; we think it works because we enjoy quirkiness. Hand-crafted and painted decorations adorn the bedrooms – one eye-catching bedroom door painted with bold green and gold made quite an impression on us.

Dunan House is strictly bed and breakfast – they don't do dinner. However, breakfast (cooked by Annie and Simon) is a highlight, with eggs coming from the resident hens and fruit from their garden. Aldeburgh has a range of restaurants within walking distance and Annie and Simon are happy to recommend.

Our most recent visit coincided with Aldeburgh festival, and the atmosphere at Dunan House provided the perfect homely backdrop to the culture. We think the prices charged are a bargain, given the size of the bedrooms and quality of service.

Bildeston, Suffolk

High Street, Bildeston, Suffolk IP7 7EB

Tel 01449 740510
e-mail reception@thebildeston-crown.co.uk
website www.thebildestoncrown.com

Nearby Lavenham, Long Melford, Constable Country, Wool Town Walks **Location** 10 mins on A1141/B115 from Hadleigh
Food breakfast, lunch, dinner
Price ££-£££
Rooms 12 double/twin; all have bath/shower and have TV, wi-fi
Facilities bar, lounge, 2 dining rooms, courtyard, 2 function rooms; fishing, riding, shooting, tennis
Credit cards AE, MC, V
Children welcome
Disabled lift, Room 2 has access, 'drop off' point with step-free access to hotel **Pets** dogs accepted
Closed Christmas Eve, Christmas Day and New Year's Day evenings
Proprietors Gillian Buckle, James Buckle

The Bildeston Crown

Village inn

This refurbished inn in sleepy Bildeston is in fact, first and foremost, a rather expensive and sophisticated restaurant. The entire ground floor is given over to tables and smart dining chairs in a series of rooms with attractive, boldly painted walls.

Chef Zack Deakin, formerly the sous chef here, is back after two years away at Maison Talbooth (page 250). *A la carte* and tasting menus (£100 including wine) are served in Ingrams, a separate, smart dining room. We would prefer it if the Crown were more inn than restaurant – simpler and less posh – where the quality of the food feels like a happy surprise rather than a big deal.

We stayed in Black Fuchsia (room no 14). It has a great bathroom, with rolltop bath and large shower, but it was done up in a slightly over-the-top colour scheme, and there was no tea or coffee. Since then, there have been further renovations, including changes to Black Fuchsia. Other rooms are lovely, with pretty fabrics and nice touches. Their weekend rates, in particular, are steep, but the Sunday-night dinner, bed and breakfast package (from £125-£170 for two, depending on the room) is a good deal. So don't let our reservations put you off – it's a useful Suffolk address.

Brancaster, Norfolk

Brancaster, Staithe, Norfolk
PE31 8BY

Tel (01485) 210 262
Fax (01485) 210 930
e-mail reception@whitehorsebrancaster.co.uk
website
www.whitehorsebrancaster.co.uk

Nearby Holkham Hall, Brancaster beach, Norfolk lavender, Burnham Market, Sandringham Estate Peddars Way
Location on A149 coast road with ample car parking
Food breakfast, lunch, dinner
Price ££ **Rooms** 15; 5 family rooms, 10 doubles (4 can be twin), all with bath and shower; all rooms have phone, TV, hairdryer, wi-fi
Facilities dining area, sitting room, conservatory, restaurant, bar, garden, terrace **Credit cards** MC, V
Children accepted **Disabled** 1 room with disabled facilities, ground floor access **Pets** well behaved dogs in 8 ground room floors **Closed** never
Proprietor Nye family

The White Horse

Village inn

Cliff Nye, proprietor of The White Horse at Brancaster, is tired of reading in guides that from the outside, his building is not exactly charming – and rightly so, because as soon as you're inside, it's something else. First you walk into a bar area for non residents, with a local community atmosphere; this melts seamlessly into a more 'residential' area with reception desk and seating; and this gives way to the big, airy conservatory dining room with its scrubbed pine tables and extraordinary view out over a network of creeks and marsh across Brancaster Staithe to Scolt Head Island – surely one of England's most distinctive coastal panoramas. You could easily while away most of a morning or afternoon here, followed by lunch or dinner, and still not be tired of the view. Your room, either upstairs or in the extension with a turf roof, will be comfortable and cleanly decorated and furnished in a modern style with seaside colours and Lloyd Loom chairs. The food is good – no more or less than you'd expect for the price – though you might hope to find a somewhat wider range of seafood on the me nu. A lesson in how to transform what was a horrible old pub in a fabulous situation into thriving 21st century operation.

Earsham, Bungay, Suffolk NR35 2AW

Tel 01986 805033
e-mail reservations@plantationfarmhouse.co.uk **website** www.plantationfarmhouse.co.uk

Nearby Norwich, Southwold, Norfolk Broads, Waveney Valley
Location 3 miles north-west of Bungay, at end of long, tree-lined drive, 1 parking space for each room
Food breakfast, afternoon tea (on day of arrival)
Price £ **Rooms** 2; both doubles, both have TV, DVD players, radio, CD player, iPod docking station, wi-fi, hairdryer, shared fridge, tea/coffee facilities, walking information
Facilities guest sitting room, dining room; separate guest entrance to house **Credit cards** DC, MC, V
Children accepted over 12
Disabled no special access
Pets not accepted
Closed no particular closing times
Proprietors Cherrie McCarron and Paul Cray

Plantation Farmhouse

Country bed-and-breakfast

Highly personalized, luxury B&B, opened in 2012, in a beautifully restored Tudor farmhouse with Victorian additions. The countryside here, in the Waveney Valley on the Norfolk-Suffolk border, is gently undulating, rather than East Anglian flat. Deep in an agricultural estate, surrounded by an acre of garden, it's about as peaceful and exclusive as you can get. The two bedrooms are beautifully done to a high standard in a stylish-traditional way. We especially like the grey-blue painted furniture, the bare, polished boards, the high fireplace, and of course the exposed timber framework. The hosts, Cherrie McCarron and Paul Cray, describe their offering as the luxury boutique hotel combined with the intimacy of a farmhouse B&B – a fair claim.

The high standards continue with tea and home-made cakes (no charge) served when you arrive; and with breakfast, using best local produce. The eggs, of course, are super fresh. Even the hens that lay them have charming names – such as Maran, Pookie, Coco, Poppy and Pixie.

Burnham Market, Norfolk

The Green, Burnham Market, North Norfolk, PE31 8HD

Tel (01328) 738777
Fax (01328) 730103
e-mail reception@hostearms.co.uk
website www.hostearms.co.uk

Nearby Houghton Hall; Holkham Hall; Sandringham House; Titchwell, Holme, Holkham and Cley nature reserves.
Location in centre of village; with ample car parking
Food breakfast, lunch, dinner
Price £££
Rooms 61; 36 doubles in main house, 8 in Railway Inn, 8 in Vine House, 9 in 3 cottages, all with bath or shower; all rooms have phone, TV, hairdryer
Facilities sitting room, conservatory, dining room, bar; garden
Credit cards MC, V **Children** accepted **Disabled** ground-floor bedrooms
Pets not accepted **Closed** never
Proprietors Bee and Brendan Hopkins

The Hoste Arms

Village hotel

Overlooking the green in a village whose main claim to fame is that it was Admiral Nelson's birthplace, this handsome yellow-and-white 17thC inn has won a clutch of awards for its bedrooms, bar and restaurant. Downstairs, it positively buzzes with life in the evenings, when locals come here to drink and eat – in that order. The brasserie-style menu includes British, European and Oriental-inspired dishes.

The man responsible for this reputation, Paul Whittome, bought The Hoste in 1989 and died tragically young, in his 50s, in July 2010. We happened to revisit the day after his funeral and found business as usual, just as he would have wished. Despite being deaf, Paul was a chatty, affable proprietor, who made The Hoste into a local institution – and helped spread its fame as far afield as the Home Counties.

Bee and Brendan Hopkins took over in April 2012, under whose ownership a new chapter is unfolding at The Hoste. Changes include the launch of a stylish new garden room in May 2013, which accommodates up to 110 people, and a lodge for 16 to 30 people. The Hoste kitchens have doubled in size and they also now have a rather large spa. Further rooms are on offer across the road in peaceful Vine House and in The Railway House on the edge of the village.

Bury St Edmunds, Suffolk

Northgate Street, Bury St Edmunds, Suffolk IP33 1HP

Tel 01284 761779
Fax 01284 768315
e-mail pott@globalnet.co.uk
website www.ouncehouse.co.uk

Nearby Cathedral; Abbey; Gershom-Parkington Collection.
Location close to town centre; with ample car parking
Food breakfast
Price ££
Rooms 5 double and twin with bath; all rooms have phone, TV, hairdryer
Facilities 2 sitting rooms, library/TV room, dining room; garden **Credit cards** AE, DC, MC, V
Children welcome
Disabled access difficult
Pets not accepted
Closed never
Proprietors Simon and Jenny Pott

Ounce House

Town house

Ounce House is a red brick, gable-ended, three-storey house, set back from the road a five-minute walk from the Cathedral and pedestrianized shopping streets in the centre of Bury St Edmunds.

The interiors are formal but homely with drawing room and dining room decorated in calm colours; these are 'statement' swagged and draped curtains, plenty of lamps, *objets d'art* and interesting pictures. Most of the bedrooms are large and one of the most attractive has a carved, crown arrangement over the bedhead, two chintzy armchairs,a decorative chimneypiece and overlooks the garden. Since our last edition, the Potts have opened up a further two bedrooms, which are decorated in the same homely style.

The owners, warm and open hosts, are good at putting people at their ease. Dinner is no longer served here, but there are several good restaurants within walking distance, with which, as Mrs Pott put it, it was hard for her to compete.

Guests have the use of the library, which is more like a den, with a large leather wing armchair, smaller easy chairs, an upright piano, shelves packed with books and an honesty bar. It is somewhere to go with a friend for a long conversation, or to watch TV.

Cley-next-the-Sea, Norfolk

Cley-next-the-Sea, Holt, Norfolk NR25 7RP

Tel (01263) 740209
e-mail info@cleywindmill.co.uk
website www.cleymill.co.uk

Nearby Sheringham Hall; Cromer Lighthouse; Holkham Hall.
Location 7 miles (11 km) W of Sheringham on A149, on N edge of village; with ample car parking
Food breakfast, dinner on request
Price ££
Rooms 9 double, all with bath/shower
Facilities sitting room, dining room, garden **Credit cards** MC, V
Children welcome
Disabled access difficult
Pets accepted **Closed** never
Proprietor Dr Julian Godlee
Manager Simon Whatling

Cley Mill

Converted windmill B&B

Imagine staying in a 'real' windmill. That is the sense of adventure that Cley Mill can induce even in the most world-weary. Memories of Swallows and Amazons or the Famous Five crowd in as you climb higher and higher in the mill, finally mounting the ladder to the look-out room on the fourth floor. Superb views over the Cley Marshes, a Mecca for bird-watchers.

The sitting room on the ground floor of the Mill is exceptionally welcoming – it feels well used and lived-in, with plenty of books and magazines, comfortable sofas, TV and an open fire. Bedrooms in the Mill feel rather like log cabins – much wood in the furniture and fittings. They are pretty rooms, with white lace bedspreads, and bathrooms ingeniously fitted in to the nooks and crannies.

Since our last edition, Cley Mill has changed hands. The new owner is Julian Godlee, a GP from Hertfordshire with roots on the Norfolk coast – the only bidder who wanted it to continue as a B&B. There has been maintenance and restoration recently, but the basic formula remains unchanged. A new bedroom has been added right at the very top of the windmill – reached by a steep ladder, it is only for the adventurous and fit, but the view makes it worthwhile. Try to book well in advance. See also our other windmill (page 35).

Stratford Road, Dedham, Colchester, Essex CO7 6HN

Tel 01206 322367
e-mail maison@milsomhotels.com
website www.milsomhotels.com/maisontal-booth

Nearby Sir Alfred Munnings Museum at Castle House, Colchester, Ipswich, Constable Country, Suffolk Heritage Coast **Location** bypass Colchester A12 northbound, take left signposted Dedham, follow signs for Maison Talbooth **Food** breakfast, lunch, dinner (at Le Talbooth restaurant); afternoon tea **Price** ££££ **Rooms** 12; all double, 7 can be twin, all have bath/shower, one has additional bunk beds; 3 rooms have hot tubs on terrace; all have mini bar, hairdryer, wi-fi **Facilities** sitting rooms, garden room, spa, pool, tennis court **Credit cards** all major **Children** welcome **Disabled** 5 downstairs rooms **Pets** dogs allowed **Closed** never **Proprietors** Milsom family

Maison Talbooth

Town house hotel

A welcome new edition to our Essex section – under an hour and a half drive from London – this smart, rather plain-looking Victorian house is hard to beat for lavish comfort. It's recently undergone some impressive embellishments: two new suites, a spa, pool, and tennis court.

The 12 poet-themed suites have a decadent Sixties feel: quilted fabrics and luxury drapes; charcoal greys and muted greens; and patterned wallpaper that contradicts the all-new modern bathrooms.

Down the road, Le Talbooth, also under the Milsom ownership, is the gastronomic hotspot of the area. It remains a popular place to eat even after 50 years, and still exudes the feel of it's 'Sixties heyday'. There's an exceptional wine list and a blend of old-and-new style cooking. If you don't feel like going out, light snacks can be served in your room at Maison Talbooth. Courtesy cars take you to and from the restaurant, or anywhere else nearby.

Church Lane, Fritton, Norfolk
NR31 9HA

Tel (01493) 484008
Fax (01493) 488355
e-mail
frittonhouse@somerleyton.co.uk
website www.frittonhouse.co.uk

Nearby Somerleyton House and Estate; Norfolk Broads; Gorleston beach, Beccles, Southwold, Aldeburgh, Walberwick
Location in own grounds with ample private car parking
Food breakfast, lunch, dinner
Price £££
Rooms 9; all double, two can be twin; all with bath or shower, phone, TV, DVD, wi-fi
Facilities bar, dining room, sitting room, private dining room, affiliation with local leisure resort (swimming, tennis, spa) **Credit cards** MC, V **Children** welcome **Disabled** no specially adapted rooms **Pets** small, well-behaved dogs **Closed** never
Proprietor Hugh Crossley

Fritton House

Country hotel

This former 15thC smuggler's inn was turned into a hotel some years back by 30-something Hugh Crossley, heir to the Somerleyton Estate of which it is a part. Interior design is by Hugh's sister Isobel, with many an old beam exposed to contrast with the mainly contemporary, easy-going feel of the place. It's as relaxed as a hotel gets, the tone set by Sarah, the young and infectiously enthusiastic manageress, but also by Hugh, who keeps a close eye and is always hatching a new plan. Ring for anything from your room – a cup of tea, a Mojito, even dinner – and it will be brought.

Downstairs there's a cosy sitting room, but the hub is the bar and restaurant, where locals come to eat. 'Simple food, well cooked' is the aim. The wine list has an unusual selection of bottles for around £12.

When we went to press, Fritton House was undergoing a major refurbishment, and is re-opening in April 2014. We would welcome reports on the place's new look.

Fritton House stands on the edge of a country park whose main feature is Fritton Lake, with rowing boats and other amusements. It's open to the public from April to October; for the rest of the year, and after five in summer, guests at Fritton House have the run of the place, free of charge. A great place to bring children.

Great Waldingfield, Suffolk

Great Waldingfield, Sudbury, Suffolk CO10 0TL

Tel 01787 372428
e-mail info@theoldrectorycountry-house.co.uk
website www.theoldrectorycountry-house.co.uk

Nearby Lavenham, Long Melford, Bury St Edmunds, Sudbury
Food breakfast included, dinner only by arrangement when booking the whole house
Price £££
Rooms 6; all double, one ground floor, all have bath/shower; 3 in the main house, 3 self-catered in The Old Stables
Facilities drawing room, honesty bar, swimming pool, tennis court, free wi-fi
Credit cards MC, V
Children welcome
Disabled access difficult
Pets clean dogs accepted
Closed rarely
Proprietor Frank Lawrenson

The Old Rectory

Country house hotel

Much of the charm of this tucked-away rectory lies in the way owner Frank Lawrenson has thoroughly restored its original character – it's in superb condition, but uncompromised by trendy, contemporary add-ons. All the rooms have bathrooms and are individually decorated: subtle pastel shades reign, with delicately floral cushions and curtains. There is a sense of space everywhere, but especially in the drawing room, and to complete the gracious but relaxed atmosphere guests get a high level of unobtrusive but personal attention from Frank and his team, including a butler. The books, the honesty bar and copious, well presented information on what to see and do in the area make you feel at home. One concession to contemporary design is the swimming pool's curved roof, open on one side, making it an indoor-outdoor pool – used mainly in the summer-time.

We sense that this place is always on the move. Currently it's making a foray into environmentally friendly technology, including a Biomass boiler and a conservation programme in partnership with local artisans. Staying here means you have the satisfaction of making a contribution to their cause.

Harwich, Essex

The Quay, Harwich, Essex
CO12 3HH

Tel (01255) 241212
Fax (01255) 551922
e-mail pier@milsomhotels.com
website
www.milsomhotels.com/thepier

Nearby Harwich sights including Electric Palace Cinema, Ha'penny Pier, Redoubt fort, golf **Location** on quayside in old town; own off-road car parking for 25 cars
Price ££ **Food** breakfast, lunch, dinner **Rooms** 14; all doubles with own shower or bath, phone, TV, wi-fi, minibar **Facilities** 2 restaurants, bar, terrace, sitting room, private dining facilities, house party service, sailing arranged on yacht or traditional Essex craft **Credit cards** AE, DC, MC, V **Children** accepted **Disabled** specially adapted room and WC on ground floor, access at rear of building **Pets** dogs allowed (in bedrooms and in the bar of the Ha'penny) **Closed** The Harbourside: Mon and Tue **Proprietor** Milsom family

The Pier

Seaside town hotel

Here's a good place for a weekend – if you like the sea, ships, and industrial seascapes. Picture-book pretty it isn't; atmospheric, absorbing and 'real' it most certainly is. The Pier, with its distinctive blue and white façade, designed to resemble a Venetian *palazzo*, was built in 1864 to accommodate overnight passengers from Harwich to the European mainland. It was from here, too, in 1620, that the Mayflower set sail for the New World.

There are two restaurants here: The Harbourside, relatively formal but specialising in locally caught seafood; and the Ha'penny Pier, a contemporary fisherman's wharf-style bar and bistro, for proper fish and chips, the chef's fish pie and daily specials. Write your order on a notepad and hand it in at the bar. Check-in is at the bar, and bags are promptly taken to your room.

All the rooms are several cuts above what you would expect for the price (deep, white-sheeted beds, natural sea colours on tongue-and-groove panelling), but with only £10 each between a 'standard', a 'superior' and a 'deluxe' it pays to go for the largest – and get the view.

The Pier has been owned for nearly 30 years by the Milsom family. Like their other establishments, Maison Talbooth (page 250) and Milsoms, it's a close-knit operation, with long-serving locals on the happy team.

Holkham, Norfolk

Park Road, Holkham, Norfolk
NR23 1RG

Tel (01328) 711008
e-mail victoria@holkham.co.uk
website www.holkham.co.uk/thevictoria

Nearby Holkham Hall, Holkham beach, Banham Zoo.
Location just off the B1105 on th A149 near Wells; with ample car parking
Food breakfast, lunch, dinner
Price £££
Rooms 10 double and twin, all en suite with shower; all rooms have TV and DVD, hairdryer, tea/coffee facilities
Facilities 2 dining rooms, 2 sitting rooms, 3 bars; garden, 2 helipads
Credit cards MC, V
Children welcome **Disabled** 1 ground-floor room with wet room
Pets dogs in some bedrooms at £10/night
Closed never **Proprietors** Viscount and Viscountess Coke

The Victoria at Holkham **Country hotel**

Part of the Holkham Estate owned by the Earl of Leicester, The Victoria (named after Queen Victoria, a year after she became queen) is an eclectic and stylish blend of colonial furniture and fabrics. Built in 1837 by Coke of Norfolk, the hotel is a five-minute stroll from the beautiful white sands of Holkham beach where there are water sports. Viscount Coke, a descendent of Coke of Norfolk, and his wife Polly acquired the hotel some time ago and undertook a major refurbishment. One of its many successful outcomes is the new conservatory.

Everywhere you turn your attention is caught by some curious object or another. Rooms contain items from the attics and basements of Holkham Hall, as well as furnishings and ornaments that have been flown in from Rajasthan. All of the bedrooms are decorated individually with flare and good taste. Although the rooms may look old they have modern comforts such as seriously comfy beds, big warm duvets and deep baths for a serious soak.

The restaurant and bar area is very much in keeping with the colonial feel, slightly hard chairs, but beautiful wall hangings and views. The food is cooked and presented to a high standard (don't overlook the fish and chips); and there's a long wine list.

King's Lynn, Norfolk

King's Staithe Square, King's Lynn, Norfolk PE30 1RD

Tel 01553 660492
e-mail info@thebankhouse.co.uk
website www.thebankhouse.co.uk

Nearby the Corn Exchange, Arts Centre **Location** on the quayside, accessible via the A10, A17 and A47; ample parking.
Price ££-£££
Food breakfast, lunch, dinner
Rooms 11; singles, doubles, large doubles and 2 suites all with TV, radio, telephones, wi-fi, tea and coffee making facilities and guidebooks
Facilities bar, brasserie, terrace, sitting area, parking
Credit cards MC, V
Children welcome; £10 per night for cot, £20 per night for children under 12 in parents' room
Disabled ramps both inside and out, and fully accessible WC
Pets allowed on request
Closed never **Proprietor** Anthony and Jeanette Goodrich

The Bank House Hotel

Town house hotel

This is the sister hotel of The Rose & Crown in Snettisham (page 262). It's just as quirky and historic as its sibling. The Grade II listed Georgian townhouse started life as the home of a rich King's Lynn merchant, but in the 1780s was set up as the first branch of what is now Barclays Bank. A dent in the wooden floor is still visible, maybe left behind by the nervous shuffling of 18thC account holders. Careful design brings out the history of the building, but this place is far from old fashioned. Traffic-light bright chairs decorate the waterside terrace outside, whilst inside the armchairs are bright green and magenta. Rooms are airy and modern, although some are a little small. Most have river views; a few look out on to King's Staithe Square.

The brasserie and bar are relaxed and welcoming, made up of a number of different areas from which you can choose according to how formal you're feeling. We think that the most sympathetic area is the former counting house – all dark, polished wood and original flooring. Dishes vary from the standard (burgers, fish and chips) to the exotic, and are prepared using local ingredients whenever possible. Bank House is brilliantly situated for the nearby Corn Exchange and Arts Centre, and pre-and post-theatre dining can be arranged.

King's Lynn, Norfolk

Lynn Road, Grimston, King's Lynn, Norfolk PE32 1AH

Tel (01485) 600250
Fax 01485 601191
e-mail
info@conghamhallhotel.co.uk
website www.conghamhallhotel.co.uk

Nearby Sandringham; Ely; Norwich.
Location 6 miles (10 km) NE of King's Lynn near A148; with parking for 50 cars
Food breakfast, lunch, dinner
Price ££££
Rooms 26; 15 in the main house, 11 garden rooms, 11 double, 2 suites, all with bath, 1 single with shower; all rooms have phone, TV
Facilities 2 sitting rooms, bar, dining room; garden, spa , tennis, croquet, putting
Credit cards AE, DC, MC, V
Children welcome (over 7 in restaurant) **Disabled** easy access to restaurant **Pets** by arrangement (outside kennels) **Closed** never
Proprietor Nicholas Dickinson

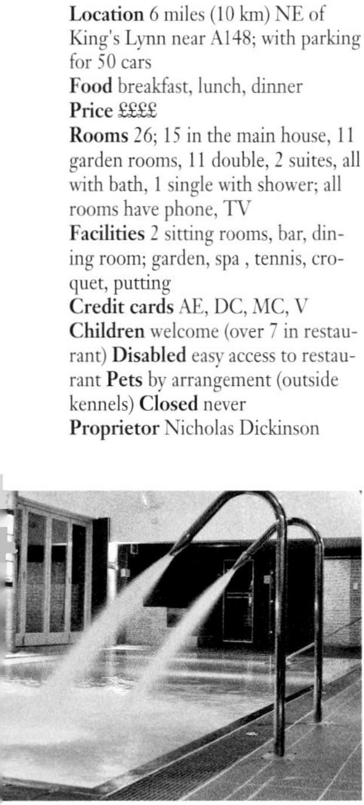

Congham Hall

Country house hotel

'Quintessentially English' is how some guests describe their stay here. Practically everything about this white 18thC Georgian house, set in 40 acres of lawns, orchards and parkland, is impressive. The spacious bedrooms and public areas are luxuriously furnished and our reporter found the service to be solicitous and efficient and the staff helpful and welcoming. Cooking (in the modern British style) is adventurous and excellent, making much use of home-grown herbs. The restaurant is a spacious, airy delight, built to look like an orangerie, with full-length windows overlooking the wide lawns of the parkland, where the herb gardens are an attraction in their own right. Visitors stop to admire the array of 600 herb varieties and to buy samples, from angelica to sorrel. The restaurant doors open on to the terraces for pre-dinner drinks and herb garden strolls.

Personal attention is thoughtful. For walkers and cyclists, the hotel will arrange to collect luggage from guests' previous destinations and deliver it onwards too. It also keeps a book of special walks, devised by the previous owners, the Forecasts, and can arrange clay pigeon shooting on site, subject to availability. Taken over in 2012 by Nicholas Dickinson, a seasoned hotelier. Reports welcome.

Lavenham, Suffolk

Market Place, Lavenham, Suffolk CO10 9QZ

Tel (01787) 247431
Fax (01787) 248007
e-mail info@greathouse.co.uk
website www.greathouse.co.uk

Nearby Little Hall Museum; National Trust Guildhall (Lavenham); Melford Hall; Gainsborough's House; Sudbury.
Location 16 miles (26 km) NW of Colchester, in middle of village; car parking
Food breakfast, lunch, dinner
Price £££
Rooms 5; 3 double with bath, 2 luxury suites with bath/shower; all rooms have phone, TV, minibar, wi-fi, some have espresso machine, hairdryer
Facilities dining room; patio, garden; bicycle hire
Credit cards MC, V
Children welcome
Disabled access difficult
Pets not accepted
Closed Jan **Proprietor** Régis Crépy

The Great House

Restaurant-with-rooms

The old timber-framed houses, the fine 'Wool Church' and the high street full of antiques and galleries make Lavenham a high point of any visitor's itinerary of the pretty villages of East Anglia.

The Great House in the market place was built in the heyday of the wool trade but was extensively renovated in the 18th century and looks more Georgian than Tudor – at least from the outside. It was a private house (lived in by the renowned artist Humphrey Spender and his brother, the poet Stephen Spender, in the 1930s) until Régis and Martine Crépy turned it into a hotel in 1985. The food (predominantly French) is the best for miles, with a well-chosen wine list – 'stunningly good', enthuses one visitor (a fellow hotelier).

If you can secure one of its five bedrooms it is also a delightful place to stay. All are different, but they are all light and elegant, with the same charm as the rest of the house. Four have their own sitting area or sitting room, with sofa or upholstered chairs. The beds (one a king-size Jacobean four-poster) are dressed with Egyptian linen and eiderdown duvets. The complimentary fruit and decanter of sherry are a welcoming touch.

In summer, the dining room French doors open on to a pretty stone-paved courtyard for drinks, lunch or dinner.

Long Melford, Suffolk

The Green, Long Melford, Suffolk CO10 9DN

Tel (01787) 312356
Fax (01787) 374557
e-mail enquiries@blacklionhotel.net
website www.blacklionhotel.net

Nearby Long Melford church; Melford Hall; Kentwell Hall.
Location in village 3 miles (5 km) N of Sudbury, overlooking village green; with car parking
Food breakfast, lunch, dinner
Price £££
Rooms 10; 8 double, 1 suite, 1 family room; all have bath/shower, all have phone, TV **Facilities** sitting room, 2 dining rooms, bar
Credit cards AE, MC, V
Children welcome
Disabled no special facilities
Pets accepted in bedrooms, £15 per pet per night, not in restaurant
Closed never
Proprietor Mr Craig Jarvis

The Black Lion

Country hotel

Long Melford is a famously attractive Suffolk village, and The Black Lion is at the heart of it, overlooking the green. It is an elegant early 19thC building, decorated and furnished with great sympathy, taste and lightness of touch. When owner Craig Jarvis took over some years ago, he reinstated its original name (the previous owners, the Erringtons, renamed it 'The Countrymen'), and transformed it into a hotel full of quirky character.

Each of the bedrooms is totally different, and all are impressively unusual. They range from the rather exotic to the more cooly romantic. The one our reporter stayed in had dark gold wallpaper, gold and brown embroidered bedspreads, exotic curtains, an ornate mirror and an oriental wardrobe.

Dinner can be eaten either in the comfortable bistro or the more formal, elegant dining room (both serve the same menu), and our reporter found it to be "absolutely delicious, first rate". The chef, known as Molly, works with seasonal and locally produced ingredients to create dishes such as Dingley Dell pork chop with Stornaway black pudding, Cavolo Nero and pomme purée. There is also homemade bread and cream teas. Reports welcome.

High Street, Mistley, Essex CO11 1HE

Tel 01206 392821
Fax 01206 390122
e-mail info@mistleythorn.co.uk
website www.mistleythorn.co.uk

Nearby Colchester 7 miles, Ipswich 8 miles, Stour Estuary
Location Mistley High Street, car park for 5 cards and street parking
Food breakfast, lunch, dinner, afternoon tea,
Price ££-£££
Rooms 11; all have television, DVD player, iPod dock, tea/coffee facilities, wi-fi; 2 rooms have small kitchen facilities
Facilities restaurant
Credit cards AE, MC, V
Children welcome
Disabled no special access
Pets well-behaved dogs in some rooms
Closed never
Proprietor Sherri Singleton and David McKay

The Mistley Thorn

Village inn

In the 1700s, a wealthy, local landowner had plans to turn Mistley into a fashionable saltwater spa, but his scheme never came off. Be prepared for a place that's semi-industrial and rough at the edges.

Two 18thC towers rise from a churchyard on the edge of the town, and the High Street has prettily painted Georgian terraces. The Mistley Thorn is a former Victorian public house, outside of which you get the smell of Horlicks emanating from the Edme Maltings factory along the road. Opposite is the Stour Estuary, upstream from Harwich. We liked The Mistley Thorn as much for its setting as for the food and accommodation.

It's now run with panache by Californian Sherri Singleton. Her menu majors on local seafood, including Mersea oysters and Colchester natives when in season. There's Suffolk Red Poll beef and Sutton Hoo chicken.

Our top-floor room, with a view of the Stour, was somewhat cramped, but it was freshly decorated and had a well-equipped, airy bathroom. Other rooms are larger. We heard some traffic noise in the morning.

Morston, Norfolk

Morston, Holt, Norfolk
NR25 7AA

Tel (01263) 741041
Fax (01263) 740419
e-mail reception@morstonhall. com
website www.morstonhall.com

Nearby Sandringham; Felbrigg Hall; Holkham Hall; Brickling.
Location 2 miles (3 km) W of Blakeney on A149; with ample car parking
Food breakfast, Sun lunch, dinner
Price ££££
Rooms 13 double and twin; all rooms have phone, TV, CD player, hairdryer **Facilities** 2 sitting rooms, conservatory, dining room; garden, croquet
Credit cards AE, DC, MC, V
Children welcome
Disabled 1 ground-floor bedroom
Pets accepted in bedrooms **Closed** Jan, Christmas, Boxing Day
Proprietors Galton and Tracy Blackiston

Morston Hall

Country hotel

Don't be put off by the rather severe-looking flint exterior of this solid Jacobean house on the North Norfolk coast. Inside, the rooms are unexpectedly bright and airy, painted in summery colours and overlooking a sweet garden, where a fountain plays in a lily pond and roses flourish. The *raison d'être* of Morston Hall is its dining room, the responsibility of Galton Blackiston, who shot to fame as a finalist in ITV's 'Chef of the Year'. He has since won huge acclaim for his outstanding modern European cuisine and, the icing on the cake, a Michelin star in 1999. His set four-course menu changes daily and might feature: confit of leg of duck on sautéed Lyonnaise potatoes with thyme-infused jus or grilled fillet of sea bass served on fennel duxelle with sauce vierge. The carefully-stocked wine cellar offers a comprehensive selection of (not overpriced) wines from all over the world. Galton and his wife, Tracy, also organize wine-tasting dinners and cookery lessons. He gives a number of half-day cookery demonstrations and runs two three-day residential courses each year. Most of the large bedrooms are decked out in chintz fabrics, with armchairs and all the little extras, such as bottled water, bathrobes and large, warm, fluffy towels.

Norwich, Norfolk

38 St Giles Street, Norwich, Norfolk NR2 1LL

Tel 01603 662944
e-mail booking@38stgiles.co.uk
website www.38stgiles.co.uk

Nearby Norwich Castle, Norwich Cathedral, shops, bars, restaurants
Location Norwich town centre
Food breakfast
Price ££-£££
Rooms 5; all have bath/shower, wi-fi, Bang and Olufsen televisions, hairdryer, bath robes, tea and coffee making facilities
Facilities wi-fi
Credit cards MC, V
Children welcome, family room available
Disabled 1 ground-floor room, but no special access
Pets not accepted
Closed Christmas
Proprietor Jan and William Cheeseman

38 St Giles

Town bed-and-breakfast

This sophisticated bed-and-breakfast in the heart of Norwich can claim to be one of the best in the city.

Owners Jan and William Cheeseman were managers of two Norwich delicatessens before buying 38 St Giles, so they know a thing or two about good food. The breakfasts don't disappoint – imaginative jams, fresh pancakes and homemade granola feature on the wide-ranging menu – and all ingredients are locally sourced. The Norfolk breakfast is a particular favourite with guests – one recent visitor describing it as 'the best British breakfast' around.

They've made the most of the breakfast room as a public space. White walls and lofty ceilings enhance the feel of Georgian grandeur – the pretty crockery adds a contrasting, feminine touch.

Bedrooms are an interesting marriage of traditional and contemporary design. Period features such as large fireplaces and generous bay windows give a lovely old-fashioned feel, while contemporary chaise longues, colourful silk curtains and modern wooden furniture make each room feel chic and cool. Welcome treats, such as homemade brownies, are left for guests.

Snettisham, Norfolk

Old Church Road, Snettisham,
Norfolk PE31 7LX

Tel (01485) 541 382
Fax (01485) 543 172
e-mail info@roseandcrownsnettisham.co.uk
website www.roseandcrownsnettisham.co.uk

Nearby Peddars Way, Houghton Hall, Holkham Hall, Sandringham, Norfolk Lavender, Brancaster, Burnham Market
Location off B1440, in centre of Snettisham village with ample car-parking
Food breakfast, lunch, dinner
Price ££ **Rooms** 16; 1 twin, 15 doubles (4 can be split for twins); all rooms have phone, TV, wi-fi, air-conditioning, hairdryers, irons
Facilities 3 dining rooms, walled garden, bar, sitting room **Credit cards** V **Children** welcome **Pets** accepted **Disabled** 2 rooms have access **Closed** never **Proprietors** Anthony and Jeanette Goodrich

Rose and Crown

Village inn

We like the way this inn keeps both locals and visitors happy. There are plenty of activities nearby, it is situated near an area of outstanding natural beauty, and it is far better value for money than its grander neighbours in nearby villages. The oldest part of the inn is the bar, originally built for workers who erected the local church, and where locals and visitors enjoy the beer and a wide selection of sandwiches whilst sitting by the open fire, then totter off to their rooms, minding the wonky old flagstones on the way.

On the way to your room, admire owner Anthony Goodrich's sporting prowess: his old school photos adorn the walls. The bedrooms are smallish, but done out in a fresh, sea-sidey way, with all the creature comforts you would expect. If you need a substantial lunch or dinner, head downstairs to one of the three dining rooms that provide fresh, locally sourced food, including beef from the salt marshes at Holkham, seafood from Brancaster and game from the gentlemen in wellies in the back bar.

Parents can rest assured that their children will be safe in the walled garden, sporting an impressive climbing frame and play area. They can be watched from the terrace or the attached dining room/sitting room. The Goodriches thoroughly deserve their Publicans' Pub of the Year award.

Stoke by Nayland, Suffolk,
CO6 4SA

Tel (01206) 263245
e-mail info@angelinnsuffolk.co.uk
website www.angelinnsuffolk.co.uk

Nearby Guildhall; Dedham Vale; Flatford Mill; East Bergholt.
Location in village centre, on B1068 between Sudbury and Ipswich; small car park for 20 cars
Food breakfast, lunch, dinner
Price ££
Rooms 6 double, 1 twin, all with bath; all rooms have phone, TV, hairdryer, wi-fi
Facilities sitting room, 2 dining rooms, bar; garden, herb garden, beer garden
Credit cards MC, V
Children travel cots in 4 rooms
Disabled not suitable
Pets accepted, 1 dog-friendly room
Closed never
Proprietors Exclusive Inns

Angel Inn

Village inn

A proper inn rather than a pub, with spick-and-span bedrooms off a long gallery landing upstairs, the Angel Inn has been in business since the 16th century. There are plenty of nooks and crannies in the bar and a variety of seating in the series of interconnecting public rooms. You'll find sofas and chairs grouped together in the lounge; and a dining room with its ceiling open to the rafters, rough brick-and-timber-studded walls and a fern-lined well-shaft 52 feet (16 m) deep. The bedrooms are a fair size, individually and unfussily decorated, and are ideal for a one- or two-night stop on a tour of Suffolk. Since the last edition, they have renovated these, re-painting them and adding new baths.

The public rooms downstairs have great character, with interesting pictures and low lighting, and are filled with the hum and buzz of contented lunch and dinner conversation. The food is excellent, with local produce used where possible, including fresh fish and shellfish from nearby ports, and game from local estates. Dishes might include griddled hake with red onion dressing, or stir-fried duckling with fine leaf salad, Cumberland sauce and new potatoes. Service is informal, friendly and helpful. Children are not allowed in the bar, and though flexible, check when booking what the rules are.

Ash Close, Swaffham, Norfolk
PE37 7NH

Tel (01760) 723845
e-mail enquiries@strattonshotel.com
website www.strattonshotel.com

Nearby Norwich; North Norfolk coast.
Location down narrow lane between shops on main street; with ample car parking
Food breakfast, lunch, dinner
Price £££
Rooms 14; 7 doubles, 7 suites, all with bath or shower; all rooms have phone, TV/DVD, hairdryer, minibar, iron **Facilities** 2 sitting rooms, dining room, bar, cafe/deli
Credit cards MC, V
Children welcome
Disabled access difficult **Pets** welcome in specific rooms **Closed** Christmas
Proprietors Vanessa and Les Scott

Strattons

Town hotel

Strattons has long summed up everything we are looking for in this guide. Perhaps it's because Les and Vanessa Scott are such natural hosts who love entertaining; perhaps it's because of their artistic flair (they met as art students) or perhaps it's because they had a very clear vision of what they wanted to create when they bought this elegant listed villa in 1990. A reader writes: '20 out of 20 for staff attitude, value for money, quality of accommodation... An absolute delight.'

Bedrooms are positively luxurious. Plump cushions and pillows jostle for space on antique beds, books and magazines fill the shelves, and the same coordinated decoration continues into smart bathrooms – one resembling a bedouin's tent. The two beautifully furnished sitting rooms, *trompe l'oeil* hallway and murals painted by a local artist are equally impressive. Yet it is emphatically a family home and you share it with the Scott family and their three cats. The food is special, too. Vanessa, a cookery writer, continues to gain awards for her cooking. There are fresh eggs every day from their own chickens, and the seasonal menu is inventive and beautifully presented. It is cheerfully served by the small team of staff in the cosy basement restaurant.

Thorpe Market, Norfolk

Cromer Road, Thorpe Market, Norwich, Norfolk NR11 8TZ

Tel 01263 832010
e-mail office@theguntonarms.co.uk
website www.theguntonarms.co.uk

Nearby Cromer, Holt, Holkham Hall, Houghton Hall, The Sainsbury Centre of Art
Location just off the A149 on Elderton Lane
Food breakfast, lunch, dinner
Price ££-££££
Rooms 8 doubles, all have bath/shower
Facilities restaurant, sitting area, bar, The Stamp Rooms
Credit cards AE, MC, V
Children welcome, £15 per night for additional bed
Disabled disabled lavatory, bar and restaurant on one level, bedrooms are on first floor
Pets accepted, dogs £10 per night
Closed Christmas Day
Proprietor Ivor Braka

The Gunton Arms

Country pub-with-rooms

One of the most impressive refurbished inns in East Anglia, possibly in the country. It's a substantial, flint-walled building in flat, spreading Norfolk parkland. Money did not deter the owner, art dealer Ivor Braka, from achieving the result he wanted. Although cash does not guarantee success, here it has come together to great effect with Braka's vision and high standards, and designer Robert Kime's flair.

Downstairs is a series of rooms which manage to feel traditional, cosy and stylish – and are full of surprises. Cropping up everywhere is outstanding contemporary art, much of it amusingly sexual. Tracy Emin's plates above the bar shocked one straightlaced couple so much that they got their solicitor to write a complaining letter. Country folk and Londoners seem to mix easily in the bar-dining area. The food is quite straightforward, including steaks cooked, memorably, on an open wood fire. The bedrooms are enchanting. If you find yourself in Ellis, look twice at the prints by the dressing table, but not if you were offended by Tracy Emin's plates.

Walberswick, Suffolk

Main Street, Walberswick, Suffolk
IP18 6UA

Tel 01502 722112 **e-mail** info@anchoratwalberswick.com **website** www.anchoratwalberswick.com

Nearby local beach and river are both a 2 minute walk, Minsmere RSPB centre, golf courses at Aldeburgh, Thorpeness and Southwold, Dunwich forest is a 45 minute walk, other sporting activities nearby. **Location** 10 minute drive from the A12 along the B1387, 15 minute drive from Southwold **Food** breakfast, lunch, dinner **Price** ££ **Rooms** 10; 6 garden rooms (3 are dog-friendly), 4 rooms in the main building; all en-suite with a bath and/or shower, all rooms have wi-fi, satellite television **Facilities** 2 sitting rooms, dining room, bar **Credit cards** AE, MC, V **Children** welcome **Disabled** one room accessible **Pets** accepted in most rooms **Closed** never **Proprietors** Mark and Sophie Dorber

The Anchor

Village inn

A place that stands out because of the hosts, says our series editor, Fiona Duncan. Some five years ago the Dorbers acquired this formerly run-down pub in the village where Sophie Dorber grew up. (She and Mark had run the popular White Horse pub in Parson's Green, Fulham. Sophie did the food, he was the landlord, with a special interest in wine and beers from the world over.)

The Anchor is far from boring now: it's a comfortable place, popular with the locals. The staff are attentive (unless over-run at peak times), and sometimes funny (watch out for Luke's unexpected quips). Sophie's food is full of flavour and Mark has done something unique with the wine list: matched dishes with not just wines but beers too. He'll even tell you what beer to drink with you breakfast porridge.

Don't be misled by the building's nothing-special exterior. The 11 bedrooms (four in the main building, six more spacious chalets in the garden) aren't as inviting as the colourful bar and restaurant – in fact they're simple, but they are priced for what they are. Bathrooms have underfloor heating.

It's a terrific weekend getaway, with much of interest nearby – the town of Southwold, and the famous Walberswick reedbeds – a birder's paradise.

Lavenham, Suffolk

Water Street, Lavenham, Suffolk
CO10 9RW

Tel (01787) 247404
Fax (01787) 248472
website www.lavenhampriory.co.uk
Food breakfast
Price ££
Closed Christmas and New Year
Proprietors Tim and Gilli Pitt

Lavenham Priory

Country house hotel

This is a very special place: the beautiful Grade I-listed house dates from the 13th century when it was home to Benedictine monks, and has been restored in keeping with its later life as home to an Elizabethan merchant, complete with original wallpaintings, Tudor fireplace and sofas covered in cushions and throws. More important, however, is the warmth of the welcome from Gilli and her husband Tim.

The house is large, and as well as the Great Hall sitting room there's a smaller room so more than one party can use the public rooms. Each of the bedrooms has a superb bed, including a four-poster in the Painted Chamber. Breakfast in the Merchants Hall is a feast. As we went to press we heard it was up for sale.

Lavenham, Suffolk

High Street, Lavenham, Suffolk
CO10 9QA

Tel (01787) 247477
e-mail bookaroom@theswanatlavenham.co.uk **website** www.theswanatlavenham.co.uk
Food breakfast, lunch, afternoon tea, dinner **Price** ££££
Closed never
Proprietor TA Collection

The Swan Hotel

Village hotel

On the news that Lavenham Priory was likely to close in 2014, we include this large but characterful inn as a useful alternative. The Swan's exterior competes head-on with the quaintest, but the recently refurbished interior is the reason to stay.

The down-at-heel, pokey old coaching inn has been made to look fresh without losing its essential character. The brasserie, overlooking the garden, works especially well. The beamy bedrooms are not as interesting as the ground floor spaces, but you may enjoy the test of finding your way back to your room through the labyrinth of passages and quirky floor levels. The Gallery Restaurant's food, in a reconstruction of a medieval timbered hall, is enjoyable, the wine list expertly chosen.

Nayland, Suffolk

The White Hart Inn

Village inn

Set in a cobbled Suffolk village, the inn dates from the 15th century. Nowadays good food and comfortable rooms still draw people in.

As we went to press, the White Hart Inn was in the process of being sold. We would welcome reports on how the new management are getting on.

High Street, Nayland, near Colchester, Suffolk CO6 4JF

Tel (01206) 240331
Fax (01206) 243396
e-mail info@whitehart-west-bergholt.co.uk
website www.whitehart-west-bergholt.co.uk **Food** breakfast, lunch, dinner **Price** ££ **Closed** never
Managers Simon and Mandy

Norwich, Norfolk

Catton Old Hall

Country house bed-and-breakfast

An impressive 17thC gentleman's residence, built from reclaimed Caen stone, local flint and oak timbers, has been transformed with great success into this genteel, family-run guesthouse. With its mullioned windows, beamed ceilings, inglenook fireplaces, polished antiques and warm colour schemes, the interior feels intimate and inviting. Owners Jean and Dianne Bowles are on-hand to welcome guests and look after them during their stay. Named after former inhabitants of the house, the bedrooms have been decorated boldly and in country-house style.

The breakfast menu is superb, making use of local produce as well as herbs and fruit from the garden. Splendid jams, preserves and marmalades are made on site.

Lodge Lane, Old Catton, Norwich, Norfolk NR6 7HG

Tel (01603) 419379
Fax (01603) 400339
e-mail enquiries@catton-hall.co.uk
website www.catton-hall.co.uk
Food breakfast
Price ££ **Closed** never
Proprietors Jean and Dianne Bowles

Orford, Suffolk

The Crown and Castle

Restaurant-with-rooms

There's been a hostelry here for eight centuries, but today's inn is a quirky, late 19th-century building that has an immediately welcoming feel.

The Trinity restaurant makes a beguiling place for an informal lunch or smarter dinner (an excellent breakfast, too). But our reporter, Fiona Duncan, felt that there were slightly jarring notes – funky wall and ceiling lights, 'no mobile phones' notices.

She thought that her room (in the outbuilding) was smart but lacked personality. It had a pretty headboard, but insistently patterned curtain fabric. Stock furniture, no desk, plain grey walls, and a 'no smoking' notice made it less of a welcoming sanctuary than other rooms she has stayed in for the same price. Despite the negatives, this is a useful address in an interesting area.

Orford, Woodbridge, Suffolk, IP12 2LJ

Tel 01394 450205
email info@crownandcastle.co.uk
website crownandcastle.co.uk
Food breakfast, lunch, dinner
Price ££££
Closed never
Proprietor Ruth Watson

Southwold, Suffolk

The Crown Hotel

Town hotel

The recently upgraded Crown is quite a characterful place, but with flaws. From the outside it looks like a substantial hotel, but inside it's more of a pub with rooms. It's on Southwold's High Street, as is its sister hotel, The Swan – see page 270, also owned and managed by Adnams, the Southwold Brewery.

On our latest visit, we noticed worn carpets on the narrow staircases and fire extinguishers rather prominent in the corridors. Our bedroom and bathroom were chilly and cramped for the price. But don't be put off. The bedrooms are well thought out and have some charming touches.

Downstairs is the vibrant bar-dining area, loved by locals, with great food, and the charming, tiny Back Bar.

High Street, Southwold, Suffolk IP18 6DP

Tel 01502 722275
e-mail crown.hotel@adnams.co.uk
website www.adnams.co.uk/hotels/the-crown
Food breakfast, lunch, dinner
Price £££-££££
Closed never
Proprietors Adnams

Southwold, Suffolk

The Swan Hotel

Town hotel

The Swan, a Southwold institution like its sister hotel The Crown (see page 269), may now need some judicious updating – but with care not to spoil its character. This comes out best in the drawing room, with its carved wood chimneypieces and Murano glass chandeliers. On a fine day the sun pours in through the windows on the market square. The bedrooms at the front are largest, but all are inviting and well decorated, most with restrained background shades but also some splashes of smart, strong colour. On the walls are interesting prints and other decorative items.

It's largish, and quite conventional for this guide, but staff are helpful and can give some individual attention.

Market Place, Southwold, Suffolk IP18 6EG

Tel 01502 722186
e-mail swan.hotel@adnams.co.uk
website www.adnams.co.uk/hotels/the-swan
Food breakfast, lunch, dinner
Price ££-££££
Closed never
Proprietors Adnams

Woodbridge, Suffolk

The Crown

Town hotel

The Crown may have stood for more than 400 years on the Thoroughfare crossroads, but its latest reincarnation combines stylish interiors and modern comforts with the centuries of architecture and period charm. It's open for breakfast, lunch and dinner seven days a week, but reservations are recommended as the restaurant – award-winning and highly recommended – can get busy. It boasts ten gorgeous bedrooms – all created by an award-winning interior designer, with an emphasis on style and comfort.

Thoroughfare, Woodbridge, Suffolk IP12 1AD

Tel (01394) 384242
Fax (01394) 387192
email info@thecrownatwoodbridge.co.uk
website www.thecrownatwoodbridge.co.uk **Food** breakfast, lunch, dinner **Price** ££-£££ **Closed** never
Proprietor Stephen David

Area introduction

The far north of England divides neatly into two areas: the north-west and the north-east. The north-west includes Cumbria, some of North Yorkshire, Lancashire and Merseyside. The north-east is a large band of territory stretching from the Humber Estuary up to the Scottish border, taking in most of the rest of North Yorkshire, the Yorkshire Dales and the large, wild county of Northumberland, together with County Durham and some heavily industrialized counties such as Teeside. Cumbria and the Yorkshire Dales have the richest crop of charming small hotels for the obvious reasons: their wonderful mountain and moorland scenery, terrific walking and many numinous ancient monuments and historic houses. For visitor numbers, Cumbria is up there with Devon and Cornwall, and getting there by train from London is much quicker.

Below are some useful back-up places to try if our main selections are fully booked:

Blakey Hall Farm
Bed-and-breakfast, Colne
Tel 01282 863121
www.blakeyhallfarm.co.uk
Interesting, luxury B&B on Leeds-Liverpool Canal.

Kelleth Old Hall
Country guesthouse, Kelleth
Tel 015396 23344
www.kelletholdhall.co.uk
Delightyful, idiosyncratic, one-room country retreat.

Seatoller House
Country guesthouse, Seatoller
Tel 017687 77218
www.seatollerhouse.co.uk
Sociable guest-house.

Goldsborough Hall
Country house hotel, Goldsborough
Tel 01423 867321
www.goldsboroughhall.com
Historic, luxurious hotel.

The Balmoral Hotel
Town hotel, Harrogate
Tel 01423 508208
www.balmoralhotel.co.uk
Upmarket, stylish hotel in central Harrogate.

Hotel du Vin
Townhouse hotel, Harrogate
Tel 084473 64257
www.hotelduvin.com
Richly furnished chain hotel overlooking The Stray.

42 The Calls
Town hotel, Leeds
Tel 0113 244 0099
www.42thecalls.co.uk
Converted riverside corn mill.

Haley's Hotel
Town house hotel, Leeds
Tel 0113 2784446
www.haleys.co.uk
Useful address for Leeds, with friendly, local staff.

The Wensleydale Heifer Village hotel, West Witton Tel 01969 622322
www.wesleydaleheifer.co.uk
Characterful, themed bedrooms in Yorkshire Dales.

Mount Pleasant Farm
Bed-and-breakfast, Whashton Tel 01748 822784
www.mountpleasantfarmhouse.co.uk Top-end B&B in 1850s farmhouse.

Askham, Cumbria

Askham, near Penrith, Cumbria
CA10 2PF

Tel 01931 712350
e-mail enquiries@askhamhall.co.uk
website www.askhamhall.co.uk

Nearby Askham village, River Lowther, Penrith, Ullswater 20 mins by car, walks from the door and fishing **Location** in own grounds, 10-minute drive from Penrith and the M6; ample car-parking
Food breakfast, lunch, dinner
Price £££-££££
Rooms 13; all with own bath or shower (26 bedrooms will be available shortly) **Facilities** restaurant, private gardens, heated outdoor swimming pool, spa, cafe, converted barn for weddings **Credit cards** all major **Children** welcome, catering arrangements to be discussed
Disabled no special facilities
Pets dogs accepted by prior arrangement **Closed** Jan and first 2 weeks of Feb **Proprietors** Charles and Juno Lowther

Askham Hall

Country house hotel

One of the most exciting developments in Lake District accommodation for a long time. The young owner, Charles Lowther (half brother of the present Earl of Lonsdale), his wife Juno and their family have created a 'hometel' – a home from home hotel out of Askham Hall, on the edge of the Lake District.

Unless you heed the detailed directions they'll give you on booking, you'll be unsure whether you've come to the right place. After driving through Lowther Park and reaching the pretty village of Askham, the hall's gates are a little way down the hill from the houses – but there's not a sign in sight. The mystery tour ends only when you see the framed message on the hall table saying ring for attention.

Charlie has given serious thought to making this place super-relaxed, more like staying in a private house than a hotel. Its one-off location in a family home gives it an added twist of originality.

Rooms have no numbers or names on the doors. Their eclectic, occasionally quirky country house style decoration and furniture is all different. A professional kitchen produces flavourful food from a small menu which is served in the informal dining room-breakfast room.

The Lowthers' other place to stay nearby is The George and Dragon near Penrith (page 279).

Austwick, North Yorkshire

Austwick, Settle, North Yorkshire Dales LA2 8BY

Tel 01524 251224
Fax 01524 251796
e-mail info@thetraddock.co.uk
website www.thetraddock.co.uk

Nearby the Yorkshire Dales National Park, Settle Carlisle Railway and 3 Peaks of Ingleborough, Whernside and Pen-Y-Ghent **Location** 1 mile off the A65 between Skipton and Kendal; with ample car-parking **Food** breakfast, lunch, dinner, bar snacks, afternoon tea
Price ££-£££ **Rooms** 12; 3 shower only, 9 bath and shower; 11 double and suites, 1 smaller double/single; all with LCD TV, phone, hairdryer, tea/coffee facilities **Facilities** 2 dining rooms, 3 sitting rooms, 1 bar; garden and patio **Credit cards** MC, V **Children** welcome **Disabled** limited access **Pets** £5 per dog **Closed** never **Proprietor** Jane, Bruce, Paul and Jenny Reynolds

The Traddock

Country hotel

'Traddock'? It means a trading paddock, and this hotel stands in a field that was forever used for just this purpose. It's a grey stone house on the edge of a mostly pretty village, part of the scenery and ideally located for the big walks in the south-western Yorkshire Dales. The feeling of being in its skin continues inside. Renovated by the Reynoldses as a new venture in the last ten years, original features and country antiques sit comfortably alongside new furniture and fabrics in confident 'country house' taste. The three sitting rooms, one spacious and well proportioned, are quirkily linked by the bar, the standing area in front of it doubling as a passage.

Our reporter's room was again in good country house taste – pine chest, pine wardrobe, rusty-red wall paper nicely offsetting cream-yellow paintwork. There were two easy chairs, but no desk and chair for writing. The shower, loo and wash basin were in a somewhat cramped cube built into the corner of the room; the shower stream was feeble; but still, the price at £140 at weekends was normal. Since our last edition, every bedroom and bathroom has been upgraded.

Worthy company for nearby Hipping Hall (page 282), with friendly owner-managed atmosphere, and just-right food.

Bassenthwaite Lake, Cumbria

Bassenthwaite Lake, near
Cockermouth, Cumbria CA13 9YE

Tel (017687) 76234
Fax (017687) 76002
e-mail info@the-pheasant.co.uk
website www.the-pheasant.co.uk

Nearby Bassenthwaite Lake; Keswick.
Location 5 miles (8 km) E of Cockermouth, just off A66; with ample car parking
Food breakfast, lunch, dinner, bar snacks **Price** £££
Rooms 15; 11 double and twin, 3 suites and 1 single; all with bath and shower; all rooms have flat-screen TV, hairdryer, phone **Facilities** sitting rooms, dining room, bar; garden
Credit cards MC, V **Children** accepted over 8, but not in the bar or dining room at night
Disabled access possible to public rooms, Garden Lodge and 3 en suite rooms **Pets** accepted in public rooms and Garden Lodge rooms **Closed** Christmas Eve and Day **Manager** Matthew Wylie

The Pheasant

Country inn

'Still a very special place,' says our most recent inspector. Nestled away behind trees just off the A66, the Pheasant was originally an old coaching inn, and there are many reminders of this within, particularly in the little old oak bar, which is full of dark nooks and crannies – little changed from its earliest days. The building is a long, low barn-like structure that has been exceptionally well maintained. There is a small but well-kept garden to the rear and grounds that extend to 60 acres.

The two sitting areas are one of the main attractions of the place. The one to the front is low-ceilinged, with small windows and plenty of prints on the walls. The second has a serving hatch to the bar; both have open log fires.

The grand refurbishment scheme was undertaken in early 2000, and smaller, more recent ones have seen the conversion of 20 old bedrooms into 15 larger, lighter, more modern rooms. They are individually decorated, partnered by *en suite* bathrooms, and some have spectacular views of the fells. The original dining room has been reorganized to make the best of its slightly uncomfortable shape; there's also a new restuarant (The Fell) at the back of the hotel. The menu changes daily and is close to achieving its second Rosette. Service is outstandingly friendly.

Borrowdale, Cumbria

Borrowdale, Keswick, Cumbria
CA12 5UY

Tel (017687) 77247
Fax (017687) 77363
e-mail
reservations@leatheshead.co.uk
website www.leatheshead.co.uk

Nearby Derwent Water; Buttermere; Castlerigg Stone Circle.
Location 3.5 miles (5.5 km) S of Keswick, off B5289 to Borrowdale, in 3 acres of grounds; car-parking
Food breakfast, dinner; half-board obligatory at weekends
Price ££ **Rooms** 11 double and twin, all with shower, some with bath; all rooms have phone, TV, hairdryer, wi-fi
Facilities 2 sitting rooms, dining room, bar; garden
Credit cards MC, V **Children** accepted over 9 **Disabled** 1 ground-floor room **Pets** dogs accepted in 4 rooms **Closed** late-Nov to mid-Feb
Managers Jane Cleary and Jamie Adamson

The Leathes Head

Country hotel

In the beautiful Borrowdale valley near Derwent Water, perched in its own wooded grounds, this Lakeland stone Edwardian house was originally built for a Liverpool ship-owner. New managers Jane Cleary and Jamie Adamson have spent the past three years refurbishing the entire house, but many of its period features, the plasterwork and a wood-panelled ceiling in the hall, are still there.

It is informal enough to attract the walkers and climbers who return year after year for the glorious fells ringing the valley. Children over nine are welcome and can have a high tea in the evenings to give their parents the chance of a quiet dinner, or drink at the bar, by themselves.

All the bedrooms are comfortable and individually furnished. Bathrooms are modern and light. The three-acre grounds include lawns big enough and level enough to play boules or croquet – and flat areas are few and far between in this region. The real challenges are the fells beyond the gate, and the hotel can help here too, with its extensive collection of walking guides. There are also lake cruises, water sports and mountain biking in the area.

As we went to press the hotel was closed for refurbishment. We would welcome any updates when it reopens in 2014.

Bowness-on-Windermere, Cumbria

Bowness-on-Windermere, Cumbria
LA23 3JP

Tel (015394) 43286
Fax (015394) 47455
e-mail kennedy@lindethfell.co.uk
website www.lindethfell.co.uk

Nearby Windermere Steamboat Museum; Lake Windermere.
Location 1 mile (1.5km) S of Bowness on A5074; with ample car-parking
Food breakfast, lunch, dinner
Price ££
Rooms 14; 12 double and twin, 2 single, 12 with bath, 2 with shower; all rooms have phone, TV, hairdryer
Facilities 2 sitting rooms, dining room, bar; garden, lake, croquet, bowling green
Credit cards MC, V
Children accepted
Disabled access possible to ground-floor bedroom
Pets not accepted
Closed 3 weeks in Jan
Proprietors Kennedy family

Lindeth Fell

Country house hotel

To stay at Lindeth Fell is like visiting a well-heeled old friend who enjoys making his visitors as comfortable as possible, who enjoys his food (but likes to be able to identify what's put in front of him), is unreasonably fond of good puddings, has a rather fine wine cellar – and is justifiably proud of the view from his house. The Kennedys' establishment hits this mark (they are always there to see that it does), and, not unsurprisingly, their approach and warm courteous welcome have been duly rewarded with a faithful following.

Approached through trees, and set in large mature gardens glowing with azaleas and rhododendrons in spring, Lindeth Fell's wood-panelled hall leads to a pair of comfortable and attractive sitting rooms and a restaurant where large windows let in the tremendous view. Weather permitting, drinks and tea can be taken on the terrace, and the same warm weather might even allow for a game of croquet. Upstairs, the rooms vary in size and outlook. Both qualities are reflected in their price but, as a general rule, the further up the house you go, the smaller the room but the better the view. All the rooms are comfortably furnished and pleasingly decorated.

Bowness-on-Windermere, Cumbria

Crook Road, Bowness-on-Windermere, Cumbria LA23 3JA

Tel (015394) 88600
Fax (015394) 88601
e-mail stay@linthwaite.com
website www.linthwaite.com

Nearby Windermere Steamboat Museum; Lake Windermere; Beatrix Potter's Hilltop
Location 1 mile (1.5km) S of Bowness off the A5074; with ample car parking
Food breakfast, lunch, dinner
Price ££-£££
Rooms 30 double and twin with bath; all rooms have phone, TV, hairdryer; wi-fi
Facilities sitting rooms, conservatory, dining rooms, bar; terrace, garden, veranda
Credit cards AE, MC, V
Children accepted
Disabled one specially adapted room **Pets** accepted **Closed** never
Proprietor Mike Bevans

Linthwaite House

Country house hotel

You could say of Mike Bevans that he liked the view so much that he bought the best place to see it from. It is our good luck that he and his wife have also created in this Edwardian country house a very professionally-run hotel with a unique style. The reception rooms are filled with palms, wicker furniture and old curios as well as antiques. Painted decoys, well-travelled cabin trunks and oriental vases help to evoke days of leisure and service in the far reaches of the Empire.

Service here manages to be crisp and amiable at the same time: you are made to feel that you are on holiday and not on parade. Whether you eat in the richly coloured dining room, the Billiard Room or the Mirror Room, the food has come from Chris O'Callaghan's kitchen (3rd AA rosette and listed in Michelin) – well-thought-out menus, beautifully presented. Bad luck, though, if you're under seven: it's an early tea for you, without the option.

Of the bedrooms, the best look directly towards Windermere, some are in a modern annexe, and there is quite a variation in size. They all have style though, with thoughtful use of fabrics and furnishings and bathrooms that are attractive rather than utilitarian. Beyond the terraces outside are 14 acres of lawn, shrubs, woods and a small lake.

Brampton, Cumbria

Brampton, Cumbria CA8 2NG

Tel (016977) 46234
Fax (016977) 46683
e-mail farlam@farlamhall.co.uk
website www.farlamhall.co.uk

Nearby Naworth Castle; Hadrian's Wall; Lanercost Priory.
Location 3 miles (5 km) SE of Brampton on A689, NE of (not in) Farlam village; with ample car parking
Food breakfast, dinner; light lunches on request
Price ££££
Rooms 12 double with bath; all rooms have phone, TV, hairdryer
Facilities 2 sitting rooms, dining room, wi-fi; garden, croquet
Credit cards MC, V
Children accepted over 5
Disabled 2 ground-floor bedrooms
Pets welcome
Closed Christmas week
Proprietors Quinion family

Farlam Hall

Country house hotel

'Charming family, quiet surroundings, excellent food,' are the phrases that encapsulate Farlam Hall. For almost 40 years now the Quinion family has assiduously improved their solid but elegant Border country house. It has its roots in Elizabethan times, but what you see today is essentially a large, Victorian family home, extended for a big family and frequent entertaining. No coincidence that it makes such a good hotel.

The dining room and public rooms are discreet and the atmosphere is one of traditional English service and comfort. The bedrooms vary widely, with some decidedly large and swish. Nevertheless, all are luxurious and charmingly done out, and some have beautiful views of the grounds that are home to a variety of llamas and sheep.

The chef, being one of the family, takes pride in his food and it shows. The menu changes daily (so guests staying for longer than one night don't get bored) and there is an impressive wine list that is overseen by Mr Quinion, not to mention the extensive English cheese board or a choice of deliciously unhealthy puddings.

Farlam Hall is well placed for the Lakes, Dales and Northumberland Coast as well as Hadrian's Wall.

Clifton, Cumbria

Clifton, Near Penrith, Cumbria
CA10 2ER

Tel 01768 865 381
e-mail enquries@georgeanddragonclifton.co.uk
website www.georgeanddragonclifton.co.uk

Nearby Ullswater; Lowther Castle
Location come off the M6 at junction 39 towards Shap, continue for 10 minutes and you will come to Clifton; has its own car park
Food breakfast, lunch, dinner
Price ££-£££
Rooms 11, all have bath/shower, 6 with shower, 5 with bath, all have TV, hairdyer
Facilities restaurant, bar, garden, courtyard
Credit cards all major
Children welcome
Disabled public areas accessible but not rooms
Pets welcome in rooms and bar but not restaurant, small charge for dogs
Closed Christmas
Proprietor Charles Lowther

George and Dragon

Country inn

In 2008, The George and Dragon – then a rather shabby village tavern – was in need of a face-lift. It was taken over by Charles Lowther and his mother, Caroline, Countess of Lonsdale, who carried out a sensitive and intelligent restoration.

Rather than transforming the whole of the ground floor into a restaurant, they kept the bar as its focal point and allowed for a virtually uninterrupted view all the way to the far side of the slate-floored, duck-egg blue panelled restaurant. Come here for lunch, dinner or to while away the time amongst regulars with a pint of ale.

Bedrooms are homely, some a little awkwardly shaped, but redeemed by luxury bath products and comfortable beds. It's a great, affordable base from which to explore the Lake District, or stopover when travelling between Northern and Southern England.

As for the food: it's tasty, uncomplicated and locally sourced. Venison and beef features large and most of the produce comes directly from the Lowther Estate – Charles breeds Beef Shorthorn cattle.

A true celebration of country life. Guests are taken hunting by the Estate's head stalker and there are one or two good fishing spots nearby. The George and Dragon is the little sister of Askham Hall, page 272, where Charles Lowther spent his childhood.

Crosthwaite, Cumbria

Crosthwaite, Lyth Valley
LA8 8HR

Tel (015395) 68237
Fax (015395) 68875
e-mail info@the-punchbowl.co.uk
website www.the-punchbowl.co.uk

Nearby Lake District National Park, Grizedale Forst Park, Windermere, Kendal
Location just N of the A5074 between Bowness and Levens
Food breakfast, luch, tea, dinner
Price ££
Rooms 9 doubles; all with bath and shower
Facilities restaurant, bar, sitting rooms
Credit cards AE, MC, V
Children welcome
Disabled not suitable
Pets not accepted
Closed never
Proprietors Richard Rose and Amanda Robinson

Punchbowl Inn

Country inn

The Punchbowl has had new owners since 2005. They have done it up in contemporary style, using mushroomy off-white shades from heritage paint makers. Tiny high-intensity downlighters make the free-standing roll-top bath and expensive taps glitter. Little bottles of as-it-were home-made shampoo and body lotion have hand-written labels. The power shower is excellent. The bath towels are enormous. The tongued and grooved wainscoting is painted Cooking Apple Green. More original is the old-style Roberts radio beside the bed tuned to Classic FM and playing when you first come in: perhaps a bit self-conscious, but not disagreeable.

Scott Fairweather's kitchen draws people from far and wide to eat quite luxurious and very imaginative dishes, made with great flair. William Nicholson's woodcuts of Twelve Sports, a polished refectory table with a bowl of fashionable green foliage and a dish of used corks give the room the air of a smart London restaurant, though the waitresses at the Punch Bowl are much nicer than their big city counterparts. The same dishes are obtainable in the bar for those who want to eat more informally. The surrounding countryside is lovely, the welcome genuine. A truly charming small hotel.

Hawkshead, Cumbria

Near Sawrey, Ambleside, Cumbria
LA22 0JZ

Tel (015394) 36393
Fax (015394) 36393
e-mail mail@eeswyke.co.uk
website www.eeswyke.co.uk

Nearby Hill Top; Lake Windermere; Grasmere.
Location in hamlet on B5285, 2 miles (3 km) SE of Hawkshead; with car parking
Food breakfast, dinner
Price ££
Rooms 8 double and twin, 2 with bath, 6 with shower; all rooms have TV, hairdryer, hospitality tray
Facilities 2 sitting rooms, dining room; garden
Credit cards MC, V **Children** accepted over 12
Disabled 1 ground-floor room
Pets not accepted
Closed never
Proprietors Richard and Margaret Lee

Ees Wyke

Country house hotel

Esthwaite Water, to the east of Windermere, has been kept safely in private hands, so has escaped the development that has ravaged some of the other Lakes. Ees Wyke, a gem of a white-painted Georgian mansion, is perched above park-like meadows that roll gently down to the reed banks on the shore, punctuated here and there by sheep and mature trees. As well as unmarred views, Richard and Margaret Lee have happily discovered the secret of making people feel instantly at home.

This is a well-kept house, with everything just so, even down to a plentiful supply of games and books for those inclement days. In the dining room are beautiful large windows to show off the view (these are new since Beatrix Potter stayed here for her holidays), Windsor chairs and crisp white tablecloths. The dinners (Richard's department, with an AA rosette) run to five generous and unhurried courses and the price/quality ratio of the wine list is definitely tipped in your favour. The bedrooms are attractive and generously proportioned, most with small but well-equipped bathrooms, and comfortable enough to allow you to build up the strength you need to tackle the truly heroic, Lakeland breakfast.

Kirkby Lonsdale, Cumbria

Cowan Bridge, Kirkby Lonsdale, Cumbria LA6 2JJ

Tel (015242) 71187
Fax (015242) 72452
e-mail info@hippinghall.com **website** www.hippinghall.com

Nearby Yorkshire Dales; Lake District; Settle to Carlisle railway.
Location on A65, 2.5 miles (4 km) SE of Kirkby Lonsdale; in 3-acre walled gardens with ample car parking **Food** breakfast, lunch, dinner
Price £££-££££
Rooms 9 double/twin; 6 with bath/shower, 3 with shower; all rooms have phone, TV, hairdryer, CD player
Facilities sitting room, dining room, breakfast room, conservatory with bar; garden, croquet, boules
Credit cards AE, MC, V
Children welcome; over 12 in restaurant **Disabled** access possible
Pets accepted in one bedroom
Closed 2 weeks in Jan
Proprietor Andrew Wildsmith

Hipping Hall

Restaurant-with-rooms

This place, long in the guide, underwent a major transformation since our last edition. The new owners have converted it from a small 'house party' country hotel into a contemporary restaurant-with-rooms. New Zealander Brent Hulena is in the kitchen, producing dishes with 'strong rustic flavours' that are still served in the spectacular beamed Great Hall. Their menu is smart, punchy and each dish comes paired with a wine recommendation. Our most recent visit confirms that the food is superlative: we couldn't remember eating so well in five years of travelling in British hotels. You might try Stewart Lambert's lamb with kidney, shallot and violet potatoes, or roast halibut with truffled pomme purée, hazelnut and sea herbs.

Parts of the Hall date back to the 15th century when a hamlet grew up around the 'hipping' or stepping stones across the beck. After a strenuous day on the fells, you can relax in the bar-sitting area with open (gas-log) fire.

There are six cool, white bedrooms in the main house and three 'cottage' rooms across the courtyard. Bathrooms are tiled in natural stone and have modern fittings. They've got a lovely calm and relaxed atmosphere, as has the rest of the hotel.

Langho, Lancashire

Northcote Road, Langho,
Blackburn, Lancashire BB6 8BE

Tel (01254) 240555
Fax (01254) 246 568
e-mail reception@northcote.com
website www.northcote.com

Nearby Ribchester Roman remains and museum; Forest of Bowland.
Location in own grounds, 9 miles (15 km) from M6 junction 32, secure car-parking
Food breakfast, lunch, dinner
Price £££-££££
Rooms 14, all double; 13 with bath, 1 with shower only; all have phone, TV, Sky TV sports channels, sound system with iPod dock, free wi-fi, boards games, hairdryer, ceiling fans.
Credit cards AE, DC MC, V
Children accepted
Disabled no specially adapted rooms
Pets guide dogs only
Closed never
Proprietor/Manager Nigel Haworth and Craig Bancroft

Northcote

Country house hotel

A gourmet oasis ideally located in the north-west (London 220 miles, Perthshire 220 miles). Half close your eyes and this solid 1880s Victorian mansion could be a restaurant-with-rooms, though in fact it offers all the comforts of a top country hotel.

But the food is the thing here, Nigel Haworth having won many local and national awards, most recently BBC's Great British Menu accolade. His cooking is firmly rooted in local ingredients, but its edge is the fresh, clean flavours and imaginative rather than trendy presentation. A cheese-flavoured ice cream partnering the summer pudding arrived in a cone on a wooden rack. Nigel's famous Lancashire hot-pot came in its own small oven-proof dish. The service is charming, the atmosphere friendly and food- and wine-oriented, much influenced by Nigel's long standing collaborator, Craig Bancroft, a great enthusiast.

Bonhomie aside, these two are shrewd marketeers and managers of staff who have a formidable local reputation. Recently re-done bedrooms are a designer's nirvana. The location is not ideal, though the Forest of Bowland is minutes by car.

Fair prices, and for kids, mini-gourmet portions. Outstanding breakfast.

Low Lorton, Cumbria

Low Lorton, near Cockermouth,
Cumbria CA13 9UP

Tel (01900) 77247 85107
Fax (01900) 77247 85107
e-mail nick@winderhall.co.uk **website** www.winderhall.co.uk

Nearby Derwent Water; Keswick; Loweswater.
Location 3 miles (5 km) S of Cockermouth, off B5289; with car parking
Food breakfast, dinner, afternoon tea **Price** ££
Rooms 7 double and twin; all with shower, 3 with bath; all rooms have TV, hairdryer
Facilities sitting room, dining room; garden, hot tub, sauna
Credit cards MC, V
Children welcome
Disabled not suitable
Pets not accepted
Closed Jan
Proprietors Nick and Ann Lawler

Winder Hall

Country guesthouse

If you take the beautiful road from Keswick by the Whinlatter Pass, you will drop down towards Lorton into the prettiest countryside you could wish for. Winder Hall is a Grade II-listed Tudor manor, oozing character and charm. A reporter was recently greeted by the proprietors, Nick and Ann Lawler, plus young daughters spilling out of the door, and invited to enjoy some of the fantastic fell walks surrounding the property.

This is by no means a hotelly hotel: you get much more the feeling of being welcomed into the family home as a close friend. Dark oak panels cover the dining room walls, but light is abundant from the long low window overlooking the beautiful medieval herb garden and fells beyond. Nick, the owner, is the breakfast chef and only uses local fresh produce, including sausages from his own pigs.

The drawing room and bedrooms are bright and airy, yet distinctly cosy. Of the seven individually decorated bedrooms, only one has a vast fireplace and priest hole. But they all greet you with fresh flowers and home-made biscuits. Perfect for large parties wanting to take over the whole house or couples looking for a romantic weekend break to experience the beauty of the North.

Newlands, Cumbria

Grange Road, Newlands, Keswick, Cumbria CA12 5UE

Tel (017687) 72948
Fax (017687) 72948
e-mail info@swinsidelodge-hotel.co.uk **website** www.swinside-lodge-hotel.co.uk

Nearby Derwent Water; Bassenthwaite Lake.
Location 3 miles (5 km) SW of Keswick, 2 miles (3 km) S of A66; with garden and parking for 10 cars
Food breakfast, dinner
Price ££££ (rate includes dinner)
Rooms 7 double, 4 with bath, 2 with shower; all have TV, hairdryer
Facilities 2 sitting rooms, dining room; garden
Credit cards MC, V
Children accepted over 12
Disabled not suitable **Pets** not accepted
Closed over Christmas
Proprietors Mike and Kath Bilton

Swinside Lodge

Country hotel

This attractive Victorian lakeland house occupies a picture-postcard setting by Derwent Water, far removed from the fleshpots of Keswick. Mike and Kath Bilton took over here in 2008, and since then it has undergone refurbishment throughout the hotel.

The chef Clive Imber produces a daily changing menu around fresh, local ingredients, including beef and lamb from a local farm. Highlights include home made breads, soups and ice creams. Each evening dinner is followed by a hot pudding, cold dessert and a selection of Cumbrian cheeses. Wine comes from growers who use traditional methods.

As for the hotel itself, it is decorated with flair (not overdone) and you are trusted with good carpets and even better furniture. Everything that should be clean is clean, and everything else has been polished. The comfortable bedrooms are no different. The hotel's prime assets, though, are outside. Lying at the foot of Cat Bells as it does, there are walks of every description through genuinely unspoilt territory – and if you haven't the energy, you can always sit and look at it. All in all a relaxed, friendly hotel.

We would welcome reports.

Sawrey, Cumbria

Near Sawrey, Ambleside,
Cumbria, LA22 0LF

Tel (015394) 36334
e-mail
enquiries@towerbankarms.com
website www.towerbankarms.com

Nearby Hilltop (NT), between Esthwaite Water and Windermere.
Location beside B5285 near Sawrey; some car parking
Food breakfast, lunch, dinner
Price ££
Rooms 4; 3 doubles, 1 twin, all with shower; all rooms have TV, tea and coffee making facilities
Facilities bar, restaurant
Credit cards AE, MC, V
Children welcome
Disabled not suitable
Pets accepted
Closed never
Proprietor Anthony Hutton

Tower Bank Arms

Country inn

Beatrix Potter pilgrims need look no further. This simple inn, a short walk from Hilltop (NT), where many of Miss Potter's books were written, is surely where Mr MacGregor allowed himself an occasional dram and it is to be seen – distantly – in The Tale of Jemima Puddleduck.

It looks more like a cottage than a pub, only the ticking clock over the porch suggesting otherwise. The inn caters for many people staying in B&Bs in the village and the owner wants the exterior to look unpretentious, feeling that walkers with muddy boots or those on budgets might otherwise be put-off. For £9.50 at lunchtime they can enjoy dishes such as Cumbrian Beef & Ale Stew ('with herby dumplings and chunky chips'), in surroundings grander than one would expect at that price, with Wedgwood china and linen napkins. It is not a posh place or a large one – three doubles and one twin room – but it is clean and tidy and the flagstoned bar offers the comfort of a wood-fired range and a number of good beers. Don't come here expecting tea on the lawn or room service. But if your imagination is fired by a view of the street where Mrs Tabitha Twitchet or the Sandy-Whiskered Gentleman strolled, this is for you.

Howtown Hotel

Country hotel

Ullswater, Penrith, Cumbria CA10 2ND

Tel (017684) 86514

Nearby Ullswater, Lake District National Park
Location just off B5320, near Pooley Bridge
Food breakfast, lunch, dinner
Price £££ (rate includes dinner)
Rooms 11; 8 double, 3 single
Facilities 4 sitting rooms, dining room, 2 bars; garden
Credit cards not accepted
Children no special facilities
Disabled access to dining room possible; not to rooms
Pets accepted in rooms
Closed 1 Nov to Easter
Proprietor Mr and Mrs Baldry

Howtown Hotel is the Real Thing. Instead of pretending to be a charming private house of some years ago, it actually is a house that has been in the same family for about a century. And little seems to have changed – except the bathrooms, which are modern and efficient. They are not en-suite, but all are private and individual, usually just across a passage. Downstairs, Toby jugs, brass warming pans, the heads of foxes hunted in the 1930s, and oil paintings make the hall seem like a pre-war antique shop. Doors are wood-grained in the old-fashioned way (no Farrow & Ball paint here). The cosy little bar with stained glass in the windows might be the snug where the Swallows & Amazons' uncle, Captain Flint, met his friends. The Smoking Room opposite has succumbed to modern diktat. Other public rooms are grander, lighter, more like drawing-rooms. The bedrooms are equally comfortable and impressive. Presiding are the Baldrys, ably supported by a very capable management and uber-friendly Poles. Nothing is too much trouble. The place is as clean as a museum. The scenery around is staggering. And they sound a gong before meals.

Mrs Baldry says she doesn't like publicity, and needs it still less. On the other hand, we feel that not a few readers of this guide will be just the right sort of guest for this unique place.

Wasdale Head, Cumbria

Wasdale Head, Gosforth, Cumbria
CA20 1EX

Tel (019467) 26229
Fax (019467) 26334
e-mail reception@wasdale.com
website www.wasdale.com

Nearby Hardknott Castle Roman Fort; Ravenglass and Eskdale Railway; Wastwater; Scafell.
Location 9 miles (14.5 km) NE of Gosforth at head of Wasdale; with ample car parking
Food breakfast, bar and packed lunches, dinner
Price ££
Rooms 18; 9 doubles, 3 suites, all have telephone and TV; also 6 self-catering apartments
Facilities sitting room, dining room, 2 bars; garden **Credit cards** AE, MC, V **Children** accepted **Disabled** 2 ground floor rooms
Pets accepted in 9 rooms, 5 self-catered apartments and all public areas except the restaurant
Closed never **Proprietors** Nigel and Lesley Burton

Wasdale Head Inn

Mountain inn

The Wasdale Head is in a site unrivalled even in the consistently spectacular Lake District. It stands on the flat valley bottom between three major peaks – Pillar, Great Gable and Scafell Pike (England's highest) – and only a little way above Wastwater, England's deepest and perhaps most dramatic lake.

Over the last decade and a half, the old inn has been carefully and thoughtfully modernized, adding facilities but retaining the characteristics of a traditional mountain inn. The main sitting room of the hotel is comfortable and welcoming, with plenty of personal touches. The pine-panelled bedrooms are not notably spacious but they are adequate, with fixtures and fittings all in good condition. There are also six self-catering apartments in a converted barn, and three suites. The dining room is heavily panelled, and decorated with willow pattern china and a pewter jug collection. Children are now allowed to eat here, but the menu is not particularly child-friendly. Food is considerably better than you would expect of a mountaineering inn, served by young, friendly staff. There are two bars. The one for residents has some magnificent wooden furniture, while tasty bar food is served in the congenial surroundings of the public bar, much frequented by walkers and climbers.

Whitewell, Lancashire

Whitewell, near Clitheroe,
Lancashire BB7 3AT

Tel (01200) 448222
Fax (01200) 448298
e-mail reception@innatwhitewell.com
website www.innatwhitewell.com

Nearby Browsholme Hall; Clitheroe Castle; Blackpool.Location 6 miles (9.5 km) NW of Clitheroe; with ample car parking
Food breakfast, picnic lunch on request, dinner, bar meals
Price ££
Rooms 15; 14 double and twin, 1 suite, all with bath; all rooms have phone, TV, CD; some have minibar, hairdryer, peat fire
Facilities dining rooms, bar; garden, fishing
Credit cards DC, MC, V
Children welcome
Disabled 2 ground-floor rooms
Pets welcome
Closed never
Proprietor Richard Bowman

The Inn at Whitewell

Country inn

Past and present come together with great effect at this welcoming inn with a glorious situation, on a riverbank plumb in the middle of the Forest of Bowland. In the 14th century it was a small manor house where the Keeper of the Forest lived. Today, some of the original architecture survives and rooms are furnished with antiques, but modern comfort is the order of the day, with, for example, hi-tech stereo systems in all the bedrooms. Most of these are spacious and attractive, with warm lighting and prints clustered on the walls; many contain an extra sofa bed; a couple have four-posters. To keep romance alive, you can book one of the rooms with a fireplace and snuggle up to a cosy peat fire while your favourite CD plays on the Bang and Olufsen, or wallow in the deep vintage baths.

Food is an important consideration here. English dishes feature predominately on the menu – seasonal roast game or grilled fish, followed by wicked home-made puddings and a selection of farm-house cheeses. Alternatively, bar meals are on offer at lunchtime and in the evening. Just past the bar is a small shop that sells a great selection of wines, books, cheeses and other bits and bobs. Be sure to check the terms and conditions of the inn before making a booking.

Windermere, Cumbria

Crook Road, near Windermere,
Cumbria LA23 3NE

Tel (015394) 88818
Fax (015394) 88058
e-mail hotel@thegilpin.co.uk
website www.thegilpin.co.uk

Nearby Windermere Steamboat Museum; Holker Hall; Sizergh Castle; Kendal; Grasmere.
Location on B5284 Kendal to Bowness road, 2 miles (1 km) SE of Windermere; with ample car parking
Food breakfast, lunch, dinner
Price £££ **Rooms** (Gilpin Hotel) 14 double and twin with bath; 6 suites with hot tubs; (Gilpin Lake House) 4 double and twin with bath, 2 double and twin with shower; all rooms have phone, TV, minibar, hairdryer.
Facilities 2 sitting rooms, 4 dining rooms; garden, swimming pool, sauna, boat house, private lake
Credit cards AE, DC, MC, V
Children accepted over 7 **Disabled** access limited, call to discuss
Pets not accepted **Closed** never
Proprietors Cunliffe family

Gilpin Hotel & Lake House **Country house hotel**

Just occasionally, whether by luck or judgement, you can arrive somewhere that tells you to congratulate yourself on your choice of hotel before you even step through the door: Gilpin Hotel & Lake House is one of these happy places. Barney Cunliffe's great grandmother lived in this Edwardian house for 40 years, and when his parents came 25 years later, it had become a rather ordinary B&B. Now, with manicured grounds and gleaming paint, quite substantially and wholly sympathetically enlarged and set on a peaceful hillside with moor beyond the boundary, you are to some extent prepared for the warm welcome and deep-pile comfort waiting for you inside. This is a highly professional and well-staffed operation, yet still driven by the enthusiasm of owners whose unmistakeable priority is the happiness of their guests.

If your tastes run to good pictures, fine furniture and immaculate service you will be happy; if they include excellent and imaginatively presented food with more than the occasional touch of outright luxury, you will be happier still; and if you want a large, thoughtfully decorated room, probably with its own sitting area, and a bathroom to talk about when you get home, then you're in luck. Since the last edition, the well-equipped Lake House has been added. Reports welcome

Windermere, Cumbria

Holbeck Lane, Windermere,
Cumbria LA23 1LU

Tel (015394) 32375
Fax (015394) 34743
e-mail stay@holbeckghyll.com
website www.holbeckghyll.com

Nearby Lake Windermere.
Location 3 miles (5 km) N of Windermere, E of A591; with ample car parking
Food breakfast, light lunch, dinner
Price ££££
Rooms 23 double, all with bath; 4 suites; all have phone, TV, DVD, hairdryer
Facilities 2 sitting rooms, 2 dining rooms; garden, health spa, tennis, croquet, Jacuzzi
Credit cards AE, DC, MC, V
Children welcome
Disabled 3 lodge rooms
Pets accepted in the Lodge rooms
Closed 2 weeks Jan
Proprietors Andrew and Jane McPherson

Holbeck Ghyll

Country house hotel

An award-winning hotel in a classic Victorian lakeland house, ivy-clad with steep slate roofs and mullioned windows – plus oak panelling and art noveau stained glass. Our latest reporter had a 'friendly welcome' and was impressed by its superb position, providing both privacy from the bustle of Windermere and grand lake views from the immaculate gardens; also indeed by the two comfortable sitting rooms, both homelike and beautifully furnished.

The buildings have been refurbished to very high standards in a traditional, slightly formal style – though proprietors and staff alike are friendly and relaxed. Andrew and Jane had managed two hotels before they arrived here. Bedrooms and bathrooms are beautifully and individually decorated, very spacious, some with their own sitting room. At the top of the house is a 'very special' four-poster room. In the Lodge nearby are six further rooms (four are self-catering), with breathtaking views. The food is a clear attraction: pre-dinner canapés are served while you select from the inventive daily-changing menu designed by head chef Dave McLaughlin, winner of a Michelin star. There is a jogging trail from which you can spot deer and red squirrels.

Arkengarthdale, North Yorkshire

Arkengarthdale, nr Richmond,
North Yorkshire DL11 6EN

Tel (01748) 884567
Fax (01748) 884599
e-mail info@cbinn.co.uk
website www.cbinn.co.uk
Food breakfast, lunch, dinner
Price ££
Closed Christmas Day
Proprietors Charles and Stacy Cody

Charles Bathurst Inn

Country inn

Charles and Stacy Cody have turned this once derelict inn in Arkengarthdale into something special. It is very popular with Dales people, to whom it is important socially, and this may have made it a bit clannish, even self-satisfied. The bedrooms have glorious views. They are light and modern, with homely touches and some period furniture. Downstairs, the ambience is darker and more masculine. A large and tempting menu of locally-sourced dishes is painted on the vast mirror at one end of the room. The Inn is halfway along the Coast to Coast walk and those setting out from here can expect a hearty breakfast and good advice, well-made sandwiches for lunch and a Thermos of something warm.

Reports welcome.

Barngate, Cumbria

Barngate, Ambleside, Cumbria,
LA22 0NG

Tel (015394) 36347
Fax (015394) 36781
e-mail info@drunkenduckinn.co.uk
website www.drunkenduckinn.co.uk
Food breakfast, lunch, dinner
Price ££–£££
Closed Christmas Day
Proprietors Stephanie Barton

Drunken Duck Inn

Country inn

So named after a Victorian landlady who found her ducks lying on the nearby crossroads. Presuming them dead, she started to pluck them; but soon realized that they were actually blind drunk, and not dead in the slightest. This inn has real character and charm. The bar/pub is delightful and exactly as you would hope an old country inn should look and feel. The menu in the bar and dining room is extensive, yet not overambitious.

Ambling round the side of the inn you will come across the 'deluxe' and 'superior' rooms. Each is individually decorated with contemporary yet comfortable furniture and fabrics, and has the added perk of private garden sitting areas. The standard bedrooms in the main house are also tastefully done out, if a little cramped.

Crosthwaite, Cumbria

Crosthwaite, near Kendal, Cumbria
LA8 8BP

Tel (015395) 68264
e-mail
booking@crosthwaitehouse.co.uk
website
www.crosthwaitehouse.co.uk
Food breakfast
Price £ **Closed** late Nov to Feb
Proprietors Sam and Tiree Dawson

Crosthwaite House

Country bed-and-breakfast

This is an attractive Georgian building with classic proportions and fine, tall rooms. Sam and Tiree Dawson (the second generation of Dawsons to run the guest-house) are the relaxed owners who make their guests very welcome. There is an open fire in the comfortable sitting room, and a collection of books and games.

Hearty breakfasts are always there in the mornings in the wooden-floored dining room. There are six bright and simply furnished bedrooms, each with their own shower room (although these can be something of a snug fit).

Crosthwaite House is now run as a bed-and-breakfast, but there are a number of pubs nearby. The Punchbowl Inn (page 280) is a short stroll away, offering dinner.

Great Langdale, Cumbria

Great Langdale, Ambleside,
Cumbria LA22 9JY

Tel (015394) 37272
Fax (015394) 37272
e-mail olddungeonghyll1@btconnect.com **website** www.odg.co.uk
Food breakfast, packed lunch, dinner, bar meals **Price** ££ **Closed** 24 to 26 Dec **Proprietors** Neil and Jane Walmsley

Old Dungeon Ghyll

Country hotel

Neil and Jane Walmsley have been the proprietors here since 1983 and have continued to improve and develop this popular family hotel retaining as many old features as possible. Once, many a climber chose to stay here. They were a pretty uncritical bunch (any kind of a roof was a luxury), but now all bedrooms have bathrooms, most of which are en suite, there is a comfortable residents' sitting room with an open fire, a busy hikers' bar (open to the public) as well as the warm guests' bar, and a snug dining room offering wholesome, uncomplicated food. Neil and Jane hold charity folk festivals twice a year, and there are music nights in the bar on the first Wednesday of the month.

Liverpool

The Racquet Club

Town hotel

A good-value place that defies the chain-hotel atmosphere of central Liverpool. Book in advance as weddings are prioritised at weekends – about 120 per year.

The design (devised by Martin Ainscough) is thoroughly quirky. For instance, stag heads line the stairs, leading up to an enormous moose head on the first floor. Throughout the corridors, there are prints of Georgian aristocracy as well as modern art – some local, some bizarre. Bedrooms are cosy and comfortable. Rooms two and three have hand-carved detail on the beds' headboards and polished antique furniture.

Sue, the bubbly general manager, has been here ever since the Ainscoughs bought the place, 11 years ago.

The Hargreaves Building, 5 Chapel Street, Liverpool L3 9AG

Tel 0151 236 6676 **e-mail** info@racquetclub.org.uk **website** www.ainscoughs.co.uk/Racquet-club/racquet-club-home.html **Food** breakfast, lunch, dinner; no lunch Sat, closed Sun **Price** ££ **Closed** 24th-26th Dec; weddings only until early Jan **Proprietors** Martin and Helen Ainscough

Bolton Abbey, North Yorkshire

Bolton Abbey, Skipton, North Yorkshire BD23 6AJ

Tel (01756) 710441
Fax (01756) 710564
e-mail res@thedevonshirearms.co.uk
website www.thedevonshirearms.co.uk

Nearby Castle Howard; Skipton Castle; Brontë Parsonage; Harewood House. **Location** on B6160 just N of junction with A59; in grounds with ample car parking **Food** breakfast, lunch, dinner, afternoon tea **Price** ££££ **Rooms** 40; 37 double and twin, 1 family, 2 suites, all with bath; all rooms have phone, TV, DVD, hairdryer **Facilities** 3 lounges, conservatory, restaurant, brasserie, 2 bars, gym, sauna, steam room, solarium, plunge pool, indoor swimming pool; garden, tennis, croquet, putting, helipad, fishing **Credit cards** all major **Children** not under 7 in restaurant **Disabled** rooms on the ground floor, and 1 specially adapted **Pets** accepted, £10 per dog **Closed** never **Manager** Andrew Mackay

The Devonshire Arms

Country house hotel

As your helicopter whirls towards its helipad, you can see that the moorland of the Dales proper comes to within a mile or so of the 17thC Devonshire Arms. Follow the path down the bank of the Wharfe, which gives the valley its name, for the half mile from Bolton Abbey village to the stone bridge and you're there. Owned by the Duke and Duchess of Devonshire, the hotel is doubly graced since it contains antiques and paintings from Chatsworth, the family seat; the Duchess has masterminded their placement and the design of the interior. This is a hotel in two parts, old and new. The elegant old wears its years well and has happily grown out of exact right angles. The new extension, which has brought with it an indoor swimming pool, gym and beauty salon, still has its sharp corners, but is settling in well.

The dining alternatives cover a similar spectrum. On the one hand is the quiet comfort of the classical Burlington Restaurant, and on the other a buzzy blue and yellow brasserie with dishes to suit most moods and a snappy wine list to go with them. The bedrooms also come in old and new varieties: the older win on character and the newer score better with their views. See also The Devonshire Fell (page 296).

Burnsall, North Yorkshire

Burnsall, Skipton, North Yorkshire
BD23 6BT

Tel 01756 729000
Fax 01756 729009
e-mail res@devonshirehotels.co.uk
website www.devonshirefell.co.uk

Nearby Bolton Abbey Estate, Leeds, Harrogate
Location Burnsall village, just off the B6160
Food breakfast, lunch, dinner
Price £££-££££
Rooms 12 doubles (some can be twin), all ensuite; 4 more planned
Facilities restaurant, bar, conservatory, wine cellar, Devonshire Health Barn **Credit cards** all major
Children welcome
Disabled no lift to bedrooms, but wheelchair access points, trained staff **Pets** not accepted, but kennels available
Closed no specific closure dates
Proprietors Duke and Duchess of Devonshire

The Devonshire Fell

Restaurant-with-rooms

Just outside picturesque Burnsall, it sits above the village and the River Wharfe, with great views. Owned by the Chatsworth Estate, this is a less formal sister hotel to The Devonshire Arms (page 295).

The ground floor leads seamlessly from one room to the other with simple wooden floors, log fires and pretty shutters in the dining room. No chintz here: the stair carpets are pink-and-grey striped; the bedrooms have bedheads and Roman blinds in bright colours. Prints, black-and-white photographs and contemporary paintings decorate the walls.

Bedrooms are very comfortable, with good sheets. On a large tray you'll find quality coffee and tea, cakes, soft drinks and fresh milk. Our reporter appreciated the large flat-screen TV, and the unusual gels and shampoos.

Drinks are generally served in a cosy conservatory, often a contradiction in terms, but this one has a log fire at one end and was 'blissfully comfortable'. Dinner, from a small menu, was 'well thought out with local fish and meat. Presentation was elegant (don't expect huge Yorkshire platefuls). Fish and chips and homemade beefburgers were just right after a day walking the fells.' A superb place to stay for walkers, and dog friendly.

Byland, North Yorkshire

Byland, Coxwold, North Yorkshire
YO61 4BD

Tel 01347 868 204
e-mail abbey.inn@english-heritage.org.uk
website http://www.english-heritage.org.uk/daysout/properties/byland-abbey/inn/

Nearby Byland Abbey
Location 2 miles from A170 between Thirsk and Helmsley
Food breakfast
Price ££-£££
Rooms 2 doubles, 1 twin, all ensuite, with TV **Facilities** breakfast room, tea room in the summer
Credit cards MC, V
Children welcome
Disabled no special access
Pets not accepted
Closed never
Proprietor English Heritage

Byland Abbey Inn

Country bed-and-breakfast

The pairing of an isolated inn with starkly beautiful Cisterican abbey ruins is rare in Britain, and as our series editor Fiona Duncan sat in the stone-walled Wass Room, she thought she could almost be in France, in a *vieux logis* overlooking a *monument historique*.

English Heritage, which maintains Byland Abbey ruins, bought the small 19thC inn some years ago and gave it a conscientious makeover: maybe a little precious in parts, with a restaurant that is possibly too smart for walkers and locals unless it's summer and they can sit in the garden with a snack. Hope to stay when there's a full moon to make the ruins more ghostly and majestic than usual.

The three bedrooms are superb, one of them, Prior's Lynn, notable for its specially commissioned Mouseman furniture made in nearby Kilburn. You can breakfast in bed, gazing at the ruins, and then wander among them free of charge, probably alone.

The Black Swan at Oldstead, a mile and a half away, is Michelin-starred,and recommended for dinner.

Cornhill-on-Tweed, Northumberland

Main Street, Cornhill-on-Tweed, Northumberland TD12 4UH

Tel 01890 882424
e-mail enquiries@collingwoodarms.com
website www.collingwoodarms.com

Nearby golfing, fishing, riding, cycling, sightseeing walks
Location near Berwick-Upon Tweed, Cheviot Hills, North Northumberland, Scottish Border
Food breakfast, lunch, dinner
Price £££
Rooms 15 all with digital televisions
Facilities brasserie, dining room, bar, library
Credit cards DC, MC, V
Children accepted
Disabled access possible, ground-floor bedroom and bathroom
Pets not accepted, but kennels available **Closed** never
Proprietor Mrs R Cook
Manager Kevin Kenny

The Collingwood Arms

Town inn

'A more relaxing, solid, reassuring and unpretentious hotel would be hard to imagine,' comments our series editor, Fiona Duncan. A former coaching inn (the words 'Post Horses' still appear above the door), it sits on an old main road to Edinburgh, with the River Tweed below.

A stone building with a plain Georgian front, its name is from its original owners: a local merchant family with strong ties to the 19thC naval hero Vice-Admiral Collingwood. They left in 1955, but current owner Mrs Cook clearly respects the place's heritage: each bedroom is named after a ship in the Admiral's Trafalgar division. Colours and fabrics have been kept muted, and Persian rugs and antique furniture are scattered throughout.

There are a few contemporary twists – a trendy, wood-floored pub-brasserie; simple, almost minimalist, headboards on beds – but these are thoughtful touches rather than needless trend-following. Attention to detail is evident, from the library-cum-sitting room to each of the 15 bedrooms.

Food is widely praised. You eat in a stylish, relaxing, parquet-floored restaurant or, if weather allows, out in the manicured gardens. Ingredients are fresh and locally sourced. When Fiona visited, she enjoyed her grilled black pudding and leek starter.

Gadds Town House

Townhouse hotel

34 Old Elvet, Durham DH1 3HN

Tel 01913 841037
e-mail info@gaddstownhouse.com
website www.gaddstownhouse.com

Nearby Durham Cathedral; Durham University; city centre
Location on Old Elvet, just off A690 and New Elvet
Food breakfast, lunch, dinner
Price ££-££££
Rooms 11; all doubles, all ensuite, all have TV, hairdryer
Facilities dining room, bar, wi-fi on ground floor, terrace
Credit Cards AE, MC, V
Children accepted, travel cot can be put in most rooms
Disabled 1 room fully equipped
Pets not accepted
Closed Christmas Day, restaurant closed on Sundays
Proprietor Nigel and Debbie Gadd

This used to be called The Fallen Angel, known for its (mostly irritating) themed bedrooms, but which could still claim to be the only interesting place to stay in Durham, a city badly in need of a characterful place to stay. Recent new owners have renamed it, and are evidently getting things right.

A trusted reporter tells us he entered the front door to see 'plastic replicas of Roman remains illuminated by a somewhat lurid, violet coloured chandelier'. But his worries disappeared rapidly. The reception staff were 'friendly and helpful in a practical way', and were just as helpful at check out.

He eulogises the food – 'one of the most excellent dinners we have had recently. Breakfast was well above average, too.'

'Our room was strange but interesting, and above all else clean, warm and comfortable.' The shower, between the bedroom and the bathroom, was open to view – encased in glass on three sides – but could be closed off with a curtain.'

The location, within walking distance (uphill) of the Cathedral and University, is fine. And it is 'very good value for money'.

Grassington, North Yorkshire

Summers Fold, Grassington, near Skipton, North Yorkshire BD23 5AE

Tel (01756) 752584
Fax (07092) 376562
website www.ashfieldhouse.co.uk

Nearby Skipton Castle, Gordale Scar, Janet's Foss, Ripon, Malham Cove, Bolton Abbey
Location in Grassington, just NW of main square; with ample car parking
Food breakfast, dinner – advisable to pre-book (not served Wed or Sun)
Prices ££
Rooms 8 double and twin with bath or shower; all rooms have TV, hairdryer, wi-fi
Facilities 2 sitting rooms, 1 with bar, dining room; garden
Credit cards MC, V
Children welcome over 10
Disabled not suitable
Pets not accepted
Closed two weeks each year
Proprietors Joe Azzopardi and Elizabeth Webb

Ashfield House

Country guesthouse

Grassington, and Wharfedale in general, is a little-known Northern gem, especially for keen walkers. Tucked away off the main street is Joe Azzopardi and Elizabeth Webb's small private stone and slate hotel, a peaceful sanctuary at the end of its own yard. What's more, and unlike anywhere else in Grassington, you can park your car there. Oak and pine furniture, bare beams and stone walls are combined with fresh flowers and neat new furnishings.

An excellent four course dinner is served in the pretty dining room every day except Wednesday and Sunday. Joe presides over the kitchen, making use of fresh local produce, and is assisted by Elizabeth. Breakfast consists of an impressive array of home-made produce – yoghurt, muesli, granola and marmalade – together with local bacon and own-recipe sausages.

The bedrooms are modestly sized with fresh, clean decoration and their own shower rooms. Since Joe and Elizabeth took over here they have upgraded all of the bathrooms and brought the whole place up to date.

Beyond the house, insulated from the bustle of the town, is a quiet walled garden with a table and chairs where you can simply sit and enjoy the sunshine if the prospect of a walk along the river seems too testing.

Harome, North Yorkshire

Harome, Nr Helmsley, North Yorkshire, YO62 5JE

Tel (01439) 770397
Fax (01439) 771 833
website www.thestaratharome.co.uk

Nearby Helmsley market town, Castle Howard, Duncombe Park.
Location 2.5 miles SE of Helmsley off the A170, ample car parking
Food breakfast, lunch, dinner (restaurant in the Inn closed on Mon) **Price** £££
Rooms 9 doubles, 3 suites, all with bath or shower; all rooms have TV, DVD, CD, radio, hairdryer, phone, tea and coffee making facilities
Facilities dining rooms, breakfast room, bar, sitting room; garden
Credit cards MC, V **Children** welcome **Disabled** 4 ground-floor rooms **Pets** accepted in a couple of ground-floor rooms
Closed never
Proprietors Andrew Pern

The Star Inn

Country hotel

'One of the most comfortable, relaxing nights I have spent in a hotel' says a recent reporter. Wellies and umbrellas wait by the front door of Cross House (the Inn's guest house) in case you feel like having a stroll around the beautiful countryside. The opulent sitting room is kept warm by the grand fire in the centre and once sat on the sofas with tea and seriously good cakes you can hardly make it to your room. When you do, you'll discover that they are immaculate, balancing the contemporary and the rustic perfectly with fantastic bathrooms (some with whirlpool baths) and music, DVDs and chocolates and crisps to tide you over until supper.

Supper and lunch can be served in the Inn itself: just across the road. The pub and restaurant are bursting with charm and decorated in keeping with the 14thC thatched image, so expect old beams and secret little loft spaces in which to enjoy coffee after the award-winning food cooked by Andrew. Upstairs the fairytale private dining room has been decorated by local artists. The restaurant was extended in 2008 and now opens out onto the rear terrace – a popular place to eat in the open air in the summer.

Hawes, North Yorkshire

Hawes, North Yorkshire DL8 3LY

Tel (01969) 667255
Fax (01969) 667741
e-mail enquiries@simonstonehall.com
website www.simonstonehall.co.uk

Nearby Pennine Way; Wharfedale; Ribblesdale.
Location 1.5 miles (2.5 km) N of Hawes on Muker road; with ample car parking
Food breakfast, bar lunch, Sun lunch, dinner
Price £££
Rooms 18 double and twin with bath and shower; all rooms have phone, TV, wi-fi
Facilities bar, lounge, brasserie, restaurant; garden, terrace
Credit cards AE, DC, MC, V
Children welcome
Disabled access possible to ground floor only **Pets** welcome
Closed never
Manager Caroline Billingham

Simonstone Hall

Country house hotel

Simonstone has undergone major refurbishment in the last few years, but still has the air of something special, helped by the friendliness of the staff. Outside, it is the same dignified, slightly forbidding, large Dales country house; but as you enter you will probably hear the lively chatter coming from the extensive bar area which is intended to re-create the hotel as a place that will attract local non-residents as well as overnight guests. To have this popular country pub within an essentially dignified old country hotel is something of a novelty – and not unpleasant. The pub is handsomely done out; bar meals and the range of wines by the glass are imaginative; waiters in black tie and apron, French bistro-style, bustle about. It gives the place an injection of life, but if you've come here for peace, or a romantic twosome, just walk down the corridor to the sitting room, hidden at the far end of the hall to provide guests with peace and quiet. You can enjoy dinner in both The Brasserie and The Four Fells restaurants.

All bedrooms now have bathrooms with showers. The superior bedrooms are handsomely done out in country house style, some with sleigh beds, others with four-posters, many of them with fantastic views of the Dales. Prices have risen, some say unjustifiably, so we would welcome further reports.

Hawnby, North Yorkshire

Hill Top, Hawnby, near Helmsley, North Yorkshire Y06 5QS

Tel (01439) 798202
e-mail info@innathawnby.co.uk
website www.innathawnby.co.uk

Nearby Rievaulx Abbey; Jervaulx Abbey; North York Moors.
Location at top of hill in village 7 miles (11 km) NE of Helmsley; with car parking
Food breakfast, lunch, dinner
Price ££
Rooms 9 double and twin with bath; all rooms have phone, TV, hairdryer
Facilities sitting room, bar, restaurant, garden
Credit cards MC, V
Children welcome
Disabled access difficult
Pets accepted in 3 rooms
Closed Monday lunchtime; Christmas day
Proprietors Dave and Kathryn Young

The Inn at Hawnby

Country hotel

After a spectacular drive through rolling valleys and the unspoilt stone village of Hawnby, you come across Dave and Kathryn Young's country inn, formerly The Hawnby Hotel. The 'village pub' façade hides an exquisite small hotel which was decorated with obvious flair by Lady Mexborough. The hotel used to be part of the 13,000-acre Mexborough estate and Lady Mexborough gave it much personal attention, refurbishing the Inn's six bedrooms which are named after colour schemes (Cowslip, Coral, Jade and so on), choosing Laura Ashley wallpaper and fabrics throughout the cosy rooms and immaculate bathrooms. Three further bedrooms are available just over the road, these ones named after stables.

The Youngs have tidied up the outside of the Inn and the gardens, as well as giving the public rooms and bedrooms some attention, aiming to make them altogether brighter and more welcoming. They have also turned their attention to the kitchen, hiring a new head chef who produces a full *a la carte* menu, all from scratch and using fresh, local produce.

Reports continue to heap praise on the Inn at Hawnby: 'This charming country hotel ... is an ideal base for touring North Yorkshire; a gem with fabulous views, home cooking and friendly service'.

Hunmanby, North Yorkshire

Stonegate, Hunmanby, North Yorkshire YO14 0NS

Tel (01723) 891333
Fax (01723) 892973
e-mail staciedevos@aol.com
website www.wranghamhouse.com

Nearby Scarborough Castle; North York Moors National Park.
Location behind church in village, 1 mile (1.5 km) SW of Filey; ample car parking
Food breakfast, lunch, dinner
Price ££
Rooms 12; 11 double and twin, 1 single, 7 with bath, 5 with shower; all have phone, TV, hairdryer **Facilities** sitting room, dining room, bar; garden
Credit cards AE, MC, V
Children welcome **Disabled** 1 adapted room
Pets by arrangement
Closed Christmas and Boxing Day
Proprietors Peter and Stacie Devos

Wrangham House

Country house hotel

Wrangham House is a well-preserved and elegant Georgian former vicarage set in an acre of wooded garden. The main part of the house was built in the second half of the 18th century. The eponymous Francis Wrangham added a wing, now housing the dining room, in 1803. Stacie Devos and her husband Peter moved here in 2005, and refurbished the kitchen, sitting room, dining room and most of the bedrooms, as well as giving the gardens some much-needed care and attention. Stacie says the improvements are an ongoing project, the aim being to restore Wrangham House to its former glory.

Peter is in charge of the kitchen and produces a few set dishes (such as roast rack of lamb), with the rest being based around what fresh, local and seasonal produce is available, ranging from game to locally caught fish and seafood – so there is always something new on the menu. Everything here is freshly made and Peter and Stacie take pride in offering a personal and flexible service – guests on long stays have the opportunity to influence the menu by discussing their preferences with Peter, and early dinners will be arranged for families with young children.

Reports welcome.

Lastingham, North Yorkshire

Lastingham, North Yorkshire
Y062 6TH

Tel (01751) 417345/417402
Fax (01751) 417358
e-mail reservations@lastingham-grange.com **website** www.lastinghamgrange.com

Nearby North York Moors; Scarborough; Rievaulx Abbey.
Location at top of village, 7 miles (10 km) NW of Pickering; ample car parking **Food** breakfast, lunch, dinner **Price** £££
Rooms 12 and 1 self-catering cottage – The Old Reading Room; 10 double, 2 single, all with bath; all rooms have phone, TV, hairdryer, wi-fi **Facilities** sitting room, dining room; terrace, garden
Credit cards MC, V
Children welcome
Disabled access to restaurant and garden **Pets** accepted in bedrooms by arrangement, not in The Old Reading Room **Closed** Dec to mid-Mar **Proprietors** Jane, Bertie and Tom Wood

Lastingham Grange

Country house hotel

Lastingham Grange – a wistaria-clad former farmhouse – nestles peacefully in a delightful village on the edge of the North York Moors. Unlike many country house hotels, it manages to combine a certain sophistication – smartly decorated public rooms, friendly unobtrusive service, elegantly laid gardens – with a large dash of informality, which puts you immediately at ease. From the moment you enter, you feel as if you are staying with friends. Recently, we had this reaction from an inspector: 'Family feeling; very child friendly; charming rooms.–'

The main attraction is the garden. You can enjoy it from a distance – from the windows of the large L-shaped sitting room (complete with carefully grouped sofas, antiques and a grand piano) – or, like most guests, by exploring. There is a beautifully laid rose garden, enticing bordered lawns and an extensive adventure playground for children.

Bedrooms are perfectly comfortable, with well-equipped bathrooms, and have been totally redecorated since our last visit, when a reporter felt that they were somewhat downbeat in places. Paul Cattaneo and Sandra Thurlow produce traditional English meals for the daily-changing menu, prepared from fresh, local ingredients. Reports welcome.

Millgate, North Yorkshire

Millgate, Richmond, North Yorkshire DL10 4JN

Tel (01748) 823571
e-mail oztim@millgatehouse.demon.co.uk
website www.millgatehouse.com

Nearby Cleveland hills; Swale valley; the Dales; Richmond.
Location in Richmond town centre
Food breakfast, dinner for larger parties
Price ££-£££
Rooms 3 double; self-catering accommodation for up to 12 people
Facilities sitting room, dining room; garden
Credit cards not accepted
Children accepted over 10
Disabled not suitable
Pets accepted (not in dining room)
Closed never
Proprietors Austin Lynch and Tim Culkin

Millgate House

Town guesthouse

Millgate House dates back to the early 1700s and, despite its relatively unassuming exterior, is full of surprises. Behind the street façade is a house of real charm and character, tastefully furnished with antiques and interesting pieces sourced from from all over the world. Below, and sloping away from the house, lies an award winning garden with excellent views across the river Swale towards the beautiful Cleveland Hills beyond.

What really sets Millgate House apart is its garden. Since scooping first prize in the National Royal Horticultural Society Garden Competition, the grounds have been featured in publications in the UK as well as internationally. The gardens are open all year round, and entry is free to house guests.

Breakfast is very good at Millgate House and dinners can be pre-arranged for parties of 16 and over. The accommodation on offer is of a high standard. All bedrooms are warm and spacious with fine views, and each has its own large, airy bathroom with great period details. All of this, together with some outstanding care and service from the owners, make Millgate House a fine choice in this area. It was named B&B of the Year 2011 by the Good Hotel Guide and now holds the prestigious César Award.

Pateley Bridge, North Yorkshire

Wath-in-Nidderdale, Pateley Bridge, near Harrogate, North Yorkshire HG3 5PP

Tel (01423) 711306
Fax (01423) 712524
email
sportsmansarms@btconnect.com
website
www.nidderdale.co.uk/sportsman-sarms

Nearby Wharfedale, Wensleydale; Fountains Abbey, Bolton Abbey.
Location 2 miles (3 km) NW of Pateley Bridge, in hamlet; with ample car parking
Food breakfast, bar lunch, dinner
Price ££
Rooms 11; 9 double, 2 twin with bath or shower; all rooms have TV
Facilities 3 sitting rooms, bar, dining room; fishing
Credit cards MC, V **Children** welcome **Disabled** easy access to public rooms **Pets** welcome by arrangement **Closed** Christmas Day, New Year's Day **Proprietors** Jane and Ray Carter

The Sportsman's Arms

Country hotel

Our latest inspection confirms that the Sportsman's Arms is going from strength to strength. The long, rather rambling building dates from the 17th century, and the setting is as enchanting as the village name sounds; the River Nidd flows across the field in front; Gouthwaite reservoir, a bird-watchers' haunt, is just behind; glorious dales country spreads all around.

Jane and Ray Carter have been running the Sportman's Arms, with the help of a young enthusiastic team, for over 30 years now, and continue to make improvements. Bedrooms (two with four-posters) have been redecorated and are light and fresh, with brand-new bathrooms. Six more rooms, four with views across open countryside, have been created in the barn and stable block. All the public rooms have recently been refurbished as well.

And then there is the food. The Sportsman's Arms is first and foremost a restaurant, and the large dining room is the inn's focal point, sparkling with silver cutlery and crystal table lights. The lively menu embraces sound, traditional local fare, as well as fresh fish and seafood brought in daily from Whitby. To back it up, there is a superb wine list – and an extremely reasonable bill.

Ramsgill-in-Nidderdale, North Yorkshire

Ramsgill-in-Nidderdale, Pateley Bridge, near Harrogate, North Yorkshire, HG3 5RL

Tel (01423) 755243
Fax (01423) 755330
e-mail enquiries@yorke-arms.co.uk
website www.yorke-arms.co.uk

Nearby Harewood House; Newby Hall; Fountains Abbey; Ripon Cathedral.
Location in centre of village; take Low Wath Road from Pateley Bridge bordering Gouthwaite Reservoir; with car parking
Food breakfast, lunch, dinner
Price ££££
Rooms 14 twin/double, all with bath; all rooms have phone, TV, hairdryer; some have minibar; 1 cottage with 2 twin/double
Facilities sitting room, 2 dining rooms, private dining room; garden
Credit cards AE, DC, MC, V
Disabled not suitable
Pets accepted in some public rooms
Closed never
Proprietors Frances and Gerald Atkins

The Yorke Arms

Restaurant-with-rooms

On the green in a pretty Nidderdale village, the creeper-clad Yorke Arms was a fully-functioning pub for 150 years. Now, it is a Michelin-starred restaurant-with-rooms. You are greeted as you enter by flagged floors, beams and, in winter, open fires. There is also a reassuring feeling of order: what should have been polished has been polished, and what should have been swept has been.

In the restaurant, wooden tables and a carpeted floor strewn with rugs are pleasantly rustic, and serve as a showcase for Frances Atkins' Michelin-starred daily changing menu: traditional and modern English dishes are her starting-point, but she also draws on other cuisines from all over the world. Old favourites such as Yorkshire hot-pot or slow-cooked shoulder of lamb usually make an appearance. The wine list is comprehensive and sympathetically priced.

The bedrooms, which have all been thoroughly refurbished, with stylish modern bathrooms, are comfortably furnished and range in size (and price) from cosy to a modest suite, 'Gouthwaite', which boasts a sofa and armchairs. Recent additions include the courtyard rooms – spacious two-storey apartments in the grounds – and a renovated two-bedroom cottage with a private garden and terrace.

Reeth, North Yorkshire

On the Green, Reeth, Richmond, North Yorkshire DL11 6SN

Tel (01748) 884292
e-mail enquiries@theburgoyne.co.uk **web-site** www.theburgoyne.co.uk

Nearby Richmond Castle; Middleham Castle Aysgarth Falls, Wensleydale Railway.
Location 10 miles (16 km) W of Richmond on B6270; with car parking **Food** breakfast, packed lunch on request, Sunday lunch on first Sunday of month, dinner; room service **Price** ££ **Rooms** 10 double and twin with bath; all rooms have phone, flat screen TV, DVD player, hairdryer, tea/coffee facilities **Facilities** sitting room, dining room; garden, fishing, drying facilities, lock-up for bicycles **Credit cards** MC, V **Children** accepted **Disabled** access possible to ground-floor room **Pets** dogs accepted by arrangement **Closed** weekdays early Jan **Proprietor** Mo and Julia Usman

Burgoyne Hotel

Village hotel

The Burgoyne Hotel stretches its late-Georgian length along the top of the sloping green in Reeth. If you turn round and look the other way, you'll see why: the Swale valley is extremely pretty, and with only the green in front of it, the Burgoyne has an uninterrupted view. Inside, time, money and taste have conspired to produce something of a masterpiece to which has been added the magic ingredient of a warm welcome. There are two elegant and richly furnished sitting rooms on the ground floor with Medieval touches here and there: stone coats of arms on the fireplaces and 'Gothic' oak doors. The restaurant, where the snowy napkins, the crystal and the silver stand out against the cool blues of the decoration, is a kind of inner sanctum where Paul Salonga's culinary art joins Derek Hickson's scientific (certainly encyclopaedic) understanding of wines.

The bedrooms, most of which face the valley, are beautifully appointed and deeply comfortable. Window seats offer pleasant perches for people who just want to sit and enjoy the view. Rather than hack space for bathrooms out of the well-proportioned rooms, one or two bathrooms are across the corridor – voluminous robes and slippers are provided for the short journey.

Richmond, North Yorkshire

Easby, Richmond, North Yorkshire, DL10 7EU

Tel 01748 826 066
Mobile 0776 967 3835
e-mail easby.hall@zen.co.uk
website easbyhall.com

Nearby The Yorkshire Dales, Easby Abbey, the market town Richmond with castle and Georgian Theatre Royal; waterfalls **Location** 4 miles from Scotch Corner (A1), 15 minutes from Darlington (2hrs 30 mins from London King's Cross); overlooks the Swale river and ruins of Easby Abbey; ample private parking.
Food breakfast **Price** £££-££££
Rooms 3; doubles (2 can become twin), 2 with bath/shower, 1 with shower, wi-fi, hairdryer, log burner/open fire, fridge, tea/coffee
Facilities drawing room, 3 gardens with a summer house and winter hut with open fire.
Credit cards none **Disabled** no special facilities **Pets** by arrangement
Closed never **Proprietors** John and Karen Clarke

Easby Hall

Country house hotel

Easby Hall stands on a country lane outside Richmond. Our first impression: here's a well-proportioned and stylish home, recently renovated. The kitchen garden is impressive, with much companion planting and not a weed in sight.

Stroll into the elegant drawing room and you will stop dead in your tracks: beyond and below the 'infinity lawn' lie the tranquil, romantic ruins of Easby Abbey, surrounded by gently rolling woods and meadows. Couples marry in St Agatha church and walk up to Easby Hall for their reception.

The house is immaculately decorated using bold wallpapers and soft paint colours. The smallest bedroom, Abbey, has the views, but each is exceptional, with quite a tea tray: home-made biscuits, fresh mint for infusions and fresh flowers. Superlative quality here, undoubtedly, but we considered the rates (£180 at weekends) uncomfortably close to a fully-fledged country house hotel, however luxurious. Dinner is currently not provided.

Breakfast was special. Each table had pretty floral china and flowers from the garden. Coffee from a silver pot; rhubarb compote flavoured with cardamom; poached eggs scattered with edible violas... had the room overlooked the abbey ruins, it would have been even better.

Ripley, North Yorkshire

Ripley, Harrogate, North Yorkshire
HG3 3AY

Tel (01423) 771888
Fax (01423) 771509
e-mail boarshead@ripleycastle.co.uk
website www.ripleycastle.co.uk

Nearby York; Fountains Abbey and Studley Royal Water Gardens; Ripley Castle
Location in village centre, 3 miles (5 km) N of Harrogate on A61; with ample car parking
Food breakfast, lunch, dinner
Price ££
Rooms 25 double and twin with bath; all rooms have phone, TV, fax/modem point, hairdryer; minibar on request
Facilities sitting room, dining rooms, 2 bars; garden, tennis, fishing
Credit cards AE, MC, DC, V
Children accepted **Disabled** 1 specially adapted room, 8 ground-floor rooms **Pets** accepted in some rooms only **Closed** never **Proprietors** Sir Thomas and Lady Ingilby

Boar's Head

Country house hotel

Anyone with a spare inn and enough paintings and antique furniture to furnish it could do worse than emulate Sir Thomas and Lady Ingilby's successful renovation of the Boar's Head in Ripley. It is a thriving establishment with helpful, pleasant staff who do not leave your comfort to chance. There are bedrooms in the inn itself, lighter more contemporary ones in its cobbled courtyard, and across the road, in the peace and quiet of Birchwood House, are four of their six best rooms. All have fresh flowers, pristine modern bathrooms and thoughtful decoration.

The public rooms are warm and welcoming, filled with period furniture; seascapes and ancestors share the walls. There is a choice for dinner: you can either go to the relaxed bar/bistro (packed when we visited) or the richer candle-lit comfort of the restaurant to agonise over a choice that includes 'Yorkshire Cassoulet' – Yorkshire duck leg, Yorkshire sausage and Easingwold pork belly – or Ripley's Famous Mushroom Stroganoff. Fresh vegetables and game make seasonal appearances from the Ingilby estate, presided over by their castle.

Romaldkirk, County Durham

Romaldkirk, Barnard Castle, Co Durham DL12 9EB

Tel (01833) 650213
e-mail hotel@rose-and-crown.co.uk
website www.rose-and-crown.co.uk

Nearby Barnard Castle; Egglestone Abbey; High Force.
Location in centre of village, on B6277, 6 miles (9.6 km) NW of Barnard Castle; with ample carparking **Food** breakfast, dinner, Sun lunch **Price** ££
Rooms 14; 13 double and twin, 2 rooms in Monk's Cottage, 1 family, 11 with bath, 3 with shower; all rooms have phone, TV, hairdryer, Bose sound systems
Facilities sitting room, dining room, bar, gun lockers, wi-fi
Credit cards AE, DC, MC, V
Children welcome **Disabled** access possible to courtyard rooms
Pets accepted in 12 bedrooms
Closed Christmas Eve, Christmas Day, Boxing Day
Proprietors Thomas and Cheryl Robinson

The Rose and Crown

Country inn

The Rose and Crown was built in 1733 in this very pretty light stone village, which owes its original layout to the Saxons and its name to the patron saint of the church. Recently refurbished by owners Thomas and Cheryl Robinson, this place has gone from strength to strength. It is set in the centre of the three-green village. The bar is comfortingly traditional: real ales, natural stone walls, log fire, old photographs, copper and brass knick-knacks. Excellent pub food is served in the 'Crown Bar'. More traditional three-course dinners, English but imaginatively so, are served in the oak-panelled dining room and, when in season, often feature local and organic produce, including fresh fish from the East Coast and locally grown vegetables. Fresh bread is baked every day.

There are seven comfortable bedrooms, attractively decorated and furnished with antiques, in the main building. Five more have been added round the courtyard at the back, and open directly on to it. Since our last edition, the Monk's Cottage has been opened to provide two extra bedrooms. It overlooks the Saxon church next to the inn. This accommodation has an honesty bar and boot room – perfect for walkers.

Grays Court, Chapter House Street, York YO1 7JH

Tel 01904 612613
website www.grayscourtyork.com

Nearby York Minster, St William's College, Railway Museum, Jorvik Viking Centre
Location Chapter House Street, off St. Maurice's Road, car parking at £15 per night
Food breakfast, lunch, dinner, afternoon tea
Price ££££
Rooms 7 doubles, 1 can be twin, all have bath/shower, with TV, safe, tea/coffee facilities, telephone, wi-fi
Facilities dining room, Long Gallery has bar, function room, library, garden
Credit cards all major
Children welcome
Disabled no special facilities
Pets by prior arrangement
Closed Christmas
Proprietor Helen Heraty

Grays Court

Town house hotel

We've never found a hotel in York that we liked enough for the guide but at last this could be it. Its strength is its young and enthusiastic staff, its hands-on owner Helen, and a wonderful old building. She converted the building with her husband John, who died in 2012.

You enter by a long, comfortable sitting room, with original 11thC walls forming one side. Above is a long, imposing gallery with wonderful oak panelling (not much enhanced by the pictures hanging on it). There's a small bar at one end, and a peaceful sitting-room/library on the same floor. Furnishings are in places an uneasy mixture of antiques, drab modern pieces and make-do.

The comfortable bedrooms have been done up in a contemporary, perhaps uniform style, mainly in off whites. Dinner was average and fairly priced, breakfast above average.

However: Grays Court is work in progress. Some two years before this edition was published the building housed a tea shop. There has been local opposition to its conversion. Once this dies down, we think it can find its form, especially if it gets an injection of buzz and atmosphere. With this, it could be a gem. The location is good, with added peace and privacy from a small tree-lined courtyard for parking.

Area introduction

From the fertile southern uplands bordering England to the dramatic mountain ranges and sensational coasts of the Highlands and Islands, Scotland is varied and breathtakingly beautiful. Within a few hours' drive the scenery changes from gently rolling hills to craggy peaks. Visitors come to hike, climb, ski, play golf, fish, and to explore Scotland's fascinating historical heritage and lively cultural life. People describe Scotland as being either 'Lowland' or 'Highland'. The lowlands, which are not all low, lie south of a line drawn between Glasgow and Edinburgh. The Highlands, though not all high, are north of this line. Our selection includes converted castles, country manors, farmhouses and town houses. This edition has a number of interesting additions, thanks to the work of Jonathan Noble. Entries are indexed in alpha order by place name, regardless of whether they are on the mainland or on an island.
Below are some useful back-up places to try if our main selections are fully booked:

One Devonshire Gardens Town hotel, Glasgow Tel 084473 64256
www.hotelduvin.co.uk
Glasgow's stylish Hotel du Vin in the leafy West End.

Ednam House Hotel Country house hotel, Kelso Tel 01573 224168
www.ednamhouse.com
Traditional fishing hotel with great location on the Tweed.

Crolinnhe Bed-and-breakfast, Fort William Tel 01397 703795
www.crolinnhe.co.uk
Guesthouse with spectacular views of Loch Linnhe.

Closeburn, Dumfries and Galloway

Closeburn, Thornhill, Dumfries and Galloway DG3 5EZ

Tel 01848 331211
e-mail info@trigonyhotel.co.uk
website www.trigonyhotel.co.uk

Nearby Drumlanrig Castle; Caerlaverock Castle; Caerlaverock Nature Reserve **Location** just north of Closeburn before the village of Thornhill; about 200 yards from the main road. **Food** breakfast, lunch Friday–Sunday, otherwise by reservation only **Price** ££-££££ **Rooms** 9; 4 doubles (2 can be twin), 4 superior (3 can be twin), one garden suite with heated conservatory and small private garden; all have bath/shower, TV, DVD and radio, hairdryer, tea and coffee making facilities. **Facilities** restaurant, gardens, bar, terrace; activities include: falconry, vintage car hire, land-rover safaris, salmon fishing **Credit cards** MC, V **Children** welcome **Disabled** no special facilities **Pets** dogs welcome **Closed** never **Proprietors** Adam and Jan

Trigony House Hotel

Country bed-and-breakfast

Owners Adam and Jan bought Trigony House Hotel 11 years ago after deciding to quit the rat-race in York and move to the Scottish countryside with their family. They've created a homely, family atmosphere founded on simple, honest comforts. Adam's food is a major draw, his unfussy classic dishes can be enjoyed in the informal bar or the slightly more formal restaurant – both have cosy wood-burning stoves.

Inside and out, it's what you would expect of a former Edwardian shooting lodge: understated and handsome, ivy creeps up the exterior and a large trim front garden is perfect for dogs. The interiors don't try too hard and suit the building; muted colours are used throughout for understated ambience and the whole building is well maintained and a perfect size for the operation.

Although tucked away in the countryside, there are lots of things to do. Adam and Jan have a wealth of suggestions for the area and often arrange things to do nearby and in the grounds. One of our favourite activities was driving around the winding Scottish country roads in a hired vintage Austin 14. Low-key walks and cycling routes are on hand, too.

Cupar, Fife KY15 5LH

Tel 01334 840206
Fax 01334 84053
e-mail stay@thepeatinn.co.uk
website www.thepeatinn.co.uk

Nearby Edinburgh; Piscottie; St Andrews; golf courses; Dundee; Perthshire; East Neuk; Falkland Palace; The Secret Bunker **Location** from the B940 and 941 follow signs to the village of Peat Inn – in prominent position with parking **Food** breakfast, lunch and dinner Tuesday–Saturday inclusive
Price £££-££££
Rooms 8; double and family suites **Facilities** private garden, restaurant, safe, parking **Credit cards** AE, MC, V **Children** welcome; under fives are free, over fives: supplement for sofa bed. Cots and high chairs available **Disabled** easy access to public areas and an adaptable ground-floor bedroom **Pets** no **Closed** Sun-Mon, Christmas and 10 days at the beginning of Jan **Proprietors** Geoffrey and Katherine Smeddle

The Peat Inn

Restaurant-with-rooms

This restaurant-with-rooms, a former 17thC coaching inn, has had a sterling reputation for more than 30 years. Originally owned by renowned chef David Wilson, it was taken over in 2006 by Geoffrey Smeddle and his wife Katherine, who are, according to one guest 'creating something quite special'.

A warm, professional welcome is ensured by Katherine and the front of house team, but the food is the big draw here. Geoffrey's dishes, which use only the best local and seasonal produce, are racking up awards. Typical dishes include Cairngorm venison, oyster panna cotta and avocado and rhubarb and connage crowdie cheesecake. This award-winning restaurant isn't intimidating, though: it's split into three small areas, which, helped by the service, create a friendly, intimate atmosphere.

Upstairs, the eight suites are each individually designed, with the bedroom and living room set on two separate levels and bathrooms finished with Italian marble. Carpets are deep, fabrics are rich, and towels are thick and fluffy. Continental breakfast (home-made, of course) is served in your suite at a preferred time – a touch that might feel intrusive to some, decadent to others. It's almost impossible to find any fault with this place.

The Howard

Town house hotel

34 Great King Street, Edinburgh EH3 6QH

Tel (0131) 557 3500
Fax (0131) 557 6515
e-mail reserve@thehoward.com
website www.thehoward.com

Nearby Edinburgh Castle; Holyrood Palace; Princes Street.
Location in New Town, E of Dundas St; private car parking
Food breakfast, lunch, dinner; room service
Price ££££
Rooms 18; 11 double and twin, 2 single, 5 suites; all rooms have phone, TV, fax/modem point, hairdryer
Facilities drawing room, bar, breakfast room, restaurant, dining room, drink service
Credit cards AE, DC, MC, V
Children welcome
Disabled access possible, lift/elevator **Pets** not accepted **Closed** never
Manager Leon Kiteley

The only indication that 34 Great King Street is a hotel is the simple brass plate to the right of the front door. The location, a cobbled street in Edinburgh's New Town (new in the early 1800s, that is), could hardly be bettered, within walking distance of Princes Street and the Castle, but almost free of traffic noise.

The 1820s building, comprising three terraced town houses, displays all the elegance and sense of proportion one associates with the Georgian era. Push open the door, and willing service is immediately on hand, including directions to the hotel's own private car park. After checking in, the charming reception staff will ask if you'd like some tea and shortbread, thus reinforcing the sense of being a guest in a friend's house.

Public rooms are elegant and captivating, although the drawing room could do with better lighting. The breakfast room is graced by delightful Italianate murals, uncovered during restoration. Bedrooms are supremely comfortable.

24 Northumberland Street,
Edinburgh EH3 6LS

Tel (0131) 556 8140
Fax (0131) 556 4423
e-mail info@ingrams.co.uk
website www.ingrams.co.uk

Nearby Princes Street, Castle, art galleries, museums and central Edinburgh shopping
Location on quiet side street with own private car parking
Food breakfast
Price ££
Rooms 3; 1 double, 2 twin bedded; 2 have bath and shower, 1 with private bathroom; all rooms have phone, TV, hairdryer, wi-fi
Facilities dining room, laundry
Credit cards DC, MC, V
Children not under 14 **Disabled** not suitable **Pets** not accepted
Closed Christmas **Proprietors** David and Theresa Ingram

Ingrams

City bed-and-breakfast

This is a conventional but well-groomed B&B in a fine four-storey Georgian town house, with handsome entrance hall and staircase lit by an oval cupola. Everywhere, pleasing architectural features have been preserved, and it is beautifully furnished with David Ingram's collection of antiques – David is a well-known Edinburgh antiques dealer. It's been his, and his wife Theresa's home for many years. David is a welcoming host and local character with an impressive knowledge of Edinburgh's history and architecture.

The rooms are all comfortably and quietly furnished in period style with smart, up- to-date bathrooms. Despite the age of the house, nothing is tired and the housekeeping excellent – there's a full-time housekeeper with back-up, which makes a difference in this type of operation.

Breakfast, a 'sumptuous affair', is served by David Ingram in the elegant dining room (our inspectors appreciated the hallmarked Georgian silver): fresh fruit salad, home-made cordial, porridge and a full traditional cooked breakfast. David prides himself on his scrambled eggs and handmade sausages. The Ingrams don't serve dinner, but you're within walking distance of a number of good restaurants; and guests have use of a fridge and microwave (likewise laundry facilities).

Coltbridge Gardens,
Edinburgh, EH12 6AQ

Tel (0131) 346 0024
Fax (0131) 346 0024
e-mail
windmillhouse@btinternet.com

Nearby The Scottish National Gallery of Modern Art next door in wooded grounds; waymarked riverside walk; cental Edinburgh sights and shopping.
Location in 2-acre grounds with ample private car parking
Food breakfast
Prices ££-£££
Rooms 3; 2 double and one twin-bedded; all rooms have TV, video
Facilities sitting room, garden.
Credit cards not accepted
Children accepted by arrangement – cots available
Disabled not suitable
Pets not accepted
Closed Christmas and New Year
Proprietors Vivien Scott

Windmill House

City bed-and-breakfast

Looking for space, fresh air, and minimal traffic noise in Edinburgh? The answer is this spacious Georgian-style house, built 1999 in a unique and spectacular position overlooking the Water of Leith. The atmosphere really is distinctly rural (the site was once used to graze sheep) despite it being only a mile – a 20-minute walk – from the city centre. The old restored windmill in the garden is home to a large family of badgers; the grounds have a weir and a waterfall.

Inside, there's an impressive staircase and galleried hall and an attractive drawing room with an open fire which guests can use. It's elegantly decorated throughout and the large, light and airy bedrooms are exceptionally comfortable. Bathrooms are warm, large and well equipped.

Vivien Scott is a thoughtful host who will book you into the local restaurants and provide torches for those who wish to walk. Breakfast is 'substantial,' served in a charming dining room; our reporters enjoyed the fresh raspberries and blueberries.

15 Woodside Place, Glasgow G3 7QL

Tel 0141 332 1263
e-mail info@15glasgow.com
website www.15glasgow.com

Nearby art galleries; all major attractions; shopping; bars; restaurants. **Location** city centre, in green area a 10 minute walk to city and West End attractions; free car-parking available on request
Food breakfast
Price £££
Rooms 5; 3 double (1 can be a twin), 2 suites, all have bath/shower, TV and DVD, iPod dock, hairdryer, tea/coffee
Facilities guest sitting room, DVD collection
Credit cards MC, V
Children welcome
Disabled not suitable
Pets not accepted
Closed Christmas
Proprietor Laura and Shane McKenzie

15Glasgow

City bed-and-breakfast

Fiona Duncan visited just before we went to press. 'It didn't happen to tick my boxes looks-wise, but for the size and quality of the rooms, it is brilliant value for money'. It's in a terrace of large, confident Victorian terrace houses near the city centre, converted from offices into a B&B in 2009 by Shane and Laura McKenzie, who live on the lower ground floor with their three children – the rest is for guests.

Period features – original shutters, fireplaces, ceilings – are preserved alongside a modish, design-led style. So modish that it might look dated sooner than it should.

'My room felt a bit gloomy and poorly lit, and I preferred the other rooms I saw, all spacious, with cool new bathrooms. One, Drawing Room, the original first floor reception room of the house, is enormous, stunning whatever your taste, with feminine touches of pink, and priced at a friendly £165 per night'.

There is a spacious ground-floor sitting room for guests, rather stiffly decorated and not much used, which would have benefitted from an honesty bar, or from use as a breakfast room. Instead, breakfast is served in your room on a tray. Laura is a warm and informative hostess and besides good value she offers a great alternative in its own right to staying in a Glasgow hotel.

Heiton by Kelso, Roxburghshire

Heiton by Kelso, Roxburghshire, TD5 8JZ

Tel 01583 450331
e-mail hotel@roxburghe.net
website www.roxburghe.net

Nearby the Roxburghe Estate and Floors Castle; The Roxburghe Golf Course; Melrose Abbey; Abbotsford
Location on the Roxburghe Estate just outside the village of Heiton, 4 miles from Kelso
Food breakfast, lunch, dinner, afternoon tea
Price £££
Rooms 22; all rooms en suite, some rooms have log fires, all have flatscreen TV, iPod stations, wi-fi, a selection of books, hospitality tray
Facilities drawing room, library, dining room, conservatory, terrace, private function room
Credit cards AE, MC, V
Children welcome
Disabled 3 ground-floor rooms, easy access **Pets** welcome **Closed** never **Proprietor** Duke and Duchess of Roxburghe

The Roxburghe

Country house hotel

The Roxburghe, under general manager Duncan Evans for the Duke of Roxburghe, shows all those personal touches that we love in privately owned estate hotels.

It's a typically solid Victorian house, scented by wood smoke and whisky. There are open fires, tartan carpets, tables piled with books, and family photographs and portraits. The drawing room, in particular, owes everything to a combination of the Duke and Duchess of Roxburghe, and a particularly sensitive designer.

The bedrooms are just right too, in classic country house style. Though our room was hardly trendy, it had character in spades. A fire crackling in a freestanding grate (logs in the basket, coal delivered on request), completed the happy mood. Our one criticism of the decoration is the oddly bleak arrangement of furniture on the wide first-floor landing.

It's also an ideal sporting hotel. Riding, golf on a championship course, fly fishing and clay-pigeon shooting (both with renowned experts) are all close and at discounted prices. World-class salmon fishing is possible on prime beats of the Tweed and the Teviot. Even when bad weather might make your visit seem in vain, the Roxburghe's charms can make the journey seem worthwhile.

Kilberry, Argyll PA29 6YD

Tel (01880) 770 223
e-mail relax@kilberryinn.com
website www.kilberryinn.com

Nearby secluded beaches, distilleries, ferries to the surrounding islands
Location on the B8024 between Tarbert and Lochgilphead
Food breakfast, lunch, dinner
Price ££
Rooms 5 double with shower; all rooms have TV, hairdryer, tea and coffee, books
Facilities restaurant
Credit cards MC, V
Children over 12 welcome
Disabled access to restaurant and 1 bedroom
Pets dogs accepted by arrangement
Closed Dec-Mar 2014
Proprietors Clare Johnson and David Wilson

The Kilberry Inn

Restaurant-with-rooms

This traditional whitewashed, red-roofed 'but'n'ben' cottage had long been run as an inn before David Wilson and chef Clare Johnson, who used to run the renowned Anchorage Seafood Restaurant in the nearby fishing village of Tarbert, took it on and set about transforming it into a modern restaurant with rooms. Gone is the former cluttered, rustic, 'twee' look. It has been replaced with minimal and contemporary decoration, with cosy log fires, beams and quarried stone-walls, hung with art from local painters. The inn has five comfortable, tastefully decorated double bedrooms with showers, in adjacent buildings.

The focus in the restaurant is on fresh, locally produced ingredients – crab, lobster, langoustine, scallops and fish are all caught within a few miles of the inn, and meat is all reared nearby. Dinner might be potted Kilberry crab, followed by Sound of Jura monkfish with pepperonata and piquillo pepper dressing, then Isle of Mull cheddar with biscuits and chutney to finish.

The inn is situated on a remote single track road on the Kintyre peninsula, with stunning views of the surrounding lochs and islands, and David thinks this remoteness makes arriving an adventure in itself. Reports welcome.

Kirkcolm, Dumfries and Galloway

Corsewall Point, Kirkcolm,
Stranraer, Dumfries and Galloway
DG9 0QG

Tel (01776)853220
Fax (01776) 854231
e-mail info@lighthousehotel.co.uk
website www.lighthousehotel.co.uk

Nearby Stranraer – ferry to Ireland, Loch Ryan, Iron Age fort, pony-trekking, golf.
Location remote; in own grounds with ample private car parking, air transfer arrangeable.
Food breakfast, lunch, dinner
Price ££
Rooms 11; 6 doubles, 5 suites, some can be twin-bedded; all rooms have phone, TV, DVD, hairdryer
Facilities 2 sitting rooms, restaurant, 20-acre grounds
Credit cards AE, DC, MC, V
Children accepted
Disabled 1 accessible room
Pets allowed in 2 of the suites
Closed never
Proprietor Andrew G Ward

Corsewall Lighthouse

Lighthouse hotel

Remote – the last mile is down a track – on a windswept promontory north of Stranraer, this is a listed, 200-year old working lighthouse. The tower itself isn't part of the hotel, but the structure at its foot, the former lighthouse keeper's dwelling, houses the restaurant, public areas and some of the rooms. Other accommodation, including the suites, are in separate buildings, none more than three minutes from the hub.

Guests come here for a unique and romantic experience, the generally light rooms and dramatic seascapes, but not for style. It's mostly done out comfortably, but in a conventional, unpretentious way – you could hardly be anywhere else but a hotel. Some of the smaller rooms may not please perfectionists – but bear in mind it's an old building.

The food ('tremendous' says a reporter) wins general approval. Service is thoughtful and the welcome personal. 'Truly magical' says one reporter of their experience there. 'Nothing beats going out after dinner to walk the shore and hear the waves exploding on the rocks' says another. Highland cattle graze the grounds, whilst seals can be seen off the coast. To climb the lighthouse tower you need permission in writing from the Northern Lighthouse Board. Reports welcome.

Burts Hotel
Melrose, Scottish Borders TD6 9PL

Tel 01896 822285
e-mail enquiries@burtshotel.co.uk
website www.burtshotel.co.uk

Food breakfast, lunch dinner
Price £-££
Closed 1 week in Jan
Proprietors Henderson family

The Townhouse Hotel
Melrose, Scottish Borders TD6 9PQ

Tel 01896 822645
e-mail enquiries@thetownhouse-melrose.co.uk **website** www.thetownhousemelrose.co.uk

Food breakfast, lunch dinner
Price £-££
Closed 1 week in Jan
Proprietors Henderson family

Burts Hotel/The Townhouse **Town hotels**

Unusually for a Scottish border town, pleasant Melrose appeals to all sorts of visitor – it offers walking and fishing, as well as shopping, museums and Melrose Abbey. Similarly, the Hendersons' two places to stay, standing opposite each other in the town centre, accommodate a range of visitors' needs.

Burts (top) is secure in its reputation as a fishing hotel with great atmosphere. Jolly flowers tumbling out of every window at the front prepare you for an unstuffy atmosphere within. Upstairs, bedroom walls are decorated in an earthy range of colours, while a lively variety of fabrics and patterns in each room add bolder colours.

Be sure to book dinner in advance, as the bistro is popular with locals – 'the hottest seats in town' we were told.

The Townhouse (bottom left) departs from the country sports ethos of its sister hotel. The rooms are similarly bold – intensely patterned walls, cushions and sofas, but more ambitious in colour scheme and size. Young city dwellers seeking a contemporary, uncluttered ambience will feel more comfortable here.

The menu offers local produce (as at Burt's), and is elegantly served, but we were underwhelmed by the drinking area in the lean-to conservatory at the back.

Portpatrick, Dumfries & Galloway

Portpatrick, Dumfries & Galloway
DG9 9AD

Tel (01776) 810471
Fax (01776) 810435
e-mail reservations@knockinaam-lodge.com
website www.knockinaamlodge.com

Nearby Logan; Ardwell and Glenwhan Gardens; Castle Kennedy.
Location 3 miles (5 km) SE of Portpatrick, off A77; in grounds; ample car parking
Food breakfast, lunch, dinner
Price ££££
Rooms 10; 9 double with bath, one single with shower; all rooms have phone, TV, video, hairdryer
Facilities 2 sitting rooms, bar, dining room; garden, croquet, helipad
Credit cards AE, MC, V
Children welcome
Disabled public rooms accessible (no ground-floor bedrooms)
Pets accepted, but not in public rooms
Closed never
Proprietor David Ibbotson

Knockinaam Lodge

Country hotel

Galloway is very much an area for escaping the hurly-burly, and Knockinaam Lodge complements it perfectly (as well as being the ideal staging post for anyone bound for the ferry at Stranraer to Northern Ireland). Succeeding proprietors of the Lodge have had a reputation for fine food and warm hospitality, and the tradition is still maintained with the help of an enthusiastic staff and the present owner, David Ibbotson.

The house, a low Victorian villa, was built as a hunting lodge in 1869 and extended at the turn of the century. It was used by Sir Winston Churchill as a secret location in which to meet General Eisenhower during the Second World War. The rooms are cosy in scale and furnishings, the bedrooms varying from the stylishly simple to the quietly elegant. A key part of the appeal of the place is its complete seclusion – down a wooded glen, with lawned garden running down to a sandy beach. Children are welcome, and well catered for, with special high teas.

Since taking over in 2003, David has brightened up the place considerably, completely redecorating, as well as turning his attention to the grounds and painting the exterior. The restaurant now has a Michelin star, and the wine list has more than 540 bins.

Edinburgh

Castlehill, The Royal Mile,
Edinburgh EH1 2NF

Tel (0131) 225 5613
Fax (0131) 220 4392
e-mail mail@thewitchery.com
website www.thewitchery.com
Food breakfast, lunch, dinner
Price ££££
Closed never
Proprietor James Thomson

The Witchery by the Castle **Restaurant-with-rooms**

It takes its name from the hundreds of witches burned at the stake nearby, but The Witchery is, thankfully, not macabre. However, it is gothic and, above all, luxurious. It occupies a pair of 16thC buildings at the gates of Edinburgh Castle. Entering from a close off the Royal Mile, candle-light reveals painted ceilings and walls covered in tapestries and 17thC oak panelling rescued from a fire at St Giles Cathedral.

Suites, either above the restaurant or in an adjacent building, are plush and opulent, with antiques, historic paintings and dramatic colour schemes, and have views towards the Old Town or over the Royal Mile.

You can eat either in the award-winning restaurant of the same name; in the Secret Garden; or in The Tower.

Gullane, East Lothian

Muirfield, Gullane, East Lothian
EH31 2EG

Tel 01620 842144
Fax 01620 8422412
e-mail enquiries@greywalls.co.uk
website www.greywalls.co.uk
Food breakfast, lunch, dinner, afternoon tea **Price** ££££
Closed Jan to Feb
Manager Duncan Fraser

Greywalls
Country house hotel

Greywalls is a slick, expensive country house hotel, with – by our standards – quite a large number of bedrooms, but despite this we cannot resist including such a distinctive place. It is a classic turn-of-the-century house, and for golf enthusiasts – it overlooks the tenth green of the famous Muirfield championship course.

The feel of Greywalls is very much one of a gracious private house, although series editor Fiona Duncan felt it would have been cosier were it still family-run.

Dinner, served in a room overlooking the golf course, is superb – it's one of Albert Roux's Chez Roux outposts. Bedrooms are attractive and well-equipped, particularly those in the original house rather than the new wing.

Jedburgh, Roxburghshire

Hundalee House

Bed-and-breakfast

Set back in the hills, this 18thC limestone manor house has been home to the Whittakers for a decade. They created the fine large garden, putting in flowering shrubs, adding peacocks and digging a pond for koi carp. Inside, the taste is even more exotic, reflecting their time in Egypt. Egyptian motifs hang on the walls and Egyptian hounds guard the fireplace in the sitting room, which has fine views of the Cheviot Hills to the south. Bedrooms may not be luxurious but one has a four-poster bed. Two others share a bathroom; these offer notable value and are useful for a family. Sheila Whittaker does not serve dinner, but her breakfasts are 'cooked and copious,' according to one teenage visitor.

Jedburgh, Roxburghshire TD8 6PA

Tel (01835) 863011
Fax (01835) 863011
e-mail sheila.whittaker@btinternet.com
website www.accommodation-scotland.org
Food breakfast **Price** £
Closed Nov-Mar
Proprietors Mr and Mrs Whittaker

Skirling by Biggar, Lanarkshire

Skirling House

Village hotel

Set in the centre of a peaceful Borders village, Skirling House was designed in 1908 by the Arts and Crafts architect Ramsay Traquair. We are delighted to report that owners Bob and Isobel are well aware of the architectural gem they have on their hands and the Arts and Craft movement is evident throughout.

Bedrooms, very much in the style of the place, have lovely views over the three-acre garden. The menu, modern and light in style, changes daily and the Hunters use local produce as well as vegetables and herbs from the house gardens.

Located by one of the main routes to Edinburgh, Skirling House makes a convenient and worthwhile stop-over.

Skirling by Biggar, Lanarkshire
ML12 6HD

Tel 01899 860274
Fax 01899 860255
e-mail enquiry@skirlinghouse.com
website www.skirlinghouse.com
Food breakfast, dinner
Price ££
Closed Jan and Feb
Proprietors Bob and Isobel Hunter

Auldearn, Nairn

Auldearn, Nairn, IV12 5TE

Tel (01667) 454896
Fax (01667) 455469
e-mail info@boath-house.com
website www.boath-house.com

Nearby Inverness, Nairn, Loch Ness, Balmoral Castle
Location off A96, near Nairn, ample parking
Food breakfast, lunch, dinner
Price ££££
Rooms 8, all with bath/shower
Facilities 2 sitting rooms, restaurant, spa; golf, fishing, riding, clay shooting all available nearby
Credit Cards MC, V
Children welcome
Disabled one ground floor cottage, restaurant is accessible
Pets accepted by arrangement
Closed never
Proprietors Don and Wendy Matheson

Boath House Hotel

Country house hotel

This Grade A listed Georgian mansion was standing derelict until Don and Wendy Matheson found and fell in love with it in the early Nineties. Having restored the house to its former glory the Mathesons decided to open their home to guests, and have since made a great success of it.

Boath House has its own spa and eight guest bedrooms, all individually decorated in rich colours in a mix of contemporary and traditional styles. All have private bathrooms, and two have four poster beds. It stands in 20 acres of grounds, including a 2-acre lake and Victorian walled garden.

The kitchen gardens provide many of the ingredients served in the award-winning restaurant. Charlie Lockley is head chef, and the focus is on organic, locally–produced and seasonal food. Local seafood is delivered daily, and meat and cheese come from a nearby farm. Wild food items, such as wild mushrooms and herbs, are also on the menu when in season, and even honey comes from the hotel's own hives – organic food is a real passion here.

The Mathesons are keen to foster a friendly, informal atmosphere and want their home to be "somewhere guests can relax and feel at ease", despite the grandeur of the house. We have heard great things about Boath House. Reports welcome.

Balquidder, Perthshire

Balquhidder, Lochearnhead,
Perthshire FK19 8PQ

Tel (01877) 384622
Fax (01877) 384305
e-mail monachyle@mhor.net
website http://mhor.net/hotel/

Nearby in the heart of Rob Roy country.
Location on private estate; turn off A84, 11 miles (17.5 km) N of Callander at Kingshouse Hotel, then follow single-track lane for 6 miles (9.5 km); well-signposted; ample car-parking
Food breakfast, lunch, dinner
Price ££-££££
Rooms 14 double, all with bath or shower; all rooms have phone, TV, hairdryer **Facilities** sitting room, bar, restaurant; terrace, garden, fishing, stalking **Credit cards** MC, V
Children well behaved children accepted over 12
Disabled access easy
Pets accepted in 2 rooms
Closed Jan **Proprietors** Tom, Dick and Melanie Lewis

Monachyle Mhor

Farmhouse hotel

A small, family-run farmhouse with a charm all its own. The setting is both serene and romantic – as well it might be: this was the family home of Rob Roy MacGregor, approached along the Braes of Balquhidder (described in Kidnapped) and set beside Lochs Doine and Voil.

Rob and Jean Lewis came here some 30 years ago from Monmouth and first farmed the 2,000-acre estate, then opened the building as a hotel as well. Since then Jean and Rob have moved to the South of France, but their children Tom, Dick and Melanie have taken over and expanded the business. A self-catering cottage has been converted into suites, and the hotel now has a total of 14 individual and very stylishly-decorated rooms; five in the main house, and nine in the courtyard buildings. As well as the farm and hotel, the Lewises now also run a fish shop (Ben Ledi), The Scotch Oven bakery and Mhor 84 – a roadside gastropub with seven rooms.

Tom Lewis is the highly-praised chef, and the hotel's restaurant – situated in a light and airy conservatory overlooking the two lochs – is popular with locals and guests alike. Much of the produce comes from the farm.

For a relaxing, country break in magnificent scenery and with memorable food, Monachyle Mhor would be hard to beat.

Brachla, Inverness-shire

Brachla, Loch Ness-Side, IV3 8LA

Tel 01456 459469
Fax 01456 459439
e-mail escape@loch-ness-lodge.com
website www.loch-ness-lodge.com

Nearby Loch Ness, Culloden, Isle of Skye, Glen Affric National Nature Reserve **Location** from Inverness follow signs for A82 Fort William/Loch Ness Road, Lodge is on the right after approximately 9 miles
Food breakfast
Price £££-££££
Rooms 7 double with flat screen TV and DVD, CD player, direct dial telephones
Facilities drawing room, spa, garden, wi-fi throughout
Credit cards AE, MC, V
Children welcome (over 12)
Disabled access possible
Pets not accepted
Closed Jan
Proprietor Scott Sutherland

Loch Ness Lodge

Highland bed-and-breakfast

Located just a stone's throw from the waters edge, this B&B offers unrivalled views across Loch Ness and the hills beyond. The lodge sits in its own cultivated gardens and acts as an ideal setting-off point to explore the surrounding highlands.

The emphasis at Loch Ness Lodge is on understated indulgence: it seems that nothing is too much for the staff (who will even provide you with satnav details for your excursions). Although dinner is no longer offered, the team are more than happy to recommend (and book) a restaurant nearby.

Breakfast is wide ranging and often centres on locally-sourced ingredients. The complimentary afternoon tea, with a variety of loose-leaf teas and home-made bakes, was a welcome addition and has proved popular with the regular guests.

Our room was particularly spacious, simply decorated in muted colours with dark wood furnishings, and came complete with whiskey and our own view of the Loch – a luxury shared by all seven rooms.

Dornoch, Sutherland

Castle Street, Dornoch, Sutherland, IV25 3SN

Tel 01862 811811
e-mail web@2quail.com
website www.2quail,com

Nearby Royal Dornoch Golf Course and Club.
Location north of Inverness, en-route to or from the Orkneys
Food breakfast
Price ££-£££
Rooms 3; all with bathrooms
Facilities library/lounge
Credit Cards AE, MC, V
Children not under 10
Disabled no access available
Pets not accepted
Closed never
Proprietors Michael and Kerensa Carr

2Quail

Town bed-and-breakfast

An exceptional B&B in a place where we've not had a recommendation until now. Dornoch, on the east coast of Scotland, north of Inverness, is a stopping point on the way to the far north and the Orkneys. It is also home to one of the largest golf courses in the world; whose springy turf is a pleasure to play on. Don't come here only if you're a golfer, but consider an unusual weekend away in this interesting place on its own merits.

When we stepped inside 2Quail, a sandstone terraced house in the heart of town, we felt as though we had entered a time warp. Much of the furniture – dainty, brown and cream upholstered armchairs, lamps with fringed sides – are family pieces. The residence is neat and furnished in a way that says 'Edwardian' or '40s' or somewhere in between; idiosyncratic, well executed and refreshingly different. There are three bedrooms. Ours was soberly furnished, yet arresting, with its wrought iron bedstead and comfortable mattress.

Owners of 2Quail – Kerensa Carr and her husband, Michael – used to run a tiny but well-regarded restaurant here as well. Now, Michael works as head chef at the Royal Dornoch Golf Club where you can easily make arrangements to eat. The club is friendly and relaxed.

Duror, Argyll

Salachen Glen, Duror, Argyll PA38 4BW

Tel (01631) 740298
e-mail enquiries@bealachhouse.co.uk
website www.bealach-house.co.uk

Nearby Oban, Fort William, Argyll Mountains, Glencoe, Ben Nevis, Skye, Mull and Iona **Location** take A82 to Ballachulish, then follow signs for Oban on the A828 for approx 8 miles, through Kentallen and Duror, you will see our sign on the left **Food** breakfast, dinner (not on Monday), home-made cakes and biscuits served on arrival
Price ££ **Rooms** 2 doubles and 1 twin, each with radio, tea/coffee making facilities
Facilities sitting room with satellite TV, book and game library, dining room, 8-acre grounds **Credit cards** MC, V **Children** accepted over 14 **Disabled** no access **Pets** not accepted **Closed** Nov-Jan **Proprietor** Jim and Hilary McFadyen

Bealach House

Country guesthouse

Set at the end of a scenic track 1.5 miles from the main road, Bealach House's biggest challenge is also its greatest asset. As the road winds onward, little signs reassure you that you are still heading in the right direction and at the end – 'absolute peace and quiet' – as one recent visitor describes it.

After taking the time to find it, this is not a place that you will be rushing to leave. The welcome from owners Jim and Hilary is always warm, home-made cakes and biscuits setting the tone from the off.

Each of the three bedrooms are simple and spacious, and each with an outstanding view of the surrounding countryside.

Dinner is universally appreciated, the three courses all made by Hilary and with three different options for every course. The same attention is paid to breakfast. There is a real feeling of home here: you might be happy sinking into an armchair to read a book or to watch TV for the evening – though, just like home, it might also mean that you never do find the final pieces of the old jigsaw you wanted to finish.

Edinbane, Isle of Skye

Edinbane, Isle of Skye IV51 9PN

Tel 01470 582266
e-mail info@greshornishhouse.com
website www.greshornishhouse.com

Nearby Loch Greshornish, Edinbane Pottery, Dunvegan Castle, Talisker Distillery, Isle of Skye Brewery Waternish peninsula, Skyeskyns Tannery, **Location** past Edinbane towards Dunvegan, sign-posted to the right, 2.5 miles down single track road **Food** breakfast, lunch, dinner, afternoon tea, all by prior arrangement **Price** ££-£££ **Rooms** 8; 6 doubles, 1 double/twin, 1 twin, all with TV, telephone, hairdryer, dial up internet, and tea and coffee facilities **Facilities** drawing room, billiard room, reception room and cocktail bar, conservatory, dining room, gardens, tennis court, croquet lawn **Children** welcome, not all rooms suitable **Disabled** access only to public rooms **Pets** dogs by prior arrangement **Proprietor** Neil and Rosemary Colquhoun

Greshornish House

Country house hotel

Greshornish House, a country house which dates from the 18th century and was once visited by Johnson and Boswell, looks towards the Trotternish peninsula. Its rather imposing appearance and history – there's been a dwelling here for close to 1,000 years – are brought back down to earth by a distinctly lived-in feel: this is the home of owners Neil and Rosemary, and their two labradors. A jumble of coats, dog leads and boots greets you as you enter the entrance hall.

The mix of country house luxury and homeliness continues in the bedrooms: fresh flowers from the gardens adorn tables; hot water bottles can be tucked under the sheets. Beds have polished wooden headboards or are four-poster, and original features are scattered throughout: brass picture rails, marble fireplaces and a rediscovered press.

Internet access is available, although Greshornish's remoteness can mean disrupted signal and interference. Wallowing in its glorious isolation is the key to enjoying this place: a walk and scramble around the Loch, then sinking into one of the drawing room's squishy armchairs in front of a roaring log fire is difficult to beat.

The candlelit dinners and summer-time fresh seafood lunches get enthusiastic reviews.

Fort William, Inverness-shire

Glenfinnan, Fort William, Inverness-shire, PH37 4LT

Tel 01397 722235
e-mail availability@glenfinnan-house.com
website www.glenfinnanhouse.com

Nearby Ben Nevis, Glenfinnan viaduct railway bridge, Shiel Cruises, Fort William, Highland activities.
Location pass through Fort William and turn off the A82 to follow the A830 'Road to the Isles', west for 15 miles to Glenfinnan. Turn left just after the Glenfinnan Monument Visitor Centre
Food breakfast, dinner, bar food
Price ££-£££
Rooms 12 including some suites and family rooms
Facilities drawing room, playroom, garden, function/wedding facilities, bar, dining room **Credit Cards** AE, MC, V **Children** welcome **Disabled** no access **Pets** not accepted in restaurant **Closed** Mid-Nov to Mid-Mar **Proprietors** Manja and Duncan Gibson

Glenfinnan

Country house hotel

The owners of Glenfinnan House Hotel clearly value family time. That perhaps explains why children are so readily welcomed, why the hotel operates a no-TV policy, and why dogs are well and truly smothered when they stay. Rooms are comfortable rather than inventive, butthe real charm lies elsewhere.

Chef/manager Duncan produces some outstanding things from the kitchen, using fine local produce such as salmon, mussels, beef or venison; some of his classic dishes, as well as various innovative options from the *a la carte* menu, can be enjoyed in both the dining room and the bar.

Most important, this is inspiring, mountainous country which adults and kids will love (the latter will enjoy the chance to visit famous scenes from the Harry Potter films). Loch Shiel cruises operate from nearby, with regular sightings of golden eagles, black-throated divers and red deer. In season, trips slightly further afield often bring you face-to-face with whales, dolphins, seals, puffins and otters.

Some reports suggest that staff can be a little over-zealous, but this can be explained by an earnest effort to keep things running smoothly; the consensus is that they know their stuff here, and do things rather well.

Grange Road, Fort William, Inverness-shirePH33 6JF

Tel (01397) 705516
Fax (01397) 701595
e-mail jcampbell@grange-fortwilliam.com **website** www.the-grange-scotland.co.uk

Nearby Ben Nevis; 'Road to the Isles'; Loch Ness.
Location on outskirts; from town centre take A82 direction Glasgow, then turn left into Ashburn Lane; hotel is at top on left; ample car parking
Food breakfast
Price £
Rooms 3 double and twin, 2 with bath and shower, 1 with bath; all rooms have TV, hairdryer **Facilities** breakfast room, sitting room; garden, sea loch close by
Credit cards by arrangement
Children not accepted
Disabled access difficult
Pets not accepted **Closed** mid-Nov to Easter **Proprietors** Joan and John Campbell

The Grange

Bed-and-breakfast

We were delighted to discover this outstanding bed-and-breakfast establishment on the outskirts of Fort William, run with great flair by Joan and John Campbell. A ten-minute walk from the fairly charmless town centre brings you to this late Victorian house, set in pretty terraced grounds overlooking Loch Linnhe.

A feminine touch is distinctly in evidence in the immaculate interior, which is decorated with admirable taste and a flair for matching fabrics with furnishings and fittings. First glimpsed, you might expect a stand-offish 'don't touch' approach from the owners, but nothing could be further from the truth at the Grange. Joan Campbell, responsible for the decoration, is naturally easy-going, with a great sense of hospitality.

All three bedrooms are superbly, and individually, decorated and furnished, their bathrooms lavish and luxurious – it all comes as rather a surprise. The Rob Roy room was the one chosen by Jessica Lange, who stayed here during the filming of Rob Roy. One of the bedrooms has a Louis XV-style king-size bed; all three overlook the garden and Loch Linnhe. A delightful place.

Harrapool, Isle of Skye

13 Harrapool, Isle of Skye IV49 9AQ

Tel 01471 820022
e-mail hopeskye@btinternet.com
website www.skyebedbreakfast.co.uk

Nearby Harrapool, Broadford, Eilean Donan Castle, Clan Donald centre, Broadford Bay, Broadford harbour.
Location in Harrapool, off the A87
Food breakfast; evening meal available on request
Price £-££
Rooms 3; 2 doubles, 1 twin/double, all with underfloor heating.
Facilities free wi-fi, sitting room, dining area, gardens, stretch of beach
Credit cards MC, V
Children welcome, but cots, highchairs etc not necessarily available
Disabled not suitable
Pets not accepted
Closed rarely
Proprietors Neil and Lesley Hope

Tigh An Dochais

Island bed-and-breakfast

Tigh An Dochais stands on a narrow strip of land overlooking Broadford Bay. It's not what immediately springs to mind when picturing a Skye B&B. Designed in 2005 by award-winning architects, it is completely contemporary: all plate glass and slate. The first-floor entrance is reached by a small wooden bridge. Stained larchwood lines the walls.

Inside, floor-to-ceiling glazing lets in the light and the landscape. Every room in the house overlooks the bay, and the views here are so stunning there's little need for further decoration: things are kept simple and uncluttered, except perhaps for a few traditional touches. Tartan fabric brightens up the bedrooms (a fair size, and with underfloor heating), and the booklined sitting room – with a part-glazed, gabled ceiling – is warmed by a log-burning stove and filled with squishy red sofas.

Breakfast is cooked by Neil, and is good old-fashioned fare. It's eaten with the other guests around the large breakfast table, which overlooks yet another breathtaking view. You can take on a full Scottish or sample the home-made bread, muffins and yoghurt: we've heard all are lovely.

Isle of Eriska, Argyll

Isle of Eriska, Ledaig, Oban, Argyll
PA37 1SD

Tel (01631) 720371
Fax (01631) 720531
e-mail office@eriska-hotel.co.uk
website www.eriska-hotel.co.uk

Nearby Oban; Isle of Mull; Inverary Castle; Glencoe.
Location on private island connected by road bridge; from Connel take A828 toward Fort William for 4 miles (6 km) to N of Benderloch village, then follow signs; ample car parking **Food** breakfast, lunch, dinner **Price** ££££ **Rooms** 17; 12 double and twin, 2 single, 3 family rooms, all with bath; all rooms have phone, hairdryer **Facilities** 3 drawing rooms, bar/library, dining room, indoor swimming pool, gym, sauna, garden; 6-hole golf course, driving range, tennis court, croquet, clay-pigeon shooting, watersports **Credit cards** AE, MC, V **Children** welcome **Disabled** access possible **Pets** accepted **Closed** Jan **Proprietors** Buchanan-Smith family

Isle of Eriska Hotel

Island mansion

A splendid hotel that has the twin advantages of seclusion, since it is set on its own remote island, and accessibility: it is connected to the mainland by a short road bridge. And for those who like to keep themselves occupied during their stay, its leisure centre, which includes a magnificent 17-metre heated swimming pool, and its sporting opportunities, will appeal.

Built in 1884 in grey granite and warmer red sandstone, in Scottish Baronial style, the Buchanan-Smith's hotel is a reminder of a more expansive and confident era. If it reminds you in feel, if not in appearance, of Balmoral, you will not be surprised to learn that the original wallpaper on the first-floor landing is also found in the royal castle. In fact the experience of staying here is very much like being in an old-fashioned grand private house, comfortable rather than stylish, with a panelled great hall, and roaring log fires and chintz fabrics much in evidence. In the library-cum-bar you can browse through the books with a malt whisky in hand, while excellent six-course dinners are served in the stately dining room. The handsome bedrooms vary in size and outlook. Since our last edition a further five rooms and two cottages on the island have been added.

Isle Ornsay, Isle of Skye

Isle Ornsay, Sleat, Isle of Skye
IV43 8QR

Tel (01471) 833332
Fax (01471) 833275
e-mail hotel@eileaniarmain.co.uk

Nearby Clan Donald Centre; Aros Heritage Centre; Dunvegan Castle.
Location on water's edge, on estate between Broadford and Armadale in the S of the island, 20 mins drive from Skye Bridge or Mallaig ferry point; ample car parking
Food breakfast, lunch, dinner
Price £££
Rooms 16;12 double, twin or triple, 4 suites; all with bath; all rooms have phone, hairdryer
Facilities sitting room, 2 dining rooms, boutique shop, Gaelic Whisky, art gallery; anchorage for yachts
Credit cards all major
Children welcome
Disabled no special access
Pets accepted
Closed never
Proprietor Lady Noble

Eilean Iarmain

Seafront hotel

Hearing the soft lilt of the voices of the staff is one of the pleasures of a stay at this traditional Skye hotel, and a sure sign that you are in the Hebrides. This is a bi-lingual establishment, and the friendly and welcoming staff are fluent in both Gaelic and English.

The hotel is part of an estate belonging to Lady Noble. Its three buildings are beautifully situated right on the water's edge, on the small rocky bay of Isle Ornsay, looking across the Sound of Sleat to the mainland Knoydart Hills beyond. If you are lucky, you may see otters on the shore.

The hotel's core is a white-painted Victorian inn, which comprises the reception area, two appealing dining rooms and six bedrooms. A further six bedrooms are in a building opposite, while the latest addition houses four split-level suites. All the rooms are traditional in character, hospitable and homely, with modern fittings and smart bathrooms. In each is a complimentary miniature bottle of whisky supplied from the distillery. The restaurant specializes in local fish, shellfish and game, and enjoys a local reputation.

Isle of Mull, Argyll

Ise of Mull, Argyll and Bute,
Scotland PA69 6ES

Tel 01681 705232
e-mail info@tiroran.com
website www.tiroran.com

Nearby Iona, Staffa, castles, mountains, beaches and wildlife.
Location countryside, by a loch with a private beach, large gardens
Food breakfast, lunch, dinner, afternoon tea, room service
Price ££££
Rooms 10; 5 double/twin, 5 double, all have shower, all have TV, hairdryer, tea/coffee facilities **Facilities** 2 drawing rooms, conservatory and dining room, gardens, beach
Credit cards MC, V
Children welcome
Disabled limited, 1 ground floor room with walk-in shower
Pets accepted, 4 rooms for pet owners
Closed rarely
Proprietors Laurence and Katie Mackay

Tiroran House

Country house hotel

An omission from earlier editions. This is about as good as a small country house hotel gets. It's secluded, but not remote, in large gardens beside a loch; you're face-to-face with terrific wildlife... but that is just a start.

One of our trusted reporters describes it as 'one of those gems' which the *Charming Small Hotel Guides* are all about, in fact it surpasses all our criteria.

He wrote of a recent visit: 'We were greeted on the doorstep by Laurence Mackay', who owns and runs the place with his wife Katie. 'The staff were a delight. The food was superb. The wine list is impressive and Laurence clearly know a good deal about single malt whisky. The freedom from intrusive modern technology was a pleasure, although had I wanted to listen to some decent music for a quiet hour, there was discreet equipment to make it possible. The old world charm of the two very different sitting rooms, then a contrasting two-level dining room, as well as the seriously comfortable and tasteful bedrooms, makes this a seriously good hotel.'

There's also self-catering accommodation in separate buildings in the garden, with access to the hotel's facilities – perfect for families.

Killiecrankie, Perthshire

Killiecrankie, By Pitlochry,
Perthshire PH16 5LG

Tel (01796)473220
Fax (01796) 472451
e-mail enquiries@killiecrankiehotel.co.uk **website** www.killiecrankiehotel.co.uk

Nearby Pitlochry; Pass of Killiecrankie; Blair Atholl; Glamis.
Location in 4 acres, 3 miles (4.5 km) N of Pitlochry, just off A9 on the B8079; ample car parking
Food breakfast, lunch, dinner
Price ££
Rooms 10; 8 double and twin, 2 single, 1 suite, 8 with bath, 2 with shower; all rooms have phone, TV, hairdryer
Facilities sitting room, 2 dining rooms, bar, conservatory, garden
Credit cards MC, V
Children accepted
Disabled access possible
Pets accepted by prior arrangement
Closed 3 Jan to 14 Feb **Proprietor** Henrietta Fergusson

Killiecrankie Hotel

Country house hotel

A sensible, reassuring sort of establishment in a delightful setting that somehow encapsulates the modest Scottish country hotel. Built as a manse for a local clergyman in 1840, it stands at the foot of the Pass of Killiecrankie, formed by the River Garry slicing through the surrounding granite hills, and it has its own attractive grounds – a lovely place in which to relax and watch out for wildlife, including red squirrels and roe deer.

The ten straightforward yet comfortable bedrooms are individually decorated in country house fabrics and custom-made furniture and fittings. An unexpected touch: beds are turned down each evening. The painted panelling in the bar helps make it a cosy, convivial place in which to gather for drinks, and a bright conservatory section is set for light lunches and supper. Guests eat breakfast in a second conservatory, overlooking the garden. In the main restaurant, chef Mark Easton, prepares a large and daily-changing 'modern British' menu. Special diets are also catered for.

Kingussie, Inverness-shire

Tweed Mill Brae, Kingussie, Inverness-shire PH21 1TC

Tel (01540) 661166
e-mail relax@thecross.co.uk
website www.thecross.co.uk

Nearby Highland Wildlife Park, Aviemore, Cairngorm Mountain Railway
Location in Kingussie just off the A9, 10 miles south of Aviemore. Large car park
Food breakfast, lunch, dinner, afternoon tea (prior booking advised)
Price ££££
Rooms 8 double and twin, all with bath; all rooms have phone, TV, DVD, hairdryer, tea/coffee
Facilities 2 sitting rooms, restaurant; garden and garden terrace
Credit cards AE, DC, MC, V
Children welcome
Disabled no special facilities; restaurant is accesible, rooms are not
Pets accepted by arrangement
Closed Christmas, Jan (open for Hogmanay) **Proprietors** Derek and Celia Kitchingman

The Cross

Restaurant-with-rooms

A trusted reporter has revisited since our last edition and met the new owner-managers, the Kitchingmans, who took over from the previous owners in 2012 and have invested steadily in the basics – including better heating and refurbished bedrooms. They've rightly maintained standards in the kitchen, with (as we went to press) a young chef from north of the border serving 'contemporary Scottish cuisine' that wins awards. A recent review in *The Scotsman* praised the hard work that goes into reasonably priced dishes, for example the chicken liver parfait, which 'seemed to be created by a nerdy perfectionist. It was silky and musky, with a sprinkle of sea salt on the top, and a dark, sticky-sweet fig and apple jam, as well as two rough oatcakes, on the side. Joy.' *Sic.*

So we believe it's business as usual in this beguiling 19thC tweed mill, though we would welcome more reports on the nature of the welcome and the atmosphere. Besides good food, The Cross's charm is its secluded 4-acre setting, in a pretty valley above Kingussie with the River Gynack alongside, where you might see salmon swimming and herons fishing. The lofty sitting room is especially appealing.

Kylesku, Sutherland IV27 4HW

Tel 01971 502 231
e-mail info@kyleskuhotel.co.uk
website www.kyleskuhotel.co.uk

Nearby Loch Glencoul and Loch Glendhu, bird watching, wildlife spotting, fishing, walking, climbing, beaches
Location good parking. Access from A894, 35 miles N of Ullapool or 95 miles NW of Inverness.
Food breakfast, lunch, dinner
Price £-££
Rooms 8 double/twin rooms: 6 with bath/shower; 2 with private shower room. All rooms have tea/coffee, TV, hairdryer
Facilities wi-fi, residents' sitting room, bar, dining area and beer garden. **Credit cards** MC, V
Children welcome
Disabled no special access
Pets welcome
Closed Dec-Feb
Proprietors T Lister and S Virechauveix

Kylesku Hotel

Lochside hotel

'It's no beauty, but it is a charmer', writes a trusted reporter of this newcomer. A group of southerners, including Tanja Lister and Sonia Virechauveix, bought it in 2010 and set about renovation in stages. 'Above all else, it is warm and comfortable, which in north-west Scotland means it has plenty going for it.'

The public spaces of this 1680s coaching inn have responded well to renovation, with wonderful views from picture windows.

The food is not far behind other grander places nearby, such as The Albannach (see opposite page) – if not behind at all. The friendly enthusiasm with which it is prepared and presented adds to the charm. Bedrooms are fresh, plain and white-and-grey contemporary, with dots of understated colour here and there. The north end of the hotel is actually the village local and makes a cheery, cosy drinking place. 'An inexpensive, helpful small hotel that deserves to succeed'.

It's a handy stopping place on the road to Cape Wrath, the far north-western tip of mainland Britain, next to the old Kylesku ferry slip, and right by the Kylesku Bridge, in wonderful scenery. Fish for the dinner table are landed on the slip.

Baddidarroch, Lochinver,
Sutherland IV27 4LP

Tel 01571 844407
e-mail info@thealbannach.co.uk
website www.thealbannach.co.uk

Nearby Suilven and Canisp peaks, Achmelvich beach, boat trips to islands
Location Lochinver
Food breakfast, lunch, dinner
Price ££££
Rooms 5; 3 suites, 2 doubles
Facilities terraces, garden, slipway
Credit cards MC, V
Children over 12 accepted
Disabled 2 specially-adapted rooms
Pets not accepted
Closed never
Proprietors Colin Craig and Lesley Crosfield

The Albannach

Country house hotel

'Up a small hill just outside the pretty port of Lochinver,' writes a trusted reporter, 'the building is not particularly attractive externally – but compared with the alternative places in Lochinver, where terms such as barracks and youth hostel come to mind – it is better than OK.'

Inside, the welcome is warm and the way they handle your booking during arrival is pleasantly personal. 'Our room was well heated, tastefully furnished and well equipped.' All the bedrooms are individually decorated and have views to the sea loch and mountains beyond.

The public parts have a Highland ambience, or as our reporter puts it, 'a slightly Gothic feel – my wife was a little anxious that on a dark staircase she might meet Norman Bates, or his mother.'

But the food is far from Gothic: as we went to press this was the most northerly Michelin-starred restaurant in Britain. Our reporter was given fat oysters as a pre-dinner appetiser, and the food thoroughly deserved its star.

Not inexpensive – without the Michelin star, it would be overpriced, but this is an interesting place in a terrific location, made better by the food. There's a self-proclaimed 'draconian' no smoking policy in the hotel, but the terrace is convenient for this purpose – umbrellas provided.

Pitlochry, Perthshire

Knockendarroch

Town mansion

Pitlochry is a particularly agreeable Highland town, and Knockendarroch House is the place to stay. Built in 1880 for an Aberdeen advocate, it displays more château-esque elegance than Scottish Baronial pomp. It stands on a plateau above the town, surrounded by mature oaks (its Gaelic name means Hill of Oaks).

Furnished in careful good taste, the house feels gracious and welcoming. There are two interconnecting sitting rooms in which to relax, with log fire, green ceilings, white cornices, pastel green curtains and new carpets – all very soothing. The dining room is light and spacious, with many windows and some attractive furniture.

Most of the bedrooms have views; those from the second floor are spectacular. They are all well furnished and two have small balconies.

Guests attending the famous Pitlochry Festival Theatre (which began here at Knockendarroch) are served an early dinner, and a courtesy bus is laid on to take them to and from the town.

As we went to press we heard from some well-travelled 30-year-olds who stayed here recently and said the description above is spot on. They enjoyed the grandeur, the comfort and the good food.

Higher Oakfield, Pitlochry, Perthshire PH16 5HT

Tel (01796) 473473
Fax (01796) 474068
e-mail bookings@knockendarroch.co.uk
website www.knockendarroch.co.uk

Nearby Blair Castle; Killiecrankie Pass; Loch Tummel, Edradour Distillery.
Location close to town centre, 26 miles (41 km) N of Perth on A9; ample car parking
Food breakfast, dinner
Price £-££
Rooms 12 double and twin, all with bath; all rooms have phone, TV, hairdryer, radio
Facilities 2 sitting rooms, dining room; garden
Credit cards AE, MC, V
Children accepted over 10
Disabled access limited
Pets not accepted
Closed mid-Nov to mid-Feb
Proprietor Liz Martin

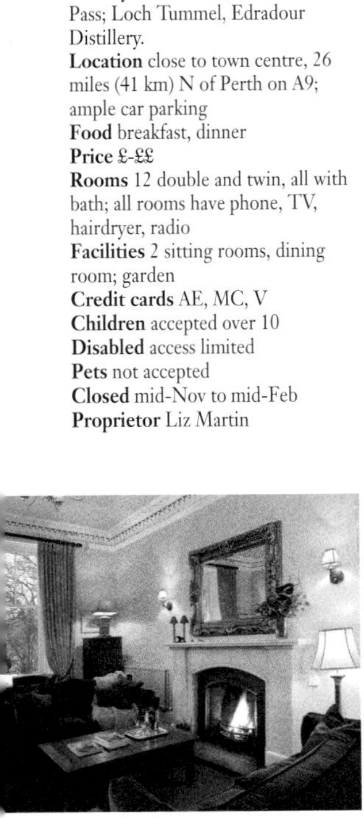

Port Appin, Argyll PA38 4DF

Tel (01631) 730236
Fax (01631) 730535
e-mail airds@airds-hotel.com **website** www.airds-hotel.com

Nearby Oban; Glencoe; 'Road to the Isles'; Ben Nevis.
Location between Ballachulish and Connel, 2 miles (3 km) off A828; ample car parking
Food breakfast, lunch, dinner; room service **Price** ££££ **Rooms** 8 double and twin, 3 suites, all with bath/shower; all rooms have phone, TV and DVD players, hairdryer; 2 self-catering cottages **Facilities** 2 sitting rooms, conservatory, dining room, whisky bar, garden and croquet lawn, shingle beach **Credit cards** DC, MC, V **Children** accepted; none under 8 in dining room after 7.30pm
Disabled no special facilities **Pets** accepted, not in public areas
Closed last three weeks Jan
Proprietors Jenny and Shaun Mc Kivragan

Airds Hotel

Ferry inn

The owners of this old ferry inn on the shores of Loch Linnhe have very sensibly taken every advantage of its superb location: the dining room, the conservatory and many bedrooms face the loch. To capitalize further, they have also created, across the road, an attractive lawn and rose garden in which guests can sit and admire the view across the loch to the island of Lismore. The sunsets here are stunning.

Despite its fairly ordinary exterior, Airds Hotel is a smart and decorous establishment, impeccably run and maintained. The interior is elegant, with two sitting rooms prettily furnished with comfortable chairs, deep-pile carpets and open fires. Rooms are full of flowers and books, and paintings are in abundance. Each of the bedrooms is individually decorated and carefully furnished, with very comfortable bathrooms. Each day the dinner menu and wine list is left in your room, so that you can consult it at leisure, give your orders by late afternoon, and relax before dinner with an aperitif, confident that there will be no unecessary delays. The dining room is somewhat formal and hushed, but the food is highly praised and often features such local delicacies as Lismore oysters, smoked salmon or venison.

Portree, Isle of Skye

Portree, Isle of Skye, IV51 9EU

Tel (01478) 612217
Fax (01478) 613517
e-mail info@viewfieldhouse.com
website www.viewfieldhouse.com

Nearby Trotternish peninsula.
Location on outskirts of town, 10 minutes walk S of centre; from A87 towards Broadford, turn right just after national garage on left; with ample car parking
Food breakfast, packed lunch, dinner
Price ££
Rooms 11 double and twin, 10 with bath; all rooms have phone, radio, hairdryer **Facilities** sitting room, dining room, TV room, washer and tumble drier for guests
Credit cards MC, V **Children** welcome **Disabled** one specially adapted room on ground floor **Pets** accepted, but not in public rooms
Closed mid-Oct to mid-Apr
Proprietors Hugh Macdonald

Viewfield House

Country guesthouse

'It won't suit everyone,' writes our reporter about Viewfield House, 'but for those seeking an age gone by, the experience would be memorable.'

This is an imposing Victorian country mansion, which, as the name suggests, has some fine views from its elevated position. The need for costly repairs to the roof prompted Evelyn Macdonald, Hugh's grandmother, to open Viewfield House to guests. The delight of it is that the distinctive character of the house was preserved; and though you will not lack for comfort or service, a stay here is likely to be a novel experience. The house is full of colonial memorabilia: stuffed animals, and birds; priceless museum relics; and a magnificent collection of oil paintings and prints.

The rooms are original, right down to the wallpaper in one instance (though all but one now have *en suite* bathrooms in the former dressing-rooms); there is a classic Victorian parlour and a grand dining room with a huge oak table, which seats up to 12 people. Guests are entertained house-party style, although separate tables can be used if they prefer not to dine communally – we admire this flexibility. Dinner can be taken each evening between 7.30 and 9pm. Breakfast features a wide selection of cooked items including Mallaig kippers, smoked haddock and porridge. Reports welcome.

Scarista, Isle of Harris HS3 3HX

Tel (01859) 550238
e-mail timandpatricia@scarista-house.com
website www.scaristahouse.com

Nearby beaches; golf; boat trips.
Location 15 miles (24 km) SW of Tarbert on A859, over-looking sea; in 2-acre garden, with ample private car parking
Food breakfast, packed/snack lunch, dinner
Price ££££
Rooms 6; 2 double, 1 twin, 3 suites in Glebe House, all with bath; all rooms have phone, hairdryer
Facilities library, 2 sitting rooms, dining room
Credit cards MC, V
Children welcome
Disabled no special facilities
Pets by arrangement
Closed Christmas, Jan
Proprietors Tim and Patricia Martin

Scarista House

Island guesthouse

Harris has little in the way of hotels, but Scarista would stand out even among the country houses of the Cotswolds.

The converted Georgian manse stands alone on a windswept slope overlooking a wide stretch of tidal sands on the island's western shore. The decoration is elegant and quite formal, with many antiques, but the atmosphere is relaxed and, by the open peat fires, conversation replaces television. The bedrooms, all with private bathrooms, have selected teas and fresh coffee, as well as home-made biscuits. Three of the bed-rooms are in the main house, with three refurbished suites available in The Glebe building, just behind the house.

Tim and Patricia Martin continue to maintain a high standard. They aim to be welcoming and efficient, but never intru-sive, and to preserve that precious private home atmosphere.

One of Scarista's greatest attractions, par-ticularly rewarding after a long walk over the sands, is the meals. The imaginatively prepared fresh local and garden produce and an impressive wine list ensure a memo-rable dinner in the candle-lit dining room.

Sleat, Isle of Skye IV43 8QY

Tel (01471) 833214
Fax (01471) 833277
e-mail reservations@kinloch-lodge.co.uk
website www.kinloch-lodge.co.uk

Nearby Clan Donald Centre.
Location in 60-acre grounds, 6 miles (9.5 km) S of Broadford, one mile (1.5 km) off A851; ample car parking
Food breakfast, lunch, dinner, afternoon tea
Price ££
Rooms 14 double, all with bath; all rooms have TV/DVD player, radio, hairdryer
Facilities 3 sitting rooms, bar, dining room, spa, wi-fi; fishing
Credit cards AE, MC, V
Children accepted **Disabled** access reasonable – one ground-floor bedroom **Pets** accepted by arrangement but not in public rooms
Closed Christmas
Proprietors Lord & Lady Macdonald

Kinloch Lodge

Country hotel

This white-painted stone house, in an isolated position with uninterupted sea views, at the southern extremity of the Isle of Skye, now known as the North House, was built as a farmhouse around 1700 and later became a shooting lodge. But it escaped the baronial treatment handed out to many such houses – 'thank goodness,' says Lady Macdonald, whose style is modern interior-designer rather than dark panelling and tartan. It has that easy-going private-house air. The guests' sitting rooms are comfortably done out in stylishly muted colours; there are open fires, honesty bar and family oil paintings grace the walls. The dining room is more formal, with sparkling crystal and silver on the tables.

Bedrooms used to be rather small, but have recently been reconfigured to give more space, and all now have en-suites, some with roll-top baths. The South House has accommodation for the Macdonalds and five more double rooms for guests. This building is quite remarkable as it looks, both inside and out, as old as its 18th century neighbour, and includes a magnificent stone spiral staircase, as wells as a wealth of books, portraits and *objets d'art.*

The food, under Marcello Tully, at Kinloch Lodge is renowned – Lady Macdonald has written cookery books and gives cookery demonstrations.

Sleat, Isle of Skye

Sleat, Isle of Skye IV44 8RE

Tel 01471 820200
e-mail info@skyehotel.co.uk
website www.skyehotel.co.uk

Nearby Knock Castle ruin, coast, mountains, wildlife, bird-watching, villages, ferry to mainland
Location just outside Ferrindonald on the A851, accessible by seaplane, ferry, train, bus and air, parking available.
Food breakfast, lunch, dinner; full and half board available, lunch not included in price.
Price ££-£££
Rooms 9 double and twin, all have bath/shower, all have TV and hospitality tray
Facilities sitting room, restaurant, gardens, yacht trips
Credit cards MC, V
Children accepted over 5
Disabled no special facilities
Pets not accepted
Closed never
Proprietors Captain Ken Gunn and Anne Gracie

Toravaig House

Country house

Toravaig House is an unimposing, plain white building nestled in Skye's Sleat peninsula. The smooth lines, silky fabrics and twinkling lights inside are a sharp contrast to what's out: craggy cliffs, an often boiling sea and the said-to-be-haunted ruin of Knock Castle.

Some of the rooms are considerably smaller than others, and not all face the sea, but each is named after a Hebridean island and individually designed. Huge, chequered headboards, spotty cushions and bold colours are found throughout, as are satellite TV and wi-fi: the decoration here is thoroughly and unexpectedly modern. That said, one room does feature a magnificent wooden sleigh-bed and the sitting room, warmed by an open log fire, is filled with squishy orange sofas.

One of the main draws of Toravaig is undoubtedly the food. Chef Joel Kirkby's menus are strictly seasonal and ingredients are locally sourced – langoustines and lobsters from local waters and home-grown leaves and herbs. The restaurant itself – The Islay – benefits from great views over the gardens and mountains beyond.

Service is described as extremely warm and welcoming: owners Captain Ken Gunn and Anne Gracie 'make the place seem like home'.

Loch Lochy, by Spean Bridge, Inverness-shire PH34 4EA

Tel (01397) 712685
Fax (01397) 712696
e-mail info@corriegour-lodge-hotel.com **website** www.corriegour-lodge-hotel.com

Nearby Cawdor Castle; Urquhart Castle; Loch Ness; Glencoe.
Location on road to Skye, between Spean Bridge and Invergarry, in own grounds, 17 miles (27 km) N of Fort William on A82; ample car parking
Food breakfast, dinner
Price £££ **Rooms** 9; 7 double and twin, 2 single, all with bath/shower; all rooms have TV, hairdryer on request **Facilities** sitting room, bar, dining room; terrace, private beach, jetty, fishing, waterfall
Credit cards AE, DC, MC, V
Children accepted over 8
Disabled access possible
Pets not accepted
Closed Dec and Jan, weekdays Feb and Nov, open New Year
Proprietors Ian and Christian Drew

Corriegour Lodge

Lochside hotel

A former Victorian hunting lodge commanding outstanding views over Loch Lochy and set in six acres of mature woodland and garden within the 'Great Glen'. With its own attractive private beach and jetty on the loch, as well as a fishing boat and the services of a private fishing school at its disposal, this is an obvious choice for keen anglers, as well walkers and climbers, pony trekkers and sailors.

When guests arrive they are greeted by Christian Drew, whose friendliness and enthusiasm for the hotel she runs with her son, Ian, are infectious. The decoration throughout the rest of the hotel is cosy and pleasant, with a log fire in the sitting room and magical views over the loch from the large picture windows in the restaurant. Many of the comfortable bedrooms have the same view.

Food is an important element here, using local meat, fish and game. For pudding you could have cloutie dumpling with rum custard.The staff are genuinely friendly and willing to help. Recent guests have complained of weak showers and patchy wireless internet, but these are to be expected in old lodges and are more than made up for by the views and food.

Strontian, Argyll

Strontian, Argyll PH36 4HY

Tel (01967) 402257
Fax (01967) 402041
e-mail enquiries@kilcamblodge.com
website www.kilcamblodge.com

Nearby ferry to Isle of Mull and Skye; Castle Tioram; Glencoe.
Location Corran ferry to Ardgour from the A82 near Ballachulish, then follow A861 to Strontian; in 19 acres with ample car parking
Food breakfast, light lunch, dinner
Price £££
Rooms 10 double and suites, all with bath; all rooms have TV, hairdryer, phone **Facilities** 2 sitting rooms, bar, restaurant, brasserie, garden, private beach, fishing, mountain bikes
Credit cards MC, V
Children not under 10
Disabled no special facilities
Closed Jan
Pets accepted by arrangement, £5 per night
Proprietors David and Sally Fox

Kilcamb Lodge

Lochside hotel

There is a sense of adventure in travelling to a hotel by ferry, particularly when it then involves a ten-mile journey, first alongside a loch and then over a pass through a steep-sided glen. Drop down through the glen, pass through the small village of Strontian, and there, in a romantic setting on the shores of Loch Sunart, is Kilcamb Lodge.

Originally built in the early 18thC, with Victorian additions, Kilcamb is a beautifully restored country house with ten bedrooms, some with a loch view. Set amidst lawns and woodland, filled in spring with the colours of rhododendrons, azaleas and many wild flowers, it is a romantic and calming bolthole, the perfect choice for nature lovers: sea otters, seals, pine martens, red and roe deer and golden eagles can all be seen.

The ground floor public rooms are pleasantly furnished with light and attractive pastel fabrics. There is a wonderful Victorian wrought-iron staircase and a large stained glass window. All the bedrooms are individually decorated and have triple-lined curtains (it stays light very late in summer). Chef Gary Phillips prepares fresh Scottish food using locally-sourced fish, shellfish and meat from the Ardnamurchan Peninsula.

Tobermory, Isle of Mull

Tobermory, Isle of Mull, Argyll
PA75 6QE

Tel 01688 302321
e-mail
enquiries@glengormcastle.co.uk
website www.glengormcastle.co.uk

Nearby Tobermory, Calgary, Dervaig.
Location on coast, easy to find with satnav
Food breakfast, lunch can be purchased in hotel's coffee shop
Price £££-££££
Rooms 5; 4 doubles, 1 double/twin, all have bath/shower
Facilities dining room, library with complimentary whisky, seating in hall area
Credit cards MC, V
Children welcome
Disabled no special facilities
Closed mid-Dec to beginning Feb
Pets accepted
Proprietors Marjorie and Tom Nelson

Glengorm Castle

Country house guesthouse

At the northernmost tip of Mull, Glengorm castle – really a grandiose Victorian country house – boldly surveys the Sound of Mull, Ardnamurchan Peninsula and, vivid at sunset in the far distance, the Outer Hebrides. It stands on a 5,000-acre estate that is yours to roam. "Everything," says Tom Nelson, "that Mull is noted for, from white-tailed eagles to whales, can be seen at Glengorm."

There are five guest bedrooms occupying the principal bedrooms of the house: spacious (two are huge) and charming, with characterful bathrooms and pretty wallpapers. These rooms are a delight, especially with the lack of televisions and telephones.

This is a family affair: Tom, Marjorie and their three children live in one wing; Tom's mother lives in the other. There's a lofty hall and sitting room (well-worn sofas, board games, big fire). You can also relax in the library, where whisky is complimentary and the fire can be lit if you wish.

Dinner isn't served at Glengorm, but the Macdonald Arms Hotel in Tobermory (four miles away) is well worth a trip. In the morning, enjoy the excellent and hearty breakfast in front of those stunning views. We thought that the prices were rather high, but the scenery, breakfast and family-feel made them worthwhile.

Aboyne, Aberdeenshire

Struan Hall
Guesthouse

Looking at the solid mass of grey stone that is Struan Hall, we could hardly believe that its original site was five miles away. The house dates back to the 1800s, but in 1904 it was dismantled, moved stone-by-stone, and rebuilt here. Set in two acres of grounds, with lawns and an Indian-style pavilion, a rockery and carp pool, Struan Hall makes a restful, comfortable base.

Tartan carpets harmonize with the pine staircase, while the dining room has a massive Victorian sideboard. Tiffany-style lamps light the hall.

Upstairs, the Scottish theme continues. The bedrooms are named after castles and have pine bedheads carved with Scottish motifs. There were new proprietors as we went to press, and reports are welcome.

Ballater Road, Aboyne,
Aberdeenshire AB34 5HY

Tel 01339 885599
e-mail info@struanhall.co.uk
website www.struanhall.co.uk
Food breakfast
Price £
Closed never
Proprietors George and Judith Anderson

Colbost, Isle of Skye

Three Chimneys
Seaside restaurant-with-rooms

For 30 years chef Shirley Spear and her husband Eddie have run Three Chimneys as an award-winning seafood restaurant in an idyllic seaside location in the north-west corner of Skye. The six suites created in a new building called the House Over-By, are luxurious – if understated – rooms designed to blend with the seascape and the changing light. Each contemporary, spacious and high-ceilinged room has direct access to the beach; bathrooms are heavenly. Breakfast is served in a room overlooking the seashore and the islands in Loch Dunvegan.

As you would expect, the menu is a mainly fishy one, but Highland beef, lamb and game are also a feature, and the puddings are just as good.

Colbost, Dunvegan, Isle of Skye
IV55 8ZT

Tel (01470) 511258 **Fax** (01470) 511358 **e-mail** eatandstay@three-chimneys.co.uk **website** www.three-chimneys.co.uk
Food breakfast, lunch, dinner
Closed 1st Dec – late Jan
Proprietors Shirley and Eddie Spear

Comrie, Perthshire

The Royal Hotel

Town hotel

From the moment you step inside The Royal Hotel, it feels right. Situated in the centre of this attractive little Highland town, and dating from 1765, it began life as a coaching inn, and earned its grand title after a visit by Queen Victoria, accompanied by her servant, John Brown.

The atmosphere is homely, yet at the same time elegant and stylish, with log fires in the public rooms as well as squashy sofas, antiques and oil paintings. The Lounge Bar is for informal dining, as well as the main restaurant.

Recent visitors enthused about the freshness of their rooms. All have been individually furnished with an eye for detail and design. It is managed by hands-on couple Jerry and Teresa Milsom.

Melville Square, Comrie, Perthshire PH6 2DN

Tel (01764) 679200
Fax (01764) 679219
e-mail reception@royalhotel.co.uk
website www.royalhotel.co.uk
Food breakfast, lunch, dinner; room service **Price** £££ **Closed** Christmas Day and Boxing Day **Managers** Jeremy and Teresa Milsom

Connel, Argyll

Ards House

Seaside hotel

This pretty Victorian villa has uninterrupted views westward over the Firth of Lorn to the Morvern Hills. Sunsets are truly spectacular.

The house itself tends to ramble, as additions have been made over the years to the original cottage. The most recent owner, Margaret Kennedy, has retained the snug atmosphere, but no longer serves dinner. Breakfasts are especially generous. You could choose not only the usual fresh fruit salad, muesli and yoghurt but also kippers, smoked salmon and scrambled eggs, pancakes and bacon with maple syrup, haggis on toast (with whisky if you want).

Special terms are available for short breaks.

Connel, by Oban, Argyll PA37 1PT

Tel (01631) 710255
e-mail info@ardshouse.com
website www.ardshouse.com
Food breakfast
Price £
Closed Christmas and New Year
Proprietor Margaret Kennedy

Muir of Ord, Ross-shire

The Dower House

Farmhouse hotel

This former Dower House of a baronial home, which burnt down in the 1950s, was converted from thatched farmhouse to charming residence in the Georgian cottage ornée style in about 1800. It became a hotel in 1989. Something of an oasis in the rugged landscape between the rivers Beauly and Conon, it is set in beautifully-maintained gardens and grounds.

The elegant, red-walled dining room makes a stunning setting for evening meals, and Robyn's self-taught cooking does not disappoint. The sitting room has comfortable chairs, flowery fabrics and an open fire.

The five bedrooms vary in size and furnishings and are fairly simple. The largest is the most luxurious, with an enormous bed and spacious bathroom.

Highfield, Muir of Ord, Ross-shire
1V6 7XN

Tel (01463)870090
Fax (01463)870090
e-mail info@thedowerhouse.co.uk
website www.thedowerhouse.co.uk
Food breakfast, dinner
Price £££ **Closed** up to a month, off-season **Proprietors** Robyn and Mena Aitchison

Strachur, Argyll

Creggans Inn

Lochside hotel

Overlooking Loch Fyne, this former hunting lodge of the 3,000-acre Strachur Estate was first opened as an inn more than 40 years ago. The MacLellan family are still in charge, and have refurbished the place, starting with the sitting and dining rooms.

The food here is excellent: drawing heavily on local products such as scallops and langoustines from Loch Fyne, it is light, inventive and delicious. The wine list is unusually good.

A major natural advantage is the position of the inn. The views over Loch Fyne and across the Mull of Kintyre to the Western Isles are breathtaking. Many parts of the Strachur Estate, including the private flower garden, are open to guests.

Strachur, Argyll PA27 8BX

Tel (01369) 860279
Fax (01369) 860637
website www.creggans-inn.co.uk
Food breakfast, lunch, dinner
Price ££
Closed never
Proprietors The MacLellan family

Tarbert, Isle of Harris

Hotel Hebrides

Town hotel

A functional, modern hotel aimed at business travellers as well as tourists – and perhaps formulaic despite describing itself as a boutique hotel. Still, it's a useful address because it's 30 seconds from the ferry pier in Tarbert on the island of Harris where until now we've not found anywhere to recommend – in fact as we went to press there was nothing that reached this standard anywhere in the Outer Hebrides. Also, unusually, it has eight single rooms where you can stay for as little as £50 including breakfast. Some of the bedroom decorations are jarring, others plainer and more successful; the staff wear low-key uniforms, but it's owner-managed and its heart is in the right place.

Pier Road, Tarbert, Isle of Harris
HS3 3DG

Tel 01859 502364
Fax 01859 502578
email stay@hotel-hebrides.com
website www.hotel-hebrides.com
Food breakfast, lunch, dinner
Price ££-£££
Closed never **Proprietors** Angus and Chirsty Macleod

Thurso, Caithness

Forss House Hotel

Country house

Sabine and Ian Richards bought this mellow country house, built 1810, in 2004. They have redecorated in a way that makes it look unchanged, though it is in fact new and fresh.

You'll find tartan carpeting, a malt whisky bar, a sunny conservatory for breakfast and a shallow Georgian staircase leading up to the light and spacious first-floor bedrooms. The food is highly rated and we thought it lived up to its reputation.

There's excellent salmon fishing at hand along the Forss, which flows in an arc around the hotel. With open, easy casting, it's well suited to beginners and children as well as the more experienced. In spring and summer the banks – thick with wild flowers – make pretty walking.

Forss, Near Thurso, Caithness
KW14 7XY

Tel 01847 861201
email relax@forsshousehotel.co.uk
website www.forsscountryhouse.co.uk
Food breakfast, lunch, dinner
Price £££ **Closed** 23rd Dec – 5th Jan **Proprietors** Ian and Sabine Richards

Urquhart, Morayshire

Meft Road, Urquhart by Elgin IV30 8NH

Tel 01343 843063
mobile 0774 8867825
e-mail info@oldchurch.eu
website www.oldchurch.eu
Food breakfast, dinner
Price £ **Closed** Nov-Apr
Proprietors Andreas Peter and Kyzysztof Plewicki

The Old Church of Urquhart **Village B&B**

A reader recommends this unusual, budget B&B – as we went to press two people can stay for as little as £66 including breakfast. Owners Andreas and Krzysztof have their own rooms in the converted church, and they are a presence, but you can feel private in the guest sitting room and dining room (dinner: £15). Bedroom decoration and furnishings are homespun and standardised. They also use the name 'B&B Parrandier'. Reports welcome.

Walls, Shetland Islands

Walls, Shetland Islands, ZE2 9PD

Tel (01595) 809307
e-mail info@burrastowhouse.co.uk
website www.burrastowhouse.co.uk
Food breakfast, light/packed lunch, dinner
Price ££
Closed Oct to Mar
Proprietor Pierre Dupont

Burrastow House
Seafront guesthouse

On the remote west side of Shetland, at the end of the single track road, on a rocky promontory overlooking Vaila Sound and the Island of Vaila, stands this calm, solid 18thC stone house. It has been run for the last nine years with enthusiasm by Pierre Dupont.

The four first-floor bedrooms in the main house are the ones to go for if you can. They are all large, one with a second bedroom which is perfect for children, and all have views. Some have splendid beds: a four-poster in one and a half-tester, draped in blue silk, in another. In the public rooms there are peat fires, books, an eclectic mix of furnishings and wonderful views from the windows. Pierre serves his natural, homely cooking in the cosy dining room.

Ireland area introduction

With a mild climate and a famously leisured way of life, Ireland (also described in tourist publications as the Emerald Isle) is a place of contrasts and changing light, of mountains, lakes and rivers, lush pastures, bog and wild moorland. There are 2,000 miles of coastline with small rocky coves, long sandy beaches and some of the highest cliffs in Europe. In the most remote parts of the country you can drive for miles without seeing anything but sheep. Among the most spectacular features are the golden beaches of Counties Wicklow and Wexford in the east, and the romantic lakes of County Sligo in the west. But if you want bright lights, music and good food, Ireland has any number of pubs that nightly celebrate the traditional Irish love of music and conversation. Northern Ireland, for a long time shunned by visitors because of the troubles, has been developing into a modestly popular destination.

Below are some useful back-up places to try if our main selections are fully booked:

Cromleach Lodge
Country house hotel, Castlebaldwin Tel 07191 65155 www.cromleach.com
Gorgeous views and high standards.

The Cliff Townhouse
Restaurant-with-rooms, Dublin Tel 01 638 3939 www.theclifftownhouse.com
Airy, stylish restautant-with-rooms in central Dublin.

Shores Country House
Bed-and-breakfast, Castlegregory Tel 066 7139196 www.shorescountryhouse.com
On Brandon Bay.

Rosturk Woods
Self-catering houses, Mulranny Tel 098 36264 www.rosturk-woods.com
Secluded woodland houses near Clew Bay.

College Hill, Armagh, BT61 9DF

Tel (028) 3752 4923
Fax (028) 3752 4923
e-mail
jill_armstrong@rocketmail.com

Nearby Armagh Planetarium; Saint Patrick's Cathedral, museums.
Location half a mile (0.8 km) from the town centre; on A3 towards Craigavon turn left at stone gate lodge; parking
Food breakfast, lunch, dinner
Price
Rooms 3; 1 four-poster with bath, 1 twin with bath, 1 single with private bath **Facilities** gardens, tennis court, boules **Credit cards** none
Children welcome **Disabled** not suitable **Pets** with advance warning
Closed Christmas and New Year
Proprietor Jill and Edward Armstrong

Deans Hill

City hotel

There have been Armstrongs in Deans Hill, a lovely Georgian house in the ecclesiastical city of Armagh since 1870. It was built for the Cathedral's dean in 1760 and, although the setting is rural, is only a ten minute walk from the historical centre of Armagh. A stone gatehouse on the road draws visitors up the long, gently curving driveway leading through green, daffodil-strewn fields, with mature trees and a large cedar of Lebanon in the rambling garden. Inside, the welcoming, easy-going house attractively wears its patina of age, with what our reporter (most enthusiastically) describes as gorgeous antique furniture, paintings and prints. Some of the tall, sash windows still carry their original glass, there are long white shutters and old floorboards covered with slightly worn carpets. Rugs are thrown over the easy chairs in the comfortable, relaxed sitting room and the huge bedrooms are wonderfully old-fashioned and elegant. One has a single brass bedstead, and plenty of pictures hung, slightly crookedly, on the walls; another has dusky pink curtains and a wallpaper of climbing roses. The bathrooms, again, are old-fashioned, with pretty papers, prints and washstands. For breakfast, there is home-made jam and fresh eggs from the Armstrong farm.

Dungannon, Co Tyrone

Grange Road, Dungannon, Co Tyrone BT71 7EJ

Tel (028) 87784212
Fax (028) 87784313
e-mail stay@grangelodgecountry-house.com
website www.grangelodgecountry-house.com

Nearby Tyrone; Ulster American Folk Park
Location in countryside 3 miles (5 km) S of Dungannon off the A 29 to Armagh; parking available
Food breakfast, dinner
Price ££
Rooms 5; 4 doubles, 1 twin; 1 with bath, 1 with hip-bath, 3 with shower; all with phone, TV, hairdryer, tea/coffee making facilities
Facilities sitting rooms; gardens
Credit cards MC, V
Children over 12
Disabled not possible
Pets welcome outside
Closed 20 Dec to 1 Feb
Proprietors Norah and Ralph Brown

Grange Lodge

Country house

Our reporter was enchanted by the setting – on a little hill in large and lovely gardens – of this rambling, ivy clad, Georgian house with later additions. But it is the Grange Lodge table that has won distinction and found it so many friends. Norah Brown, who is self-taught, has several awards for her outstandingly good cooking and she and her husband, Ralph, are relaxed, easy-going, welcoming hosts. Much of the fruit, vegetables and herbs she uses are homegrown and sometimes a second dining room is opened up to outside groups looking for her special talent and dishes from her "best friend", the Aga. Admirers praise the ageless quality of her food and her sure touch; she says people have just forgotten what real home cooking is. Ralph has the happy task of bringing breakfast out from the kitchen: try Mrs Brown's porridge with brown sugar, cream and Bushmills whiskey, rhubarb compote, soda bread and full Ulster grill with potato cake. The sitting room – there's a 'den' with TV, too – is immaculate, in elegant dark colours; most surfaces are crammed with ornaments, family photos, pewter and plates. Upstairs, ivy pushes at the window panes of the bedrooms. Some of Mrs Brown's biscuits are always to be found on the hospitality tray.

Magheralin, Co Armagh

58 Newforge Road, Magheralin, Craigavon, Co Armagh BT 67 0QL

Tel (028) 9261 1255
e-mail enquiries@newforgehouse.com
website www.newforgehouse.com

Nearby Belfast (25 km); Mountains of Mourne (50 km).
Location clearly signposted, just off A3, through Magheralin, 1st left onto Newforge Road, with ample private car parking
Food breakfast, dinner
Price £££
Rooms 6 doubles with bath/shower; all rooms have phone, TV, DVD player, hairdryer, wi-fi
Facilities drawing room, dining room; large garden
Credit cards MC, V
Children welcome
Disabled dining room accessible
Pets not accepted
Closed 3 weeks over Christmans and New Year
Proprietors John and Louise Mathers

Newforge House

Country guesthouse

For Northern Ireland, this is about as sophisticated as a guesthouse gets, in fact it's almost a small hotel. Instead of sharing the owner's home, you have the run of it, not least the graceful drawing room. John and Louise Mathers, the young owners, live in one outbuilding, while John's father has another. Six generations of Mathers (a linen family) have lived here; the latest bowed to the fact that it was too big and converted it to a guesthouse, restoring it in the process. The Georgian interior has been respected, but the walls have that clean, smooth modern finish and there's an optimistic, airy atmosphere – windows are tall. The dining room has separate tables, so no communal dining. Another bonus: John is a trained chef, with a professionally fitted kitchen and the food is good: three courses (£40) with two choices at each course, ingredients fresh each day. There's a license, and a wine list. Give a day's notice for dinner.

Even the smallest of the six bedrooms, named after family members, is roomy, and all are individually decorated in the best of taste. In fact, they're as smart as many we've seen in chic city hotels, and the spacious bathrooms gleam.

You're guaranteed a peaceful night here since the house stands well back from a quiet road just outside Newforge.

Bushmills, Co Antrim

9 Dunluce Road, Bushmills, Co Antrim BT57 8QG

Tel (028) 2073 3000
Fax (028) 2073 2048
e-mail mail@bushmillsinn.com
website www.bushmillsinn.com
Food breakfast, lunch, dinner
Price ££
Closed never
Proprietors Alan Dunlop

The Bushmills Inn

Converted coaching inn

Chickens once lived on the first floor when this charming little inn was going through hard times. All that changed in 1987 when the present owners spotted the potential of the building. The oldest part – now the restaurant – dates back to the 17th century. Almost the first thing to be seen, once inside, is a glowing fire, which is always lit. There's a warren of ground-floor rooms, with a roaring fires and old flagstones; the Victorian-style bar has gas lighting, leather chairs and dark wood panelling. The older bedrooms have been converted into a cinema and conference room; newer ones in the Mill House extension – with river views – are larger, with wood panelling, rough white walls and their own sitting area.

Downpatrick, Co Down

Tyrella House. Downpatrick Co Down

Tel (028) 4485 1422 **e-mail** tyrella.corbett@virgin.net **website** www.hidden-ireland.com/tyrella **Food** breakfast; dinner on request, a day's notice needed. **Price** £ **Closed** Nov-1 Mar, parties of 3 couples together welcome at any time **Proprietor** David Corbett

Tyrella House

Country house bed-and-breakfast

Staying at Tyrella as David Corbett's guest is to experience in a genuine way the vanishing lifestyle of the Northern Irish landed gentry. It's a fine country house, dating from the 18th century, down a longish drive, not another building in sight. The nicely proportioned rooms contain the accumulated brown antique furniture and possessions of four generations of Corbetts. Don't expect immaculate paintwork or a trim drive; do expect a relaxed welcome, a large bedroom, a comfortable bed and the feeling of being in a home. The food gets some pleasant compliments in the visitors' book. The house still stands in some 300 acres of its own, now used for equestrian events (David is a horseman) and has its own private beach, which guests can use.

Aghadoe, Co Kerry

Aghadoe, Lakes of Killarney,
Co Kerry

Tel (064) 31711
Fax (064) 31811
e-mail charming@indigo.ie
website www.killeenhousehotel.com

Nearby Killarney, 4 miles (6 km); Muckross House; Gap of Dunloe.
Location in countryside, 4 miles (6 km) from Killarney; car parking
Food breakfast, dinner
Prices €€-€€€
Rooms 23; 8 championship, 15 standard; 8 with king-size double and single; 2 double, 5 twin, 2 single, 6 double and single; 22 with bath, 1 with shower; all rooms have phone, TV, radio, hairdryer
Facilities bar, sitting room; garden, terrace, tennis court
Credit cards AE, DC, MC,V
Children welcome if well-behaved
Disabled not possible
Pets welcome
Closed 1 Nov to 1 Apr
Proprietors Michael and Geraldine Rosney

Killeen House Hotel

Country hotel

We had to visit a hotel with 'charming' as its e-mail address. And there it was: a charming small hotel, a rectory built in 1838 and given a bright new white front and architectural twiddly bits painted in red by Michael and Geraldine Rosney, who took it over in 1992. Michael is a jolly, amusing – and kind – person who used to manage the Great Southern Hotel in Killarney. He has created a warm, cosy, entertaining and lively little place, where he spoils his golfing clients and indulges their every whim. He sees them off in the morning and waits for their return in the evening, like an anxious parent. Then he is to be found in The Pub, 'possibly the only place in the universe that accepts golf balls as legal tender', where he dispenses Guinness and sympathy. Nothing is too much trouble for him: he puts phone messages in envelopes and distributes them himself. All this activity provides loads of fun for everyone, especially Michael, and you don't have to be a golfer to benefit from his generous spirit. Comfortable, spacious bedrooms are decorated in checks and plaids; there's a special one with a spa bath that he gives to regular guests as a 'thank you' for coming back again and again. Good showers; excellent food at Rozzers restaurant, one of the most popular in the Kerry area, with chef Paul O'Gorman at the helm.

Ardara, Co Donegal

Tel 074 9541546
website www.thegreengate.eu

Nearby Ardara (for tweed); Glenveagh National Park.
Location 1 mile (1.6 km) from Ardara, up a hill; with car parking
Food breakfast
Price
Rooms 4; 2 double, 2 triple; all with bath
Facilities garden, terrace
Credit cards not accepted
Children welcome
Disabled access possible
Pets not accepted
Closed never
Proprietor Paul Chatenoud

The Green Gate

Cottage bed-and-breakfast

This little place, a tiny farmhouse with stone outbuildings, owned and converted by a Frenchman who came to Donegal 15 years ago to write about "life, love and death", is bursting with charm. The book never got finished, but Paul Chatenoud, who left behind his musical bookshop and flat in Paris for a wilder existence on the top of a hill overlooking the Atlantic, has created what must be the most beautiful small B&B in Ireland. So much love and care has gone into this enterprise; he's done most of it with his own hands, from thatching the cottage roof to plumbing and whitewashing the four guest rooms. Simple they may be, but he thinks of everything: hot water bottles, a map in each room, and a bath in which you can rest your head back and gaze out of the window at the sky and the sea. His garden is filled with primroses, fuchsia and small birds, and he has planted hundreds, if not thousands, of orange montbretia up the lane. Breakfast is taken *chez lui*; in his own cosy kitchen he serves coffee/tea, cornflakes, bacon, eggs, sausage, toast and 22 types of home-made jam and marmalade – any time before 2 pm. And you get his delightful company. An English composer came for a night and was still there a week later. 'A treasure' says an entry in the visitor's book.

Ballylickey, Co Cork

Ballylickey, Batry Bay, Co Cork

Tel (027) 50071
Fax (027) 50124
email ballymh@eircom **website** www.ballylickeymanorhouse.com

Nearby Ring of Kerry; Killarney; Bantry.
Location in gardens and grounds, on N17 between Bantry and Glengariff; car parking available
Food breakfast
Price ?
Rooms 11; 7 suites, 4 double; all with bath and shower, phone, TV, hairdryer
Facilities 3 sitting rooms, restaurant; garden, terraces, swimming pool **Credit cards** AE, DC, MC, V
Children welcome **Disabled** poolside cottage **Pets** not accepted
Closed end Oct to beginning Apr
Proprietor Paco Graves

Ballylickey Manor House **Country guesthouse**

This Former Shooting Lodge, with romantic view of the sea from the front door, is a former grande dame of the Irish country house hotel scene – the first to be accepted by the Relais and Chateaux group in 1967. So it has all the requisite comfort and style – and some extra very French touches added by Christiane Graves' talent with colours, fabrics and antiques. As a private family house, it was visited many times by the writer and poet, Robert Graves, uncle of owner George Graves, whose mother, Kitty, laid out the lovely gardens. Some rooms are in the main house; one has doors opening on to a little sheltered patio with table and chairs for sitting out; or you may choose simply to let in the sound of birdsong and the wonderful damp smell of the plants and foliage. You are even closer to nature in the blue-grey wooden cottages in the trees and shrubs by the swimming-pool. With the sound of French staff chattering away in the kitchen of the poolside Le Rendez-Vous restaurant – covered in May with pink clematis – it is not hard to imagine oneself in a Relais and Chateaux in the South of France. Full marks should go to Mr Graves for his decision – possibly an unpopular one with some guests – not to allow parking in front of the house, which wrecks the sea view, by placing obstacles on the gravel driveway.

Ballymacarbry, Co Waterford

Glenanore, Ballymacarbry, Co Waterford

Tel (052) 6136134
Fax (052) 6136540
e-mail hanorascottage@eircom.net
website www.hanorascottage.com

Nearby Dungarvan, 18 miles (29 km); Clonmel, 15 miles (24 km); Blackwater Valley.
Location in Nire Valley, 4 miles (6 km) out of Ballymacarbry; parking available
Food breakfast, packed lunch, dinner
Price
Rooms 10; all double/twin; all with Jacuzzi; all rooms with phone, TV, hairdryer; tea/coffee making facilities
Facilities garden, terrace, spa tub
Credit cards MC, V **Children** not accepted **Disabled** not possible **Pets** not accepted **Closed** Christmas week **Proprietors** Wall family

Hanora's Cottage

Riverside guesthouse

Changes have taken place since our last edition at award-winning Hanora's Cottage, built by a little bridge over the river in the beautiful Nire Valley for late owner Seamus Wall's great-grandmother. With the village school and church next door, the picturesque group of buildings and their setting made our inspector think of somewhere in the Pyrenees. The guest-house is a favourite with walkers, who come for the Comeragh Mountains and nearby forests and lakes. Mary Wall puts comfort high on her list and pampers her guests. She has added five new rooms, each with a spa tub, where guests may rest aching limbs and emerge refreshed for a candle-lit dinner in the new dining room. Food is prepared by the Walls' talented Ballymaloe-trained son, Eoin, and his wife Judith. In the new extension, brilliantly designed to fit with the rest of the building, Mary has put in a drying and boot room. Bedrooms are large, calm and peaceful, with thick carpets, and most have spa baths (superiors have double Jacuzzis). There are books by the beds, some Tiffany lamps, and quality bedlinen. The breakfast room looks out on to the little stone bridge and Seamus's renowned bread recipes are still being used. Plenty of fruit and freshly-squeezed juices, too. Ask for a front room if you want to fall asleep to the sound of the river.

Ballymote, Co Sligo

Ballymote, Co Sligo

Tel (07191) 83329
e-mail stay@templehouse.ie
website www.templehouse.ie

Nearby Sligo, 12 miles (19 km); Yeats Country; Lissadell House; Carrowkeel megalithic passage tombs.
Location on 1,000-acre estate, 4 miles (6 km) from Ballymote; parking available
Food breakfast, dinner
Price €
Rooms 6; 3 double, 2 twin, 1 family room; 2 with bath, 3 with shower; all rooms have hairdryer
Facilities garden, woodland, farm, lake fishing, boating
Credit cards MC, V
Children welcome, high tea in kitchen for under-5s
Disabled access difficult **Pets** dogs on leads (sheep); sleep in car **Closed** 15 Nov to 1 Apr **Proprietors** Roderick and Helena Perceval

Temple House

Country house

Is this a dream? It begins as you enter the gates of what is a gentle, gracious world of its own. In parkland filled with fat sheep, this is a whopper of a Georgian mansion, the home of the Percevals since 1665. Much of what you see was refurbished in 1864; electricity was not put in until 1962. To be overcome by awe and wonder would be easy were it not for the charm and kindness of Roderick and Helena Perceval together with their children and four dogs. Temple House is very much a home, and they want it to be enjoyed.

Bedrooms, with marble fireplaces and much of their original Victorian furniture, seem to be the size of football pitches – one is called the 'half-acre'. All the bedrooms and bathrooms have been revamped since 2005, when Roderick and Helena took over from Roderick's parents, and there is now wi-fi throughout the house.

As shadows fall, you could take a walk across the farm land to the ruins of a 13thC Knights Templar castle and a Tudor house down by the lake. The family silver comes out for dinner – an experience in itself; delicious dishes and freshly-baked bread. Guests dine together at a vast mahogany table and the atmosphere is that of a friendly house party. Big breakfasts.

Caragh Lake, Co Kerry

Caragh Lake, Killorglin, Co Kerry

Tel (066) 9769105
Fax (066) 9769105
e-mail reservations@ardnasidhe.com
website www.ardnasidhe.com

Nearby Killorglin, 4 miles (7 km); Killarney, 21 miles (34 km); Dingle peninsula; Caragh Lake; golf; boating.
Location in lakeside gardens, 4.5 miles (7 km) from Killorglin; parking available
Food breakfast, dinner, afternoon tea **Price** €€€
Rooms 18 double, all with bath/shower; all rooms have phone, hairdryer; ironing board, wi-fi
Facilities gardens, terraces, boating, fishing, riding, free entry to leisure centres and spas at sister hotels
Credit cards AE, DC, MC, V
Children not suitable
Disabled ground-floor room
Pets not accepted
Closed Oct to 1st May
Proprietor Killarney Hotels

Ard na Sidhe

Lakeside hotel

When we visited Ard na Sidhe (Gaelic for Hill of the Fairies), there seemed to be no-one about. The lovely wooded prize-winning gardens, with paths leading down to little grassy areas by the lake where there are benches to sit on and dream, were deserted. Most of the guests, we were told, were out playing golf. These golfing hotels are left like the Marie Celeste during the day, and lucky non-golfers may have the place to themselves.

This handsome Victorian stone house was built in 1913 by a Lady Gordon, and is so romantic that you can be as fanciful as you like. It certainly feels as if there are fairies about; indeed, behind the house is a fairy hill, with passages said to lead to a large cave. But these little creatures do not like to be seen.

All credit must be given to Killarney Hotels for keeping the house quite uncommercialized and unspoiled, and bringing in Roy Lancaster to advise them on the gardens. There are no facilities here, except natural ones. But guests are given complimentary use of the leisure centre and spa at the group's nearby sister hotels. Bedrooms (spacious) are in the main house and in the Garden House (very quiet and tranquil); all have impressive antiques Lady Gordon might well have chosen herself; excellent bathrooms.

Cashel Bay, Co Galway

Tel (095) 31111
Fax (095) 31117
e-mail info@zetland.com
website www.zetland.com

Nearby Connemara, Roundstone, Clifden, Westport, Aran Islands, fishing (some deep sea), shooting, golf, scuba diving, horse-riding, climbing.
Location in gardens overlooking Cashel Bay, on N340 to Roundstone from Galway; car parking
Food breakfast, dinner
Price ?
Rooms 22 rooms, all with television, shaving points, hairdryers and tea and coffee making.
Facilities gardens, bar, restaurant, open fires, lounge, Wi-Fi
Credit cards AE, MC, V
Children welcome
Disabled ground-floor room
Pets dogs with baskets permitted in bedrooms **Closed** never
Proprietors Colm Redmond

Zetland House Hotel

Country house hotel

Guests remark that they feel as if they are stepping back in time as they drive up to the Zetland House. It's an imposing, 19thC sporting lodge, which broods over a landscape of bogs, mountains, beaches, lakes and little else.

Inside, it's all soft, golden lighting, polished wood, open fires and plaid armchairs. The bedrooms are furnished chintzily but luxuriously, with carved wooden furniture and floral fabrics. Most have mesmerising views. Standard rooms are uniformly comfortable, but the deluxe rooms are truly charming: one has a king-size, four-poster bed, and all have sea views.

Downstairs, the restaurant's main feature is its stunning views over Cashel Bay and the surrounding area. Guests shouldn't just expect to feast their eyes, though – the Zetland has recently won several awards for catering and hospitality. The chef uses only locally-produced, fresh products and seasonal herbs and vegetables, and the wine list is interesting. The bar is cosy and wood-panelled, and offers a selection of Irish whiskys, as well as the black stuff. 'Life moves at a different pace, here' says one guest. 'People have time to stop and chat to you.'

Clifden, Co Galway

Ballyconneely Road, Clifden,
Co Galway

Tel (095) 21460
e-mail info@mallmorecountry-house.com
website www.mallmorecountry-house.com

Nearby Clifden; Connemara National Park; Kylemore Abbey.
Location a mile out of Clifden town centre; in own 35-acre grounds on Ardbear peninsula; car parking
Food breakfast
Price €
Rooms 6; 3 double, 1 twin, 1 family room with 1 double and 2 singles, 1 with 1 double and 1 single, all with showers and spring water; all rooms have wi-fi, most have hairdryers
Facilities gardens and woodland
Credit cards not accepted
Children welcome; 20% discount
Disabled possible
Pets not permitted in rooms
Closed 1 Nov to 1 Mar
Proprietors Alan and Kathleen Hardman

Mallmore House

Country bed-and-breakfast

The Hardmans breed Connemara ponies, for showing and dressage; these hardy little natives are often kept beside the drive to the family's lovingly restored house with a cheery red front door and late Georgian porch. The place is stiff with historical interest: Baden Powell, founder of the Boy Scouts, used to spend his holidays here. Alan and Kathleen Hardman came from The New Inn at Tresco on the Isles of Scilly to work for themselves and found the house in a derelict state: only one room had been used since the 1920s. From the back of the house there is a lovely view through trees over the bay to Clifden and out to the Atlantic. You can walk down to the sea through the orchard and past the old cottage. Rooms in this unusual and intriguing, mainly single-storey house, with original pitch pine floors, have a variety of views; for water ask for Room 4. One room has the original washbasin, and wallpaper with a pattern of birds; another original wide shutters, yellow paper, a Bonnard print and spotless bathroom. Award-winning breakfasts are served in the dining room, which also has its original shutters; tables have pink cloths. On the menu: smoked salmon pancakes; smoked mackerel; Irish bacon. Very much a family affair; a daughter bakes brown bread each evening.

Clifden, Co Galway

Beach Road, Clifden, Co Galway

Tel (095) 21369
Fax (095) 21608
e-mail thequay@iol.ie
website www.thequayhouse.com

Nearby Connemara National Park; Galway, 50 miles (80 km).
Location on quay, 3 minutes by car from Clifden town centre; car parking in road
Food breakfast
Price €€
Rooms 14; 5 superkings, 9 double (4 twin); all with bath and shower; all rooms with phone, TV, radio, hairdryer, balcony
Facilities sitting room; garden, terrace
Credit cards MC, V
Children welcome
Disabled ground-floor rooms
Pets not accepted
Closed end Oct to end Mar
Proprietors Paddy and Julia Foyle

The Quay House

Town house hotel

Paddy Foyle is a celebrated mover and shaker in this rapidly-getting-very-hip little seaside town, where he was born in room 12 of Foyle's Hotel. He is also the owner of the stylish Quay House, down on the harbour wall where the fishing boats tie up. A natural interior decorator, he has the boldness and panache of a set designer: the house, built in 1820 for the harbourmaster, is a stage for his fanciful ideas and outbursts of colour. You have the distinct sense you are in a production of some kind – is it an opera? a film? – as you pass through the wondrous rooms. A favourite theme is Scandinavian: washed-out, distressed paintwork; plenty of grey and Nordic blue; wooden panelling; striped fabrics. One room is a riot of blue *toile de jouy*; there's a Napolean Room at the top of the house; another has a frieze of scallop sea shells. It's pretty; it's fun. But Paddy is a restless pacer, always moving on, so expect changes. He's already stuck a bay on to the old flat-fronted house, bought the place next door and turned it into studios.

On a recent visit we were once again enchanted by the originality of the place, and found Paddy as full of charm as ever. A must if you are in this part of Ireland, and well worth a detour.

Clones, Co Monaghan

Clones, Co Monaghan

Tel (047) 56007
e-mail mail@hiltonpark.ie
website www.hiltonpark.ie

Nearby Castle Coole and Florence Court (National Trust); Armagh.
Location 3 miles (5 km) S of Clones, near Clones Golf Club; in 500 acres of parkland, woods, lakes; car parking
Food breakfast, dinner
Price €€€
Rooms 6; 5 double, 1 twin; all with bath; all rooms have hairdryer, electric blankets and hot water bottles.
Facilities gardens; games room; grand piano; pike and brown trout fishing; rods; boating on lake
Credit cards MC, V
Children over 7 by arrangement
Disabled not possible
Pets by arrangement
Closed end Sep to end Mar except for group bookings
Proprietor Fred and Joanna Madden

Hilton Park

Country house hotel

In the Hidden Ireland group of country houses taking paying guests is Hilton Park – home of the Madden family since 1734 and remodelled in the Italianate manner in the 1870s. It is grand, beautiful, and most evocative of the great days of the Irish country house. Fred, having trained in London, is now in charge of the cooking. He prepares breakfast, which is served in the old servants' hall below stairs. He and his wife Joanna, who manages the front of house, are memorably delightful hosts. Many family stories are to be told about the guest bedrooms: one was Johnny's when he was a child.

Little seems to have changed over the years, though one of the rooms has been renovated since our last visit. The wallpaper in the Blue Room, with a four-poster bed and stunning view down to the lake, was put up in 1830. On our visit, the lace curtains had just come out of a box opened for the first time since 1927. Next door, a roll-top bath, marble washstand, print of Landseer's Hunters at Grass, and the scent of jasmine from plants in pots arranged at the foot of the tall window, all add to the grace and charm. Lucy's dinner is by candle-light, with fresh produce from her garden.

Dingle, Co Cork

Upper John Street, Dingle,
Co Kerry

Tel (066) 9151518
Fax (066) 9152461
e-mail info@pax-house.com
website www.pax-house.com

Nearby Killarney, 42 miles (68 km); Mount Brandon; Tralee, 30 miles (48 km).
Location in countryside, half a mile (0.8 km) out of Dingle town; sign-posted on N86; car parking
Food breakfast
Price €€€
Rooms 13; 8 double, 4 double and single, 1 single; 5 with bath, 8 with shower; all with phone, TV, radio, hairdryer, trouser press, tea/coffee making facilities
Facilities lounge, dining room; garden, patio, terraces **Credit cards** AE, MC, V **Children** accepted **Disabled** not possible **Pets** if well-behaved **Closed** 1st Dec to 1st Mar **Proprietor** John O'Farrell

Pax House

Guesthouse

There is an abundance of wild fuchsia in the hedgerows of the little lanes around Pax House, high on a green hill looking down over Dingle Bay. Before breakfast, you can take an early walk down to the shore, or, from the terrace, count the cows coming out of the milking parlour of the farm below this rather odd building that was once a retirement home. John O'Farrell took over from the Brosnan-Wrights in the summer of 2006, having worked in the hospitality business for more than 30 years, in such diverse places as Switzerland, Thailand, America and Spain. He has since repainted the house, all bedrooms have fresh flowers, and a collection of original paintings, prints and sculptures fill the house.

Most rooms have showers; cold taps produce water from the house's own spring well. John serves a notably varied breakfast, from a full Irish to pears in white wine, honey and clove syrup, and kippers in a lemon butter sauce. From the dining room you can see the field on Sleahead that starred in a film with Tom Cruise, and over to the Ring of Kerry. The silence on the green hill is blissful, but Dingle, a swinging little town, with its full share of traditional music, pubs and restaurants, much frequented by celebs, is only a short walk away.

Drinagh, Co Wexford

Drinagh, Wexford, Co Wexford

Tel (053) 58885/58898
Fax (053) 58885
e-mail killianecastle@yahoo.com
website www.killianecastle.com

Nearby Wexford; Rosslare; Waterford Harbour; Kilmore Quay.
Location in farmland, 3 miles (5 km) from Wexford; car parking
Food breakfast
Price €
Rooms 8; 3 double, 3 twin, 2 family; 6 with bath; 2 with shower; all rooms with TV, hairdryer; iron in corridor; tea/coffee making facilities under stairs
Facilities garden, terrace; tennis court; public telephone
Credit cards MC, V
Children welcome
Disabled not suitable
Pets not in house
Closed 1 Dec to 1 Mar
Proprietors Jack and Kathleen Mernagh

Killiane Castle

Farmhouse bed-and-breakfast

Those who have already found Killiane Castle tend to have that special expression worn by people who have a secret they want to keep to themselves. For this is a remarkable place and farmer's wife, Kathleen Mernagh, a most charming and thoughtful hostess. The Mernaghs' early 18thC house was built inside the walls of a largely intact Norman castle, complete with tower (now listed) and dungeon. From the back rooms, you see the ruins of a small chapel in a field and the marshes running down to the sea. Down a leafy lane, miles from the main road, it seems centuries away from everywhere else. Twice a day, you can hear the hum of machines as the cows file in and out of the milking parlour. Kathleen Mernagh, mother of five boys, loves what she does and she does it extremely well. Long before she married a farmer she worked in hotel management. Our reporter heard one guest say to another at breakfast (Jack Mernagh serves his wife's dishes): "It's just like a small hotel." Some bedrooms overlook the weeping ash at the front of the house; more interesting ones overlook the courtyard and over the castle walls to green countryside beyond. All are spacious, well-equipped and comfortable. Happy birds twitter and swoop over the rooftops of this historic place, only a short drive from Rosslare.

Dublin

70 Adelaide Road, Dublin 2

Tel (01) 475 5266
Fax (01) 478 2841
e-mail info@kilronanhouse.com
website www.kilronanhouse.com

Nearby Grafton Street; National Gallery; Trinity College.
Location 5 minutes walk S of St Stephen's Green; private, secure car parking
Food breakfast
Price €€
Rooms 15; 11 double (8 twin), 2 single, 2 family; all with shower; all with phone, TV, hairdryer; safe and free internet in reception
Facilities sitting room
Credit cards AE, DC, MC, V
Children over 10
Disabled no special facilities
Pets not accepted
Closed never
Proprietor Leon Kinsella
Manager Seán Finnegan

Kilronan House

Town guesthouse

This veteran, reasonably-priced Georgian guest-house in a quiet, leafy, residential street near St Stephen's Green has been in business for more than 35 years and is perfectly situated for walking to some of the city's most famous landmarks and shops. A new owner has recently taken over and refurbished the place, bringing it up to date. Our reporter was impressed with the warm, yellow walls and parquet floor of the entrance hall and the welcoming reception area tucked under the stairs. Bedrooms are on four 'creaking' floors, and it is a long climb to the top. Some are on the small side. Colours tend to be yellow again, with elegant fabrics and pretty, white-painted wrought-iron bedheads, some pine furniture, heavy off-white curtains and the odd print on the walls. We were told of one room – below ground level – that was described as 'tiny', so it is clearly advisable to check in advance which rooms are available. The yellow sitting room has a big, gilt-edged mirror over the fireplace, antique furniture and a chandelier. The yellow extends to the breakfast room, with silver and white linens on the tables. The overall feel of the place is old-fashioned and relaxed. In late 2013 they refurbished the bedrooms and general areas – reports, please.

Dublin

31 Leeson Close, Dublin 2

Tel (01) 676 5011
Fax (01) 676 2929
e-mail info@number31.ie
website www.number31.ie

Nearby St Stephen's Green; National Gallery; Grafton Street, Trinity College.
Location just off Lower Leeson Street; 5 minutes walk from St Stephen's Green; car parking
Food breakfast
Price €€€-€€€€
Rooms 20; 15 double (12 twin), 5 family; 17 with bath, 3 with shower; all with phone, TV, DVD player, hairdryer, wi-fi; safe at reception
Facilities sitting room, breakfast room, conservatory; garden
Credit cards all major
Children welcome
Disabled not suitable
Pets not accepted
Closed never
Proprietors Noel and Deirdre Comer

Number 31

Town guesthouse

This is a very special and visually pleasing place: a mews house designed in the mid-1960s by controversial Dublin architect, Sam Stephenson, and the Georgian house across the garden that was acquired giving much more space. The delightful Noel and Deirdre Comer, former owners of Kilronan House (page 375), loved the originality from the outset. Only a plate on the wall with '31' on it indicates this is somewhere you may stay. The Stephenson building is modern and open-plan, with painted white brickwork and much glass, wood and stone; kilims hang on the wall. There's a little sunken sitting area, with a black leather sofa custom-built around the fire. French windows and wooden decking lead to the garden and the back of the Georgian house. Deirdre's generous and delicious breakfasts (home-made breads, jams, potato cakes, granola) are served in a white upstairs room on long tables with fresh flowers, sparkling silver, and white linen napkins. Five stylish bedrooms are in the mews house (two have patios). Fifteen more are in the Georgian house, with moulded ceilings and painted in National Trust colours. The Comers completed a thorough refurbishment in 2007, replacing all bathrooms and beds and bringing the place up to modern standards.

Dunkineely, Co Donegal

St John's Point, Dunkineely,
Co Donegal

Tel (07497) 37022
Fax (07497) 37330
e-mail info@castlemurray.com
website www.castlemurray.com

Nearby Donegal.
Location a mile (1.6 km) off the main N56 from Donegal to Killybegs, signposted in Dunkineely; parking
Food breakfast, dinner, Sunday lunch; bar lunch, afternoon tea in Jul-Aug
Price €€
Rooms 10 (9 with sea view); 7 double, 3 twin; all with shower and some with bath; all with phone, TV, hairdryer, tea/coffee making facilities, wi-fi **Facilities** bar; garden, terrace **Credit cards** MC, V
Children welcome
Disabled not possible
Pets small dogs in rooms
Closed end Jan to beginning Feb
Proprietors Martin and Marguerite Howley

Castle Murray House

Country restaurant-with-rooms

This charming little place has been run by father and daughter Martin and Marguerite Howley since 2002. The setting of Castle Murray House could be called magical. In front of the hotel, bright green fields with low, drystone walls run down to the sea and a small ruined castle on the point is illuminated as night falls. Across the bay, the sun goes down over the Slieve League, the highest sea cliffs in Europe.

The restaurant is renowned for its locally-caught seafood, including lobsters which potter about in a tank by the raised, open fire. Head chef since 1995, Remy Dupuy creates 'French dishes with an Irish touch' and the menu is based on local, seasonal produce.

Up a pine staircase, bedrooms we felt were a touch basic on our last visit have since been redone, with modern bathrooms. The Howleys have also turned their attention to the gardens and added a new deck.

Reports welcome.

Goleen, Co Cork

Gurtyowen, Toormore, Goleen, Co Cork

Tel (028) 35324
Fax (028) 35324
e-mail fortviewhousegoleen@eircom.net
website www.fortviewhouse.ie

Nearby Goleen; Mizen Head; Schull peninsula; Skibbereen; Bantry.
Location in countryside, 6 miles (10 km) from Goleen; car parking
Food breakfast
Price €
Rooms 5; 2 with 2 double, 2 with double and single, 1 with double and 2 single; 1 with bath, 4 with shower; all rooms with hairdryer
Facilities sitting room; garden, terrace **Credit cards** not accepted
Children over 6 welcome
Disabled not possible
Pets not accepted
Closed 1 Nov to 1 Mar
Proprietor Violet Connell

Fortview House

Farmhouse bed-and-breakfast

This place is a labour of love, and it radiates an appropriately warm glow. Richard Connell built the newer part of this house on the West Cork family dairy farm himself, out of stone, and roofed it in slate. The interior is the inspired work of his delightful wife, Violet. With her own ideas, and pictures from magazines, she has created something so fresh, welcoming and comfortable that it is hard to tear oneself away. You can tell what's in store by the two small bears in the retro pram in the hall and the boxy blue-and-red chairs in the sitting room. Violet's bedrooms are named after wild flowers: periwinkle; lavender; daffodil; fuchsia. In one, she has hung straw hats on the wall. She has made curtains out of striped mattress ticking and stencilled a bathroom with sea shells. In a family room with two single beds and pretty patchwork quilts, she props teddy bears up on the pillows as if they are waiting for new, young friends to come. The beamed dining room has a long table, terracotta tiles, wood-burning stove, and old pine furniture. Violet's breakfasts reflect the same attention and care: eggs from the Connell's own hens; freshly squeezed juices; hot potato cakes, salmon and crème fraîche. She has many admirers. Be sure to book early.

Goleen, Co Cork

Goleen, Co Cork

Tel (028) 35225
Fax (028) 35422
e-mail suehill@eir.com.net
website www.heronscove.com

Nearby Mizen Head; Cork, 75 miles (120 km); Bantry, 25 miles (40 km); Skibbereen, 24 miles (39 km).
Location on Goleen Harbour; car parking
Food breakfast, lunch, dinner
Price €
Rooms 5; 1 double, 2 twin, 2 double with a single bed; 1 with bath, 4 with shower; all with phone, TV, CD/radio, hairdryer, electric blanket, tea/coffee making facilities; small fridge on request
Facilities terraces, garden
Credit cards AE, MC, V
Children by arrangement
Disabled not suitable
Pets not accepted
Closed Christmas and New Year
Proprietor Sue Hill

The Heron's Cove

Restaurant-with-rooms

A fisherman in a trawler brings Sue Hill's order to the door of her white-painted, waterside restaurant, which offers 'fresh fish and wine on the harbour' and, most likely, a view of a heron. It is an idyllic spot, on this rugged stretch of the West Cork coastline. It is not surprising to hear from Sue that some of her guests do not want to do anything but simply sit and watch the tide come in and go out again. Three of the bedrooms in this modern house open on to balconies overlooking the little sheltered cove, and from the terrace of the restaurant on the ground floor – which is open from May to October – there are steps down to the beach. Guests are clearly those who relish the peace and quiet.

Along the upstairs landing runs a long shelf with a row of books. Bedrooms are well-equipped. There are posters of Aix-en-Provence on the walls and Sue has turned the staircase into a gallery for local artists. She is also very switched on to IT and offers guests e-mail and fax facilities. It's only a short walk to the village of Goleen and Sue sends all visitors off on the spectacular drive to Mizen Head, which is Ireland's most southwesterly point.

Gorey, Co Wexford

Gorey, Co. Wexford

Tel (053) 942 1124
Fax (053) 942 1572
e-mail info@marlfieldhouse.ie
website www.marfieldhouse.ie

Nearby Waterford; Kilkenny; Wexford; Rosslare; beaches.
Location in 35-acre gardens and woodland, 1 mile (1.6 km) out of Gorey on R742 Gorey-Courtown road, or exit 23 off NII from Dublin/the south; with car-parking
Food breakfast, lunch, dinner
Price €€€€
Rooms 19; 17 double, 2 single, all with bath, phone, TV, hairdryer
Facilities sitting room, bar, dining room, sauna; garden, terraces, tennis, croquet
Credit cards AE, DC, MC, V
Children welcome; high tea for those under 8
Disabled access possible **Pets** dogs welcome by prior arrangement
Closed 2nd Jan – beginning Mar
Proprietors Bowe family

Marlfield House

Country house hotel

A sign in the drive of this stunning Regency house, once owned by the Earls of Courtown and now a Relais and Chateaux hotel (one of the best in Ireland), reads: 'Drive carefully, pheasants crossing'. Not only is this a preserve of all good things for people, but it is pretty comfortable for animals, too. There's a little dog basket for a terrier beside the 18thC marble fireplace in the semi-circular architect-designed hall. Mary Bowe's peacocks, bantams, ducks and geese are cherished and indulged almost as much as her guests. This is a gorgeous, overblown place, a feast for the eyes because of Mary's passion for interior decoration. Her taste is reflected in Waterford crystal chandeliers, little French chairs, gilded taps and a domed conservatory dining room. Garlanded with awards – Hostess of the Year, Wine List of the Year, Best Breakfast, One of the World's Most Enchanting Hideaways – the hotel has a tradition of warm hospitality and the Bowes' daughters, Margaret and Laura, are now at the helm. Bedrooms are sumptuous and charming. Jewels in the crown are the State Rooms, decorated with rich fabrics and fine antique furniture: the French Room, with marble bathroom, overlooks the lake; the Print Room has views of the rose garden. Outstanding food.

Inis Meáin, Co Galway

Inis Meáin, The Aran Islands, Co. Galway

Tel +353 86 8266026
e-mail post @inismeain.com
website www.inismeain.com

Nearby coastal and cliff walks, bird and wildlife watching, the island pub, ferry to other islands and mainland. **Location** on Inis Meáin Island, reachable by ferry, plane, private boat or helicopter. **Food** breakfast and packed lunch included, dinner in restaurant **Price** €€€€ **Rooms** 5; 4 suites, 1 suite-apartment. Each has seating area, mini-deli, wetroom shower, books. Apartment has lounge, dining area with wood-burning stove and guest rest-room. **Facilities** restaurant, bicycles, fishing rod and binoculars provided **Credit cards** MC, V **Children** welcome **Disabled** not suitable **Pets** no specific facilities **Closed** Nov-Mar; suite-apartment available for longer stays during this time **Proprietor** Ruairi and Marie-Therese de Blacam

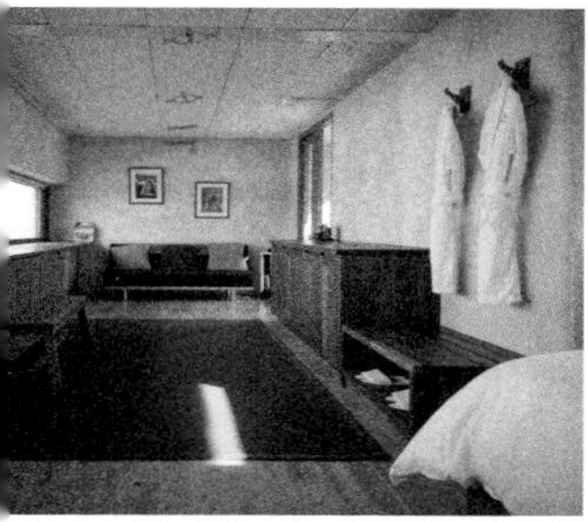

Inis Meáin Restaurant and Suites **Island hotel**

15 miles off the west coast of Ireland, Inis Meáin is a landscape of terraced limestone, higgledy-piggledy fields and hundreds of miles of dry-stone walls. Irish is the first language of the islanders, and traditional methods of farming, fishing, sport and music are a large part of their lives.

This place sits by the coast on a rocky outcrop. It's owned and run by Ruairi – a native – and his wife, Marie-Therese. Alongside winning a host of awards, they've stuck to their aim of showcasing the best of the island (quite literally: huge windows offer amazing views). The restaurant, headed up by Ruairi, uses main ingredients sourced mostly on Inis Meáin: lobster and crab caught by local fishermen, wild food from the surrounding countryside and home-grown vegetables, fertilised with seaweed. It's great food: cooked simply, but by all accounts superbly.

The bedrooms offer views of the coastline and island, and are uncluttered to let the landscape do the talking. Walls are painted in natural lime and furniture and flooring is simple polished wood. The de Blacams want the guests to 'appreciate the peace and quiet' so bicycles, books and fishing rods are provided in place of TVs. This is characteristically thoughtful: the couple are praised by guests for their 'warm welcome and attention to the small things'.

Inistioge, Co Kilkenny

Cullintra House

Country house

The Rower, Inistioge, Co Kilkenny

Tel (051) 423614
e-mail info@cullintrahouse.com
website www.cullintrahouse.com

Nearby Kilkenny, 19 miles (31 km); New Ross, 6 miles (10 km); Jerpoint Abbey; Waterford, ancient cairn nearby on farm.
Location in wooded countryside, 6 miles (10 km) from New Ross; car parking
Food breakfast, dinner
Prices €-€€ (minimum stay 2 nights)
Rooms 6; 5 double/twin, 1 family; 2 with bath, 4 with shower; hairdryer; all rooms equipped with hot water bottle **Facilities** courtyard; gardens, terrace, bridge for viewing countryside **Credit cards** extra charge of 3 per cent **Children** welcome
Disabled 1 ground-floor room but no special facilities
Pets welcome
Closed never
Proprietor Patricia Cantlon

Patricia Cantlon is known for her long, leisurely, candle-lit dinner parties at the 250-year-old ivy-clad farmhouse where she was born. Guests have reported moveable eating times. When our reporter called, Patricia had several important jobs to do before getting under way in the kitchen: station herself outside the front door with palette and brushes to finish off a painting; race off to the vet with one of her cats. The day begins when a guest knocks on her door to alert her that people are up and about and waiting for breakfast (could be noon). Her informality and originality have won friends and admirers all over the world. They leave messages in the visitors' book such as 'Great fun'; 'The house, the surroundings, the food, and most of all Patricia, were a magnificent find'.

She has, indeed, created a bewitching retreat. The low-ceilinged house abounds in artistic extras such as the imaginatively-designed rooms in the green-roofed barn, and the conservatory, where Patricia lights banks of candles for pre-dinner drinks. There are log fires, long walks (there are countless acres of woodland to explore), conversations with cats and foxes, swimming with Patricia in the river. She's a natural hostess, with persuasive powers to make her guests feel they have entered a place that is not quite of this world. It works.

Leenane, Co Galway

Leenane, Co Galway

Tel (095) 42222
Fax (095) 42296
e-mail stay@delphilodge.ie
website www.delphilodge.ie

Nearby Westport; Kylemore Abbey; Clifden; golf.
Location by the lake in wooded grounds on private estate; with car parking
Food breakfast, lunch, dinner
Price €€€
Rooms 12; 8 double, 4 twin, all with bath; all rooms have phone; hairdryer on request **Facilities** drawing room, billiard room, library, dining room; garden, lake
Credit cards AE, MC, V
Children welcome
Disabled 2 ground-floor rooms
Pets not accepted
Closed mid-Dec to mid-Jan
Manager Michael Wade

Delphi Lodge

Fishing lodge

The 2nd Marquess of Sligo – who had been with Byron in Greece – thought this wild place as beautiful as Delphi, and built himself a fishing lodge here in the mid-1830s. When Peter Mantle, a former financial journalist, came across the house, it was semi-derelict. Falling under the same spell, he restored it with great care and vision, and Delphi is one of the finest and foremost sporting lodges in Ireland. Fishing is its main business, but everyone is made welcome here. He stepped back in 2011, and as we went to press the new manager was Michael Wade.

On our visit, wood smoke was rising from the chimney, a new delivery of Crozes Hermitage was stacked up in the hall and Mozart was playing in the snug library overlooking the lake. Among the guests were a couple of bankers in their waterproofs, a novelist, and some Americans. Salmon are weighed and measured in the Rod Room, creating frissons of excitement and stories for the communal dinner table; the ghillies come in during breakfast to discuss prospects for the day ahead. Bedrooms are unfussy but pretty, with pine furniture; larger ones have lake views. Book well ahead. Our most recent inspector was impressed: 'a unique and stunning location; the absolute country house experience.'

Lisdoonvarna, Co Clare

Lisdoonvarna, Co Clare

Tel (065) 7074025
Fax (065) 7074025
e-mail
ballinalackencastle@eircom.net
website www.ballinalackencastle.com

Nearby The Burren; Ballyvaughan; Doolin Crafts Gallery.
Location in 100-acre grounds, 3 miles (5 km) S of Lisdoonvarna on R477; car parking
Food breakfast, dinner
Price €€
Rooms 12; 2 suites, 10 doubles; 10 with bath, all with shower; all with phone, TV, radio, hairdryer
Facilities sitting room, bar, restaurant, wi-fi; garden
Credit cards MC, V
Children welcome
Disabled not suitable
Pets well-behaved dogs in room; not in public areas
Closed end of Oct to end of Apr
Proprietors O'Callaghan family

Ballinalacken Castle Hotel **Country hotel**

This fascinating house, high on a green hillside with uninterrupted Atlantic views, was built as a 'villa' in the 1840s for John O'Brien, MP for Limerick. Not only does it have its own ruins of a 15thC O'Brien stronghold, but the entrance hall with cupola and green Connemara marble fireplace remains more or less unaltered. There is a newish, discreetish extension, but main house bedrooms have large, dark, old-fashioned pieces of antique furniture, huge wardrobes, and original shutters. From the bed in Room 4, you can see the Aran islands; and Room 7 has a view of the Cliffs of Moher. The lay-out is intriguing – mostly on one floor.

Chef Michael Foley uses fresh local ingredients to create dishes such as cannelloni of crab meat in a light salmon mousse, with shellfish jus, and Barbary duck with celeriac purree and Guinness and fresh honey sauce. The dining room has another cracker of a fireplace, turf fire, original wood floor, pink tablecloths. Nightcaps are served in the lounge bar, and you can steep yourself in the history of the place with locals and join in sing-alongs on weekend evenings, when live entertainment is laid on.

The O'Callaghans also offer self-catering accommodation in nearby Gentian Cottage.

Lisdoonvarna, Co Clare

Lisdoonvarna, Co Clare

Tel (065) 7074026
Fax (065) 7074555
e-mail info@sheedys.com
website www.sheedys.com

Nearby The Burren; Ballyvaughan; Doolin Craft Gallery.
Location in centre of Lisdoonvarna, on edge of the Burren; car parking
Food breakfast, lunch, dinner
Price €
Rooms 11; 5 double, 6 twin; 9 with bath, 2 with shower; all with phone, TV, hairdryer; ironing board available
Facilities south-facing sun lounge, seafood bar, sitting room, restaurant
Credit cards AE, MC, V
Children welcome
Disabled not possible
Pets not accepted
Closed end Sep to end Mar
Proprietors the Sheedy family

Sheedy's Restaurant & Hotel **Restaurant-with-rooms**

This small hotel was originally a farmhouse where the Sheedy family began looking after visitors to this little spa town (it has sulphurous springs) in 1855. John Sheedy, ex-Ashford Castle head chef, has come home to cook; his delightful wife, Martina, looks after front of house and the wine list and adds her taste for contemporary design. John Sheedy's food is highly acclaimed and the restaurant has been given a completely new look to complement his celebrated 'Modern Irish' cooking. Walls are painted in a moody grey colour called 'Muddy River'. Martina, who used to work at Mount Juliet, has also transformed the hotel, bringing in help from the nearby Doolin Craft Gallery, renowned for sharp, simple design in wool, crystal, linen and tweed. The lobby heralds the exciting shape of things to come, with shiny wood floor, little curved reception desk, a bit of exposed natural stone, paintwork in gentian blue and terracotta red.

Upstairs, bedrooms have been upgraded; the priority is comfort, but with some modern design. A place to watch; reports, please.

Mallow, Co Cork

Mallow, Co Cork

Tel (022) 47156 **Fax** (022) 47459
e-mail info@longuevillehouse.ie
website www.longuevillehouse.ie

Nearby Mallow Castle; Anne's Grove Gardens at Castletownroche.
Location on wooded estate, 3 miles (5km) W of Mallow on Kilarney road; ample free car parking
Food breakfast, snack food, afternoon tea, Sunday lunch, dinner
Prices €€-€€€
Rooms 18; 12 double/twin with bath; 6 suites; all with central heating, phone, hairdryer
Facilities drawing room, bar, 2 dining rooms; fishing, clay & game shoot, brandy distillery
Credit cards MC, V
Children welcome
Disabled easy access to public rooms only
Pets small dogs accepted by prior notice **Closed** midweek Jan – Mar; Mon and Tue all year
Proprietors William & Aisling O'Callaghan

Longueville House

Country house hotel

One of the finest country house hotels in Ireland: this elegant and imposing pink listed Georgian house on a 500-acre wooded estate on the Blackwater River has a three-storey block in the centre built in the 1720s, later wings, and a pretty Victorian conservatory. Inside, it is full of ornate Italian plasterwork, elaborately framed ancestral oils and graceful period furniture. The drawing room overlooks lawns and rows of oaks in the parkland; in the distance are the ruins of the family's Dromineen Castle, demolished under Cromwell, who dispossessed the family. But, after 300 years, they are back.

Longueville House has everything, including internationally recognised chef William O'Callaghan, who, according to one leading food critic, cooks 'some of the finest food in Europe'. Many of his ingredients come from the estate farm and the walled kitchen garden. Some 25 acres of apple orchards provide apples for Longueville House's craft apple cider, some of which William distils into brandy.

Bedrooms are comfortable and filled with antiques. The ones at the front of the house have the best views. The Presidents' Restaurant is named after the portraits of Irish presidents that hang on the walls. The wine list is superb, as is William's seven-course Surprise Tasting Menu.

Mountrath, Co Laois

Mountrath, Co Laois

Tel (0502) 32120
Fax (0502) 32711
e-mail roundwood@eircom.net
website www.roundwoodhouse.com

Nearby walking, horse-riding, fishing; Slieve Bloom mountains.
Location in countryside, 3 miles (5 km) N of Mountrath on Kinnitty road; with gardens and ample car parking
Food full breakfast, dinner
Price €€€
Rooms 10; 8 double (3 twin), 2 family rooms; all with bath; all rooms have central heating
Facilities sitting room, study, dining room, hall, library; croquet
Credit cards AE, DC, MC, V
Children very welcome
Disabled not suitable
Pets accepted by arrangement
Closed 3 weeks Jan and Christmas
Proprietors Hannah & Paddy Flynn

Roundwood House

Country house

A recent reporter reacted very well to the Flynns' operation. The house is 'not in perfect repair, but for the type of place they run, this didn't seem to matter': it's a 'wonderful place, and Hannah and Paddy really are charming and informal hosts'. The perfectly proportioned Palladian mansion is set in acres of lime, beech and chestnut woodland. The Kennans have wholeheartedly continued the work of the Irish Georgian Society, who rescued the house from near-ruin in the 1970s. All the Georgian trappings remain – bold paintwork, shutters instead of curtains, rugs instead of fitted carpets, and emphatically no TV. Despite this, the house is decidedly lived in, certainly not a museum.

For Paddy's plentiful meals, non-residents sit at separate tables; residents usually sit together (though not obligatory) – fine if you like to chat to strangers, not ideal for romantic twosomes. After-dinner conversation is also encouraged over coffee and drinks by the open fire in the drawing-room. You may well find the hosts joining in.

Four pleasant extra bedrooms in a converted stable block we thought were cosier and of a better standard than those in the main house. It's very child-friendly (the Flynns have two girls), with a lovely big playroom at the top of the house, full of toys.

Multyfarnham, Co Westmeath

Multyfarnham, Co Westmeath

Tel (044) 937 2191
Fax (044) 937 2338
e-mail stay@mornington.ie
website www.mornington.ie

Nearby Mullingar, Lough Crew, Tullynally Castle, Belvedere House, Newgrange, Lock's Distillery, Kibeggan.
Location in private grounds outside Multyfarnham
Food breakfast, dinner
Price €-€€
Rooms 4; 3 double and 1 single, with private bathrooms with power showers **Facilities** drawing room, dining room, sitting room, walled gardens and 50 acres of grounds, wi-fi and broadband
Credit cards AE, DC, MC, V
Children by arrangement **Pets** not accepted **Closed** Nov 1st – Mar 20th. Open for groups on weekends in Nov **Proprietors** Warwick and Anne O'Hara

Mornington House

Country house

Mornington House stands a little apart from the tiny village of Multyfarnham, deep in the Westmeath countryside. Set back from the road by an acre or so of gardens, rolling up the drive to this place feels like taking a dip into the 1930s. It's not for those seeking glossy interior design and state-of-the-art equipment: it's proudly old-fashioned. Rooms have shelves of books and encyclopaedias rather than TVs; brass bedsteads and wooden dressing tables.

Guests eat together house party-style at a long, polished dining table after gathering in the drawing room for drinks. Candlesticks, chandeliers and family portraits adorn communal rooms (most with open fires and oriental rugs). There's an air of elegance, and the antiques are to be used rather than simply admired.

Cooking is done by owners Anne and Warwick, and is wonderfully hearty – their Guinness stew is a firm favourite with guests. Whenever possible, ingredients come straight from the walled garden and local suppliers. It's worth checking that you're staying on a night when dinner is served: the O'Haras take occasional breaks from cooking. According to reports, they're wonderful hosts: welcoming and full of stories about the building which has been in their family for hundreds of years.

Nenagh, Co Tipperary

Ardcrony, Nenagh, Co Tipperary

Tel (067) 38223
Fax (067) 38013
e-mail magaret@ashleypark.com
website www.ashleypark.com

Nearby Lough Derg; Limerick, 27 miles (43 km); Shannon.
Location on private estate, with lake, 3.5 miles (6 km) out of Nenagh on Borrisokane road; car parking
Food breakfast, dinner
Price €€
Rooms 6; 3 double, 2 twin, 1 family; 3 with bath and shower, 3 with shower; TV and hairdryer on request **Facilities** garden; lake, boat, fishing rods, riding; public telephone
Credit cards not accepted
Children welcome
Disabled not possible
Pets accepted
Closed never
Proprietor Sean Mounsey

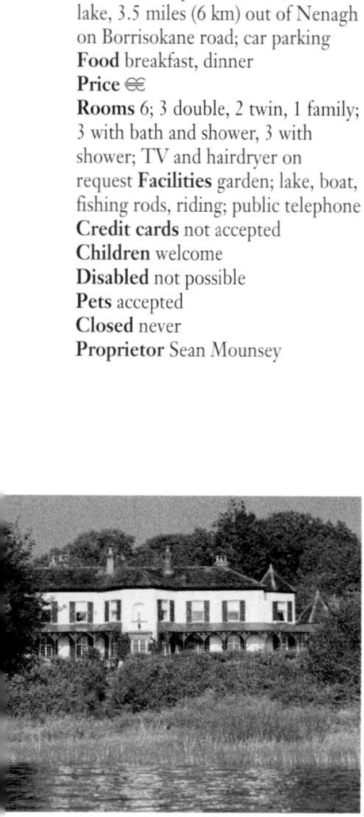

Ashley Park House

Country house bed-and-breakfast

A peacock was sitting, wailing, on the rail of the green veranda when we visited Ashley Park: one of the owner's beloved birds that are fed every morning in a ritual of the household. Mr Mounsey is insistent that nothing here should be like a hotel. He need have no fears on that front. This wildly atmospheric early 18thC house comes complete with ballroom, ruined chapel on an island on the lake, original stabling and farmyard in a more-or-less untouched state, and a scheduled Neolithic ring fort in the woods. The whole place is a nature reserve, too. Mozart is played at breakfast and Frank Sinatra at dinner.

We were unable to see any bedrooms, as they were occupied by a sleeping film crew, but, like all the other rooms in the house, they are huge, as are the bathrooms with their Victorian fittings. The former Irish President, Mary McAleese, has stayed in Room 2. Roses trail along the veranda that runs the length of the house and, to relax, you can sit and read in the octagonal Chinese Room. There are turf fires; Mr Mounsy's daughter, Magaret, bakes a delicious scone; fresh eggs can be ordered straight from the hen. Hotels just don't come like this.

Newmarket-on-Fergus, Co Clare

Newmarket-on-Fergus, Co Clare

Tel (061) 363739
Fax (061) 363823
e-mail info@carrygerryhouse.com
website www.carrygerryhouse.com

Nearby Shannon airport, 8 miles (13 km); Limerick, 20 miles (32 km); Ennis (32 km).
Location in gardens and grounds; car parking
Food breakfast, dinner
Price €€
Rooms 11; 6 superior double, 4 double, 1 twin, 1 family room, 10 with bath, 1 with shower; all rooms have phone, TV, hairdryer on request
Facilities restaurant, bar, courtyard
Credit cards AE, DC, MC, V
Children over 12
Disabled access possible
Pets accepted
Closed 24 to 27 Dec
Proprietors Niall and Gillian Ennis

Carrygerry Country House **County house hotel**

Being so conveniently close to Shannon airport – a ten-minute drive away – this could have settled for being a commercial hotel. But the kindness and warm hospitality of Niall Ennis and his wife, Gillian, have made this old manor house a place to remember for those staying for either their first or last night in Ireland.

In gardens, woodland, and pasture, Carrygerry – built in the 18th century with a gable end and a remarkable courtyard entered through an archway – was a private house until as recently as the 1980s. Gillian is passionate about her house and she has filled it with antiques and pretty things. The two cosy sitting rooms, either side of the front door, are delightful places to pass away the time, with blazing fires, deep sofas, striped cushions, oriental carpets, and rich, dark colours. The house really seems to come alive in the evenings, when it positively glows in candle light. In the former coach house in the courtyard is a bar; some bedrooms are there, too.

At the end of a flight or a long drive, this is a comfortable, welcoming traveller's rest.

Rathnew, Co Wicklow

Newrath Bridge, Rathnew,
Co Wicklow

Tel (0404) 40106
Fax (0404) 40338
e-mail reception@hunters.ie
website www.hunters.ie

Nearby Mount Usher Gardens, Powerscourt Gardens; Russborough House; Glendalough; golf.
Location in gardens on River Vartry, in countryside half a mile from Rathnew; car parking
Food breakfast, lunch, dinner
Price €€€
Rooms 16; 15 double/twin, 1 single, 15 with bath, 1 with shower; all rooms with phone, TV, hairdryer; hot water bottle
Facilities gardens, terrace
Credit cards all major
Children welcome
Disabled ground-floor room
Pets not accepted
Closed 24 to 26 Dec
Proprietors Gelletlie family

Hunter's Hotel

Coaching inn

The area around it is fast becoming part of Dublin commuterland, but not much changes here in this little island of constancy. In 1840, some Victorian travellers touring Ireland reported: 'We strongly recommend Mr Hunter's Inn at Newrath Bridge, which is, according to our experience, the most comfortable in the county.' The same applies today. This is a delightful, proudly old-fashioned place, built as a coaching inn for several big houses in the vicinity. You would not be surprised if you were to hear the sound of horses' hooves and carriage wheels clattering into the enormous stable yard, or trunks being carried into the beamed front hall, which still has the tiled floor laid in 1720. Nothing clashes, nothing jars, to spoil the old world charm that brings people from far and wide. Present owners, Richard and Tom Gelletlie (great-great-grandsons of the original Mr Hunter) get complete strangers talking in the small bar, with bare, wide wooden floorboards, beams, and a print of the 1900 Grand National winner, Ambush 11, on the wall. There is good, plain cooking; a lovely garden by the river; courtesy; glowing fires; charming bedrooms (ask for garden view); tea on the lawn; billowing wisteria.

Recess, Co Galway

Inagh Valley, Recess, Co Galway

Tel (095) 34706
Fax (095) 34708
e-mail inagh@iol.ie
website www.loughinaghlodgehotel.ie

Nearby Recess; Oughterard; Clifden; Galway.
Location in open country on shores of Lough Inagh; car parking
Food breakfast, lunch, dinner
Price €€€
Rooms 13; 1 triple, 4 twin, 8 double; all with bath and shower; all rooms have phone, TV, radio, hairdryer, trouser press; ironing board on request, room service
Facilities garden, lake, fishing, bicycles
Credit cards AE, DC, MC, V
Children welcome
Disabled suitable ground-floor room **Pets** acccepted
Closed mid-Dec to mid-Mar
Proprietor Maire O'Connor

Lough Inagh Lodge Hotel **Country hotel**

This solid, well-proportioned Victorian shooting lodge, romantically placed on one of the most beautiful lakes in Connemara, was boarded up when Maire O'Connor and her late husband, John, came across it looking for somewhere suitable to run as a small hotel. Remarkably, some of the old sporting record books survive and may be read by guests. Little has been overlooked in the way of comfort. Each bedroom, named after an Irish writer, has a dressing room with trouser press (not that we rate these very highly as creature comforts, but they're useful for damp Connemara days). Views are of water and The Twelve Bens mountains. Maire has kept to rich dark Victorian colours and polished wood; her careful attention to detail and service is reflected throughout the comfortable, cosy house. She arranges the fresh flowers, which are sent from Clifden. Rooms downstairs have inviting log fires and warm lighting. The green dining room with yellow curtains and gleaming, dark wood floor is delightful. Seafood and traditional wild game dishes are specialities of the kitchen. Loughs Inagh and Derryclare are on the doorstep; for walkers, there are miles of tracks through the wild and rugged landscape. The hotel also has a stable of bicycles.

Riverstown, Co Sligo

Riverstown, Co Sligo

Tel (071) 9165466
Fax (071) 9165108
e-mail ohara@coopershill.com
website www.coopershill.com

Nearby Sligo, 12 miles (20 km); Lough Arrow; Lough Gara.
Location 1 mile (1.5 km) W of Riverstown, off N4 Dublin-Sligo road; in large garden on 500-acre estate, with ample car parking
Food breakfast, light/packed lunch, dinner; restaurant licence
Price €€€
Rooms 8; 7 double, 1 twin, 7 with bath and shower, 1 with shower; all rooms have phone, tea/coffee
Facilities sitting room, dining room, snooker room, wi-fi; fishing, tennis, croquet **Credit cards** MC, V
Children welcome if well behaved
Disabled no access
Pets welcome if well behaved, but not allowed in public rooms
Closed Nov to end Mar
Proprietor Simon O'Hara and Christina McCauley

Coopershill

Country house hotel

Simon O'Hara runs this delightful country house with his partner and the chef, Christina. They took over from his parents eight years ago and have continued to subtly improve the style of the place without interfering with its essential appeal.

It is a fine house with splendidly large rooms (including the bedrooms, most of which have four-poster or canopy beds). It is furnished throughout with antiques; but remains emphatically a home, with no hotel-like formality.

The grounds are extensive enough not only to afford complete seclusion, but also to accommodate a river. Four-course dinners are available from a daily changing, seasonal menu. Much of the food is produced in the grounds, and the restaurant can make the unusual boast that the distance travelled from farm to plate for many of its ingredients is just 200 metres. The O'Haras rear fallow deer on the 500-acre estate, producing award-winning venison. The Restaurant Association of Ireland awarded them Best Hotel Restaurant in Sligo in 2013.

Slane, Co Meath

Rossnaree, Slane, Co Meath

Tel 041 982 0975
website www.rossnaree.ie

Nearby Dublin (40 mins); Newgrange, Knowth and Dowth (Bru na Boinne)
Location the Boyne Valley; in own grounds with ample car-parking
Food breakfast included; dinner (for 4 or more) to be booked in advance, afternoon tea
Price €€
Rooms 4; 3 double, 1 twin; all with own bath or shower
Facilities guided tours; Rossnaree School of Art; fishing on the River Boyne; summer cooking courses
Credit cards DC, MC, V
Children welcome
Disabled access difficult
Pets acccepted on request
Closed Nov – Feb
Proprietor Aisling Law

Rossnaree House

Country hotel

This 200-acre wooded estate is a true taste of Ireland. The north side of Rossnaree looks towards the Hill of Slane, where St. Patrick lit his paschal fire in defiance of the pagan King of Tara; the neighbouring glen is where the Battle of the Boyne took place. The house was purchased by the Law family in the early days of the Irish Free State (1925). It is now managed by Aisling Law, great granddaughter of Irish revolutionary Maud Gonne.

Aisling is a talented artist. Each of the four bedrooms has a unique and carefully considered theme: the 'bird' room with its subtle Oriental influences and murals with hand-painted birds and blossom trees; the 'tiger' room with its four-poster bed, draped with Congolese wall hangings; the period style 'William Morris' room, with original William Morris wallpaper; and the 'river' room, with magnificent views across the River Boyne and the Megalithic sites of Bru na Boinne.

Breakfast happens in the dining room during winter, beside a crackling open fire, on a pretty mahogany dining table laid with antique china and silverware. In summer, you can take a picnic basket to the River Boyne. They have a small farm with geese, guinea fowl, hens and roosters.

Tours of Rossnaree are also available for visitors who book in advance.

Ardmore, Co Waterford

Cliff House Hotel

Restaurant-with-rooms

Outside our usual territory, this modern steel, glass and slate building drops down a cliff to the sea in a series of levels. They're connected by a lift and a spiral staircase; all the rooms face the water. The decoration is somewhat bland, except for the shell mirrors and lamps in reception, the jazzy bar and the lime-green spa. The charm is in the special seaside setting, in the quality of the light that results, and in the charming local staff. A Relais & Chateau member. Food (Michelin star) by Dutchman Martijn Kajuiter.

Ardmore, Co Waterford

Tel 024 87800
e-mail info@thecliffhousehotel.com
website www.thecliffhousehotel.com
Food breakfast, lunch, dinner
Price €€€€
Closed 24th-26th Dec
Proprietors Barry and Gerri O'Callaghan

Ballingarry, Co Limerick

The Mustard Seed at Echo Lodge **Country house**

Dan Mullane won his spurs in 1985 with a restaurant in a tiny thatched cottage in Adare, often called the prettiest village in Ireland. A decade later he moved his chefs to a new kitchen in a former convent a few miles away. The Mustard Seed Country House is painted yellow, and has blue pots on the doorstep. 'Foodies' flock to his blue-walled dining room with the yellow laburnum outside the window. Service is smooth and professional. Breakfast could be stewed prunes with an Earl Grey and lemon syrup, or porridge with cream and Irish whiskey. Dan designs a pretty bedroom, too. He likes wallpaper striped like a Jermyn Street shirt, and gleaming white bathrooms; two of his most successful rooms are in black and white.

Ballingarry, Co Limerick

Tel (069) 68508
Fax (069) 68511
e-mail mustard@indigo.ie
website www.mustardseed.ie
Food breakfast, lunch, dinner
Price €€€
Closed Feb
Proprietors Dan Mullane

Ballylickey, Co Cork

Sea View House

Country hotel

Kathleen O'Sullivan grew up in this white Victorian house, a stone's throw from Ballylickey Bay. In 1978 she turned it into a successful small hotel. 'Kathleen is a delightful hostess,' writes a recent reporter, and Sea View is a 'very nice, quiet comfortable hotel'.

The bedrooms are beautifully decorated in pastel colours and floral fabrics with stunning antique furniture – especially the bedheads and wardrobes. The rooms in the old part of the house are more irregular and individual.

There are two sitting-rooms – a cosy front room adjoining the bar and a large family room at the back. The menu changes daily, and Kathleen is forever experimenting with new dishes – roast smoked pheasant on the day we visited.

Ballylickey, Bantry, Co Cork

Tel (027) 50462
Fax (027) 51555
email info@seaviewhousehotel.com
website www.seaviewhousehotel.com
Food breakfast, lunch (Sun only), dinner **Prices** €€-€€€
Closed Nov-Mar
Proprietor Kathleen O'Sullivan

Cashel, Co Tipperary

Cashel Palace Hotel

Converted bishop's palace

This exquisite 18thC former archbishop's palace is in the historic market town of Cashel, with its famous and dramatic Rock, one of Ireland's most visited sites. In the garden are two mulberry trees planted in 1702 for the coronation of Queen Anne, and the descendents of the original hops planted by one of the Guinness family in the mid-18thC (there's plenty of the 'black', velvety stuff in the Guinness Bar, with flagged cellar floor and terracotta walls). There are four-poster beds, fine antiques and pictures and spacious bathrooms. You have the choice of two restaurants – The Bishops Buttery serves modern Irish cuisine. We felt that some of the rooms were lacking in charm and atmosphere, but the exceptionally friendly and knowledgeable staff are a great asset.

Main Street, Cashel, Co Tipperary

Tel (062) 62707
Fax (062) 61521
e-mail reception@cashel-palace.ie
website www.cashel-palace.ie
Food breakfast, lunch, dinner
Price €-€€
Closed 24-26th Dec
Proprietors Patrick and Susan Murphy

Clifden, Co Galway

The Ardagh Hotel

Coast hotel and restaurant

The view from the restaurant over Ardbear Bay is fabulous: light and colours constantly change; sunsets are memorable. This small family hotel has an Alpine flavour that gives it charm. Monique Bauvet's the chef, housekeeper and gardener; her rooms are pristine and have recently been redecorated in a bright and contemporary style; she made the garden among the rocks. Her husband, Stéphane, can be found behind the front desk, or serving wine, and is always ready to help. Their hotel has a satisfying combination of friendliness and reliable, discreet efficiency. Not all the well-equipped rooms have sea views; ask when booking. Tucked under the eaves, a sunny sitting room for residents has piles of magazines and a profusion of greenery.

Ballyconneely Road, Clifden, Connemara, Co Galway

Tel (095) 21384
Fax (095) 21314
e-mail ardaghhotel@eircom.net
website www.ardaghhotel.com
Food breakfast, bar lunch, dinner
Price €€ **Closed** Nov to Easter or April 1 **Proprietors** Monique and Stéphane Bauvet

Cloyne, Co Cork

Barnabrow House

Country house and restaurant

This could be called a 'cutting edge' country house. No faded chintzes or family portraits here. Semi-minimalist interiors, with bold, bright colours and vast expanses of gleaming wood floors look as if they have come out of glossy magazines. Behind the rejuvenated main house is a coach house with floors painted white and elsewhere much orange, pink and yellow; a rustic cottage; and restaurant with an outdoor timber terrace. Hens provide fresh eggs; organic produce for the table comes from the kitchen garden.

Barnabrow House's main business is now weddings, but B&B is still available Sunday to Wednesday, and all week in the quieter months. Barnabrow, under chef Stuart Bowes, is now also open for lunch on Sundays.

Cloyne, Middleton, Co Cork

Tel (021) 4652534
Fax (021) 4652534
e-mail barnabrow@eircom.net
website www.barnabrowhouse.ie
Food breakfast, lunch, dinner
Price €€€
Closed Christmas week
Proprietor Geraldine Kidd

Dublin

Trinity Lodge
Town house hotel

Owner Peter Murphy opened this three-storey Georgian house (since the last edition two more buildings have been added) in the heart of Dublin opposite Trinity College in 1997. It's an elegant, little guesthouse that doesn't have any of the things he hates about hotels. It's in a handsome building and in order to keep its character, Peter chose not to put in a lift, or carve chunks out of rooms for bathrooms. But, he's got almost everything else in the way of comfort and convenience, such as air-conditioning and personal safes. There's a sitting area in the entrance hall with a window looking on to the street and comfortable armchairs. You can walk easily to all the local sights from here.

12 South Frederick Street, Dublin 2

Tel (01) 617 0900
Fax (01) 617 0999
e-mail trinitylodge@eircom.net
website www.trinitylodge.com
Food breakfast
Price €€
Closed never
Proprietor Peter Murphy

Innishannon, Co Cork

Innishannon House
Country hotel

This attractive, imposing 18thC house on the banks of the Brandon River was taken over by new proprietors the Roche family, whose son, David, is now manager. While maintaining the rustic country house style, the new owners have been redecorating the place since they took over in 2004. No. 16 is a cosy attic room with an antique bedspread, No. 14 a fascinating circular room with small round windows and a huge curtained bed.

Jean-Marc is still in change of the cooking – duck *confit*, fillet steak, smoked salmon – earning the place two rosettes. Innishannon is not the last word in seclusion or intimacy; there are facilities for conferences and wedding receptions.

We would welcome reports.

Innishannon, Co Cork

Tel (021) 4775121
Fax (021) 4775609
e-mail info@innishannon-hotel.ie
website www.innishannon-hotel.ie
Food breakfast, lunch, dinner
Price €€
Closed mid-Jan to mid-Mar
Proprietors Roche family

Kenmare, Co Kerry

Castletownbere Road, Kenmare, Co Kerry

Tel (064) 41252
e-mail muxnawlodge@eircom.net
Food breakfast;
Price €
Closed Christmas Eve and Day
Proprietor Hannah Boland

Muxnaw Lodge

Bed-and-breakfast

Charming, gabled Muxnaw Lodge was built in 1801, one of the oldest houses in Kenmare, set on a hillside overlooking the suspension bridge.

Hannah Boland has created an attractive period style for her lovely old house, with painted magnolia and blue walls, brass beds and lovingly-polished antique furniture. In the bedrooms, she hides the modern electric kettles away in wooden boxes so they don't spoil the general look. In a bathroom at the back of the house, you may sit in the corner bath and look at the sea. For breakfast, fresh eggs from the butcher are cooked on Mrs Boland's big red AGA in the kitchen. She is such a delightful hostess that guests may find themselves getting away rather later than planned.

Kilgraney, Co Carlow

Kilgraney, Bagenalstown, Co Carlow

Tel 059 9775282
Fax 059 9775455
e-mail bobbie@lorum.com
website www.lorum.com
Food breakfast, dinner
Price €€
Closed Dec-Feb
Proprietors Bobbie Smith

Lorum Old Rectory

Country guesthouse

There will come a moment in your stay at Lorum Old Rectory – perhaps during conversation at dinner, or in the afternoon as you glimpse owner Bobbie Smith collecting herbs from the garden – when everything clicks. That is when you will realize just how refreshed you are after such a short time and just how pleasant a place Lorum is. Much of this is down to Bobbie, whose warm manner gets people talking, and whose quirky but clever grip of flavours in the kitchen oils the wheels.

The rich Irish heritage helps too, whether in the form of a fine view of Mount Leinster from your bedroom; the inviting furniture in the communal areas; or perhaps a trip into nearby Kilkenny, a historic town with medieval roots

Kilkenny, Co Kilkenny

Butler House

Town house

This tall, grand Georgian house was once the dower house to Kilkenny Castle, family seat of the Earls of Ormonde. In the 1970s, the house was refurbished in contemporary style by Kilkenny Design, and the result is stunning.

The house has been refurbished again recently, with large spacious rooms, oak furniture and muted colours. The effect, with acres of white walls, is ordered, quiet and restful. Breakfast is now served in the Kilkenny Design Centre, a short stroll through the walled garden. Morning coffee, biscuits and cake are served on a pale oak table in the entrance hall. Superior bedrooms have bay windows and garden and castle views. Butler House is now run by the Kilkenny Civic Trust.

16 Patrick Street, Kilkenny,
Co Kilkenny

Tel (056) 7765707
Fax (056) 7765626
e-mail res@butler.ie
Food breakfast
Closed 24 to 29 Dec
Proprietors Kilkenny Civic Trust
Manager Gabrielle Hickey

Kylemore, Co Galway

Kylemore House

Country house hotel

Once the home of the poet Oliver St John Gogarty – who features in James Joyce's *Ulysses* – there's still a strong artistic flavour about this white house on the edge of Kylemore Lake. Owner Nancy Naughton says her regulars – mostly fishermen – don't want any changes; so the somewhat off-beat charm of the house seems to be unchanging. Quite so: the pictures alone would keep anyone engrossed for hours. She says her fishermen don't care much where they sleep, but the bedrooms are spacious and filled with interesting pieces. Downstairs rooms have welcoming peat fires in beautiful fireplaces. The kitchen is always busy: Mrs Naughton making her home-made marmalade, brown bread and packed lunches.

Kylemore, Co Galway

Tel (095) 41143
Fax (095) 41143
e-mail kylemorehouse@eircom.net
website www.kylemorehouse.net
Food breakfast, packed lunches; dinner for groups
Closed Oct to Easter
Proprietor Mrs Nancy Naughton

Shanagarry, Co Cork

Shanagarry, Midleton, Co Cork

Tel (021) 4652531
Fax (021) 4652021
e-mail res@ballymaloe.ie
website www.ballymaloe.ie.
Food breakfast, lunch, dinner
Closed Christmas
Proprietors the Allen family

Ballymaloe House

Country house hotel

We can't resist this rambling, creeper-clad house set in rolling green countryside. Readers have been 'immensely impressed' and found the staff 'well-drilled as an army, but jolly, with abundant charm'.

The Allens have been farming here for almost 70 years, started offering rooms in the 60s, adding more facilities and rooms over the years – those in extensions and converted out-buildings now outnumber those in the main house.

Despite quite sophisticated furnishings, the Allens have managed to preserve intact the warmth of a much-loved family home. Reporters have been impressed by the standard of food. Jason Fahey prepares the Classic French and Irish dishes. Just as much care is lavished on breakfast, and the famous children's high tea.

Woodstown, Co Waterford

Woodstown, Co. Waterford

Tel (0)51 382 549
Mobile (0)87 248 6283
e-mail gaultierlodge@yahoo.ie
website www.gaultierlodge.com
Food breakfast
Price €
Closed winter months
Proprietors Sheila and Bill

Gaultier Lodge

Beach B&B

Well above average B&B in a handsome, 18thC Georgian house with a five-star location beside the beach on Waterford Bay. Step straight out on to the broad sands. Busy, characterful hosts – Sheila (Irish) and Bill (American) – who know their own minds. Smart, period-furnished bedrooms. Generous brunch. A guest reports confusion over bookings: get written confirmation, and pay any deposit required to be 100 per cent of the reservation.

Index – Hotel names

In this index, hotels are arranged in order of the first distinctive part of their name; other parts of the name are also given, except that very common prefixes such as 'The' and 'La' are omitted. More descriptive words such as 'Hotel', 'B&B', 'St', 'Maison' and 'Auberge' are included.

I

J

K

L

Index – Hotel locations

In this index, hotels are arranged in order of the names of the cities, towns or villages they are in or near. Hotels located in a very small village may be indexed under a larger place nearby. An index by hotel name precedes this one.

Other Duncan Petersen titles

Buy your *Charming Small Hotel Guide* or other titles by post or e-mail directly from the publisher and you'll get a worthwhile discount. *

Titles:	Retail price	Discount price
Austria, Switzerland and the Alps	£14.99	£13.50
France	£14.99	£13.50
Germany	£14.99	£13.50
Italy	£16.99	£15.50
Spain	£14.99	£13.50

The *On Foot City Guides* are great companions for the *Charming Small Hotel Guides*. These books feature unique aerial-view maps, which show not only the city's street layout but the look of your surroundings too.

Titles:	Retail price	Discount price
London Walks	£9.99	£8.50
New York Walks	£9.99	£8.50
Paris Walks	£9.99	£8.50
Prague Walks	£9.99	£8.50
Rome Walks	£9.99	£8.50
Venice Walks	£9.99	£8.50

We also publish an innovative series of country walking and cycling routes on cards in boxes, including *Walker's Britain in a Box* the perfect companion to *Charming Small Hotels Britain & Ireland*. All these guides are stocked by Amazon. You can also e-mail us for more information on this series at duncan.petersen@zen.co.uk.

Please send orders to: Book Sales, Duncan Petersen Publishing Ltd, Studio 6, 82 Silverthorne Road, Battersea, London, SW8 3HE; or: duncan.petersen@zen.co.uk, giving: the title and number of copies; name and address; cheque made out to: Duncan Petersen Publishing Ltd, or card details.
*Offer applies to this edition and UK only.

Exchange rates

As we went to press, $1 bought 0.73 euros and £1 bought 1.21 euros